The Florida History and Culture Series

UNIVERSITY PRESS OF FLORIDA

Florida A&M University, Tallahassee
Florida Atlantic University, Boca Raton
Florida Gulf Coast University, Ft. Myers
Florida International University, Miami
Florida State University, Tallahassee
New College of Florida, Sarasota
University of Central Florida, Orlando
University of Florida, Gainesville
University of North Florida, Jacksonville
University of South Florida, Tampa
University of West Florida, Pensacola

The Columbia Restaurant

Celebrating a Century of History, Culture, and Cuisine

By Andrew T. Huse

with Recipes and Memories from Richard Gonzmart and the Columbia Restaurant Family

University Press of Florida

Gainesville · Tallahassee · Tampa · Boca Raton · Pensacola · Orlando · Miami · Jacksonville · Ft. Myers · Sarasota

14 13 12 11 10 09   6 5 4 3 2 1

Library of Congress Cataloging-in-Publication Data

Huse, Andrew T.
The Columbia Restaurant : celebrating a century of history, culture, and
cuisine / by Andrew T. Huse.
p. cm.
ISBN 978-0-8130-3365-5 (alk. paper)
1. Columbia Restaurant (Fla.)—History. 2. Cookery, Spanish. 3.
Cookery, Cuban. 4. Cookery—Florida. I. Title.
TX945.5.C65H87 2009
641.59759—dc22
2008055190

The University Press of Florida is the scholarly publishing agency for the
State University System of Florida, comprising Florida A&M University,
Florida Atlantic University, Florida Gulf Coast University, Florida In-
ternational University, Florida State University, New College of Florida,
University of Central Florida, University of Florida, University of North
Florida, University of South Florida, and University of West Florida.

University Press of Florida
15 Northwest 15th Street
Gainesville, FL 32611-2079
http://www.upf.com

Contents

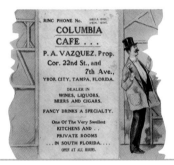

Photo By Rob/Harris

Acknowledgments

This book would not have been possible without the support and encouragement of Richard and Melanie Gonzmart, the Columbia's reigning president and its first lady. They welcomed me into their lives in ways that still surprise me. Their daughters, Lauren and Andrea, generously shared their insights. Casey, Richard's brother, offered keen and articulate observations that always enlightened me.

Other members of the extended Columbia Restaurant family helped shape the story through interviews. Veterans such as George Guito, Luis and Helen Diaz, Charlie and Melba Hero, and Joe Roman shared many precious memories. Relatively new employees—those who have been with the company for fewer than twenty-five years—illustrated the recent past with humor and sincerity. Curt Gaither, Jim Garris, Dennis Fedorovich, and Geraldo Bayona all brought unique perspectives of their own and are all crucial characters in this story.

Behind the scenes, I received invaluable assistance from Karen Mayo. At the earliest stages of research and writing, she typed, proofread, transcribed, and shared the workload. Helen Dean Design created a wonderful layout in a cooperative spirit. Angela Geml at the Columbia provided help and good cheer on countless occasions. Mary Jane Park's proofreading cleaned up the text in its roughest stages.

The reviews of other colleagues improved the book in a variety of ways. Leland Hawes, Rodney Kite-Powell, and Barbara Cruz read the text and offered astute advice. Jane Duncan and my brother Tim Huse endured many late-night readings of the text. Their helpful comments often led to more marathon readings. Rue McKenzie, Noel Smith, and Stefanie Boyar all contributed to the text in special ways.

Working in the Special Collections Department at the University of South Florida Tampa Library has always been a pleasure and a great advantage. My research materials were never far away, especially after the Gonzmarts donated their family's papers to USF in 2005. The department's director, Mark I. Greenberg, has always been an indispensable colleague. His encouragement and understanding facilitated my research and writing in countless ways.

Colleagues in the USF Tampa Library's Oral History Program processed the interviews, and became instant fans of the restaurant and family's rich history. Rebecca Willman, Kimberly Norton, Arlen Benson, Maria Kriser, Cyrana Wyker, and Rachel Lisi's excellent transcripts provided a huge haul of material for the book. Program coordinators Nicole Cox and Catherine Cottle brought the project to fruition. Elizabeth Tucker and Mary Beth Isaacson provided an excellent index.

Gary Mormino, Florida historian par excellence, has been an inspiration for as long as I've known him. Ray Arsenault, or "Dr. Ray," provided his own example as an "outside agitator." I've even had the pleasure of teaching in their innovative Florida Studies Program at USF's St. Petersburg campus. I continue to learn through their fine examples.

Though he is no longer with us, journalist Paul Wilder's writing gave me a treasure trove of older material to draw from. The original *Columbia Spanish Restaurant Cookbook* (1995) by Adela Gonzmart and Ferdie Pacheco, provided some vital stories as well. The honor of following in their footsteps has been humbling.

Special thanks to Andrea Gonzmart for handling the recipes and Geraldo Bayona for his proofreading.

Finally, I must thank my parents. You know who you are.

Research note: The bulk of research for this book was conducted using the Gonzmart–Columbia Restaurant Collection and Columbia Restaurant oral history project at the University of South Florida Tampa Library. The archival collection is available at the Special Collections Department and the interviews can be accessed through the library's online catalog.

Introduction

The average restaurant lives a tragically short life: two years, five years, ten. Few survive long enough to have substantial stories to tell. The very best restaurants create a "sense of place" through food, service, and atmosphere. The Columbia Spanish Restaurant has ambience in spades, carefully created and preserved for over a century. The Columbia, as locals call it, began in a small immigrant enclave in Tampa called Ybor City. Over the next century, the Columbia became a part of the Florida experience and carefully expanded around the state.

Family has always come first. Without family, there would be no Columbia Restaurant as we know it. Nothing can extricate the two. Like all families, the Hernandez-Gonzmart clan has had difficulties in and out of the business. Where many families and businesses failed, the Gonzmarts and the Columbia have survived and flourished. It was not easy, as this book will demonstrate. They only have made it look easy.

In the last fifteen years, the fourth generation of the Columbia, led by Richard Gonzmart with his brother, Casey, has reinvented the restaurant in a dramatic fashion while preserving the essence of the business and the family. In family and business, there is no standing still. The fifth generation is now staking its place in the Columbia dynasty.

Restaurants are sensitive barometers of culture. The Columbia's history is not one of staid, changeless uniformity, but quite the opposite: to prosper, the restaurant has undergone nearly constant change, much like Florida. Even today, the menu changes several times a year, and specials grace the tables daily. Owners and employees preserve key fixtures with a curator's dedication: Spanish tile, the enigmatic fountain, the old-time bar, and the crystal chandelier. Classic recipes have been restored with profound reverence. Over a century old, the Columbia has reached a new height of fame and prosperity.

As a scholar of culinary history, it is difficult for me to imagine a more fertile single subject than the Columbia Spanish Restaurant. It is grand but not jaded, fine but not pretentious, and so important that it has become part of the landscape. The Columbia Restaurant is so inescapable in Tampa that it almost disappears from view. It is Ybor City's virtual axis, economically, culturally, and historically. Ybor City would not be complete without it. The same could be said for Tampa, Florida, and beyond.

As so often with family lore and recipes, the Columbia is often taken for granted by those close by. To those doubters, we say, this is no tourist trap. This is history in a glass, family traditions garnished with love. New generations of Floridians have discovered the Columbia like clockwork, providing a steady clientele. Visitors from farther afield arrive with enthusiasm and curiosity and leave with satisfaction. The restaurant and family always find their way back into the public eye, back into the greatness that has been the hallmark of this restaurant.

The following complete recipes have been thoroughly tested for the home chef. They also reflect the restaurant's balance between tradition and modernity. When desirable, the Columbia chefs have preserved and updated recipes to obtain the best results.

For those interested in history and good stories, you are in good hands. The Columbia family bares its soul in the pages ahead. Tales of triumph and woe punctuate a century of taste and toil. Without the cooperation of the Gonzmarts and the extended Columbia family, such a complete account of the restaurant's life would have been impossible. I have had the honor of interviewing legends in their own time. I have long dreamed of being able to interview those no longer with us.

The cast of characters goes on and on in the pages ahead. The recipes are just as vibrant. It is our earnest hope that you enjoy them all.

Six Generations of The Columbia Restaurant

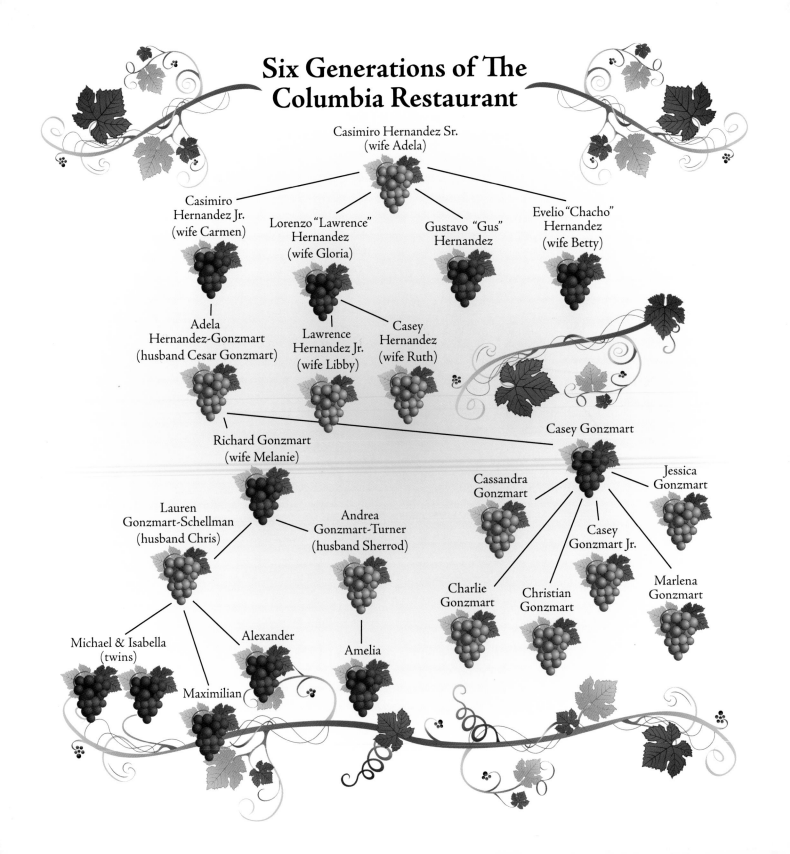

Casimiro Hernandez Sr. (wife Adela)

Casimiro Hernandez Jr. (wife Carmen)

Lorenzo "Lawrence" Hernandez (wife Gloria)

Gustavo "Gus" Hernandez

Evelio "Chacho" Hernandez (wife Betty)

Adela Hernandez-Gonzmart (husband Cesar Gonzmart)

Lawrence Hernandez Jr. (wife Libby)

Casey Hernandez (wife Ruth)

Richard Gonzmart (wife Melanie)

Casey Gonzmart

Cassandra Gonzmart

Jessica Gonzmart

Casey Gonzmart Jr.

Lauren Gonzmart-Schellman (husband Chris)

Andrea Gonzmart-Turner (husband Sherrod)

Charlie Gonzmart

Christian Gonzmart

Marlena Gonzmart

Michael & Isabella (twins)

Alexander

Amelia

Maximilian

The 1st Generation, 1905–1929

With his family, Casimiro Hernandez came to Tampa, Florida, from Cuba at the beginning of the twentieth century. His tiny Saloon Columbia served the workers of boom-time Ybor City, the immigrant enclave known as the cigar capital of the world. In under thirty years, the bar grew into one of Tampa's most popular restaurants. The Hernandez family navigated the Columbia Spanish Restaurant through World War I and Prohibition.

Casimiro chose a potent symbol as the Columbia's mascot: a Spanish galleon. It not only conjured the Spanish empire, but also reminded Tampa's immigrants who had arrived at the America, Gem of the Ocean, how much they had to be thankful for. In northern Spain, which many thousands of hungry emigrants had left to find sustenance and wealth in the Americas, the departing ship became a reminder of all who had gone. The Columbia's galleon is arriving, sailing to the shores of wealth and freedom.

No one at the time could foresee just how popular the symbol would become. In 2005, Casimiro's descendants used the galleon as the hundredth-anniversary logo.

The 1st Generation, 1905–1929

Havana and Tampa

For the Hernandez family, the American dream began in an unassuming way. They had little to start with. They couldn't speak the language, but they could work, earn, and share. They struggled on and found a way together.

Our story begins with Casimiro Hernandez Sr., a Cuban citizen of Spanish descent. He ran his first restaurant in Havana during Cuba's War for Independence, or the Spanish-American War. When the Spanish Navy pressed him into service, he would not serve against his own people: He jumped ship, swam ashore, and avoided Spanish authorities until war's end. He hoped to provide a better home for his four sons—Casimiro, Lorenzo, Gustavo, and Evelio—someplace else.

In 1902, the Hernandez family hopped a steamer to Tampa and a new start. Lured by opportunity in Ybor City—Tampa's cigar-producing Latin Quarter—Casimiro Hernandez saw a prosperous future in the land of plenty.

Cigar factories served as Ybor City's economic hub. Immigrant cigar workers demanded coffee, pastries, and Latin food to remind them of home and create a new beginning.

Casimiro Hernandez Sr. built a thriving business in Ybor City. Generous to a fault, Hernandez was also known as "Fatty."

The Latin Quarter

The Wild West wound down at the end of the nineteenth century, but the Florida frontier refused to be tamed. Yellow fever struck cities and coastal villages. Mosquitoes and alligators swarmed from the swamps. Tampa originally coalesced in the 1840s around Fort Brooke, an Army outpost erected against the defiant Seminole Indians, who refused to be forcibly resettled to the West. Fewer than 1,000 hardscrabble settlers populated Tampa in 1880.

The next twenty years brought some amazing changes, the most notable being the coming of the railroad and the rise of Ybor City. During the 1870s, Vicente Martinez Ybor produced cigars in the politically unstable Spanish colony of Cuba. For decades, Cuban insurgents and Spanish troops fought over the island, and the cigar industry moved to Key West. The small, isolated island had a scant water supply, and Ybor found it difficult to shake the labor unrest he encountered in Cuba. In 1884, two of his friends visited to tell him about the favorable conditions on Florida's west coast.

With a humid climate, deep port, and a rail hub courtesy of railroad baron Henry Plant, Tampa proved an ideal site for the cigar industry. Following Ybor's example, other cigar producers arrived in 1885. Large factories of wood and brick sprang up with their long rows of windows. By 1900 Ybor City became a cosmopolitan colony of Spaniards, Cubans, and Sicilians. The same urgent need for safety and sustenance drove immigrants from their homelands to settle in Ybor City. The cigar industry provided a prosperous economic hub, giving rise to a vibrant new business

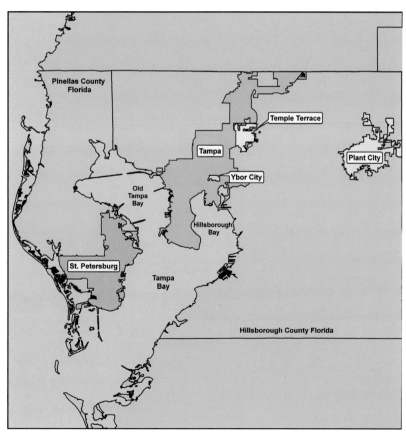

Ybor City is located in the center of the Tampa Bay region. Map by Pete Reehling.

district. City fathers in nearby Tampa annexed Ybor City in 1890.

By all accounts, contrasts and contradictions riddled Tampa, a Cracker town with a Latin Quarter, an industrial enclave isolated in vast wilderness, where white and black men and women worked side by side. Tycoons planned Ybor City while they anticipated profits. Proud artisans, anarchists, and communists arrived with fresh memories of hunger, violence, and rebellion. Ybor City became a liberal union redoubt in a rather conservative community.

Tampa's immigrants worked together to create social services and a vibrant cultural scene.

The Cherokee Club provided hospitality to Ybor City's upper-class residents. As illustrated here, the new immigrants brought their colorful culture and a lust for life never seen before in Tampa. Later known as El Pasaje or The Passage for this long gallery, the building still stands today.

By 1927, Seventh Avenue (then known as Broadway) was the only street in Ybor City with electric street lights.

A boom town based on cigars in 1885, Ybor City thrived economically and culturally by 1900. This photo from 1919 shows Ybor City in full blossom, with automobiles, streetcars, and horse-drawn carriages along 7th Avenue.

Lectors read news, political tracts, and literature to workers in the cigar factories.

If the cigar factories served as Ybor City's economic hub, the elaborate social clubs became the cultural centers. Boasting theaters, cantinas, clinics, and cemeteries, these ethnic mutual aid societies sustained members from cradle to grave, with many good times in between. Games, dances, and banquets at the lavish recreation centers known as "labor temples" punctuated the social calendars of the immigrants. In sharp contrast with Tampa, the rough frontier post, Ybor City percolated Old World culture. Ybor City's newspaper *La Gaceta*, founded in 1932, brought the scoop in three languages (Spanish, English, and Italian), and still does.

In the shadows of the great cigar factories and labor temples, merchants maintained a bustling trade along the brick and wooden streets. The aromas of roasting coffee, tobacco, and savory Latin cooking mingled with the stench of horse manure. The staccato of Spanish dominated most conversations, but one could hear the drawls of the Crackers in the saloons and the strains of Italian opera in the theaters.

Above the rattle of horse-drawn carriages and clatter of streetcars, literature spilled from the factories onto the streets. Cigar workers enjoyed a quiet work environment by industrial standards, and even the illiterate became remarkably "well read." Factory *lectores* (readers) read news, novels, and political literature to cigar workers from their elevated chairs. In the days before widespread literacy and the radio, cigar workers hired professional *lectores* for their strong, cultured voices and intellectual bent. Workers voted on which *lector* to hire and the daily selection of news, literature, and political tracts to be read. Families often picnicked outside the factory's open full-length windows to listen to favorite stories such as *Don Quijote*.

The rhythm and impulses of the cigar industry ruled Ybor City. With the factory lunch whistles came waves of hungry workers to an impressive variety of eateries. Cafes supplied the simple pleasures of coffee, conversation, bread, and sweets. Restaurants specialized in familiar immigrant foods, from peasant staples to Europe's finest dishes.

Columbia Café

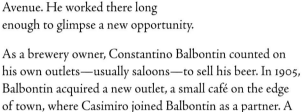

As a boom town still on the rise, Tampa's Latin Quarter required plenty of labor. No stranger to hard work, Casimiro Hernandez Sr. found it at the Florida Brewery on Fifth Avenue. He worked there long enough to glimpse a new opportunity.

As a brewery owner, Constantino Balbontin counted on his own outlets—usually saloons—to sell his beer. In 1905, Balbontin acquired a new outlet, a small café on the edge of town, where Casimiro joined Balbontin as a partner. A certain P. Vasquez established the 60-seat Columbia Café in December 1903 with turkey dinners and a rousing band.

Back then, saloons occupied all four corners of the intersection at Twenty-second Street and Broadway (East Seventh Avenue), then on the edge of Ybor City. Locals knew that junction as the "Seminole" because Native Americans had used the spot as a trading post in the mid 1800s. In the early 1900s, the area still served as a marketplace, especially for fish. Before cars and traffic lights cluttered the road, a large water trough for horses and livestock had stood in the middle of the intersection. Legend had it that while training his Rough Riders in Tampa, Teddy Roosevelt had watered his horse there regularly. Casimiro Sr. arrived too late to meet the Rough Riders, but he bathed in a patriotic afterglow, proud of his adopted city and nation.

Grateful for his asylum in the land of opportunity, Casimiro adopted the name of his new café from the popular song "Columbia, Gem of the Ocean." The Saloon Columbia was born.

As a rotund and fun-loving man, Casimiro lived up to his nickname, "Fatty." He was generous to a fault, offering three daily meals to workers for five dollars a month. He made a modest living and gave most of it away. "It is democratic in the extreme," a reporter noted of Casimiro's timeless café. "If a working man wants a Cuban sandwich and a glass of Tropical Ale, he enters the corner door, dressed however he may be, and sits down to one. All day long, workers sit around as if at home."

Casimiro Sr. soon became known for more than his generosity and strong drink: His occasional food specials were always delicious. His granddaughter Adela said of Casimiro Sr., "An intrepid and innovative person, he was very knowledgeable about Spanish cuisine."

Being familiar with the vagaries of weather and commerce in Ybor City, Casimiro remained prepared for disruptions of business, whether from a hurricane or the cigar industry. With profitable factories and happy workers, business thrived in the Latin Quarter. But labor strikes wreaked havoc on the local economy, as unpaid cigar workers refused to shop and relied on union-run soup kitchens. Stubborn negotiations between producers and unions could last a year or more, prolonging hardships. But Casimiro's foresight, kindness to strangers, and good food pulled his business through.

The Florida Brewing Company towered above Ybor City Ice Works.

Casimiro gambled on a new life in an unfamiliar city, and the basic elements are in place to begin our story. The saloon became the beginning of something far greater, much like sofrito, the base of many Spanish recipes—garlic, onions, tomatoes, and green peppers sautéed in olive oil. Casimiro and his family built upon a strong and simple foundation.

Saloon Columbia

"Don't fail to visit Ybor City: The Havana of America," the *Tampa Tribune* urged in 1905. "The largest cigar factories in the world. Mingle with a cosmopolitan people, dine in the Spanish restaurants—see life in cafés and theaters." The Saloon Columbia, a unique hybrid of the American-style

saloon and the European-style café, might not have been what the journalist had in mind.

Like most other Ybor City residents, Casimiro Hernandez was a newly arrived immigrant in search of his fortune. He offered liquor, wine, and cigars to the thirsty workers of Ybor City. He later added sandwiches and snacks to the menu, but a neighboring restaurant called "La Fonda" furnished complete meals. Casimiro had built a thriving business by 1912, when he bought out the Balbontins' inter-

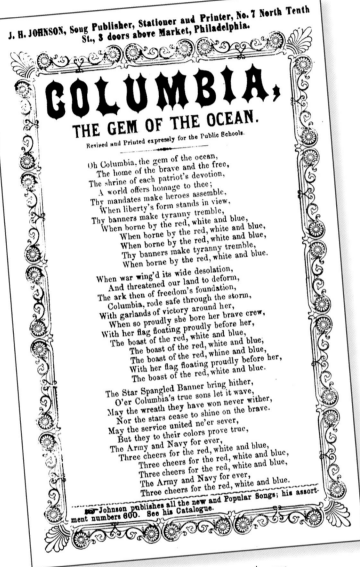

A patriotic song inspired the Columbia Restaurant's name.
Image courtesy of the Library of Congress.

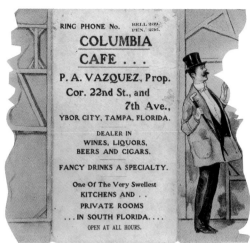

This folding advertisement clearly "reveals" the masculine bent to Ybor saloons in 1905.

est. The Hernandez family owned a restaurant for the first time. Casimiro Jr. left work in a cigar factory to join his father in the family business. The Columbia became the newest member of the Hernandez family.

Although Ybor had been an industrial town since the cigar factories arrived in the 1880s, it still retained the rough-and-tumble feel of the Florida frontier. At the same time, farmers and ranchers staked out parcels to tame the land. The workers and farmhands, many of them young single men, could not subsist on coffee alone. When not working, most of the men needed a strong drink to soothe their ills and pass the time.

Tampa became Florida's hardest-drinking city. Most of the Latin men had left their families behind in the old country, and they felt free to pursue pleasure while not eking out a living. The simple Saloon Columbia filled the needs of the workers nicely.

The Columbia closely followed the template for saloons at the time. Swinging wooden doors greeted patrons from the sandy street. A long bar acted as a serving area with a large mirror behind it, which made the narrow room appear larger. Standing at the bar or sitting at tables drinking and discussing issues of the day in various languages, the clientele tended to be rough and hard-drinking. No women dared to enter.

It is a mistake to imagine all saloons as depicted by Prohibitionists or in films set in the Wild West. Saloons were neither as depraved nor as violent as those sources would suggest. In reality, the saloon served as a social clearinghouse for men to blow off steam and develop networks for employment and recreation. Single men living in boarding houses or rented rooms needed a place to relax, and the saloon offered much more comfort and dignity than their spartan rooms could provide.

Whether or not Casimiro knew it, his business was a unique blend of Old World and New. Across the Atlantic, European cafés offered the exotic stimulants imported from New World colonies: coffee, tea, and chocolate, all liberally sweetened with New World sugar. Spaniards had become especially attached to coffee. The invading Moors brought coffee to Spain after AD 711, centuries before the

rest of Europe drank the dark brew. Sweet pastries and baked goods accompanied the beverages. Cafés—sometimes known as salons—became places for discussion of the arts, sciences, politics, and gossip.

America produced a rowdy equivalent known as the saloon. The name is derived from the European salon, but the similarities end there. The American saloon specialized in hard liquor, beer, and wine. Workers in industrialized America had less use for coffee and tea, often sipping drams of alcohol throughout the day. Many saloons offered simple lunches free with the price of a couple of drinks, so the saloon served hungry and parched workers alike. It was not until the twentieth century that breaks involved more coffee than alcohol for most of the nation, but in Ybor City, *cafeteros*, or traveling coffee vendors, serviced workers in cigar factories for a weekly fee.

The delights offered by the Columbia did not satisfy every worker. Some sought out the forbidden fruits of gambling, drunkenness, and prostitution, common vices in America. A nationwide movement to ban the sale of alcohol gathered momentum for decades, culminating in the so-called

Noble Experiment, or Prohibition. Florida went legally dry in 1918, the United States a year later.

As the Prohibition movement gained steam, Casimiro faced a bitter dilemma. He could lose his saloon or find a new use for the Columbia. He did not have to look far for partners. The Garcia brothers, who owned La Fonda, the restaurant next door, agreed in 1920 to join him and retain the name "Columbia." The two businesses had depended upon one another anyway, even opening a joint bakery in 1916. With the Garcia brothers, the size of the restaurant doubled overnight, and Casimiro became a more legitimate restaurateur.

While it was illegal to sell alcohol in Florida, it was by no means uncommon, especially in Ybor City, where citizens had a healthy disdain for Prohibition laws. Italians continued to make their wine, and Crackers inland cooked up their moonshine in the woods, far from prying eyes. Rumrunners plied their cargoes into Florida's many inlets, beaches, and barrier islands. Bolita, an illegal lottery brought in from Cuba, became Tampa's favorite pastime.

Casimiro Sr. partnered with a neighboring restaurant to survive Prohibition, giving its name, La Fonda to the new dining room. The Columbia doubled in size overnight. Casimiro Jr. is on the right.

In defiance of their elders and the law, young women in the 1920s flouted tradition. Their footloose lifestyle was symbolized by their unlaced boots, whose tongues flapped loose while they danced, earning the women the moniker "flappers." This reveler had an elegant Latin flair.

Bootlegging revenue elevated small-time hoods to fearsome heights of power.

The Columbia's bartenders were never without work, but demitasse cups replaced shot glasses. Management still bought liquor; it was just more expensive and from less scrupulous distributors. Bartenders filled bottles from barrels of contraband liquor.

With America victorious and productive after World War I, business flourished in the 1920s. The Florida land boom—when speculators feverishly traded parcels of land they had never seen—provided an added boost. Intoxicated with imagined profits, high rollers from out of town spent money lavishly. Tourism increased, and Tampa became known for delectable food and fine cigars. Columbia classics such as Spanish bean soup, Cuban sandwiches, and arroz con pollo (chicken and yellow rice) became the highlights of many a visit.

Although the alcohol never disappeared entirely, Prohibition made it safe and acceptable for women to dine out virtually anywhere. The ladies with more Victorian attitudes just enjoyed the food. On the other hand, Prohibition didn't dissuade the dance-crazed flappers, many of whom drank and smoked in public for the first time in their families' history. The flappers appreciated the discreet demitasse cups.

Immigrants like Casimiro held fast to the traditions of their homelands, but were also open to change. Spanish bean soup serves as a good example of this, made with garbanzos, potatoes, ham, chorizo, and saffron. The soup was based upon a massive stew called cocido madrileño, which Spaniards serve in several courses—the broth with vermicelli, the beans with cabbage, and finally, the meats. The original dish was too heavy to be practical at the Columbia, and had a debilitating effect on diners. It also took too long to serve rushed lunch customers. The Columbia served the meal altogether for a change, minus the vermicelli and cabbage. The new twist on tradition quickly became popular. Newspapers in the 1920s boasted that Tampa had three major attractions: sun, cigars, and soup. It is a wonder that such a heavy dish remained so popular in sunny Florida.

"The way you typically would eat it, it's just too big of a meal. And you'd have to take a nap or whatever. When I go to Spain and eat it, I can't eat the rest of the day or that night and I usually take a siesta." Richard Gonzmart on cocido madrileño, the inspiration for Spanish Bean Soup.

El Rey, Pete, and Prohibition

The Columbia acquired one of its most loyal employees quite by accident. Gregorio Martinez worked in a nearby speakeasy during Prohibition. When federal agents stormed the bar, he fled across the street to the Columbia. Already dressed in a tuxedo, he behaved as if he worked there. Amused and impressed by his composure in such circumstances, management hired Martinez as a waiter.

Worried that the feds were still looking for him, Martinez grew a mustache. Coupled with his customary grace, it made him look exactly like King Alfonso XIII of Spain, earning him the nickname "El Rey" (The King).

The Roaring Twenties lived up to their name. The restaurant was no longer on the Florida frontier, but at the limits of law enforcement. Because the Columbia lay just inside Tampa city limits, brawlers, criminals, and bootleggers had only to run across Twenty-second Street to escape the jurisdiction of city police. Small hollows in the columns of the bar held stashes of hooch for special customers.

The Twenties roared when a group of civic leaders and businessmen held a memorable banquet at the Columbia. A doctor and a wholesaler took El Rey to the side and asked him to participate in a prank. After being seated, the doctor insulted the wholesaler, who sprang from his seat and shouted back. As the shocked party looked on, the doctor pulled a pistol and fired in the air. Doing his part, El Rey turned off the lights. Amid a clattering commotion, the guests fumbled to the exits in the dark. When the lights came up again, only the antagonists remained—everyone else had run to avoid the violence. It seems justified that the two men would be stuck with the bill after their prank.

Pete Scaglione was a Columbia bartender never to be forgotten. A firm and talented barkeep, he devoted himself to his craft and the Columbia. Beginning in 1927, Pete worked at the bar and helped out in the back of the house—with the smugglers. When asked by reporters years later about

Gregorio Martinez, also known as "El Rey," enchants the guests in the 1940s.

his alleged Cuban rum smuggling, Pete never denied it. He just smiled and changed the subject. Some even say he distilled the Columbia's hooch himself.

Prohibition made law-breakers out of all kinds of citizens. Take a certain federal judge who will go unnamed. One night during the dry years, he sat at the bar and intoned, "As an officer of the court, I know it is illegal to drink under the American flag." Pete quickly replaced the U.S. flag with the Cuban one. The judge then continued, "Ah well, let's drink a toast to Cuba." Every drinker raised glasses with the judge that night.

Pete spent many nights with regrettable company. He got into enough barroom fisticuffs to learn one important les-

They roared in the 1920s: bartender Pete Scaglione and his wife.

Pete Scaglione, mixing drinks and making history.

cooking for army generals. He found the Spanish monarch favored hearty stews and meat dishes. After cooking in Havana for a spell, Pijuan came to the United States in 1923, smuggled aboard a fishing boat at Tarpon Springs. He eventually found work at the Columbia, where he raised the quality of the cuisine to new heights.

After he decided to stay in Tampa, he sent for his wife and children, who quietly slipped into the country. A congressional act had grandfathered illegal immigrants such as Pijuan, but his family arrived too late for blanket amnesty. When the immigration authorities learned of this, they announced that Pijuan's family would be deported. Local politicians sprang into action to help Pijuan and Casimiro, preserving the Columbia's incredible cuisine for themselves and their grateful constituents. Private Law 225, "For the Relief of Mrs. Pacios Pijuan," passed in Congress to right the situation.

With his immigration issues resolved, Pijuan could resume his artistry in the kitchen. A local reporter once noted: "Dominating—and we do mean dominating—the vast cooking regions, is Senor don Francisco Pijuan Alsina. At the slightest raising of eyebrows or snap of fingers, when he is concocting a special dish himself, the staff chefs and cooks dash hither and yon producing just exactly the right amount" of whatever he required.

Adela said, "Pijuan was a special favorite of my father, who appreciated genius wherever he found it."

son: Always wear a clip-on tie instead of the real thing. If a brawler grabs a clip-on tie, it will simply come off. Wearing the real thing produces an unpleasant result: The patron can pull an unwitting bartender over the bar by his neck. Pete always preferred unassuming short ties.

Like the speakeasy across the street, the Columbia sold illegal alcohol and needed cool heads in the house should the feds raid—and they did. Today, the family still has a search warrant dating back to 1932. Congress repealed the fruitless Prohibition laws a year later, ending the game of cat and mouse. Trucks, rail cars, and steamships converged on Tampa delivering beer, wine, and spirits.

Pijuan and Citizenship

Francisco Pijuan became the head chef after relocating from Spain, where he was said to have served as King Alfonso's personal chef. He began his career at age fourteen

Chef Pijuan circa 1945. He elevated the Columbia's cuisine to new heights.

The 2nd Generation, 1930-1955

Casimiro Hernandez Jr. paid off his father's heavy debts and guided the Columbia through the Great Depression. He navigated the difficulties of World War II and rationing. He nurtured the business until it reached a plateau of quality and popularity that attracted national and global attention.

Each Hernandez brother shined in his respective roles. Lawrence's connections and boundless generosity paid dividends long after his death. Gustavo's coconut ice cream could satisfy the most discerning sweet tooth. Evelio's coffee was the best in a very selective city of café con leche. Casimiro managed the restaurant itself, and demanded nothing less than excellence from his employees and his food.

The next quarter century vaulted the Columbia to unprecedented heights among Florida restaurants. Casimiro hired journalist Paul Wilder to share the Columbia's story "after hours" from his job as a reporter. The press and recipes lured hungry throngs to the restaurant. With notoriety came swarms of patrons, seemingly from every corner of the globe. A restaurant three times as large as the Columbia couldn't have handled the mobs. Wilder penned many of the following stories from the Columbia's ascent to greatness during the first 12 years after the war.

The Columbia, Gem of Spanish Restaurants, made more than good food—
it made memories, and it made history.

After Casimiro's death, his massive debts almost put the Columbia out of business.

The 2nd Generation, 1930–1955

 ## Hard Work and Hard Times

Just when the Columbia began to soar financially in the late 1920s, events near and far away seemed to conspire against it. The Florida Land Boom went bust in 1926, and the high rollers disappeared. Casimiro Sr. died in 1929, leaving a massive debt of $78,000, probably $1 million in today's currency. To make matters worse, the stock market crashed a few months later, sending the nation into an economic tailspin. As the Depression worsened, beggars went door to door looking for work or handouts. The Columbia floundered into the 1930s, surrounded by an Ybor City in steep decline. Over the next three decades, the hand-rolled cigar industry steadily disappeared.

Casimiro Jr. faced a crisis that made Prohibition look like a honeymoon, but hard times were nothing new to Ybor City's citizens. Starvation, poverty, and violence had forced

Young Adela Gonzmart, Casimiro's granddaughter, already being groomed as a princess.

The café in 1929 with Cusimaro Jr. at right. Young Casimiro Jr. inherited an ugly business situation and never quit.

many of them to emigrate there from their homelands in the first place. The cycle of feast and famine, driven by strikes in the cigar factories, reminded all how tough things could be on a regular basis.

Cuban bread in Ybor City served as a symbol of discipline amid adversity. When Cuba struggled for independence from Spain in the late 1800s, its citizens faced hunger and hardship. One response was the stretching of Cuban bread into long, thin loaves to make it easier to cut small slices for rationing. The practice never changed in Tampa.

Casimiro and his neighbors turned misfortune to their advantage. Tampa's most famous sandwich would not be possible without the stretched Cuban loaf. In Havana, workers ate "mixto" sandwiches of various meats on Cuban bread. Ybor City split the loaf and filled it with mojo roast pork, sugar-cured ham, salami, Swiss cheese, pickles, and mustard. Each of the main ingredients symbolized Ybor City's dominant ethnic groups: fine glazed ham for the Spaniards, bread and mojo pork for the Cubans, and salami for the Italians. People at the time probably did not think of the sandwiches in such terms—they were simply good to eat. With such food, the Columbia's future was assured.

 ## The Great Depression

As eldest son, Casimiro Jr. (hereafter referred to as Casimiro) inherited the restaurant in 1929. He also became responsible for his father's debt on the eve of the Great Depression. The Columbia's profit and loss reports reveal a struggling business in the early 1930s. Many of the cigar factories had closed down or moved away. The international scene was bleak, with fascism on the rise in Europe.

THE GREAT DEPRESSION	
Year	Profit
1924	26,027
1926	20,990
1929	-2,168
1930	891
1931	5,206
1933	-1,902
1934	-1,065
1935	4,183
1937	10,981
1938	3,542

As In The Olden Days—

You will find this the same busy corner. Why? We are going to be just as exacting in the quality of your favorite Beer as you found here in the olden days and assure you of one thing— your confidence will soon be gained in our service today!

Come and Enjoy Real Spanish Meals With **Good Old Time Beer**

The quality of our Spanish Dinners has won thousands of friends in Florida. With the serving of good old Beer they will be a real treat.

COLUMBIA CAFE Corner 7th Ave. and 22nd St.

The boom and bust economy of the 1920s and 30s took a toll on the Columbia's profits.

During the low point of the Great Depression, only eight patrons visited the restaurant one day, and they spent only $12.42. Casimiro looked out the window at somber Seventh Avenue, nervously picking his eyebrows. "If you saw him picking at his eyebrows, he was mad," his grandson Richard Gonzmart said. "When he did that, you knew, stay away."

Casimiro walked to the hardware store to buy nails. Upon his return, he convened a meeting of his employees and placed the nails on the table. "Another twelve dollar day," he announced, "and I nail up the damned joint." His waiter, Gregorio Martinez, or El Rey, quietly left and withdrew his life savings of $50 from the bank. "Don't close the place," he said upon his return. Casimiro refused the money and never publicly wavered again in the face of adversity.

> "El Rey had faith in my grandfather and his dreams. So he believed. To come with your life savings and offer it to somebody…. He believed what my grandfather was doing was valid. Sometimes we all have our doubts. When you have somebody who assures that they believe in you, that gives you the strength to go forward." Richard Gonzmart

Not even the Depression could dampen Casimiro's generous instincts. When he learned that a local teacher, Leva Dopp Grebenstein, would not eat her lunch each day because her students had nothing to eat, Casimiro intervened. He insisted on sending soup and bread for the remainder of the school year. Mrs. Grebenstein had a long standing connection to the Columbia: Her father ran the Seminole Saloon across the street in the early days.

Both families must have rejoiced when the news arrived from Tallahassee. On May 8, 1933, the Florida Legislature followed a national trend and voted to legalize alcohol. With Prohibition repealed, Casimiro recovered his primary source of revenue, though he never gave it up entirely.

The Grand Cashier

One of the Columbia's only female employees was Dolores Jimenez—Lola—the unerring cashier. She became so obsessed with keeping a balanced drawer that when men replaced tile near her register, coworkers joked that Lola had lost a quarter and ripped up the floor looking for it. The joke was barely an exaggeration.

During the Mexican Revolution of 1910, Lola came to Tampa with her family. Her distinguished father became employed as the Spanish Consul. Her 15 years of experience as a secretary scarcely prepared her for some of the most colorful days of her life at the Columbia.

When Casimiro hired Lola on May Day 1930, she didn't know a single word of English, though she had been well educated in Mexican schools. The Columbia's American patrons gradually taught her to speak English, but she continued to count in Spanish. Her impeccable sense of timing served the restaurant well, for she was never late for work.

Shortly after being hired, she must have wondered if she should look for another job. Few customers came to dine, and the ones who did ran up tabs they could not pay. Not a good place for a cashier.

Business picked up over the 1930s and Lola trained more cashiers. One New Year's Eve—when any cashier would be lucky to be only ten or twenty dollars short—Lola burst into tears when she found the drawer short by twenty-five cents. Early in the morning of New Year's Day, Lola insisted on filing through the stubs to find the discrepancy. When management dissuaded her, she returned home for a fitful sleep. The next morning, a new calculation revealed a shortage of only two pennies. Lola grudgingly let the matter go.

The war years brought a flood of fortune. Then came the day when she almost lost a fortune. She typically stored the day's checks in a bag under the counter. A customer once asked her to hold his paper bag, which held several neckties. When he paid his bill and asked for his ties, Lola handed over the checks. Still thinking he had his ties, the man went home. She did not discover her error until sometime later. "That's when I, how do you say, sweat blood," Lola said. Thankfully Lola knew the man's name, and she tracked him down through a frantic series of telephone calls. He discovered the mistake and recovered his ties. Thus ended Lola's greatest ordeal.

To celebrate Lola's twentieth anniversary with the company in 1950, Casimiro gave her an extended vacation. For one of the first female employees at a time few women worked in restaurants at all, this was quite an honor. The male dominated unions had gone on strike for such privileges. Despite her unceasing devotion to her profession, they would never admit her as a member.

The Good Wine

After the repeal of Prohibition, Casimiro could only afford to stock the cheapest wine—most customers could not afford better. The house had only three bottles of fine wine priced at fifteen dollars each. Those bottles crowned a wine cabinet display, and had become symbols that the humble and struggling Columbia still had some class and self-respect.

Headwaiter Joseph Fernandez remembered the day that a dirty looking Cracker man ordered one of the fine bottles to accompany a Cuban sandwich. When he pointed to the bottle and said, "I want that," the waiter balked. He doubted that the disheveled backwoods boy had the money, so he suggested a cheaper brand. The thirsty Cracker insisted and drank the entire bottle of fine vintage with his pedestrian sandwich.

The cooks leered at him from the kitchen door when they heard some uncouth character was drinking *the* wine. Gathered in clusters, the waiters whispered with sinister envy. "It was like watching the passing of an old friend— that bottle of wine," Fernandez remembered. "I do not

know what would have happened to this poor man if he had tried to beat his bill."

The man proudly paid for the meal with a fifty-dollar bill, a handsome sum in those days. Then the customer asked for another bottle, this one for his wife. When she smelled the wine on his breath, he explained, she would demand some wine of her own. So he bought a 75-cent wine and poured it into the expensive bottle. Nothing could have disgusted the waiter more, who briefly had hoped to double his tip.

The old Columbia Café in the 1940s.

The Restless Perfectionist

A restless perfectionist, Casimiro Jr. took over the business as the eldest son. Spanish tradition dictated this, and the young man was more than qualified. The Columbia once received a review by a Florida journalist complaining of the most surly service he'd ever seen. Casimiro kept the clipping and even reprinted it in the newspaper "to remind us that we ain't perfect," he said.

It is no wonder that Casimiro often fretted about the business. He grew up from age twelve working in every position at the restaurant. He'd seen his father spend too much and make too little. He upheld the strictest discipline to survive the Depression and extract the Columbia from debt. His father had established a small business with partners. Casimiro Jr. took it to an entirely new level.

A *Saturday Evening Post* reporter once described Casimiro as "a rumpled and restless individual who speaks a peculiar mixture of English and Spanish that only his close associates understand well." When asked about his business principles, Casimiro responded, "When a man finish eating with me, I want he should say, 'By heaven, I full. I got plenty.'" And they did.

A humble and hardworking man, Casimiro did not seek the limelight. His picture rarely appeared in the newspapers and never appeared in any ads. Casimiro remained quiet and rather stoic. The only sure way to get a rise out of him was to prepare bad food or offer bad service.

His suppliers bore the most scrutiny and ridicule, as Casimiro inspected the fish, pressed the meat, and muddled olive oil in his hand as he tasted it for acidity. He eyed fresh produce with suspicion and bought only the best. To meet his standards, chefs sometimes prepared dishes four or five times.

It was not unusual to hear him mutter in the kitchen as he poured out whole pots of imperfect soup. He once ordered 675 Thanksgiving pies. One by one, he tasted the apple, pumpkin, and mincemeat pies and found each lacking. He threw them out and improvised dessert rather than serve an inferior product.

Above: *Casimiro Hernandez Jr.'s stoic exterior hid a compassionate heart.*

Left: *Casimiro Jr.'s wife, Carmen.*

When he saw a chef or cook rest on his laurels, Casimiro pulled his original creations from the menu to goad him into new experiments. He sometimes slipped out the back door to watch departing customers walk back to their cars and to listen to their assessment of his fare.

No one in the restaurant worked harder. He slept in his chair, often spending the night at the restaurant, as it was open twenty-four hours during the 1940s. It was said he could even sleep standing up at the cash register.

Casimiro's taciturn nature did not extend to civic and family affairs. He boosted any event and supported many charities, earning him the Ybor City Optimist Club's Outstanding Citizen Award.

Casimiro's brothers founded enterprises of their own to help the Columbia. Gustavo (known as Gus) ran the ice cream plant, and Evelio (known as Chacho) operated the coffee mill. Lorenzo (Lawrence) dabbled in local politics and insurance before buying a share of the restaurant in the 1930s.

It was said that Casimiro Jr. could sleep propped up at the cash register.

Despite his earnest nature, Casimiro Jr. had a playful side. Here, he hoists a drink at a Rotary Club meeting while wearing sunglasses and a baby bonnet.

"You probably heard this story a thousand times. If he go in that kitchen, taste some food and didn't like it, he'd dump the whole damn thing in the garbage can. You know, or in the toilet. I've seen him. Whatever it was. If he didn't think it was good, he'd say in Spanish, 'This isn't worth a damn. I won't serve it to nobody…'" Charlie Hero

Coconut Ice Cream

In the 1890s, Cuba faced a dairy shortage during the war with Spain. Cubans substituted coconut milk for the dairy when preparing rice pudding and did the same with ice cream. At that time, Casimiro Sr. was working in a Havana restaurant and he recorded the recipe for coconut sherbet. He never used the recipe at the Columbia, but his sons found it after his death.

Casimiro Jr.'s brother Gustavo (Gus) ran a restaurant across the street for a while, regularly "borrowing" ingredients from the Columbia. When Gus bragged about his low prices, Casimiro wondered why Gus charged anything at all—the food came from the Columbia's pantry. Later, Gus

Gus Hernandez, the king of the Columbia's coconut ice cream.

opened Jordan's Bakery there, which supplied all of the Columbia's pastries.

Intrigued by the salvaged ice cream recipe, Gus experimented with the dish by adding various amounts of cream. Late at night he whipped up ten different versions of the recipe. By day, employees and patrons taste-tested the specimens. Once he had perfected the recipe, Gus opened Tropical Ice Cream Company to make his helados.

To add flash to the dish, Casimiro served it in hollowed-out coconut shells. Casimiro was forced to find a hardened steel blade, because the band saw went dull after splitting just six or seven shells. The hardened blades lasted six months. Kitchen personnel used a special curved knife to scoop the meat from the shells. Forty coconuts went into every gallon of ice cream. To streamline service, the staff froze individual portions in their own shells, ready to be served.

By the mid-1940s, the Columbia sold ten gallons a day during the slow summer season. In winter, sales averaged between forty and eighty gallons. Gus's ice cream became the Columbia's most distinctive dessert for many years.

Connections

Hearty and cheerful, Casimiro's brother Lawrence became his partner in the mid-1930s, eventually owning his own shares. Before then, he worked in several banks, dabbled in insurance, and served as a justice of the peace beginning in 1932, gaining many influential friends. Behind the scenes, Lawrence found helpful union contacts for the Columbia.

Lawrence counted politicians and gangsters as his close associates. Back then, the two circles were not much different. Organized crime underwrote almost every local candidate from the 1920s to the 1950s. Like today's lobbyists, the mob hedged its bets by funding opposing politicians.

In 1940, redistricting took Lawrence's post, and he left public service to work at the Columbia full-time. He continued to serve in a variety of public appointments. President Franklin D. Roosevelt asked him to serve on the National Cigar Wage Board in 1941; he sat on the Tampa Housing Authority; and he was vice consul for Honduras in Tampa.

Lawrence Hernandez could work any system: businessmen, labor unions, gangsters, and customers.

When not fulfilling his civic duties, Lawrence wore the Columbia's jovial public face. His lust for life shown through in his big smile and he held court over cocktails in the small package store behind the café. He delighted in giving away valuable gifts such as liquor and perfume, even when they were scarce during World War II. A single compliment on an item of clothing or jewelry prompted Lawrence to give it away to its admirer. Clearly, Lawrence had inherited his father's sense of generosity.

He devoted himself completely to the restaurant, using every contact at his disposal to work the system. In Tampa, there existed many hidden levels of power.

Don Quixote

Casimiro's instincts told him to consolidate and expand the business, but his partners, the Garcia family, resisted. By the early 1930s, Manuel Garcia held his family's shares of the Columbia. Casimiro's brother Lawrence bought an official share of the restaurant at that time. This weakened Garcia's hold on the business. Determined to fulfill his dreams of a lavish new dining room, Casimiro bought Garcia's share of the Columbia. Garcia went on to revive an old restaurant down the street, Las Novedades, which had originally opened in 1890. A healthy rivalry ensued between the former partners for almost forty years.

The Columbia became a family business again, shared by Casimiro and Lawrence Hernandez. Lawrence's involvement increased as spokesman and diplomat. He drummed up business and mingled with Tampa's elite: businessmen, politicians, and gangsters. Casimiro's unerring hand selected the finest ingredients and managed the employees. Consolidated ownership also allowed them to take risks. A massive $75,000 loan from friends financed a new kitchen and dining room, thanks in part to Lawrence's influence. Any time they needed money for improvements, the Hernandez brothers raised money from friends and paid them back at fixed rates.

The elegant Don Quixote Room debuted in 1935. The repeal of Prohibition brought back legal alcohol sales and a thirsty clientele. Here, El Rey regales a young couple with his expert service.

Casimiro's aptly named Don Quixote Room boasted air-conditioning, a bandstand, and a dance floor. The A/C was primitive by today's standards, but it was a rare luxury then, Tampa's first air-conditioned dining room. No one likes to eat while uncomfortably warm, and air-conditioning revolutionized the experience of eating out in the South. The expanded and modernized kitchen turned out Spanish food fit for royalty. Cuban and Italian specialties rounded out the menu, making it a reflection of Ybor City's population.

Some people had doubts about the wisdom of such a risky venture in the midst of the Depression. Ybor City's future was in question. Many of its cigar factories and restaurants had closed down during the mid-1930s. All of the most obvious signals dissuaded expansion. To some, Casimiro must have seemed a little like Don Quixote himself, charging at windmills in a fantasy world.

Casimiro had his own doubts. He confided to his wife, Carmen, one night, "Carmita, if this room is not a successful venture, I'll have to blow my brains out." Carmen Hernandez was the Columbia's greatest silent partner over the years, wielding great influence and holding her own shares in the restaurant.

She responded, "Casimiro, this room is going to work. Never say a thing like that to me again!"

He scarcely looked back.

Casimiro sensed the times were on his side. Prohibition and the Depression brushed aside much of his competition. Tourism had increased a decade before with the Florida land boom.

The years of Prohibition allowed women to explore restaurants usually reserved for males. Ladies had even sampled the brew of speakeasies and became more comfortable imbibing with meals. Jazz reflected the excitement of the 1920s, and dancing became a social obsession.

Casimiro Jr. began his collection of Don Quixote themed art in the 1930s.

The demographics of Casimiro's patrons changed. Beside the traditional working men sat ladies out shopping, families celebrating, young folks on dates, and married couples rekindling romance.

People living in the Depression sought escape, entertainment, and romance. They wanted to live the lighthearted, glamorous escapades they saw in the movie theaters. They wanted, if only once a year, to put on their very best clothes, splurge on a fine Spanish dinner, taste the wine and champagne, and dance the night away like Fred Astaire and Ginger Rogers. Casimiro's instinct told him that a great opportunity lay cloaked in those dark years.

The Don Quixote Room opened to immediate success in 1935. Casimiro's beautiful renovations brought a cheerful and bright atmosphere to a place that had relatively little to be happy about.

Tiles depicting the story of Don Quixote lined the walls and brought splashes of color and a touch of Spanish romance. The finest musicians and orchestras graced the stage with big band jazz. Music brought the Don Quixote to life, when the room alone could make the ladies swoon. And if they couldn't get their men on to the dance floor, a few Cuban Manhattans, mojitos, or Cuba Libres could do the trick. State-of-the-art air-conditioning relieved the exuberant dancers. The Columbia had the coolest dining room in Tampa, in every sense of the word.

Ever since the restaurant expanded into the dinner business in 1920, the Columbia faced two challenges. The first, to provide quick, cheap lunches prepared in bulk and fancy dinners cooked to order. The second challenge was far more intangible: to provide atmospheres to accommodate lunch time bolting *and* the prolonged pleasures of the Spanish dinner table.

Over the next 10 years, Casimiro paid off his debts and the Columbia became the most famous restaurant in Florida. His big risk had paid off.

The Patio room has aged quite well. The opulent
new rooms of the 1930s heralded a new age of dining
at the Columbia, with heightened expectations for
food, music, and romance.

Paella

Food remained the Columbia's main attraction. Pijuan's talents fully bloomed in the new kitchen, and his amazing dishes embodied the romantic atmosphere. Paella became his most distinctive dish.

The origins of paella are not in Spain, but in Persia, where it was known as "pilau." For centuries, the Persians made a dish of rice, spices, and various meats and vegetables. They cooked pilau in a heavy, broad pan until the flavors melded and a golden crust of rice formed on the bottom. The invading Moors brought the dish to Spain in AD 711. People in the Americas and beyond—India, Africa, and the Caribbean—interpreted the dish in their own ways over the years. Spaniards devised an especially savory version using the culinary equivalent of gold—saffron, which is worth more than gold by weight. Saffron is expensive because it is so difficult to harvest. Workers painstakingly remove the tiny stamens from the crocus flower. Arroz con pollo, or chicken and yellow rice, is a simplified version of pilau.

A dish of paella Valenciana evokes the same passions as the colorful Don Quixote Room. As a rice-producing region in Spain, Valencia is a natural home to great paella, originally made in the orchards and rice paddies with snails, green beans, and other prominent ingredients in the area. Paella cooks usually used orange wood for their paella fires, a fuel perfectly suited for the dish: it burns hot at first, bringing the water to a boil, then smolders at a lower temperature, simmering the rice. Valencians never mix meat with seafood in their paella, but immigrants in America departed from this custom.

Paella made in the Valencia region contains a dazzling array of seafood, perfect for Florida's fertile waters. The shrimp, oysters, scallops, mussels, clams, crab, snapper, lobster, plus chicken and pork lend their juices to the rice as it cooks, with the blended flavors permeating the entire dish. The saffron lends taste as well as a vibrant yellow color, which is complemented by the green of bell pepper, asparagus and peas, and the red of tomato and roasted red pepper.

Gambling

Other gambles never panned out. Lawrence and Casimiro planned new delights that almost led to an Ybor City gang war. Such was the success of the Don Quixote Room that in 1937 they built the beautiful Patio Room, with its fountain and natural light. They hired Ivo de Menici from Italy to design the space. Sculptors fashioned the enigmatic fountain from a design found in Naples—"Love and the Dolphin"—supposedly recovered from the ruins of Pompeii. The statue romanticized a brutal depiction: a sea monster crushing a nymph. The retractable skylight proved to be a novelty, offering al fresco dining most of the year.

A pan of paella is a feast for the senses.

The room that caused all of the trouble was the planned casino upstairs, Vista Hermosa. The Hernandez brothers knew Santo Trafficante, the powerful mob boss. Prohibition had unwittingly created a thriving criminal underworld financed by bootleg liquor and gambling, raising gangsters like Trafficante and his sons to positions of great power. Lawrence and Casimiro planned to take the Trafficantes as partners and open a casino, offering slot machines and bolita tickets. A stairwell in a hidden entrance led to the casino. But Charlie Wall, the Anglo king of Tampa's underworld at the time, did not look kindly upon this violation of his territory. Gangsters battled for control of Tampa's rackets throughout the 1930s, and a new war threatened.

Trafficante and the Hernandez brothers tried to negotiate over territory to no avail. The potential clientele for a casino grew with army air corps bases in Tampa and ex-

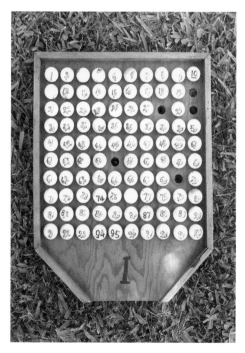

Bolita, an illegal lottery imported from Cuba, became Tampa's favorite pastime by the 1940s.

panded port facilities. The gorgeous Columbia Restaurant drew more customers than ever, and could surely rule the casino business, Wall feared.

One night Lawrence walked out the restaurant's side door with the pharmacist J. B. Pacheco. A shotgun blasted buckshot out of the alley and struck Lawrence. J. B. rushed him to the Trelles Clinic down the street to patch him up and avert disaster.

In the aftermath of that salvo, the Hernandez brothers decided not to build their casino after all. Bolita remained and financed organized crime for another twenty years. The Columbia focused on what it did best—great Spanish food and atmosphere.

"Eat Chicken and Divide"

When gangsters in Tampa talked about splitting profits from a scheme or heist, they said they would "eat chicken and divide." Few immigrants could ignore the delights of southern-fried chicken.

For the first 60 years of the 20th century, it seemed every restaurant in Tampa served fried chicken. Chinese restaurants cooked up the southern classic in their woks. Italian restaurants listed the dish on menus beside pasta classics. Ethnic eateries offered the dish to mollify unadventurous patrons.

The Columbia sometimes served fried chicken that looked the same as most others in town. But when they "taste what they get," journalist Paul Wilder wrote, "their eyes widen in surprise and one patron remarked: 'It's fried chicken, all right, but what country?' So all we can tell you is it's 'country style the Columbia way.'" The kitchen did its best to improve upon the Southern specialty by soaking the chicken overnight in milk, lemon juice, onion, garlic and pepper. Bathed in milk and egg and then dipped in Cuban bread crumbs, it is understandable that the extra flavor took patrons by surprise.

War, Mobilization, and Rationing

Everyone in Ybor City saw the storm clouds long before lightning struck at Pearl Harbor. In the 1920s, Mussolini brought fascism to Italy. Hitler and Franco followed suit in Germany and Spain in the 1930s. The Japanese attack at Hawaii shocked the nation on December 7, 1941. The following New Year's Eve was quiet in Ybor City, with no fireworks or bright lights.

The silence of shock and mourning did not last long. Tampa shook off the malaise of the Great Depression with a boost from military projects. The shipyards and naval repair facilities just down the street from the Columbia worked day and night, employing men, women, blacks, and whites. Three Army air fields settled around Tampa—MacDill, Drew, and Henderson—bringing pilots and support personnel to the area. Tampa's port and shipbuilders brought visitors from all over the globe, from Russia to Australia.

Dinner at the Columbia, preferably with a date, was the dream of many a sailor and soldier. Fantasies came true every night by the bar, at the tables, and on the dance floor. The sights, sounds, aromas, and tastes of those nights burned into the memories of the men, comforting recollections in a foxhole.

The war was not a complete bonanza—it brought endless complications. Beyond the terrible price of lost loved ones overseas, the restaurant felt the pinch of the war. Skilled employees left for the front. Rationing of sugar and meats hampered business, but it could have been much worse. The government calculated allocations of rationed goods to restaurants by business levels in December 1941, the month the United States entered the war. Florida's tourist season is well underway in December, so restaurants there found themselves with a relatively generous portion after all.

Despite tight wartime rationing, Columbia ads boasted in Spanish, "We have it all at La Fonda."

In its ads, the Columbia sent out conflicting messages on the effects of rationing. As regulations tightened in 1943, a Columbia ad read, "The present times are difficult for citizens, restaurants, and bars. The Columbia fights to please its customers while complying with the government. We ask your patience if our friends and customers can't get all of the commodities available in normal times."

Later, the Columbia flaunted its ability to obtain virtually anything for its exclusive dining rooms. With Prohibition experience and shady friends, the Hernandez brothers negotiated the new black market with ease. A 1945 ad read, "Food is short due to wartime rationing, but we have it all at La Fonda." Lawrence's well-placed gifts of liquor and perfume won many new friends.

A Home Front Restaurant

The war brought difficulties no well-placed friend could fix. The military and wartime industry made employee retention difficult. Wage and price controls presented their own difficulties. Casimiro admitted, "We paid a $2500 War Labor Board fine because at the time we were over-paying the chef, a pantryman, and our musicians." With the country short of manpower, retaining good help could be difficult. It is no wonder that Casimiro overpaid his employees.

Maintaining low prices became a constant struggle. Influential friends could alleviate some of rationing's burdens, but not the federal Office of Price Administration, which had the power to freeze or roll back prices. The OPA once fined the restaurant a whopping $1,200 for a price on crawfish that did not comply with regulations. Still, through thrift and government regulation, Casimiro did not raise 1940 prices until after the war.

"We thought today you might like to know how the restaurant gets by despite increasing labor, equipment and food costs," management shared in an ad. "The answer is volume." Buying, selling, and cooking in bulk saved money and kept patrons happy. Casimiro found other ways to maintain profits. To avoid escalating beef prices, he prepared "extravagant seafood dishes that cost us less to produce." Rationing of meat encouraged fish and organ (liver, kidneys, tripe, etc.) consumption well after the war. The growing use of chicken livers in the kitchen bulked up meat dishes such as steak capuchina and enriched sauces.

Rationing of coffee, sugar, meat, and other foods also threatened to hurt business. The war put an end to the

FOOD PRICES, 1940–1947		
Bulk Product, per pound	1940	1947
Chicken	.23	.45
Rice	4	12.50
Beef Filet	.35	.75
Olive oil, per gallon	1.50	10.00
Menu Item, per Order	1940	1947
Arroz con Pollo	.75	.90
Spanish Bean Soup	.25	.40
Beef Stew	.35	.40
Lunch Combo	.50	.75

Columbia's short-lived chicken farm in 1946, as an ad announced: "We got about 4,000 from there. Now we're buying chickens again." The losses didn't end there. Besides café con leche and Cuban toast, Casimiro shut down the kitchen for breakfast. The surges of lunch and dinner business brought most of the profits anyway.

"A lot of servicemen, and a lot of ships of the Navy would stop right here on Thirteenth Street, and when they get off they would come here to Ybor City. They'd ask a cab driver, 'Where's a good place to eat?' 'The Columbia Restaurant!' That was one of those things, and the hotel people knew also. They brought four or five cabs parked all the time here." Joe Roman, Columbia waiter

It seems that parking has always been scarce in Ybor City: the Columbia in the 1940s.

bread—12 feet long in all—washed down with six bowls of Spanish Bean Soup. "We only charged him 25 cents for the pound [of butter]," Paul Wilder wrote in an ad, "It seems fantastic now when we pay 70 cents wholesale."

"Once the Columbia bought Minnesota butter, already cut and racked," Wilder mused, "and each patty was stamped with the name 'Columbia'; now we're lucky to get any Minnesota butter at all." One pat of butter per customer still amounted to four thousand pounds a month. The

During World War II, the Columbia was attracting people from all over the world. The steady business required large stocks of scarce resources, such as meat, oil, butter, sugar, and alcohol.

Management coped with an onion shortage during the war, and bought them whenever they could. When no onions remained, Casimiro bought them dehydrated. "We still have a few cans left in the warehouse, and we hope we never have to use them again." During the war, the Columbia cured its own pimientos "and many of our patrons easily detected the difference." Saffron was not so easily replaced. The Spanish Civil War had driven the already-high price up to ninety-five dollars a pound. During the global war, prices settled to forty-eight dollars a pound. Today, saffron sells for over forty dollars per *ounce!*

Butter and Olive Oil

In the days before the war, a customer once ordered an entire pound of butter with four loaves of Cuban

kitchen resorted to cooking with three parts margarine to one part butter. Butter ran out just once, when cream cheese had to suffice on Cuban bread.

The Columbia's clientele demanded fifteen to twenty gallons of olive oil a day. Sometimes the kitchen employed butter during shortages, which drained the kitchen of another scarce resource. The Spanish Civil War cut off olive oil shipments from Spain, so management bought up stocks from Greece and Italy until those were exhausted. Casimiro was pleased to find some domestic oil almost as good as the imports. Unable to obtain large drums of oil, he bought the product in containers as small as a pint. Somehow, the restaurant never ran out.

The security of the oil required extreme measures. "The olive oil is kept hidden now," Wilder wrote, "and only [headwaiter] Angel Leon has the key to the hiding place." When an absent-minded waiter left the spigot to the oil barrel running one day, the mistake was not discovered until the precious oil formed a puddle running into the dining room. He must have been lucky to keep his job—if he did.

The Clumsy Wartime Waiter

A young waiter was lucky to keep his job—and his life— after an awful day on the job. Ferdie Pacheco, a young man of fourteen years, watched the Columbia's older waiters practice their craft during the war. He felt justifiably awkward in their presence.

Just as Ybor City's Latins made a craft out of soup, sandwiches, and cigars, the waiters practiced an elite art form. They memorized every order, writing nothing down. Customers could rely upon the knowledge and opinions of the waiters as experts in food and drink. They carved fish and fowl tableside with a flair. They selected and uncorked the finest wines with the assurance of sommeliers. They carried the plates lined down their arms, yet maintained a graceful walk across the dining rooms. They comported themselves with the dignity Pijuan's majestic cuisine deserved.

Ferdie found himself in Pijuan's crosshairs after trying to carry five plates of spaghetti on one arm, the same way he'd seen experienced waiters do it. All five dishes spilled to the floor when he fumbled. After his fellow waiters laughed, they wondered what fate awaited him in Pijuan's kitchen. Ferdie shuffled back into the kitchen and asked Pijuan for five more orders of pasta.

"Five orders of spaghetti and meatballs?" Pijuan said mildly, taking a huge bite out of a head of lettuce.

"I nodded," Ferdie remembered, "knowing he was letting me off the hook. Not another word was said about it, then

New waiters endured ridicule and intense scrutiny from coworkers. A group of self-assured waiters in the 1940s look confident except for the young man at the bottom right. He'd probably been rushed into service when a waiter was drafted into the armed forces. A three-year apprenticeship was an unaffordable luxury in times of war.

Waiters prided themselves on grace and dexterity. It is said that a waiter once balanced 14 plates down his arms at once. Needless to say, the restaurant went through a great deal of plates and glasses broken in accidents.

or ever, by Pijuan, who despite his feared persona was a softie at heart."

Santo Trafficante, one of the most powerful gangsters in the state, was known as a popular and gentle man in Ybor City. Trafficante ordered vermicelli soup from fresh-faced Ferdie one morning. Trying to impress Ybor City's elder statesman, with a flourish he poured the soup from a tureen into the bowl. The steaming soup splashed out of the shallow bowl and on to the old man's lap.

Pacheco's feelings of clumsiness can be especially understood by the grace of his fellow waiters. He was rushed

into service as a waiter, after all, because so many able-bodied men were off fighting in World War II.

Ferdie went on to become one of Ybor City's great success stories. He became a doctor, served as Muhammad Ali's ringside physician, a boxing analyst, and an artist. With Adela Gonzmart, he penned the Columbia's first cookbook.

Pompano and Steak Capuchina

Wartime rationing cramped lifestyles and intensified appetites. Shortages of sugar, butter, coffee, and liquor prompted hoarding and a thriving black market. The rationing of meat left many Americans craving a good steak. The police apprehended several "meatleggers" in Tampa during the war.

In the 1930s, the Columbia began to sell arroz con pollo in large volumes, and found itself discarding thousands of chicken livers. The cooks didn't need many giblets for sauces and gravies. Pijuan experimented with ways to use the livers. He bundled five or six with strips of bacon and browned them in a pan with wine sauce, calling it "Chicken Liver Steak." It took a while for the dish to catch on, but by 1946, the kitchen served ten thousand orders a year.

Chopped livers topped steak capuchina, which was baked in a paper bag with Spanish gravy, mushrooms, and nuts. Customers ate six thousand orders a year. Another dish called for broiled chicken liver skewers. The browned nuggets graced a length of battered and fried Cuban bread, all topped with oil and vinegar. With Pijuan's help, the Columbia served forty thousand pounds of chicken livers annually—not bad for what passed as trash for so many years.

The Rationing Board encouraged citizens to eat fresh seafood, and there was no shortage in Florida's fertile waters. Pijuan mastered Spanish and French cooking, and his talents shone with every order of pompano en papillot. He placed the fish filets into a pouch of parchment, providing a delicate oven. Inside, they baked in a creamy sauce with onion, lobster, and shrimp. Pijuan's pompano made one forget all about rationing—and everything else.

At one time, waiters served the fish still sealed in its browned parchment bag. Out of ignorance, some early customers enjoyed a less than ideal order of the fish. They ate the paper bag. "One customer wrote to my father praising the pompano papillot," Adela said. "Noting at the end, 'I particularly liked the crust.' At that point, we decided to let the waiter remove the paper at tableside and serve the pompano."

Meat rationing encouraged domestic fish consumption and the Columbia offered lavish seafood dishes in lieu of meat.

OPA CHARGES 8 FIRMS BOUGHT STOLEN MEAT

Restaurant and Seven Markets Sentenced

A thriving black market circumvented government rationing. The Columbia coped with shortages, but Laurence could obtain the most sought-after items with ease.

Patriotism

The most resonant message in the Columbia's ads was the owners' dedication to the Allied cause. Spain may have gone fascist, but the hearts of the Hernandez family identified with their home, the United States. As the Christmas holiday approached in 1942 and the outcome of the war still in question, a large Columbia ad in *La Gaceta* declared in Spanish:

> *The Columbia Restaurant wishes its thousands of clients and friends during this Christmas the happiness[…]that each human being deserves. Distance all the worries with a Nochebuena dinner in the Columbia Restaurant or awaiting the New Year in one of our rooms.*

> *NATIONAL UNITY*
> *This restaurant, one of the best known in the country, during these difficult days for the American people, wants to express one more time its profound devotion to the United States, everybody's country, and recommends unity and cooperation in Tampa and all the Republic. The Columbia offers its collaboration to win the war over the common enemy, and delivers through its employees and owners an offering on the altar of the attacked nation.*

The ad was especially poignant because it was written and published in Spanish, for an immigrant audience. Forget the past, Casimiro suggested. *We are all Americans now.* During the war, Tampa's immigrant communities underwent a profound change. Fascist Spain and Italy seemed worlds away to the immigrants, many of whom became G.I.s themselves.

The Fighting Waiter

Casimiro Yanez Jr. began work as a waiter in 1939. Three years later during the war, he became a pilot in the Air Transport Command. The Columbia's own waiter flew big C-47 transports and B-25 Mitchell bombers to places like Casablanca, Cairo, Naples, and Marrakech. No matter how far he traveled, there always seemed to be someone around to swap Columbia memories with. Of course, they always missed the food.

In a Madrid nightclub during the war in neutral Spain, a man heard Yanez's familiar accent, a Spanglish dialect with Cuban and Italian inflections known only in Tampa. The other patron turned out to be a Cuban who had frequented the Columbia Restaurant.

In 1942, Yanez was stationed in Casablanca, French Morocco. He enjoyed a surprise visit with Eddie Diaz, who once worked at the Columbia as the sandwich man. After exchanging news and favorite memories, they went straight to the dining hall where Diaz worked as mess sergeant. Raiding the stores, they prepared a special meal for their fellow soldiers. They gathered rice, onions, pimientos, and chicken. They obtained saffron at a nearby Moroccan shop and went to work. Four thousand miles from home, the

men nonetheless enjoyed a taste of arroz con pollo. It was the first Spanish meal Yanez had enjoyed in about sixteen months. Morale soared that night in the mess hall.

Yanez returned from the service healthy, if a bit hungry for the Columbia's food. Management promoted him to headwaiter soon after his return. Yanez found the transition from soldier to civilian somewhat strange. He often saw familiar faces, people he'd met during the war in more trying circumstances. Instead of reminiscing about the Columbia overseas, they found themselves remembering the war at the Columbia. That suited them just fine.

A fascinating variety of characters told their stories to Yanez. One man "waited eight thousand miles" for his meal after hearing about the Columbia in some South Pacific hellhole. Three women—two English and one French—

The Columbia's extensive use of rice required dedicated specialists.

Soldiers missed more than sweethearts and hometowns as evidenced in the numerous letters received from troops oveseas longing for a taste of Columbia's Spanish fare.

An artist's rendition of the Columbia chow hall on Ie Shima Island, where American soldiers endured snipers, typhoons, and kamikaze attacks.

learned of the Columbia's storied cuisine in Marseilles. A Tampa boy dreamed of the Columbia as he forced down K-rations in the jungles of Burma.

Yanez's biggest struggle as a civilian was to convince patrons of his Spanish ancestry. His light hair, rugged features, and blue eyes made him suspect. Customers sometimes accused him of being a faux Spaniard. One patron became especially annoyed, saying, "I think you say you're Spanish just because you work in a Spanish restaurant and don't want to admit you're really Irish."

Yanez bowed coolly and replied, "Well, madam, if it will please you, then I am Irish." Only then was the customer convinced of his Spanish nature. In fact, Yanez was a "Gallego," or a person born in the Spanish province of Galicia.

Like so many of Tampa's Spaniards, Yanez hailed from the "unconquered" northern provinces of Spain, which remained untouched by the Moorish invasion.

Ie Shima

While the bloody battle for Okinawa proceeded in 1945, a small ray of hope beckoned on nearby Ie Shima Island. Less than two miles from where the beloved journalist Ernie Pyle and General Simon Bolivar Buckner died, Tampa native Mike DiBona assembled his own Columbia Restaurant using scrap lumber and canvas.

A mess sergeant in the Tenth Army, DiBona scrounged for spices, had coffee sent from Tampa, and cooked Spanish meals, all in the midst of storms and exploding kamikazes.

Ie Shima Island after the typhoon of 1945.

The seventy Florida men in his unit couldn't have been more appreciative of his efforts. DiBona even placed a board sign on the crude tent reading "Columbia Restaurant, Ybor City."

A typhoon ravaged the island after the Japanese surrender, sweeping away several buildings, including DiBona's Columbia. In the wreckage, DiBona found the sign and salvaged his pots and pans. A new mess hall with prefabricated walls sprang up. The old sign went up once again, this time adorned with painted palm trees.

When DiBona's deployment ended, he passed his Columbia on to an Atlanta man who had been to the restaurant several times. DiBona's company planned a reunion at the real Columbia in 1947, hopefully without the intrusion of typhoons and kamikazes.

Hero Wedding

Hernandez family friend Charlie Hero served as a radar specialist accustomed to ducking buzzbomb attacks late in the war in Europe. He helped plot the planned invasion of Japan. After not receiving leave in over two years, Charlie went home and visited his family before his next bloody assignment. He also saw his girlfriend, Melba. They got married quite unexpectedly in the Columbia's Patio Room while other G.I. couples were getting hitched there.

Ever the gift-giver, Lawrence gave Charlie plane tickets to Miami for their honeymoon and Melba a bottle of fine perfume. Charlie tried to refuse the plane tickets to no avail. Air travel seemed so ostentatious in the 1940s. Lawrence insisted, and Charlie took the tickets. Miami seemed so exotic, like another country, even for a Florida resident.

The Heros chose a good time to get married. While on honeymoon, they heard news of the atomic bombs and the Japanese surrender. Charlie enjoyed a fine wedding reception at the Columbia—and would never have to invade Japan. They still felt they did not take enough time to get married. Charlie Hero explained, "Years later we had our marriage blessed."

Charlie and Melba Hero shortly after being married at the Columbia. They remained lifelong friends of three generations of owners.

Peace, Cooked Two Ways

The first victory, V-E Day (Victory in Europe) on May 8, 1945, was a kitchen blitzkrieg. Jubilant crowds overwhelmed the restaurant when news broke of Nazi Germany's surrender. The kitchen kept up for many hours before all the ingredients ran out. The coolers didn't even have cold cuts for sandwiches. On-duty chef Sarapico raised the white flag at ten that night, turning out the lights in the kitchen. The celebration continued at the bar.

Balbino Alvarez Lopez went to the Columbia to eat in the early 1920s and never stopped, dining there every day for over a quarter century. On August 14, 1945 (V-J Day), he found the restaurant closed and the streets packed with revelers.

The nation had good reason to celebrate. News of the Japanese surrender meant the end of the war and prompted a spontaneous national celebration, a giant block party in Ybor City. The biggest party in history roared in the streets, and Alvarez didn't care. He peered into the Columbia's darkened windows. To his surprise and delight, he saw Casimiro deep in thought. A hopeless workaholic, Casimiro happened to be in the restaurant checking the books. He let Lopez in and made him some bacon and eggs, the only meal served at the Columbia on V-J Day.

 ## Tampa Fusion Food

"It seems funny for the Columbia, a Spanish restaurant, to be serving a German dish, but that's the way we operate," read a Columbia ad. Sauerkraut stewed in the Columbia's kitchen. "The specialties are Cuban and Spanish dishes, but that doesn't mean other nations don't have good ideas in cooking, too. Columbia chefs borrow flavor combinations from French, Italian, German, Mexican, and American chefs, adapting the different ideas to the Columbia's own way of doing things."

The biggest party in history: VJ-Day in Ybor City.

On St. Patrick's Day, the kitchen usually prepared special dinners, such as the green theme meal: corned beef and cabbage, green pea puree, salad, and lime sherbet. The cooks made the meal all the more Irish by adding green coloring to the boiled potatoes, dubbing them "Potatoes O'Hara" after Ybor merchant Phil O'Hara.

Tampa boasted fusion cuisine long before the word became trendy. It wasn't just good food—it was good for business. With familiar American classics—even meatloaf!—Casimiro made unadventurous businessmen and tourists comfortable. The more open-minded eaters had a twenty-five-page menu to explore.

The lunch and dinner specials reflected Casimiro's unpretentious ambition to please all: Stuffed cabbage. Pig knuckles in sauerkraut. French oxtail ragout. Spaghetti gumbo. Picadillo. Country-fried chicken. Frog legs dusted in spices and wrapped in bacon. Macaroni and eggplant. Meatballs and pasta. Seafood empanadas and plantains. Baked beans and sausage. Long before tourists ever heard of a grouper sandwich, the Columbia cooked the neglected fish Galician style with sliced potatoes, sofrito, vinegar, oregano, and bay leaf. And for dessert: Roquefort and Camembert cheese with French champagne, guava shells with cream cheese, and crepes Suzette.

A Taste of Italy

As a matter of courtesy to their Italian neighbors and tourists, some Spanish and Cuban restaurants offered spaghetti and other *squisito* (tasty) specialties. Italian food was a well-kept secret in most of Tampa and the United States. Then came the war. Some GIs tasted the food while serving in Italy. Many others ate approximations of Italian cuisine in the mess halls. For many a country boy, noodles and red sauce were a revelation. Some had never tasted garlic or olive oil, never mind basil or oregano.

The restaurant served almost four hundred pounds of pasta a week during the mid-1940s. Macaroni and rich tomato sauce—cooked with meat or topped with cheese—appeared routinely as a daily special. Crab enchilado—seafood and tomato sauce over pasta—remained a revered and messy favorite.

In 1950, Casimiro must have been happy to find Giovanni Garzia, an accomplished Italian chef. He had become a cook's helper at sea at age thirteen. He was quickly recognized as a cook in the Italian merchant marine during World War I, for he soon moved to a general's mess in the army. He worked cruise liners and glamorous hotspots in New York City before relocating to Florida for the sake of his wife's health.

His Italian specialties soon became Columbia mainstays. Toward the end of 1950, the Columbia rolled out a new Italian menu. Italian dishes had appeared on the menu for some time, but the new menu was an effort to cash in on America's postwar craze for Italian food.

For a full week, the Columbia's ads trumpeted the Columbia's new Italian specialties to the public: Minestrone.

Pasta fagioli. Chicken cacciatore. Ravioli. Veal cooked four ways: "scallopini, rolitini, pizziola, and parmigiana." Garzia even served pizza. Patrons could order his pies topped with crab, ground meat, or cheese. Management made every effort to import vital ingredients from Italy. Local Italian dairy farmers supplied fresh mozzarella.

By 1953, Garzia had left the Columbia, but his Italian specialties remained. Most of the regular Italian menu disappeared, but many of the dishes resurfaced as daily specials.

Café con Leche

Everyone was crazy about the Columbia's coffee. Café con leche—strong Cuban coffee and boiled milk—embodies the thrift and passion of Cuba.

Customers sought the Columbia's coffee urns with a passion of their own. Joe Diliberto drove to the Columbia three miles from the Farmers' Market to get the best coffee in town. He repeated this procedure five or six times daily, downing about twenty cups altogether. Streetcar conductors gulped down scalding coffee during unauthorized stops. One Tampa man bought a round of java for everyone in the house every time he visited. One day his charity provided coffee for sixty-eight other patrons.

Anglos drank 80 percent of the Columbia's joe in 1946. The Columbia offered "American" style coffee for the faint of heart. Most of the coffee beans came from Mexico, Colombia, Venezuela, Haiti, and Central America. Cuban coffee mills roasted the beans for as much as twice as long as typical mills. The longer roasting time decreased caffeine levels by up to 80 percent, while strengthening the flavor of the coffee to help "stretch" the beans.

Pascual Soto, the Columbia's coffee maker, did not take well to the new electric coffee urns during the 1940s. Casimiro bought the new twin-urned mechanism thinking it would come in handy during the winter rush. He thrust it into service three days later when his old urn broke down. Casimiro installed the new equipment overnight, and Pascual soon ran into trouble.

When the salesmen demonstrated the equipment, all seemed clear. But the first time Pascual used the urn, he could not figure out how to turn off the dispenser. As steaming coffee streamed from the faucet and dripped down to the floor, Pascual ran around the restaurant in panic, shouting in Spanish: "It's no good! I don't like these newfangled coffee urns. Send them back!"

Waiters rushed to assist, pulling levers and turning knobs to no avail. Finally, a waiter arrived and calmly turned a small wheel. The torrent subsided, and the crisis passed. By the end of the day, Pascual decided the new urns—which produced more coffee with less maintenance—could stay at his station.

Soup of the Day

Many of Ybor City's oldest restaurants kept weekly soup schedules to provide variety for daily diners. The Columbia always provided Spanish bean soup and vermicelli soup. White bean soups were quite popular. On Sundays, patrons enjoyed caldo Gallego, a rich soup with white beans, turnip greens, ham, and chorizo. Today, patrons still enjoy this dish at the Columbia's Ybor and Sarasota locations. The cooks experimented on Mondays and Tuesdays, trying their hands at gumbo, split pea, beef barley, and lentil. The kitchen served some variety of soup with seafood on Wednesdays and Fridays. On Thursday, the kitchen offered Berzada, with blood sausage, bacon, and collard greens. On Saturdays, ham, bacon, and sausages mingled with fava beans and rich broth, a stew called fabada, the beloved staple of Asturias.

Inspiration from Spain and Cuba constantly reinvigorated the Columbia kitchen. During the postwar period, the kitchen took many cues from Cuba, including olla, a stew inspired by the Indians of the island, replete with several varieties of potatoes, meat, and vegetables. One cook brought his grandmother's recipe for carne Pinarena from the Pinar del Rio province. Mojo-marinated beef cubes were braised with butter and then simmered in gravy with pearl onions, new potatoes, string beans, carrots, green peppers, tomatoes, capers, and olives. The stew thickened while being baked.

The Columbia used mild fish for making seafood soup, which appeared on the menu several times a week. The cooks found that the oils in pompano and mackerel transmitted too much "fishiness." The cooks preferred white meat from red snapper and trout.

By the 1950s, even lowly black bean soup became recognized as a sophisticated dish. Once a specialty of Cuban peasants, *Gourmet* magazine reprinted the Columbia's recipe for black bean soup in 1953. According to Paul

Wilder, Spanish bean soup became Tampa's most-eaten dish, "with a possible exception of mashed potatoes." On busy days, the Columbia sold four to six thousand bowls of the favorite. Wilder intoned that the Columbia made the soup "in much the same way Castillian peasants prepared bean soup a century and more ago." Even then, the Columbia's soup stood head and shoulders above the competition. A new waiter from Cuba said it was the best soup he'd ever eaten.

The kitchen made a forty-gallon pot of Spanish Bean soup four times daily, using the following ingredients:

180 pounds of garbanzos (usually from Mexico)

35 gallons of garbanzo purée

100 pounds of potatoes

20 pounds of chorizo

20 pounds of bacon

24 cans of tomatoes

4 pounds of garlic

15 pounds of onion

4 pounds paprika

2 gallons of olive oil

Black bean soup, once known as Cuba's national dish, became a mainstay in Tampa.

Sandwiches

From a small sandwich stand beside the cash register, a two-man crew served 175,000 sandwiches every year, most of them the Cuban variety. Angel Fernandez must have been good with a knife. Without the aid of a modern deli slicer, everyday he precisely cut 85 pounds of smoked ham, 60 pounds of roast pork (or 60 pounds of turkey), 15 pounds of Swiss cheese, and 15 pounds of Genoa salami. When Fernandez called it a day, another man served sandwiches until 2:00 AM.

The sandwich station's warming oven—in the days before the sandwich press—held sixteen sandwiches. During the lunch rush, Fernandez enlisted the main ovens in the kitchen. Angel claimed there was no better sandwich anywhere than the Columbia's Cuban.

Children especially loved the sandwiches. Most patrons knew better than to ask for lettuce or tomato. Customers seldom requested mayonnaise, consuming only five gallons annually in the 1940s. Those ingredients were confined to the triple-decker club sandwiches.

Steak, Symbol of Success

One customer proved to be an extreme diner, regularly ordering a rib-cut sirloin a foot long and three inches thick. The weight was not recorded, but the steak fit for a lion cost about twenty dollars and took forty-five minutes to cook. "He was willing to wait while it was being prepared," management recalled.

For many years, steak had been a favorite indulgence in America. The lean years of the Depression and rationing of the war elevated the demand for good meat. The rationing authorities made all good cuts of beef steak quite costly, with organ meat at the bottom.

After the war, while most of the world picked up the pieces of civilization, the United States lived "high on the hog," earning paychecks and consuming dinners worthy of global envy. Steak became much more than a passing indulgence in the 1950s and 1960s. It became a celebratory rite and symbol of success, and the Columbia cashed in.

Together with arroz con pollo and pompano en papillot, steak was the Columbia's top seller. The kitchen could handle up to seventy orders of steak at a time, cooked a dozen different ways with as many sauces.

The kitchen employed a butcher to slice twelve-ounce filets from the tenderloins. Butcher Jose Rivas once served as a chef, but "tired of arguing with the waiters." Scar tissue covered his hands through slips of his blade and handling sharp bones. People knew Rivas as "El Capitan" because he worked at sea for much of his life. He had spent so many years on the ocean that the proud butcher refused to trim

another fish. At the Columbia, he trimmed the tenderloin tips for beef stew. With nothing wasted, cooks simmered loose trimmings into stocks. Casimiro sold excess fat to a nearby soap factory.

Steak el Patio was most extravagant with fat. Seafood was layered on top of a broiled steak surrounded by several deep-fried items: onion rings, breaded ham, and battered asparagus tips, all garnished with parsley and red wine sauce. Steak capuchina packed even more flavor with a sauce of chopped chicken livers, nuts, mushrooms, and wine, all baked in parchment paper.

Some customers requested steak tartar—raw chopped steak with raw onion and raw egg. Other steak varieties included Creole (broiled and surrounded by potatoes and plantains with a gravy of onions, green pepper, and wine); Milanesa (breaded and fried covered in rich tomato sauce); Catalana (broiled with rich tomato sauce, peas, chopped ham, and pimiento); mushroom (covered with butter or gravy with sliced mushrooms); sautéed (grilled and covered with brown gravy, chopped ham, peas, and red wine baked in a casserole); and planked (broiled and served surrounded with mashed potatoes, carrots, string beans, and beets).

 ## Pride and Character

Casimiro knew that his business brimmed with distinctive personality, and he would even tolerate some inefficiency to preserve that quality. He once hired a specialist to study his operations and offer ways to optimize them. While McDonald's invented fast food in California, the Columbia's employees were too proud to produce their culinary creations on a soulless assembly line.

Columbia employees often displayed strong personalities and individual style. No one dared to tell Ramonin Lopez how to mix drinks.

Casimiro reflected through an ad:

> *Every employee of the Columbia is an expert in his field and takes pride in his own particular ability so sometimes there may be a seeming lot of confusion around the Columbia. You may hear the biggest argument going on in arm-waving Spanish and think somebody is going to get killed. The argument may be merely over whether a dish should have one pinch of oregano or two. But the outcome of the argument will result in a better Columbia dish.*
>
> *Our resolutions for assembly-line efficiency didn't all work out. And now we know why the Columbia is unlike any other big restaurant and why our efficiency expert is so despairing. We found the Columbia is a human institution, catering to the human whims of thousands of wonderful patrons from all over the world. And the greatest motivating force producing the Columbia's famed food and service is human pride.*

Diplomatically, the ad did not mention the most intractable obstacle to change: the Cooks' and Waiters' Union. It resisted many new practices (such as the hiring of women until the 1990s).

The Dancing Waiter

Tampans recognized Jimmy Rochey as a Columbia waiter, but people all over the country had seen him perform as a stilt dancer. He began dancing at age twelve, performing the first time at seventeen. He met his wife, Ann, at his first gig. They became a performing vaudeville act called The Two Aces.

FLOOR SHOW TONIGHT
Featuring
THE GREAT ROCHEYS
NATIONALLY KNOWN STILT DANCERS FROM STAGE AND SCREEN

WE ARE PROUD OF—
AND YOU WILL ENJOY OUR—
- Western Prime Ribs of Beef
- Broiled Steaks
- Genuine Red Snapper Steaks
- Jumbo Fried Shrimp
- Well Prepared Fresh Vegetables
- Home-made Pies, Cakes and Biscuits

SUNDAY DINNER
SIX COURSE DINNER FROM $1.50 TO $2.00
SERVED FROM 11:30 A. M. TILL 9:30 P. M.

For Your Listening Pleasure Nightly
EDDIE FORD
At the Console of the Hammond Organ

The Crystal Ball Is Closed All Day on Mondays
NO COVER—NO MINIMUM—NO ADMISSION
(Air Conditioned)
Dine In Tampa's Most Unusual Restaurant
Delightful Atmosphere

AT THE   For Reservations
                          TELEPHONE
                          W-5501
CRYSTAL BALL
5013 BAYSHORE BOULEVARD, TAMPA 6, FLORIDA

Jimmy Rochey found fame as a stilt dancer, but he made a lousy waiter at first.

Gregorio Martinez, also known as "El Rey," made every guest feel like royalty at the Columbia.

With stiff competition on the dwindling vaudeville circuit, The Two Aces elevated their act onto stilts. They waltzed, ran, rhumba-ed and tap-danced for amazed audiences. The novelty brought abundant bookings in theatres, nightclubs, and hotels. They toured Europe in 1938, and a movie short featured their act, bringing unprecedented exposure.

While dancing a Hawaiian number in New York, Jimmy's stilt slipped on a flower petal and he crashed to the floor, shattering his knee cap. He soldiered on and finished his act, but knew his career as a stilt dancer was over. The couple relocated to Tampa to be close to Jimmy's father.

He sought work at the Columbia, bragging that he "once had been at the Astor." He began as the reputedly worst Columbia waiter of all time, and management discovered that Jimmy had merely *dined* at the famous hotel, but never worked there. But Casimiro gave him a chance, and he became "one of Tampa's most expert Spanish waiters."

Four years after Jimmy retired The Two Aces, they performed a single gig at Tampa's Latin carnival. The applause began as a "polite ripple." When they took their bows after a spectacular flourish at the end, the crowd went wild. Jimmy wept at the swelling applause. "It's so good to know," he said, "the folks still like us."

King of the Waiters

Headwaiter El Rey's notoriety did not end with the repeal of Prohibition. When first hired in the 1920s, he worked as the only waiter and often performed double duty as a cook or dishwasher. He rose to be one of Tampa's most noble waiters.

He set the tone for future Columbia waiters by performing the most difficult tasks with graceful nonchalance. Like some other Spanish waiters, he rejected trays, instead lining multiple dishes down his outstretched arms. A Columbia waiter once set a record by carrying fourteen plates on one arm. The older waiters could balance eight cups of coffee, one on top of the other. It is little wonder that Casimiro claimed to spend ten thousand dollars on broken dishes every year.

Unlike other waiters, El Rey wrote down his orders. But his Old World charm and regal demeanor more than compensated for his lack of memory. Utterly dedicated to the restaurant, he was so busy running the dining room when his twin daughters were born that he couldn't get away to see them until five hours later.

El Rey received the greatest tribute in 1937 from a regular customer. The patron asked him for his jacket. The dining room was slow, so the noble waiter complied, thinking it was some kind of joke. After putting on El Rey's coat, the patron offered him his own and proceeded to take El Rey's order. He insisted on serving his favorite waiter and dutifully brought El Rey a Spanish salad, steak, and fries.

By 1946, he could count on forty fellow waiters in the dining rooms, but he continued to work shifts just like the rest. While most waiters could carry six salads lined up on one arm, Rey carried ten. Certain patrons ordered pompano just to watch him artfully de-bone the fish, then dress it to make it look as if no one had ever touched it. He was such a good waiter that when Casimiro offered him positions as headwaiter and manager, he refused them. The younger waiters looked to Rey for guidance and the tricks of the trade. If Pijuan dominated the kitchen, El Rey was king of the dining rooms.

In the mid-1940s, El Rey began working the lunch shift for the first time. The consummate night owl complained that the light hurt his eyes. Beyond that minor irritant, two aspects of the lunch trade made him incredulous. First, the sheer number of lunchgoers surprised him, as he'd always assumed that Columbia patrons only came by night. Second, the rock bottom fifty-cent luncheon greatly disturbed him—the tips were correspondingly low. He could not understand how the same nice meals served so cheaply by day cost so much more at dinner. "He's finding out about mass production," Wilder wrote.

While some kitchen techniques had passed him by, El Rey would always be the ideal Spanish waiter: dignified, professional, and charming. Younger waiters tried to follow his example, but there was only one El Rey, Tampa's most famous waiter.

New Recruits

Joe Roman worked as a waiter during World War II at a young age. Back then, becoming a waiter required a union membership and an apprenticeship of several years. All Columbia waiters started in the café, with its constant flurry of customers and small bills. Graduating to the dining rooms meant a leap in pay as well as status.

Joe Roman: "I tell you, when I was seventeen and half I was a waiter. I was doing it all, there was no men here. Everybody was taken away to the service. So that is how I was able to start so young as a waiter. There were a few restaurants and a lot of Cubans, Puerto Ricans, Spaniards, and Italians came to Tampa in those years."

Joe got a job at the Columbia in the 1950s.

"I always wanted to come to the Columbia. But in those days we used to have a union, and I used to go to the union. [The shop steward said,] 'Roman, there's no opening' until there was an opening in the coffeeshop. I was a waiter already [at age twenty-one]. I says, 'I don't mind working in the café.' I was five years in the coffee shop before I was able to come in [to the other dining rooms]."

With his apprenticeship over, Roman worked in the restaurant itself:

"There was only men working, especially Spanish gentlemen who used to be waiters who probably came from Spain, and their families were from Spain. There weren't

any women in the restaurants. Especially the Spanish restaurants.

"We used to have a grilled pompano that you had to serve in front of the customer, and you had to take the head off and the tail. In the center a chef would [split the fish]. You'd cut the tail or you cut the head off, and you just move the filets to the side . . . lemon, butter . . . close the fish again and serve it. Take all the spines off it and serve it like that.

"Paella has always been served in front of the table. You serve right there in front of the customer.

"Pompano papillot comes in a paper bag, and you get the knife and fork and you cut around the seams of it, you turn it around. You turn it, and you put some lemon on the side. The lemon is always in the dish, and there's always a little parsley green.

"I always wanted to work at the Columbia since I started really. The Columbia has always been number one."

The Elite

"Spanish waiters have undoubtedly glorified their calling," a reporter once mused. "The accomplished waiter scorns pad and pencil. He can listen to the varied requests from a table of six, carry the items in his mind, transpose them into Spanish and shout the whole thing to a battery of cooks in the kitchen, while a dozen other waiters are doing the same thing." They were also some the highest-paid waiters in the world. They never rushed and rarely fumbled. They always walked gracefully with something in their hands—a saucer of sliced lemon, a shaker of salt, salad dressing on the side.

Just as cigar workers first worked as apprentices doing menial tasks, Columbia waiters began as bus boys. Once qualified, bus boys could stand in for waiters and pitch in on busy days. They also filled in for absent dishwashers

Waiters like El Rey, left, were at the very top of the profession.

Manager Pete Deemer in the old wine cellar.

and salad men. "Some day the Columbia bus boys will be waiters," Wilder wrote. "No longer neophytes, they then will be able to say: 'It's the bus boy's fault.'"

The top waiters included Gregorio Martinez, a veteran of twenty-five years; and Lorenzo Olivera, who worked the Columbia for nine. Headwaiter Joseph Fernandez possessed a remarkable memory for names and faces and a "full-throated voice of the raconteur and a bountiful flow of malarkey," as one journalist put it.

Maitre d' Joe Fernandez Pepin had a knack for remembering faces and names. It became common for the Columbia to pay for him to attend the World Series and meet the players so he could remember every player. As a good maitre d', Pepin would then know their status, and treat them accordingly. After being away for several years, a customer came to the restaurant with a challenge for Pepin: remember his name and win a bowl of soup. One can only wonder what kind of soup Pepin ate that night. They're all good at the Columbia.

Serafino Martinez (father of future Florida Governor Bob Martinez), a seven-year employee at the time (he went on to serve a total of 18 years), never wrote down a single order. For one party, he memorized the orders of thirty-six customers. One New Year's Eve, he served 211 with no pen or paper.

With the help of the kitchen, waiters did not have to memorize every order. Bartenders garnished similar-looking cocktails differently. Cooks used garnish to provide cues to waiters. For steak, pimiento meant rare, chopped egg meant medium, parsley meant well-done.

Columbia waiters and bartenders employed an unusual method of grabbing food from plates. They held forks and spoons much like chopsticks, forming a useful claw. They never slid food from one plate to another, but picked it up with their improvised tongs.

Some visitors did not know what to make of the imperious waiters. In 1959, the *Saturday Evening Post* observed, "All of Spanish extraction, they speak English only when absolutely necessary, and their Latin temperament sometimes results in spectacular behavior not seen in most eating places. Some time ago, for instance, one waiter turned a plate of soup over the head of a customer who he believed had insulted the soup."

Once, a patron with a bill of $1.30 tipped with thirteen pennies. At the time, ten percent tips were acceptable (today, between fifteen or twenty percent is advisable). As the customer left the restaurant, the furious waiter pelted him with the handful of pennies, growling, "I take no centavos,

The restaurant's exquisite collection of Don Quixote–themed art adds brilliant color to the dining rooms.

Señor Stingy!" On another occasion, a waiter handed a small tip back to the customer with the remark, "you forgot your change." Management found the remark inexcusable and reportedly fired the waiter.

It could be difficult to fire even the most surly waiter. Casimiro would have to deal with the union, which essentially controlled dining room policy, or lack thereof, for most of the century.

The First Strike

Labor difficulties forced the Columbia's closing in 1946. The waiters in eight other Spanish restaurants in Tampa also participated. All 250 of the workers belonged to the Cooks and Waiters Union of the American Federation of Labor. Membership was capped at three hundred, and the waiting list was lengthy. Out of the nine Spanish restaurants that the union lorded over, the Columbia's staff comprised a third of the membership, a testament to its impressive size even then. The union's name was impressive in itself: Local 104, Hotel and Restaurant International Alliance League of America. Years after the great cigar-maker unions were crushed, the waiters and cooks still exercised considerable power through their union.

As a loyal union member, Joe Roman took part in the strikes. "Truly the waiters were making very little; they didn't have no insurance, they didn't have nothing," he said. The union demanded new contracts with higher wages, as the cost of living had risen sharply after the lifting of price controls at war's end. Two of the fancier Spanish restaurants—the Columbia and Rubin's—closed down. A handful of others—such as the Barcelona, Valencia Gardens, and Las Novedades—soldiered on with coffee and sandwiches.

It was the first time that a union shut down the Columbia. The union shrewdly chose to strike at the height of tourist season in mid-January, a move that achieved some measure of surprise. The owners asked for more time but were refused. Imagine the disappointment of a patron from Bartow when she discovered she would not be entertaining visiting family there. The Columbia alone lost the sale of three thousand meals every day. The Spanish Restaurant Owners Association insisted that its members and customers could not afford the new wage scale, which entailed twenty-five dollars weekly for waiters, and seventy dollars for senior (or first) cooks. The deal included two weeks of paid vacation and free meals.

The strike affected a cluster of other businesses that supplied the restaurants: bakeries, produce companies, food wholesalers, dairies, and linen companies. Casimiro took advantage of the lull to have the restaurant thoroughly scrubbed.

The strike lasted only three days before the owners gave into demands. "Many of our workers have been with us since the days when the Columbia was just a tiny café, and economic questions cannot quickly end such association," management announced. Simultaneously, management raised prices for the first time since 1940. The price of a cup of coffee doubled to a dime, and Cuban sandwiches went from twenty-five to thirty-five cents.

"Little Bird"

Growing up in Tampa, Vincenzo Perez always knew he wanted to become a chef. At fourteen he fought his first and only boxing match to raise money for travel to New York, where he could fulfill his dream. Perez won the match and the purse of fifty dollars. He gave ten to his mother and with the rest went to the Big Apple, where he found work as a dishwasher in a Chinese restaurant.

After learning to cook with a wok, he moved on to a Jewish deli, then to an Italian restaurant. Perez worked as a grill man, fried fish and chips, and worked his way through several restaurants and cafeterias. He met a girl from Tampa while in New York City. When she returned to Tampa with Perez in 1938, he took a job as a waiter at the Columbia. He eventually moved into the kitchen, and when Pijuan fell ill he filled in.

He flitted about the kitchen in nervous spurts, earning the nickname Sarapico, or Little Bird. His behavior resembled "a little bird like a sand crane," Wilder wrote, "that makes so much noise when a hunter approaches. Sarapico makes

Vincenzo Perez was known as Sarapico, or "little bird," for the way he darted around the kitchen.

a lot of noise, all right, but it is generally of help to the hunter of good food." Sarapico's memory lives on through his most enduring dish, shrimp supreme. Many would rather forget some of his misguided recipes in the 1950s.

Exit Pijuan

Pijuan lay sick in the hospital in 1946, but he refused to sit out Thanksgiving. He could not stay away from his kitchen kingdom. Pijuan surprised all by coming in and preparing the sixty gallons of cranberry sauce. The Columbia stuffed its turkeys with a dressing of chopped Cuban bread, nuts, raisins, pork, and beef.

The Columbia's most illustrious chef died in 1949, an irreplaceable master of the kitchen. Pijuan's last request was to be buried with a Columbia menu on his chest. Casimiro himself placed the menu in Pijuan's arms at the funeral, to be sure he held it just right.

 ## A Charming Duet

A wedding would have more impact on the Columbia than Pijuan's funeral.

Casimiro's daughter, Adela, found her calling in music, and proved to be a promising classical pianist. With her glowing personality and obvious beauty, she did not need to boast of her Columbia connections to be popular, but she didn't hide them, either. Most of all, she was known as a prodigy on the piano.

She met a tall, young violinist while performing in the Tampa WPA Symphony. They both attended Hillsborough High School, and the young man offered her rides to school from band practice in his old Plymouth. After Adela turned sixteen, he asked her out to the movies. Her uncle Lawrence saw her out with the boy at the Park Theater. When Casimiro found out, he was furious that neither Adela nor her mystery date had asked him for permission.

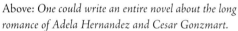

Above: *One could write an entire novel about the long romance of Adela Hernandez and Cesar Gonzmart.*

Left: *A gifted musician and charismatic performer, Cesar played his audiences' heart strings with every draw of his bow.*

owner's only daughter. He invited her to come see him play at the restaurant.

Asking for permission was never Cesar Gonzalez Martinez's way. The charismatic boy was raised to be a performer first and foremost. Afraid the future violinist would injure his hands, Cesar's mother did not allow him to participate in sports. With or without his violin, Cesar commanded attention. Handsome, talented, and charming, he was a lot like Adela.

Those traits explained his greatest feat yet—attaining position of first violinist in Columbia Restaurant's orchestra at age sixteen. They also brought about his downfall. Cesar had bragged to Adela about his gig at the Columbia, but she never volunteered the information that she was the

Adela came to the Don Quixote Room with her mother, Carmen, and an aunt. Between sets, Cesar saw Adela. Surprised and delighted, he glided over to meet her family. Casimiro saw the introductions taking place from across the room. He immediately identified an unsuspecting Cesar as Adela's mystery date. He fired the talented first violinist right then and there.

The two musicians went their own ways. Cesar studied music at Stetson College and got his Ph.D. Adela enrolled at the Juilliard School of Music in New York in 1941 and studied under the respected concert pianist Jose Iturbi and composer Carl Friedberg. She played with the greats in

private parties and performed at recitals. Mother Carmen lived with Adela and acted as constant chaperone. Casimiro unfailingly visited once a month, enduring long train rides to and from Florida.

Imagine Adela and Carmen's surprise when they saw Cesar selling ice cream in Flushing Meadow, New York World's Fair. How far he had fallen, the ladies thought of him, dressed in an awful zoot suit. Although he tried to explain he was auditioning in New York, the ladies didn't really believe him. When he begged for a date, Adela agreed but gave him an old address. She asked the landlord not to give her new address to any cocky young men.

She graduated from Juilliard in 1944 at age twenty-four. Carmen moved back to Tampa and Adela stayed in New

By her early 20s, Adela Hernandez became a gifted classical pianist with a distinctive style. Young Cesar Gonzalez Martinez got his first gig playing violin at the Columbia at age 16.

York to pursue her career in music. In 1946, Adela visited her parents and met a man in Tampa. Casimiro took an immediate dislike to her Italian fiancé. Adela rebelliously proclaimed her love for the man. For Casimiro, the last straw came when he tried to patch things up at a Father's Day brunch in his home. When Casimiro offered his guest some prized Cuban rum, the uncouth Italian said, "That's what the low-class people drink." The brunch ended suddenly, but Adela's romance did not.

Casimiro asked Adela and Carmen to accompany him to Cuba for a couple of weeks. He hoped to convince Adela not to marry her boorish fiancé. While Adela and Carmen enjoyed the beach, Casimiro wandered into a tailor's shop. To his surprise and delight, he met Cesar Gonzalez Martinez, who was being fitted for several new suits. Casimiro never would have imagined being so glad to see Cesar.

The young man's fortunes had indeed changed since his days as an ice cream vendor. The young man explained that the Havana Symphony had recently hired him, where he held positions as first violinist and concertmaster. He had also gained a second Ph.D. in music from Havana's Mu-

nicipal Conservatory. Cesar had landed back in the Cuban capital after a tour of South America and an eighteen-month gig as orchestra leader and master of ceremonies at the Copacabana in Rio de Janeiro. He changed his name to Gonzmart to differentiate himself from the countless entertainers named Gonzalez and Martinez.

Although Casimiro told him of Adela's impending marriage, Cesar insisted that the family join him for dinner that night at one of Cuba's finest restaurants, La Zaragozana. The usually stoic Casimiro rushed to the beach to tell Adela she had a date with Cesar Gonzmart.

"Oh, him," Adela sighed to her father. "The zoot suiter?"

Adela remembered, "My dad was uncommonly excited."

He explained breathlessly, "You should see him now. . . . He is doing very well. I saw him at the tailor's buying a whole new wardrobe. He's first violinist with the symphony."

Adela recalled, "My mother looked at me as if my dad had lost his mind." When Casimiro rushed them back to the hotel to get ready to go to dinner, she thought to herself, "Well, it's a way to spend a nice evening."

Cesar poured on his considerable charm at the outset, wooing both Adela and Carmen. Carmen liked Cesar from the start. He never did have to ask for a date with Adela—Casimiro offered. After Cesar signed the imposing restaurant bill with a blithe flourish, he took Adela to the trendy nightclub El Zombie.

"After that," Cesar remembered, "we had dinner together every night." Adela rebuffed Cesar's flirting repeatedly, explaining she would be married soon. But she never told him to stop.

This racist image of Mr. Zombie promoted a Havana nightclub where Cesar and Adela danced in the 1950s.

When the Hernandez family said good-bye to friends before leaving for Tampa, Carmen fell down a flight of marble stairs, suffering bruises and a broken collar bone. Casimiro and Adela remained in Cuba to nurse her back to health at a friend's home. Cesar used his connections to arrange club dates for Adela, the beautiful pianist who had yet to make a splash in Cuba. She won a job as soloist in the Havana Philharmonic Orchestra. He busied himself with his own position and rebuilding his own band, then known as the "Rhumba Society Orchestra."

Left to right: father of the bride Casimiro, mother of the bride Carmen, groom Cesar, bride Adela, and other relatives.

A glamorous couple, Adela and Cesar wed December 27, 1946.

One night, her fiancé called with suspicions. A mutual friend had seen Adela dancing with Cesar in the Tropicana. Adela called off the wedding that same night. When he caught wind of the breakup, Cesar rushed to Adela with an engagement ring.

Adela remembered balking at his proposal. She remembered saying, "'I haven't even said yes.' Cesar had confidence and a winning way. 'You will,' he said, smiling his onstage smile. 'You will.'" Adela and family were shocked to discover later that Cesar, Adela's new fiancé, was already married to an actress in Cuba. He claimed to be separated from his wife and son, with divorce proceedings already begun. He even told a fanciful story that Walt Disney had named his film *Fantasia* after his ex-wife after he had seen her dance.

Despite all the crises and drama, Adela agreed to marry Cesar on December 27, 1946, in Tampa. Adela went to her seamstress asking for a new wedding dress. She modified the first wedding dress to wear for recitals. It would be the wedding of the year for Ybor City.

Cesar thanked his lucky stars that a thief had stolen his only suits several months before. Without that loss, he would never have met Casimiro in the tailor's shop. The tailor welcomed all the new business: Cesar's suits and one groom's tuxedo with tails.

Succession

Lawrence knew of his heart condition and suffered several minor heart attacks in the 1940s. His doctor told him

A Hernandez family dinner with Cesar. His charm quickly won over the family.

Left to right: Casey Hernandez, Cesar's father Marcelino, Cesar, Adela, Lawrence, and Casimiro on the eve of the wedding. This is one of the last photos ever taken of Lawrence.

Lawrence Hernandez, Columbia Restaurant Owner, Drops Dead

Lawrence Hernandez, prominent Ybor City businessman, died suddenly this afternoon after suffering a heart attack as he sat in his office at the Columbia Restaurant.

It was reported that the 46-year-old Tampa resident, who came to Tampa from Havana in 1905, suffered the attack shortly after 1 o'clock, was rushed to a hospital but died enroute.

Co-owner of the famed Ybor City restaurant with his brother, Casimiro, Mr. Hernandez attended Tampa schools and was granted his citizenship papers in 1929. At one time he was a teller with the National Bank of Commerce and later was assistant cashier and member of the board of directors of the Columbia Bank of Ybor City.

He was elected justice of the peace in the old District 1 in 1932 and served in that office until the County's peace justice districts were reduced to two. He had served as a member of the Tampa Housing Authority since his appointment by Mayor Chancey in June, 1939.

During the City Charter change campaign last year, the restaurant operator openly joined the group which asked for adoption of the new type municipal government.

He was a 32nd degree Mason. His residence was at 161 Bosphorus.

Besides his brother, he is survived by his widow, Mrs. Gloria Hernandez; two sons, Lawrence Jr., United States Naval Academy midshipman, and Casimiro; two other brothers, Evelio and Gustavo, and his mother, Mrs. Adela Hernandez, all of Tampa.

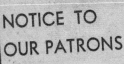

LAWRENCE HERNANDEZ

Gloria, Lawrence's widow, insisted that the wedding take place as planned.

NOTICE TO OUR PATRONS

Due to the death of Lawrence Hernandez, one of the Columbia owners, the restaurant will remain closed until after his funeral Saturday afternoon.

+ +

Dec. 28, 1946

The Columbia

to rest and to take better care of himself, but Lawrence could not give up smoking, drinking, or the Columbia. He continued to work, smoke, drink, and laugh, and died at the restaurant, just as he expected.

He'd just begun to enjoy a visit with his sons—Lawrence Jr. was in the Navy and Casey was attending school in Maryland—and anticipated Adela and Cesar's wedding the next day. He died suddenly while chatting with friends and planning the wedding reception in the restaurant's office.

The Columbia shut down on December 26, the day before the wedding, to mourn Lawrence's death. All the wedding flowers went to the cemetery for the burial. There, Lawrence's widow, Gloria, told Adela, "I insist that you go through with your wedding."

Casey Gonzmart was born on June 2, 1948.

Immediate family attended the ceremony and a handful of close friends came to the restrained reception. Nothing went as planned, certainly not the honeymoon. Instead of speeding off to Washington, D.C., and New York City, the newlyweds broke down in remote Wildwood, Florida. They spent the night at the home of some kind folks who took them in. A mechanic said he wouldn't be able to get the part for days. Cesar and Adela limped home in a clunking car. They surprised the family with their arrival in Tampa on New Year's Eve.

The family erupted with joy when the newlyweds made their unannounced return. Lawrence Jr., Annapolis graduate and accomplished boxer, committed the final act of the wedding episode. Happy and full of drink, Lawrence went around the room hugging everyone. A man of passion, he saved the greatest bear hug for Carmen and unwittingly

broke her ribs. Cesar and Adela must have been relieved to repair the car and take their honeymoon.

In 1948, Adela gave birth to a son, named Casimiro, or Casey. The Gonzmart family went on tour with Cesar's band in 1948. They would never wander away for long.

Casimiro began an unsettling search for a successor to the dynasty.

 ## Reflections and Resolutions

On New Year's Eve 1947, Casimiro reminisced about a past celebration when patrons formed a conga line and snaked through the restaurant, into the kitchen, through the back door, and back into the dining rooms. Management probably did not feel inclined to celebrate so raucously that year

Casimiro's rare smile at a large Columbia dinner with local notables. Lawrence Jr. sits on the far right.

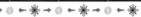

Lawrence's sons, Lawrence Jr. and Casey, having coffee at the Columbia.

since Lawrence Hernandez, Casimiro's jovial brother and Columbia partner, had died only days before.

His two sons—Casey and Lawrence Jr.—inherited his shares of the restaurant. Neither worked in the restaurant at the time. A split in ownership threatened, with Lawrence's sons controlling much of the company without actually working in it.

Casimiro must have pulled a few eyebrows over that dilemma, thinking about how far he had come. He reflected on all the hard work and sacrifice leading up to 1947. He inherited his father's share of the restaurant in 1929. Amid the Depression in the mid-1930s, Casimiro had dreamed big with his brothers and staked his fortune on the lavish Don Quixote Room. Lawrence's investment had allowed

> A Columbia ad suggested a New Year's resolution for Tampa's married men: "Take the little lady out for a few more outings during 1950. She would appreciate a holiday from the kitchen."

him to expand the business and buy out the Garcia brothers.

In the decade after the Patio Room opened in 1937, the Columbia had focused on promotion and expanding the clientele, and then the war swept millions of patrons into the restaurant. By the mid-1940s, the Columbia had won devoted fans from all over the world.

The restaurant struggled to serve the hordes it attracted. Daily business grew by leaps and bounds during the war, doubling in the first year. Lack of space and facilities meant that the cooks and waiters strained to keep up, like workers on an assembly line that got a little faster every day.

The waiting list grew long on the busiest nights. Bored and hungry patrons—some who traveled many miles to dine—scrawled in the guest book: "This food better be worth the wait." Loath to turn anyone away, Casimiro responded. On New Year's Day 1947, days after Lawrence's death, Casimiro resolved to renovate. He devoted more space to tables. Construction crews gave the Columbia's kitchen a makeover. Only growth could keep pace with increasing demand. Crowd-pleasing Lawrence would have approved of his brother's aggressive strategy.

Any questions of the Columbia's viability vanished during the war. Casimiro went from a struggling, civic-minded entrepreneur to a hugely successful VIP. The momentum

TOTAL ANNUAL SALES, MEASURED FROM OCTOBER TO SEPTEMBER	
1941–42	$313,517
1943	$637,811
1944	$684,775
1945	$790,306
1946	$824,446
1947	$972,718
1948	$932,581
1949	$979,324

gained during the war did not subside, and the business continued to grow. The Columbia fed about one million patrons in the year before April 1949, more than ever before. The surge of tourists from January to April provided an increasingly generous spike in business. He hoped to expand in time for the next winter's onslaught.

Lack of space cost Casimiro an estimated 15 percent in additional sales in the 1940s. A series of renovations between 1949 and 1952 allowed the business some breathing room, but not nearly enough. Seating expanded from seven hundred to nine hundred. Casimiro reluctantly opened the Don Quixote Room—previously reserved for upscale dining at night—to luncheon diners. The growing crowds changed his mind.

The Chaotic Kitchen

In the age before computers, the kitchen functioned in a rather chaotic manner. Waiters memorized every order and proceeded to the kitchen, where they yelled the orders to the cooks before they forgot them. In turn, the cooks memorized the orders of the waiters. The whole system would have collapsed but for the strict division of labor. The grill man listened only for the orders that concerned him, the cook at the fish station paid attention only to fish orders, and so on.

The loud, jarring ordering system was enough to cause most new employees to fall to pieces. When the time came to pick up their orders, waiters shouted, "Lleno, lleno!" or "I'm taking," while pushing aside the waiters trying to submit orders. All the jostling and yelling contributed to a steamy atmosphere rightly known as "the kitchen madhouse." Instituting written tickets would have only slowed the cooks, so the system remained in place.

The kitchen dealt with so much volume by 1950 that new employees wrote down and kept track of orders for the waiters and cooks. After a waiter submitted an order to the kitchen, he gave his order card to a female "checker" or "kitchen secretary." The checker looked up the prices and did the math for every tab. If the waiter forgot any detail of an order, the checker answered all questions for waiter, kitchen, and management.

This procedure relieved waiters of a heavy burden and ensured accuracy for management. It also bypassed the unions, which sometimes resisted further accountability for workers. Today, it seems ironic that the same women excluded by the unions handled some of the Columbia's most important roles: cashier, ticket checker, and bookkeeper.

During rush hours the kitchen kept a frenetic pace, occasionally overwhelming even the checkers. Gladys Blazo often dreamed of pressures in the kitchen, "I'd wake up, my head tumbling with stone crabs, fried shrimp, chicken and rice, stone crabs." Color-coded order cards helped checkers to keep the dining rooms straight. During peak hours, one

Master chef Pijuan (left) approved the upgrading of the old kitchen.

woman did all the math, while two others organized the tickets according to waiter and customer. Because waiters rotated through the restaurant daily and were assigned numbers, keeping track of everything from day to day could be tricky.

"When the checkers first started, they thought the waiters were all mad at each other," the journalist Paul Wilder, who wrote ads for the Columbia, once remarked. "Now that they have learned some Spanish, they know the men are merely shouting out orders or bantering with the cooks, in good-natured relief from the pressure. The checkers, or 'waiters' secretaries,' banter now, too."

In the late 1940s, Casimiro remodeled the kitchen to accommodate the increased volume in the kitchen. Once the service ended and the crowds went home, workers moved in to renovate by night. The staging ground of hundreds of meals per hour had been less than five feet long, but the renovations tripled the kitchen's space. Although banks of new appliances lined the walls, the brick oven and charcoal grill remained. The project cost forty thousand dollars in all, much of it spent on the kitchen.

The surge in business in the 1940s and 1950s demanded new adaptations at the restaurant. The new bar annex to the Don Quixote Room allowed customers to enjoy cocktails while they awaited tables.

The renovations also included an updated ladies' room and the new Don Quixote lounge. Beginning in October 1948, Casimiro began work on a new lounge in what used to be a storeroom near the Don Quixote Room. Patrons waiting for open tables could toss back drinks just outside the dining room. Illuminated photographs of famous Florida scenes glowed from niches in the walls. An artist painted the Columbia's ship on the front of the bar, punctuated with chrome nails. A nearby freight elevator brought down supplies without disturbing the dining rooms.

By 1952, Casimiro claimed to have "one of the most compact kitchen layouts of the U.S." If his claim wasn't true then, it was certainly true by the late 1990s, when a new round of renovations began.

Don Quixote and Music

When he expanded the restaurant in 1935, Casimiro identified with Don Quixote, the hopeless dreamer. Fascinated by the beauty of art, Casimiro sought a collection of his own to charm customers. Over time, the restaurant itself became a work of art, both fine and functional.

He began collecting everything Quixote after the 1936 Chicago World's Fair. Spain's ambassador visited the restaurant and gave Casimiro a "tile plaque" once displayed at the fair's Spanish pavilion. Casimiro had no pretensions to build a world-class Quixote collection, but he began his own humble assembly of art while traveling in Cuba. He obtained the doors to the Don Quixote Room from an old Cuban convent. He went shopping for a rocking chair in Marianao, near Havana, but instead found some exquisite hand-painted Sevillian tiles and could not resist them. In the late 1940s, he added three thousand dollars' worth of new tiles from Cuba, Spain, and Mexico to the Don Quixote room, a huge cosmetic investment at the time.

Casimiro also added colorful light to his dining rooms. Albert Schwartz of Atlanta created the Columbia's stained glass. Schwartz had built the windows of chapels for years, then retired to Anna Maria Beach, Florida. He took a fancy to the Columbia, and Casimiro commissioned the windows. The first set of four windows drew so many comments that Casimiro commissioned the rest. He valued his collection "in the thousands of dollars."

When on vacation in exotic locales, friends and well-wishers bought antiques and Quixote art for the restaurant. Banker A.J. Grimaldi brought gifts after a trip to New York City: tissue-wrapped ceramic figurines, all inspired by tales of Don Quixote. Their origins could not be confirmed, but Casimiro prized them as collector's items. The banker George B. Howell gave him a set of tiles obtained while traveling in Spain.

The Columbia earned a reputation for good music in the Don Quixote Room starting in the 1930s. The difficult days of the war eventually curtailed the entertainment. After the war, the Columbia offered limited music. During dinner hours, Casimiro hired piano players during the week and bands during weekends. In the 1940s, songs such as "Siboney," "La Malaguena," "Fire Dance," and "Near You" enjoyed popularity.

The musical taste of the Columbia's clientele amazed newly hired pianist Jean King in the late 1940s. "I had to do some fast brushing up," she said, delving into the likes of Chopin, Debussy, and Tchaikovsky. "I had to go out, get the music, and refresh my memory." She interspersed her accustomed boogie with the more refined music Columbia patrons came to expect. King boasted a strong pedigree of employers. Much as the waiters eschewed trays and note pads, she did not refer to sheet music instead of playing from memory. Casimiro's daughter, Adela, often played from memory herself during her days at Juilliard.

In the Patio Room, Casimiro placed small signs bearing painted Spanish proverbs. Wilder offered some rough translations for the public.

"In eating and drinking there is no losing."

A plaque in the Don Quixote Room read, "If somebody gets rich, some other gets poor."

Quixote Court and Patio

NUMBER SIX

$6.00

SOUP: CHOICE OF

Soup
or
Shrimp Cocktail

SALAD: Lettuce and Tomatoes

MEAT: Columbia Selected:
U. S. Choice 18 oz. Sirloin Steak
with French Fried Potatoes
Garnished with Mushrooms
and Peas

DESSERT: Choice of Ice Cream
or
Cream Cheese with
Guava Preserves

Hot Cuban Bread and Butter

Coffee or Tea

Quixote Court and Patio

NUMBER SEVEN

Special Dinner

$3.75

SOUP: CHOICE OF

Spanish Bean Soup
or
Shrimp Cocktail

SALAD: Lettuce and Tomatoes

FISH: Pompano Papillot
or
Red Snapper Papillot

DESSERT: Choice of Ice Cream
Egg Custard
or
Cream Cheese with
Guava Preserves

Hot Cuban Bread and Butter

Coffee or Tea

Management continually upgraded the menu and décor at the Columbia Restaurant.

The Wilder Years

The cocktail reigned in the United States beside soda pop (see "Columbia Mixology" below). And no proper journalist went without cocktails. Paul Wilder—the reporter Lawrence and Casimiro hired to hang around the Columbia, eat the food, drink the booze, and distract his employees with interviews—stirred more than his cocktail. Wilder's newspaper columns created a stir of their own.

Their clever, articulate promotions won a clientele too large for the Gem of Spanish Restaurants. Wilder already wrote award-winning features for the *Tampa Morning Tribune*. His Columbia column—which was actually an ad—appeared in the same newspaper, facing the editorial page. The ads began running every weekday in 1946, with a list of specials, a recipe, or Wilder's witty banter.

To the surprise of many readers, the Columbia shared its woes for all to read. For a decade beginning in 1946, Wilder frequently wrote witty columns for the restaurant, featuring its delights and difficulties. The stories of glory and vulnerability resounded with readers, and the ads won many fans. Locals sent Wilder's clippings to acquaintances around the world. Some of those pen pals came to Tampa just to experience the Columbia for themselves.

If management's choice to run column-style ads was savvy, its choice as writer proved just as wise. As a talented journalist, Paul Wilder knew the kind of material that appealed to people, and stories of bad news (or at least near disasters) dominate the headlines during

Paul Wilder's Columbia newspaper column became an instant hit with its mix of funny stories, quirky characters, recipes, and descriptions of lunch and dinner specials.

Paul Wilder's columns (right) brought throngs of curious customers to the restaurant from 1946 until the mid 1950s.

Strangest Story 12/6/51

We at the Columbia are accustomed to many bizarre stories, for our guests come from all over the world. But the other night we heard one of the most unusual incidents in our experience. Perhaps you'd like to hear about it, too.

A tall, ruddy-faced stranger sat down in the Don Quixote court and ordered a dinner. He was all by himself.

After eating and leaning back in relaxation, he motioned to Joe Fernandez, the night headwaiter. Joe went over to ask how he enjoyed his dinner and see what the guest had on his mind. After the pleasantries were exchanged, the stranger made this remark:

"You know, I'm here tonight because of a dead man."

Fernandez, as we told you, has heard many strange things in his restaurant career, but this surprised him the most. He asked for details. And this is what the guest told him:

"I'm a member of the Royal Northwest Mounted Police," he said. "I've been in it for 11 years.

"Eight years ago I was on duty in the Yukon territory when we found a drowned man. I searched him for identification and among his papers was a card from the Columbia Restaurant in Tampa, Florida, with a picture of a statue and fountain.

"For some strange reason, I kept the card, after all the other details were taken care of. I guess it was because I had been in that cold territory so long that I wondered what Florida really was like, and what a place like the Columbia restaurant could be. I thought that some day I would visit there."

Eight years passed. Finally the Mountie was transferred a few weeks ago to the Mounted Police headquarters in Montreal, and he had a chance for a vacation. He decided to get in his car and drive to Florida, and that's why he visited the Columbia.

As he left, he said his picturization of the Columbia in the years was fulfilled, and that he will be back again in three more years.

any age. Thankfully for us, Wilder's Columbia writing did not "toot a big horn," but lured the reader with stories of risk, accident, and victory, all involving the kinds of outsized personalities that the Columbia attracted.

While Casimiro welcomed praise from the public, Wilder explained, "Nobody will read that sort of thing all the time, and the Columbia likes to present advertising that people will read. We at the Columbia have found it much better just to tell what happens as it happens, without embellishment, and to let each patron decide for himself whether he likes the food and the service." The self-deprecating ads cultivated sympathy among readers who had never heard of the restaurant before.

Only Casimiro's close associates and friends could understand everything he said. His mangled Ybor City Spanglish made him more shy. Wilder visited the restaurant nightly to discuss ideas for stories and knock back countless coffees and cocktails. Wilder gave him a charming and fluent voice he never otherwise would have had. The columns often read as if the writer were taking one into confidence, telling a joke, revealing a secret, or making a heartfelt apology.

"The ads are double checked now," the newspaper read. There had been yet another mishap at the Columbia Restaurant, this time involving an ad. The promotion erroneously listed the price of an elaborate Sun-

"As an ex-newspaper woman (and a gourmet) your ads in the *Tribune* are the most literate I have ever read in any newspaper or magazine. I want to congratulate you on your ad writer, and equally on the courage you show—in contrast to so many places which shroud their specialties in secrecy—in giving all those recipes. They not only magnetize people toward your restaurant but teach people the *art* of good food." Carolyn Wilson, Mystic, Connecticut / Nokomis, Florida, 1951.

"This fellow, Paul Wilder, is certainly doing a nice job for you folks in the *Tribune*. This boy seems to have a bright future when it comes to writing." Eli Witt, Eli Witt Cigar Company, Tampa, 1946.

"You know that the column you are running in the *Tribune* is one of the best advertising ideas that I have ever seen. I have eaten many meals at the Columbia, but I never knew that they served all those unusual dishes." John H. Simmon, Tampa, 1946.

"Congratulations on your articles that have been appearing in the *Tampa Tribune*. They are excellent and create a new personal interest in your place of business. After reading them a stranger could walk in feeling that he was eating with close acquaintances. No reply will be necessary to this letter as I presume you are receiving many of them these days." J. C. Webster, Lakeland, Florida, 1946.

"I read with much enjoyment your daily ads in the *Tribune*, for I am a retired proofreader and also a native of New Orleans, where the cuisine is an important thing to epicures. Particularly do I enjoy your departure from the dull and un-entertaining ads which your rivals force on the public. In your ads there is daily delight, for they always have a surprise for me. That item today about 'bi-lingual' napkins hit me hard." George Parke, Crystal Springs, Florida, 1951.

"I don't know who writes the advertisement for the Columbia which appears in the *Tampa Tribune*; however, it has always been my opinion that, instead of it being a paid advertisement, they should pay you for allowing them to print it. I find it intensely interesting." Olga Carlson, Tampa, 1951.

"Well written letters is an art, and the writer of the Columbia advertisement is an artist in his individual style. The column is engaging and unique. Stands out by itself from all others. Between the lines one feels the pulse and spirit of genial, harmonious, and most considerate hosts. It was kind of Mr. Casimiro Hernandez Jr. and Mr. Lawrence Hernandez to send their friends the leaflet of appetizing recipes. Thank you for remembering me." Iown Kingson, Auburndale, Florida, 1946.

"Really enjoy reading these squibs. I personally think you have got something on the ball there." John Rast, Augusta, Georgia, 1946.

day dinner as seventy-five cents instead of $1.25. Confusion reigned all day, and management apologized in print through new ads.

Wilder apologized to his audience in his column on many occasions. Fans had called asking why their beloved ad did not appear the day before. One man wrote to the restaurant admitting that Wilder's column had changed his daily reading habits. "Lately I find myself looking over the headlines," he wrote, "then right to the middle of the paper looking for the Columbia report on what's happening at the best of restaurants."

Other readers asked for recipes, especially arroz con pollo. Popular Spanish and Cuban cookbooks did not yet exist, and newspaper food sections contained more Jell-O and canned hot dog recipes than for flan and chorizo. America was ravenous for decent food writing.

Wilder piqued curiosity about more than Spanish food. The Columbia itself fascinated the public as a tourist attraction and business. One woman called from Orlando to make a reservation to visit the wine cellar described in a column. Another patron could not believe that management replaced ten thousand dollars' worth of broken dishes a year.

Some thought Wilder would soon exhaust subjects to write about. But the dynamic Columbia restaurant supplied a decade of material for hundreds of quirky articles.

Trade journals paid the biggest compliment, reprinting the stories for thousands of restaurateurs to read as examples of excellent advertising. Wilder gave up drinking in the 1960s after the Columbia's bar became a bit too familiar. His wife confessed, "Paul was drained" of inspiration.

Those who knew him could identify Casimiro's keen business instincts in the Columbia's column. One could imagine him picking at his eyebrows as he fussed over the obstacles. For more than ten years, Casimiro Hernandez and Paul Wilder shared the Columbia's dreams and sorrows with Tampa Bay. Many of those stories can be found in the first half of this book.

Hushpuppies

Casimiro might have wondered whether the curious correspondent had ever set foot in the Columbia. A recent letter to management requested the Columbia's hushpuppy recipe. No one in the Spanish-speaking kitchen knew how to make that Cracker staple. It seemed a strange request, but it made for an interesting column.

Finally, the bookkeeper, Mrs. Jeter, spoke up in her Southern drawl. "I can cook hushpuppies," she said. "On every fishing trip I have to make the hushpuppies while the men folks eat them. Last trip I didn't get a one myself."

Women rarely cooked in any Latin restaurant back then, certainly not in the Columbia. Men dominated the unions. Women couldn't even wait tables. It must have been an amusing scene to watch the Latin cooks wearing union badges that day.

Mrs. Jeter cooked by feel as they did, and they watched her toss the ingredients together and fry them up. She demonstrated the golden brown art of hushpuppies to the Columbia's chefs in their sacred kitchen. A prolonged discussion followed in Spanish on how best to put the Columbia's spin on those classic corn meal fritters. It comes as little surprise that the elite Columbia cooks chose not to

By the 1950s, many of the Columbia's most famous dishes were in place, such as shrimp supreme, roast pork, and paella. The strong Columbia sangria was not added until the 1960s.

embellish Jeter's recipe, which included grated onion and sweet milk.

Kitchen Basics

Customers and *Tribune* readers constantly asked for recipes, so Wilder shared them in his column. Over the next ten years, the Columbia essentially paid the newspaper to share an entire cookbook with the public for free. Wilder also explained the secrets of basting and braising, key techniques in turning simple cuts of meat into something special. Other tips informed readers about the Columbia's basic sauces.

The Columbia's *salsa madre*, or "mother sauce," served as a base for many of the kitchen's creations. Each morning at seven, the cooks simmered cauldrons of meat and giblets to create a rich broth. Added to other ingredients, it formed mignon sauce (with chicken liver and onions), habanera sauce (with plantains, yams, green pepper, and

wine), hollandaise (with eggs, flour, and oil), and Catalana (with tomato sauce). The kitchen used thirty gallons of rich Catalana sauce a day, as it formed the basis for the Columbia's Creole and pasta sauces.

Casimiro took pride in using "a minimum of grease." Cooks blotted French fries with napkins. They skimmed olive oil from the surface of dishes with ladles or basters. The kitchen replaced lard with olive oil in most of the recipes, and used olive oil in the preparation of fresh mayonnaise. Nonetheless, the fry cook used forty pounds of lard every day.

Week after week, Wilder disseminated daily lunch specials to readers. He announced the launching of seasonal menus, holiday offerings, and special menus and combinations. In 1953, the kitchen introduced a light and fast summer menu, including many cool dishes with meat, fruit, cheese, and vegetables.

Casimiro shared helpful tips with frustrated readers who found themselves unable to reproduce their Columbia favorites at home. He also admitted that the Columbia's atmosphere and service had much to do with the way the dishes tasted. One reader claimed to make a better flan with the Columbia's recipe. Still, she made regular pilgrimages to the restaurant and ordered the flan every time.

Press

The Columbia didn't have to create its own press. "No one who writes about Florida ever leaves the Columbia out," Wilder insisted. "How can he?"

In December 1946, *Esquire* magazine ran a story called "Food with a Spanish Accent." Paul Wilder wrote the piece on Ybor City dining, with emphasis on the Columbia. Management offered thousands of reprints to curious patrons.

In the following years, food writer Duncan Hines lauded the Columbia in his famous travel guides. "This restaurant is outstanding," he wrote. "Particular attention is given to seafoods, and their grilled red snapper steaks are acclaimed as perfect. Many people go for their meat dish of beef baked in a bag with amazing mushroom and chicken liver sauce." In *Dining Out in America's Cities*, Raymond Ewell wrote, "The Columbia is indubitably the outstanding Spanish restaurant in the United States." Over the following 30 years, publications covering the Columbia included magazines such as *National Geographic*, *Ladies Home Journal*, *McCall's*, *Fortune*, and *Holiday*.

An article in the Saturday Evening Post featured the Columbia, by then a restaurant of national significance.

Attention increased as the Columbia's fame spread. A high point came in 1959 with a glowing article in the *Saturday Evening Post*. The writer admired the restaurant's "tempestuous atmosphere" of waiters, revelers, and tourists. He also marveled at the service given by the waiters and management:

> While the personal, emotional manner in which the restaurant is run has resulted in some monumental faux pas, it has also succeeded in giving the place undoubted color and personality. The management has been smart enough to see that examples of its tempestuous temperament make the kind of news the public likes to read about; so, when something goes wrong, the Columbia, instead of trying to conceal it, will buy newspaper space to air all the details publicly.

The *Post* reporter, Rufus Jarman, had grown tired of the same overhyped, expensive, and unimaginative Spanish and Cuban restaurants in Miami and south Florida. The Columbia resided in "shopworn" Ybor City thirty miles away from any beach worthy of the name. It had become a destination unto itself. Jarman called the restaurant a "resolute nonconformist."

"The Columbia's exterior is undistinguished," Jarman wrote, "a hodgepodge of bleak windows, grillwork, tiles, one heavy portal and patches of stucco that struggle along the width of a block." It should be noted that all the beautiful tile now on the restaurant's exterior did not yet exist.

Unlike the flashy eateries in Miami, the Columbia did not take pains to feature citrus for the sake of tourists. Even without it, for ten straight years beginning in 1961, *Holiday* magazine recognized the restaurant as "One of the Outstanding Restaurants in the United States."

Novel Merchandise

Casimiro did not stop with mere food and publicity. He merchandised. Some readers suggested that Wilder's columns be compiled in a book. Always interested in trying new things, Casimiro printed a souvenir booklet featuring recipes, photographs, and Wilder's text, and sold it for 50 cents. Customers took home many millions of Columbia matchbooks over the years. Cigarette companies distributed millions more around the state.

Columbia — GEM OF SPANISH RESTAURANTS SINCE 1905

Merry Xmas

COLUMBIA
Gem of Spanish Restaurants
TAMPA FLORIDA

CLOSE COVER BEFORE STRIKING

Merry Christmas
happy New Year

Those matchbooks got around. In 1948, the manager of the Patio Theatre in Brooklyn wrote to Casimiro after seeing an image of the Patio Room on a Columbia matchbook.

> *You certainly must be famous from coast to coast. One of our patrons who had visited your restaurant was so impressed with the similarity of the fountain in your patio that they sent one of your match folders to our attention. It is remarkable that there is such a close resemblance, since we at the Patio Theatre have a very similar arrangement in our lobby and our fountains seem to be identical.*

The theatre's manager asked for boxes of the Columbia's matchbooks, as they would generate conversations in Brooklyn and bring publicity. Casimiro duly shipped a case of free matches. (They didn't cost him anything in the first place. He'd only paid for the *advertising* printed on matchbooks supplied free by tobacco interests.)

Customers snapped up 100,000 free postcards between 1942 and 1946. The crowds also squirreled away countless Columbia menus, costing management thirty-five cents apiece. Casimiro estimated the loss of six thousand menus a year. Souvenir hunting had become so prevalent that the restaurant began using swizzle sticks stamped with the text, "Stolen from the Columbia Restaurant."

Postcards and matchbooks spread word of the Columbia far and wide.

Ever the tinkerer, Casimiro sought novelty. "The Columbia was talked into buying 1,000 plastic fiber bibs by an enterprising salesman who, it seems, may yet know what he is talking about." Emblazoned with the words "I have been to the Columbia, Gem of Spanish restaurants, Tampa, Florida," each bib protected shirts and promoted the restaurant. Originally purchased for children, the bibs caught on with adults, too. The popularity of saucy spaghetti and notoriously messy crab enchilado made the bibs a sought-after accessory. They disappeared in a matter of weeks.

With memories of rationing and shortages, patrons rarely left food behind, but the "doggie bag" concept had not yet caught on. People felt ashamed to take food home for their dogs, never mind themselves. The five-course "No. 3 dinner" overfilled many patrons. When waiters noticed guests tucking uneaten food into the cloth napkins, management provided cardboard containers for leftovers. "Please leave the cloth napkins," Casimiro admonished. "They cost money."

Hernando De Soto Discovers Espiritu Santo Bay, Tampa

In the year 1539, the Spanish explorer Captain Hernando De Soto, searching for gold, discovered what is now called Tampa Bay. At this spot, starting with a small fishing village, the city of Tampa grew to metropolitan proportions. Next to it grew Ybor City, now a part of Tampa, with its colorful Latin Quarter, Spanish Restaurants, Cafes and Cigar factories. Ybor City, with a population of 25,000, still retains its old-world charm. A trip through Ybor City is not complete without a visit to the Columbia Spanish Restaurant.

View of air-conditioned "QUIXOTE COURT", Columbia Restaurant. Here fine Spanish dishes are served, and you leisurely dine and dance to music by a Spanish Orchestra playing from a beautiful Cypress balcony. Note the famous "Wishing Well" Bar in the rear.

A view of the "Cortijo Room" where private parties up to 40 persons are accommodated. Columbia Restaurant has seven additional private dining rooms, seating from 4 to 16 persons each

PLACE STAMP HERE

FROM

Columbia Restaurant

Spanish Restaurant and Bar

7th Avenue   Ybor City.

Photographed in "QUIXOTE COURT" of the

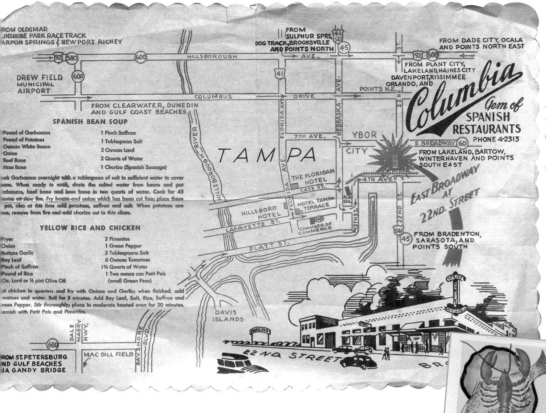

Neither the regular customers nor the waiters liked to use the paper doilies (left), and Casimiro found himself "stuck with 100,000 useless pieces of ruffled paper."

A trip to the "spotless kitchen" is part of your visit. The chef takes pride in our 30-year reputation for Spanish and Sea Food Dishes.

ARROZ CON POLLO (Chicken and Rice)

MAIN DINING ROOM — In this dining room the crowds who daily patronize Columbia

Casimiro's penchant for novelty included bilingual cocktail napkins bearing Spanish proverbs. One read, "Don't sign anything you can not read; don't drink wine that you can not see." Some simply read "Welcome" and "Good journey." Casimiro did not care for one of the proverbs: "Eat plentiful, laugh hearty, for tomorrow you may be gone." Wilder explained, "We're really not that pessimistic. That one got on the napkins by mistake."

Some of the novelties didn't work as well. To decorate the Formica tops of the café tables, Casimiro ordered ruffled paper doilies. He printed recipes and maps of Tampa with various landmarks on the placemats. Neither the regular customers nor the waiters liked to use them, and Casimiro found himself "stuck with 100,000 useless pieces of ruffled paper."

Tourists and newcomers loved the paraphernalia, so Casimiro left stacks at the exits and cash registers. Anyone could find their way around town provided they began at the Columbia, which appeared most prominently on the map. "So even though the doily idea fizzled," Wilder reflected, "the map-and-recipe combination proved more than popular. So if you need a little map in a hurry—just drop by the Columbia. We've got nearly 90,000."

Despite a few duds, Casimiro often found the combination of the novel and practical. In small folders the size of cigarette papers, he provided female customers with soft lipstick blotting tissues imprinted with the Columbia's logo. "In a moment of weakness, we ordered 50,000," Wilder announced. "They are due any day now."

Casimiro always thought of the ladies. Though men usually paid for meals, women were the greatest excuse for a lavish evening. He installed an expanded ladies' room and repaved the parking lot when the attendant observed that the old rough surface was difficult to walk on in high heels. He designed small private dining rooms upstairs called *Los Privados* for romantic couples and discreet mistresses. An artist painted the intimate dining rooms' ceilings with the moon and stars that seemed to glow, inspired by Tampa Theatre.

Columbia waiters watched women store their purses and handbags on the crowded tables or at their feet. Always the problem-solver, Casimiro affixed hooks below the corners of every table to accommodate purses. They presented only

one problem: Having forgotten about Casimiro's considerate fixture, women could not find their bags at meal's end. He even considered larger hooks as hat racks, but dismissed the idea as impractical.

"While the where-to-put-the-bag problem hasn't been entirely solved," Wilder wrote, "the Columbia gallantly and proudly announces that at last a step has been made in the right direction. So ladies, we may have to admit it took the Columbia nearly half a century to adopt such an innovation, but at least you will admit we finally did it." With a wolfish touch, he added, "It is now correct Columbia etiquette to peer under the table to find the pocketbook hooks."

Columbia Mixology

After the war, cocktails enjoyed a new heyday, and the Columbia served millions of them. In 1951, the restaurant listed more than forty-five house cocktail specialties.

When *Esquire* magazine asked the Columbia for a refreshing rum drink recipe, the bar offered a Columbia Collins. It called for a dash of lime juice, a half ounce of grapefruit juice, three dashes of crème de cacao, one teaspoon of brown sugar, and 1¼ ounces of rum. After the article ran, several bartenders had not yet learned how to make it. A Columbia Collins on the menu called for gin. The mix-up prompted Casimiro to print new menus featuring both.

The year 1950 ushered in many improvements. The kitchen added a new glass-washer and brilliantly colored vessels for specialty drinks. Back then, different cocktails required many different shapes: slim beer goblets, broad double martini glasses, short-stemmed frappe glasses, tall hourglass-shaped daiquiri cups, stout highball glasses, and exact replicas of the Columbia's original cocktail glasses from 1905. When patrons asked to buy them as souvenirs, Casimiro quickly caught on to the opportunity and sold them.

The Columbia's creative bar invented many drinks, some noted by national publications like Esquire.

One of Florida's oldest bars can be found in the Columbia Café.

One labor-intensive novelty was the Pousse Café cocktail, a multilayered concoction of many colors. The standard Pousse Café contained six layered cordials; the Columbia's contained nine. Each required five minutes of careful pouring. Grenadine provided the red at the bottom of the glass, followed by anisette (white), crème de Yvette (blue), triple sec (white), crème de menthe (green), chartreuse (yellow), fleur d'amour (pink), green chartreuse, and light brandy, which was set afire at the table. Customers often requested the drink just to watch the show.

Spanish republicans favored the Spanish flag (later known as "The Spanish flag on fire") of grenadine (red), chartreuse (yellow), and crème de Yvette (purple). Café Diablos took fifteen minutes to make, at a whopping $1.25 each. After carefully peeling an orange, bartenders fashioned the skin into a bowl that held the fruit and a cocktail of Cointreau, Curacao, brandy, sugar, cinnamon sticks, cherries, and pineapple. During Prohibition, Babe Ruth downed two dozen at one sitting.

A cocktail called "angel tips" included crème de cacao with cream floated on top and a cherry. One could enjoy a brandy Alexander, pink lady, or grasshopper, all made with milk or cream. The Columbia served frothy eggnog all year long, spiked with bourbon or rum. Patrons especially like the Ramos fizz, with sugar, lime juice, crème de cacao, and gin mixed with sweet cream and orange flower water.

Holiday magazine noted the Columbia's "unusual Spanish wines." The Columbia's bars kept 140 different brands of wine, liquor, and cordials on hand. The restaurant even boasted its own California wines, including Sonoma Red, Dry Semillion, and Mountain White Chablis. During the holidays, the package store marketed Spanish cider, cognac, Spanish anisette, house wines, Benedictine, and various liquers as gifts, with vintages dating as far back as 1908.

Edible Merchandise

Ever crafty, Casimiro captured the taste of Spain and sold it worldwide. In the 1950s, the Columbia developed its own line of edible merchandise, including Spanish bean soup, coffee, guava paste, coconut ice cream, chocolate bars, and honeyed almonds.

Casimiro marketed traditional turron, Spanish almond nougat, over the holidays. Beginning in 1934, the Columbia supplied the soft and moist Jijona and the hard and brittle Alicante. Casimiro carried a very distinctive nougat from the Hijos de Galiana company. The secret to its fine candy was the honey, harvested only in May, when the fruit trees of Spain enjoyed full bloom. The blossoms imbued the honey with a fruity taste and aroma. The treat caught on until the war interrupted supplies in 1941. Ten years later, Casimiro continued the holiday tradition, buying a ton of nougat and wondering if people would remember. They did, buying up half of it in just two weeks.

The next year, he doubled his holiday stock of nougat to four thousand one-pound boxes and doubled it again a year later, selling out each time. Ever the salesman, Casimiro offered to mail packages of the confections anywhere. Regulars sent the candies as gifts, while others ordered them from afar. In 1956, he stocked eleven thousand pounds of the confection in anticipation of the holiday sea-

Genial Tony Schiro, for 37 years a barman, has mixed favorite drinks for many a world celebrity at the famous Columbia Bar. Built in 1907 by C. Hernandez, Sr., it has been operated by his family continuously ever since without alteration.

A street in Ybor City, Latin Quarter of Tampa and home of Columbia Restaurant

Casimiro loved Cuban crackers. He opened two bakeries over the years to supply the restaurant with crackers, bread, and pastries.

son. Two years later he added marzipan and yema, a very soft nougat with an egg-yolk base.

Over the Easter holidays in the 1950s, the Columbia offered variety packages of dulce fino, cookies and cakes soaked in syrups such as rum, almond, coconut, and cinnamon. Because they kept for more than a month, the packages could be shipped anywhere. In a rare acknowledgement of the latest war, Wilder suggested, "Some mail them to men in Korea, especially to Tampa youths of Latin heritage, who have delighted in the candies since childhood."

Yellow rice, black beans, pastries, and quince paste were added to the Columbia brand lineup in 1956. Later, management added new items such as candied coconut with orange shells, olives, soup (canned by Lykes), and Cuban crackers. Casimiro even added a full line of tropical marmalade: tangerine, mulberry, kumquat, orange, grape, and the deluxe orange-cherry-pineapple.

GI Smokes

Casimiro and the Columbia staff sent off merchandise of a different kind in 1951. As a token of his appreciation, he

mailed cartons of cigarettes to soldiers fighting in Korea. An attached note read: "Give 'em Hell!" This relatively small gesture made a difference to soldiers freezing in foxholes with nary a cigarette on Christmas Eve.

Many wrote grateful letters and telegrams to the restaurant. "Everyone of my command are very thankful as they were received when the company were without cigarettes," Cavalry Lt. S. S. Wilson wrote from Chip-Yong-Ni, Korea. "To them a token of appreciation for their efforts means so much individually and collectively, for I have a really fighting command. P.S. We Are Giving 'em Hell."

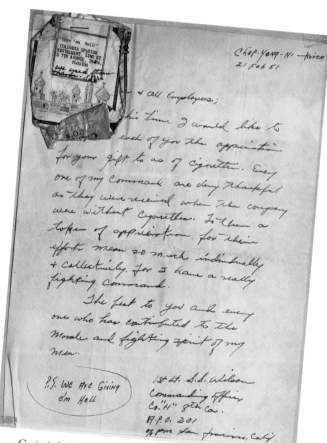

Casimiro's shipments of cigarettes to GIs fighting in Korea boosted morale and made a name for the Columbia

Assorted Mobs

The Columbia attracted all kinds of people, and the most enthusiastic and dedicated are still remembered today. Tourists, revelers, and celebrities made the Columbia the stage of their lives, and they all played interesting parts.

Hurricanes

"We don't know how much of the Columbia will be left this morning," Wilder wrote, "but if there's a coffee urn remaining, you can be sure the Columbia will be open." The Columbia had closed only two days in its history until then, neither time for a storm. The hurricane of 1921 brought flood waters over Palmetto Beach and up to Ybor City's First Avenue. Partly flooded with a battered roof, the Columbia served patrons until it ran out of coffee. Even then, management scrambled through the elements to obtain more. Five years later, a hurricane dampened the Columbia's coal supply, and it took some doing to start a fire.

Hurricanes and tropical storms flooded Tampa regularly. This image comes from the 1920s.

Determined to stay open through a hurricane in the mid-1940s, management dispatched a car to pick up cooks and waiters. A malfunction of the retractable patio skylight allowed rain to pour in throughout the ordeal, flooding the Patio Room and sending goldfish from the fountain onto the floor.

Regulars trudging through the storm found the Columbia's windows boarded up. Their despair turned to delight when they found the usual conviviality in the café behind the improvised shutters. Casimiro merely covered the stained glass windows to protect them. Hotel guests found happy respite in the café—their hotel dining rooms had closed.

Steak and Fish Breakfast

At seven-thirty one morning, the first waiter to arrive was just waking up to a cup of coffee. A party of four came into the café with an unusual request. On their way to Miami, they had heard about the Columbia and had gone out of their way to seek a luxurious dinner. Casimiro had phased out breakfast years before, and lunch service would not begin for several hours.

A bit surprised but not unprepared, the kitchen came to life, cranking out steaks for the men and pompano Almendrina—butter braised fish with chopped almonds—for the women. Morning regulars began to filter in for their coffee, amused by the curious scene. While they sipped coffee and munched on Cuban bread, a foursome of strangers enjoyed a fine dinner the next table over. The Columbia could do it all.

Eating Time

One extravagant party enjoyed a progressive dinner with different courses, wines, and waiters in each dining room, which took three hours. They started in the café with cocktails, ate soup in La Fonda, enjoyed salads and entrees in the Patio, and concluded with champagne in the Vista

Hermosa banquet room. Presumably, they would have to return to experience the Don Quixote Room.

Other patrons arrived in a rush, especially for lunch. Wilder gave several tips for speedy service, the most obvious being, don't arrive during the lunch rush. Management also urged customers in a hurry to order the lunch specials, which the kitchen mass-produced.

A Pleasant Hazing

If the Columbia had a dress code, it would have been tested one day in 1953. As part of an initiation rite, five fraternity pledges from the University of Florida arrived dressed as Indians complete with war paint. They arrived at 1:00 A.M., just as the restaurant was about to close. Unable to close his doors to customers, Casimiro fed the young braves before sending them back to Gainesville. They completed their hazing when they obtained the signature of the maitre d'.

Gasparilla

In 1904, Tampa's city fathers created a holiday from a dubious episode in Florida history. Accounts of a pirate named Jose Gaspar are sketchy at best. Legend has it that he committed suicide off Florida's west coast rather than be captured by authorities. Somehow, that story was parlayed into an annual pirate invasion and parade roughly equivalent in atmosphere to Mardi Gras in New Orleans. The city's business elite dressed up as pirates and threw coins and bullet casings to bystanders from parade floats (beads would largely replace those souvenirs over the years). According to the ritual, Tampa's mayor gives away the key to the city to the swaggering pirates.

Gasparilla festivities always brought a surge of business. In 1948, thunderstorms may have dissuaded revelers from watching the parade, but not from dining at the Columbia. Under raincoats, umbrellas, newspapers, and cardboard

boxes, loyalists scurried through the rain to find warm comfort inside their beloved restaurant. The headquarters of Gasparilla's Latin carnival set up shop in the banquet room. It was an ideal spot for a rendevous. When crowds and storms split one party, they reunited at the restaurant. It was the most obvious place to celebrate.

The holidays and Gasparilla brought such volumes of business that management employed a "kitchen cop" to direct

The Columbia often found itself at the epicenter of Gasparilla festivities, Tampa's answer to Mardi Gras.

traffic in 1951. Five thousand guests ate there on Gasparilla day that year. During the night parade, the next day, the Columbia served almost as many patrons in just three hours. Wilder proudly reported that maitre d' Joe Fernandez maintained his urbane composure through it all.

The Columbia also entertained the Queens of Gasparilla and the Memphis Cotton Carnival that year. Headwaiter Angel Leon pulled out all the stops, arranging napkins like water lilies and nobly serving stone crab cocktail, baked chicken with vegetables over yellow rice, and the trademark coconut ice cream.

While the queens dined in royal finery, the King, Gregorio "El Rey" Martinez, directed two catering operations at the Cuban Club, one for the Krewe of Gasparilla. That feast included fried chicken, stuffed potatoes, picadillo, fried shrimp, turkey sandwiches, and Danish pastry with guava and apple.

The dishwashers could not always keep the pace and were sometimes forced to stack dirty pans and dishes in the kitchen. Somehow the cooks themselves kept up, though they cursed the complicated dishes. Every order of planked red snapper el Patio or trout Sarapico threw another wrench into the works. Chicken la Pinta had to be deboned, stuffed with ham, and wrapped in bacon. Every order required the attention of three cooks, as they prepared nothing in advance.

Through Wilder's column, Casimiro apologized to his customers: "The rush during Gasparilla day was just too much for us to handle, large as the Columbia is."

The restaurant served seven thousand people on Gasparilla day 1952. About two thouand carried off sandwiches and baked goods: the dining rooms were filled to capacity. Predictably, Casimiro printed a new column offering heartfelt apologies and asking the public "to try us again under more normal circumstances." If such incredible business was a problem, his problems were just beginning.

Parade Fever

Casimiro caught parade fever in 1937, never to find a cure. After he expanded the restaurant with the Don Quixote and Patio rooms, he wanted publicity. In the days before television, parades offered businesses the opportunity to employ live-action advertising. The local parade circuit provided a promising and treacherous route for the Columbia's many floats. "Running the largest Spanish restaurant in America often seems simple compared to entering one float in a parade," Wilder confessed. "Sketches have to be rushed, pretty girls have to be hunted to add decoration to the float, schedules have to be worked out, all sorts of things."

Although they won prizes around the state, the Columbia's floats seemed to be jinxed. In Sarasota, a driver rear-ended a float depicting Columbus's three caravels. Casimiro once built a float so tall it smashed into an awning on Tampa's Franklin Street. On another occasion, a float would not fit through an underpass and snagged power lines wherever it went. It took Casimiro's steel determination to persist in such ruin, float by float.

The war and gasoline rationing stopped floats in 1942, but parades crisscrossed Florida again four years later. The Columbia did amazing things with tin foil and papier-mâché. No theme was too fanciful or ambitious. Casimiro ordered the construction of dragons, genies emerging from bottles, seascapes with "live mermaids," and surf-tossed beaches.

In 1946, the Columbia's annual Gasparilla float cost about one thousand dollars to construct. It weighed three tons. A later float held a piano and orchestra. Another contained a replica of the Patio's fountain. A live girl's face peered out from the papier-mâché statue. A float depicting the struggle between Don Quixote and a windmill required six weeks of labor.

It is also notable just how many things could go wrong in so many places. Most Florida cities celebrated winter fes-

Columbus's caravels sailed again on this Columbia parade float. Many of the restaurant's floats met unfortunate ends.

tivals with parades, and Casimiro entered Columbia floats in as many as possible. So many tired paraders once sat on a float that it dragged along the street. On other occasions, a float ran out of gas on the way to Sarasota; the masts of Columbus's three ships had to be lowered to pass safely under power lines; and the engine overheated during a St. Petersburg parade, billowing smoke and alarming spectators.

During another parade in St. Petersburg, a float's gas line became clogged. A resourceful crew member stretched himself under the open hood and poured gas into the carburetor so the float could pass the reviewing stand under its own power. On another occasion, the zipper broke on a girl's dress. Instead of basking in glory, she spent the rest of the parade sitting on the back of the float, huddled in a coat.

One of the more ambitious floats—"Love's Young Dream"—met an unfortunate end during Tampa's Gas-

parilla parade. It passed the reviewing stand in Plant Park without incident. After being parked in a warehouse at Drew Park for two hours, it caught fire. Crews scrambled to drive other floats away from the smoke and flames. Harry Burnett, who built the float, burned his hands trying to smother the flames. The fire department kindly avoided spraying undamaged parts of the float.

With the help of his wife, Burnett patched up the float, replacing cardboard and floral paper in time for the night parade the next day. The cosmetically restored float made the starting line. Then the generator failed. Without lights and music, the float would serve little purpose in the night parade. The crew from the Pan-American Airways float helped install a new generator.

"Love's Young Dream" shone bright that night until the new generator died three blocks from the end of the route. The embattled float went to Winter Haven the next week. "If anything happens, we apologize in advance right now," management explained. "You just can't out figure the obstinacy of inanimate floats."

Every year, the Columbia's parade floats demonstrated Casimiro's dogged determination to soldier on. He eliminated flimsy building materials such as tissue and tinsel. In 1950, he resolved to build new floats to serve multiple parades.

Preparations paid off the next year, when Casimiro equipped his float with a fire extinguisher. In a Sarasota parade, a nearby float caught fire at the starting line. The Columbia saved the day by suppressing the flames until firefighters arrived. Shortly afterward, the float trouble officially ended: During a Strawberry Festival parade in Plant City, no crashes took place, nothing caught fire, and nothing broke down. Not a single mishap occurred.

Perhaps the jinx just skipped a few years. In the Gasparilla parade of 1955, four birds in cages adorned the restaurant's massive fiftieth-anniversary float. Bystanders along the parade route watched one of the homing pigeons slip between the bars and fly away, presumably home, wherever that was. The crew then tied the others in place so they wouldn't finish the parade with four empty cages. Undeterred, Casimiro doubled the contingent of birds for the night parade that year.

In 1956, he left nothing to chance. He equipped the float with two generators—one for the float and one for the truck—to provide illumination during the night parade. Of course, the unthinkable happened. While flamenco dancers cavorted around thatched Cuban huts, all the lights on the float suddenly went out. One of the generators had died, and so did the Columbia's illuminated entry into the night parade. "We at the Columbia, you may guess, were just crushed, plain crushed," Wilder wrote. "The parade is over now, and things are beginning to look bright again."

The posing ladies and caged birds on the Columbia's fiftieth-anniversary float in 1955.

Free Soup

When the city of Tampa held a Million Dollar Day in 1949, an annual event to stimulate Tampa's businesses, the Columbia participated with special lunch and dinner entrees. Casimiro liked to take part in civic events and celebrations. He could express his genuine love for Tampa and Florida while creating publicity.

In 1954, he accepted the largest order of Spanish bean soup in the Columbia's history—four hundred gallons. He served it all free on the street, provided by the Ybor City Chamber of Commerce. A consummate worrier, he regretted accepting the order so blithely, but it seemed like a good idea at first.

Wilder wrote of Casimiro's grief:

> But that was before all the headaches came up. Now we find the Columbia kitchen will be piled with nothing but soup containers Thursday on one of the busiest days of the year. It looks right now as if the Columbia will have to do the impossible. We'll let you know how we come out.

Four bakeries supplied the Cuban bread necessary for the event. Starting at 2:00 A.M., Columbia cooks prepared that day's soup in ten stages, eight hundred gallons in all, half to be given away.

1,000 pounds of garbanzos
350 pounds of potatoes
150 pounds of chorizo
60 pounds of onions
5 pounds of garlic
40 pounds of bacon
10 pounds of paprika
40 pounds of lard
10 pounds of salt

The Columbia's truck distributed soup to three stations along Seventh Avenue. That afternoon, the stations ran out of Cuban bread first. They resupplied with a reserve of 100 loaves delivered in a police squad car; then a courier ran to the Wohl and Son Wholoesale warehouse for more disposable bowls.

The soup stations were to be closed at six that evening to make way for the night parade. As the clock struck the hour, a block-long line of people still awaited soup. Through fast ladling, everyone was served and the stations were broken down in twenty minutes. Almost 5,000 visitors tasted Tampa's famous soup on Seventh Avenue that day, consuming five hundred gallons, one hundred more than originally planned.

"So the Columbia is pleased to report that what seemed like such a hazardous undertaking was highly successful and went off without a serious hitch," a proud Casimiro reflected in Wilder's column. To satisfy curiosity, the kitchen calculated how many free garbanzos people ate that day and came to a conservative estimate of 900,000 beans. The restaurant's partnership with the Chamber of Commerce became an enduring tradition. No other restaurant joined the exclusive promotion that year.

Every year, crowds line up for free soup from the Columbia. Once served during Gasparilla, it is now ladled out on Fiesta Day.

In 1973, the Columbia served a whopping 1,200 gallons of soup on the street, tripling the 1953 supply. The celebration in 1976 saw 1,500 gallons. These days, the tradition continues on Fiesta Day.

Chorizo

Starting in 1912, Andres Sanchez and his wife prepared the Columbia's chorizo in a tiny factory about five blocks north of the restaurant. His father in Spain passed the family recipe to Sanchez, using pork, beef, garlic, paprika, and other seasonings. His wife, Amanda, stuffed the casings and pinched them off at such regular intervals—about 4 inches—that she was accused of using a ruler. He smoked the fresh sausages over oak coals for four days, then dried them for five more.

Chorizo played a key role in many Columbia recipes, from soups to sauces and stuffings. Much like Casimiro, Sanchez was never fully satisfied with his work, so in 1956 he and his wife visited Galicia, Spain, for three months to learn the methods of sausage makers there. He worked in several factories for free to immerse himself in the process. To Casimiro's amazement, Sanchez returned with a superior recipe, adding even better flavor to the Columbia's food. Confident of the product, Casimiro canned the chorizo in lard for retail sale, affixing the Columbia's name to the label. In 1956, the Columbia's kitchen used two hundred pounds of chorizo every week.

Hollywood

When actors Robert Wagner and Terry Moore arrived with journalists and studio press agents in 1953, the scene did not remain subdued for long. The actors had taken a break while filming *Twelve-Mile Reef* in Tarpon Springs, enjoying steaks and flaming rum omelets.

Word of the celebrity visit traveled fast, and carloads of giddy teenagers rushed into the Patio Room for a look at real Hollywood stars. The famous pair graciously signed autographs and said goodnight. Thankfully for them, the hordes of paparazzi in SUVs lay far in the future.

In 1954, Paramount Studios filmed *Strategic Air Command* with Jimmy Stewart at MacDill Air Force Base and Plant Field in Tampa, and Al Lang Field in Pinellas County.

Cesar poses with actor Jimmy Stewart on the set of Strategic Air Command *in Tampa.*

Paramount asked the Columbia to cater during one of its shooting days in St. Petersburg.

For service scheduled at noon, the truck set out at 10 A.M. with tables, silverware, refreshments, and warm food. As many Tampa Bay area commuters are aware, the flow of traffic on the causeways and bridges can be unreliable at best. Ensnared on the Gandy Bridge for close to an hour, the catering crew nearly panicked, knowing full well that Paramount adhered to a tight filming schedule.

Meanwhile, a Paramount official was phoning all over town trying to locate the tardy caterers. "I didn't know whether just to jump overboard then or wait to shoot myself when I faced those Paramount people," the chef reportedly said.

The truck arrived just ten minutes before serving time, and the film crew pitched in, arranging tables, place settings, and hauling food from the truck. When the crew of more than one hundred arrived, the scene appeared orderly and undisturbed.

Baseball

Back in the 1940s and '50s, baseball was truly America's favorite pastime, and the Columbia stood in the midst of the sport's spring training grounds. The Chicago White Sox and the Cincinnati Reds (then the Redlegs) trained in Tampa, the Phillies warmed up in Clearwater, and the Yankees and Cardinals trained in St. Petersburg. During the World Series, the Columbia typically piped radio coverage into the dining rooms. This pleased the guests but irritated Lola, the cashier, who could not keep count with

so much noise. Waiters often paused to listen to the plays pan out.

One night in 1951, onlookers were surprised to see an Atlantic Coast train make an unscheduled stop behind the Columbia on Sixth Avenue. Jaws dropped when forty men emerged from the train wearing Boston Red Sox uniforms. The team's manager had persuaded the engineer to make the stop; he wanted to hasten their farewell feast after spring training in Sarasota. As the grateful team anticipated dinner, the engineer waved and tooted his whistle. After their meal, the players took cabs to Union Station.

The chefs experimented with fireworks for a Major League Baseball banquet in 1952. A special circular table set up around the Patio fountain held large casseroles with one thousand baked stone crab claws—caught off Anna Maria Island—in butter. The waiters added five bottles of brandy and set it alight in a colorful "swoosh." Despite the reputation of baseball players' appetites and their preference for stone crabs, the 181 guests could not finish the succulent claws.

At the end of spring training in March 1954, the National Baseball League planned a press conference in the Don

Baseball players have always loved the Columbia. Babe Ruth, top, snuck out of training camp in St. Petersburg to visit the Columbia. Goose Goslin, left, ate multiple orders of custard in one sitting.

Quixote Room. The American Baseball League held a press conference the same night, accepting an invitation to hold a joint event. The reservations specified two hundred guests, but three hundred showed up, followed by throngs of regular customers.

"You should have seen the shuffling," Wilder wrote, "as tables were shoved together, tablecloths flapped, plates and cutlery rushed out," as the event spilled over into the Patio Room. "In a near-frenzy, waiters hopped up the stairs" to open the Vista Hermosa Room and the Sancho Panza Room, making 130 more seats available. Iced bottles of champagne filled the fountain. The crowd devoured hundreds of flaming stone crab claws. The *Tampa Times* sportswriter "Salty" Sol Fleischman set a record of twenty-eight claws in a sitting.

That night, the staff and kitchen "worked at full speed" to keep up with demand. The *Tampa Times* printed a glowing review calling the evening "one of the most enjoyable events of any spring training event in history. Columbia officials, too, are due a large pat on the back for jam-up service." Still, Casimiro acknowledged that service suffered that night and asked forgiveness for anyone who felt slighted. Nothing was too troublesome for such influential company.

The heroics proved to be a worthy investment—the party returned two years later with 550 guests and $11,000. Another home run.

King-Size Diner

3/28/51

Al Tomaini of Gibsonton has several complaints against the Columbia.

For one thing, the doorways are too low. Al has to stoop every time he comes in.

For another thing, the tables are too small. He has to turn sideways and sit with his knees beside the table.

In case you may not know, Al Tomaini is the Columbia's biggest patron, and probably Florida's biggest permanent resident. He's the 8-foot, 4½-inch giant who owns the Giant's Tourist Camp at Gibsonton.

Al, who takes pride in the special size 22 shoes he wears, has been coming to the Columbia for 15 years, ever since he first began living at Gibsonton.

There have been periods of the year when he has not been in, because then he was on the road with shows as one of the world's tallest men. But this year, Al retired from carnival business and now he spends full time at his Gibsonton place where he has a trailer camp, fishing camp with 36 boats, 14 tourist cottages—and his own restaurant. He dines at his own restaurant while he's in Gibsonton, but visits the Columbia each time he comes to Tampa.

When Al Tomaini first visited the Columbia he was a little fearful about the chairs supporting his 356-pound weight. But he tested one, gingerly sat down, and nothing collapsed. So he has achieved confidence in the sturdiness of Columbia chairs.

The other day, a friend, marveling at Al's height and build figured he must run up quite a bill when he eats in a restaurant.

"How many meals do you order at one time to get filled up?" the friend asked the giant.

Al grinned.

"Well," he said, "one Columbia dinner is enough to satisfy even a big man like me."

The huge, lumbering Primo Carnera was not a great heavyweight boxing champion, but he was the undisputed champion of consumption at the Columbia.

The Gibsonton giant Al Tomaini often enjoyed king-sized dinners at the Columbia. Paul Wilder penned this column about Tomaini in the 1950s.

Professional Athletes and Champion Eaters

A young lady enjoyed a modest dinner at the Columbia in an attempt to lose weight. Her order included shrimp cocktail, soup, Pompano en Papillot, salad, steak with mushrooms, and guava shells with cream cheese.

The hungry patron was also the female champion of professional wrestling. Mildred Burke visited the Columbia once a year with her manager, Billy Wolfe Jr. She defended her title more than one thousand times between 1938 and 1951, and dined at the Columbia every time the wrestling circuit brought her to Tampa. She found the guava shells so tasty that she bought some to serve at a party in her Los Angeles home.

Athletes always came to the restaurant with king-sized appetites. When Babe Ruth trained with the Yankees in St. Petersburg, he'd often sneak from camp to enjoy late dinners at the restaurant. A man of great appetites, he'd call for six orders of stone crabs for one sitting or twenty-seven Café Diablo cocktails. Outfielder Goose Goslin had a special affinity for the custard- and fruit-based "Harlequin Dessert" and consumed them en masse. Other baseball stars double-ordered shrimp or steak.

Wrestlers out-ate all the competition. "Two-Ton" Tony Galento reigned as the undisputed champ of spaghetti consumption, downing fourteen servings with two full loaves of Cuban bread and fourteen beers after a match in Tampa. His record-breaking meal took two hours, considerably longer than the wrestling match.

Primo Carnera, a huge boxer turned wrestler, held the undisputed Columbia title for eating. In 1950, he celebrated the return of his wife and children from Italy. At the Columbia that night, he feasted upon four bowls of Spanish bean soup, a forty-ounce steak cut two inches thick, a double mixed salad, two loaves of Cuban bread, more than three servings of paella, and five bottles of wine. The waiters who thought they'd seen everything were rightfully amazed.

 ## Holidays and Occasions

The Columbia's ads and columns relentlessly pushed Thanksgiving dinner at the restaurant, making special mention of the carefully prepared turkey. Casimiro soon became a victim of his own success, running out of turkey on Thanksgiving for several years in a row. Each year, the kitchen ordered additional fowl, assuming business would increase but without anticipating the growing turkey frenzy.

In 1952, patrons devoured almost 2,500 pounds of turkey in just four hours. Only three cooked birds remained at four-thirty that afternoon. The kitchen quickly roasted ten more, hoping to make it until eight o'clock, when the special ended. At seven, a fresh rush of customers stormed the restaurant and emptied the kitchen. In just twenty minutes, the last of the turkey disappeared, along with the last of the steak (900 pounds), snapper fillets (450 pounds), Valencia soup (80 gallons), and even 90 gallons of Spanish bean soup cooked under duress. Casimiro vowed he would

HOLIDAYS AND OCCASIONS		
Christmas	Pigs	Turkeys
1950	14	80
1952	28	150
1954	40	[140?]
1956	80	140

never leave his Thanksgiving customers without turkey ever again. If the kitchen prepared too much, he reasoned, they would slice it the next day to augment the Cuban sandwiches.

Casimiro found Thanksgiving 1954 almost as embarrassing. The ad for that night's dinner failed to list the fish course separately. "So when one good patron was expecting his turkey," Wilder explained, "he gazed first in amazement, then in anger, at the three small pieces of fried crawfish placed before him. 'Do you mean to tell me,' he demanded of the waiter, 'that I drove a hundred miles to get *this?*'" The waiter's explanation that the crawfish represented only the fish course mollified the puzzled guests.

Then supplies began to run out. Casimiro ousted Gus from his own Thanksgiving table to prepare more coconut ice cream desserts. When the supply of fresh roasted coffee dwindled, the coffee mill reopened to grind more. The bakery fired up the ovens to bake twenty more pumpkin pies—and the restaurant still ran out. Despite roasting 2,400 pounds of turkey, the kitchen served the last of it by 10 o'clock that night.

Over the 1950s, the Columbia's roasted Christmas pig rose in popularity, outselling turkey by far. Management always tried to offer alternatives to turkey, which diners grew tired of by the Christmas and New Year's festivities. The Columbia kitchen lovingly marinated and roasted Noche Buena mojo pork as countless Cubans did.

The Columbia's Cuban roast pork was popular during the winter holidays, when people tired of turkey. Roast pork on Christmas Eve is a Cuban holiday ritual.

When the Columbia still maintained its own butchery in-house, Casimiro bought prizewinning beef from national competitions. Chef Pijuan stands with his knife at the ready.

For the less adventurous, the kitchen offered brown gravy over "country-style" pork. In that variation, cooks stuffed the pigs with a dressing of almonds, filberts, capers, stuffed olives, raisins, black beans, rice, beef, pork fat, and bread crumbs. Cooks sewed up the roast and baked it, complete with an apple in the pig's mouth.

Prize Beef and Blue Ribbons

The American obsession with steak became stronger in the 1950s, and Casimiro aimed to please. To support Florida's cattlemen, he bid on prize-winning Ocala beef. Casimiro thought it was a bargain despite the high prices, and displayed the meat's blue ribbon at the cashier's counter.

He urged curious patrons to let him know how they liked the steak, which could be requested while stocks lasted. He willingly lost money on every order to help promote the state's cattle industry.

On New Year's Eve 1952, the Columbia's kitchen thought it a risk to offer steak beside the turkey and roast pork. "Apparently, guests had so much turkey and trimmings through the holidays they were ready for something different—because we ran out of steaks in the kitchen and had to send to the warehouse for more." As in years past, Casimiro sought out prize-winning beef, this time blue-ribbon selections judged at the International Livestock Exhibition in Chicago. The restaurant aged the 2,100 pounds of beef in its own lockers and offered them at a fair price.

On the eve of 1953, he stocked another two tons of blue-ribbon beef, offering full steak dinners for a special price of $4.75, complete with salad. "You could not obtain the same dinner anywhere else in the United States for less than six dollars," Casimiro claimed.

He worried that he had bought too much meat, leaving a surplus over Lent, when steak orders decreased by 40 percent. During this meatless time for Catholics, the Columbia promoted seafood such as yellowtail and clam chowder. He shouldn't have been concerned about the beef. Patrons devoured more than a half ton of steak in just one week that February. By Easter, Casimiro had ordered another three thousand pounds of beef to prepare for a post-Lenten rush on steaks.

Waiters wore small blue ribbons on their jackets to promote the steak special. Casimiro gave the large blue ribbon provided by the packing house to El Rey as a sign of his status at the Columbia.

Regular customers and other employees ridiculed the headwaiter mercilessly as if he'd been chosen as Casimiro's favorite heifer. Wilder reported that in a short time, "he finally ripped the prize ribbon off and refused absolutely to wear it any more—a little one yes," like the rest of the waiters. "A big one, no."

Tourists

In the 1940s a myriad of groups and clubs held banquets at the Columbia: Pharmacists of Florida, the Business and Professional Women's Clubs of Florida, the State Elks Association, and the Florida Institute of Accountants. An increasing number of patrons came from out of state, participating in business trips, honeymoons, and family vacations.

The restaurant's guest book revealed from whence customers came. All parts of Florida were represented: Miami, Jacksonville, Key West, Pensacola, Daytona Beach, and all parts of the Tampa Bay region. Others covered many more miles before dining at the Gem of Spanish Restaurants: from Sweden, Japan, France, Italy, Spain, China, Germany, Denmark, Cuba, England, Greece, and of course, Canada.

From within the United States, New York and Illinois led in numbers, followed by Michigan, Ohio, Pennsyl-

vania, and all parts of New England. A serviceman once left his military issue hat in one of the dining rooms, and his officer was none too pleased. The soldier wrote to the restaurant from Alaska, begging for his hat. Management sent it off to that frosty land.

Part of the beauty of the Columbia experience was the sense of discovery and adventure. It took several decades for the greater Tampa area to sample Ybor City's cuisine. By World War II, Tampa Bay had fallen in love with Latin cooking, while the rest of the country was just catching on. Countless GIs who trained or docked in Hillsborough County took treasured memories home and often vowed to return. Others moved to Florida to resume civilian life.

Postwar affluence allowed an unprecedented number of families to take vacations, and emerging air travel offered greater mobility. Visitors from Chicago had often sampled ethnic cuisines before, but most rural midwesterners had nothing in their previous experience comparable to the Columbia's food. Many had never even tasted garlic, so Spanish food provided many revelations for rural Americans accustomed to bland diets.

On her visit in 1941, a writer for the *Hastings Banner* in Michigan reported the Columbia safe for cautious midwesterners. "The Columbia will always be tops for us for the meal was a perfect one," she wrote. The Columbia's charms put the uptight reporter at ease, though her writing displayed a rather provincial attitude: "Then, the Spanish music and songs, the faultlessly groomed dark-skinned waiters, who might pass for college students; the distinguished gray-haired major-domo, who might be the deposed president of some Latin-American republic, all combined to make it a restaurant that was 'different.'"

Of the food, she noted, "Spanish beans are round like marbles and were combined with vegetables and a few little pieces of round sausage, like the Brookfield kind; with it came a crisp well done section of Spanish round loaf bread still warm from the oven."

After offering a recipe, she prodded her provincial readers, "Don't be afraid to use garlic, you'll soon get the habit, and use it for many dishes." To assuage any guilt from enjoying lusty garlic, she helpfully reminded readers of its "medicinal" value.

Happiness Tours

During the 1950s, group travel and "Happiness Tours" became increasingly popular. Chartered Greyhound buses carried throngs of vacationers from all over the country on weeklong tours of the Sunshine State. Florida Circle Tour, the company behind the bus excursions, extended their scheduled stays in Tampa in light of the Columbia's popularity.

For many years, Happiness tourists visited Tampa for one night, eating at their designated hotel. "But more and more people riding with us asked about the famous Columbia Restaurant and wanted to visit," the director of the Happiness Tour said. "So we had to shift our whole schedule around on the Florida West Coast, but we decided to do it—and stay in Tampa another night so the folks could visit the Columbia." Once a week, groups of thirty-five to one hundred came to the Columbia via Happiness Tours.

Occasionally, they became too much of a good thing. One night, the travelers found the Columbia "all jammed up." Waiters crowded the tourists into the upstairs banquet room, about one hundred in all. The famished party discovered the kitchen had run out of the famous arroz con pollo.

As they awaited the preparation of more chicken, the tourists became testy. Then a woman, perhaps even Adela, sat at the piano and began to sing. Before long, the grouchy patrons became revelers under the influence of music, cocktails, and the Columbia's charm. "I really think they had a better time than if the food had been served as usual," the tour director said.

Crepes Suzette and Rum Omelets

Patrons young and old tend to enjoy the Columbia's tableside service. Waiter Pedro Demer (otherwise known as Pete Deemer) specialized in making crepes Suzette tableside. Management admitted that diners could obtain this French specialty in the fine restaurants of most cosmopolitan cities. Nonetheless, the Columbia continued to offer the dish as an eye-catching crowd pleaser.

Demer began by warming a pan over a small portable alcohol stove. He then rubbed two lumps of sugar against the inside of orange and lemon peel, allowing the sugar to absorb the citrus oils. After stirring the sugar into butter melted in the pan, he squeezed the juice from an orange to form his sauce.

The kitchen supplied freshly prepared crepes, which Pedro dropped into the sauce, carefully folding them. When ready to serve, Demer splashed in three liquors: Benedictine, Cointreau, and brandy, tipping the pan to set them alight. The dessert encouraged generous tips, but management rarely promoted it, due to its French heritage and excessive preparation time.

Only one dessert of the era could exceed the famous crepe, a neglected classic of yesteryear. A Columbia favorite for many years, the rum omelet dazzled the senses. The cooks blanketed fruit (such as guava, apple, or pineapple) in a delicate omelet and dusted it with sugar. Waiters flambéed the dessert tableside with rum and served it from a hot skillet. The flames caramelized the sugar on top of the omelet to create a lovely smell and taste.

Catering and Mass production

The Columbia provided personalized service and a commissary under a single roof. It is not surprising that Casimiro used the words "mass production" to describe the methods of the restaurant's kitchen in the 1940s and 1950s. The capacity of America's factories ensured the Allied victory in World War II. Casimiro's cocina ensured everyone could enjoy the peace.

Centro Español picnics regularly demanded 1,500 orders of arroz con pollo. The night before, when they would normally close down the kitchen, the cooks went to work on the next day's order. At 2:00 A.M., they simmered 80 gallons of broth with chicken necks and gizzards. To this rich stock, they added their winning blend:

> 400 chickens
> 75 pounds of rice
> 72 cans of tomatoes
> 100 pounds of onions
> 14 gallons of olive oil
> 1 pound of bay leaves
> 15 pounds of salt
> and a side of white bacon.

Cooks hustled forty-two huge pans in and out of the oven beginning at 6:00 A.M. Workers drove them in the Columbia's truck, arriving at 11:30 that morning, and the feast went off without a hitch. A local orphanage received the leftovers that afternoon.

Casimiro tried to apply mass-production techniques in the restaurant as well. He numbered the most popular menu combinations, offering quick, standardized dinners

Pijuan was perhaps the best chef the Columbia ever saw.

at lower prices. Wilder's columns often featured different combinations, of which there were about fifty. Incidentally, the numbers did not tax the memories of his paperless waiters.

The demand for banquets at the restaurant grew so quickly that Casimiro refused new clients. Booking large banquets would mean turning away regular customers. Instead, he rented the patio of the Circulo Cubano (Cuban Club) down the street and carted the food over. A catering crew of thirty-five could then serve banquets of up to one thousand guests without taking up a single seat in the restaurant. In turn, the Cuban Club welcomed the frequent rentals.

Large catering operations presented their own hazards. When removing a large pan of arroz con pollo from the oven, the cooks tipped some grease onto the gas stove, which promptly burst into flame. Reacting to shouts of

"Fuego! Fuego!," the kitchen sprang into action, and Paul Wilder was on the scene. "As one helper ran for the telephone to call the fire department, another leaped for the 'liquid-ice' fire extinguisher and a third dumped a box of soda into a bucket of water."

Through fast action, the employees extinguished the fire and called the fire department to report that all was right again. The brief mishap did nothing to delay the arrival of the food to the Centro Asturiano's fiftieth-anniversary banquet. "It was a good dinner, too, we might add."

Special Deliveries

"Your wonderful bags of Cuban sandwiches were waiting for us at the plane and my daughter was so excited for she had never had one and could hardly wait until lunch," a prominent Chicago woman gushed in a letter to Casimiro. "We waited until we called my husband, who came home from his office and we all had a beautiful luncheon party of Cuban sandwiches."

Word of the Columbia traveled far and wide, and so did the food. Casimiro saw the potential in takeout and delivery. Such business literally took off on airplanes headed for cities across the country. The Columbia sent hams to New York, stone crabs to Chicago, and fish to Atlanta.

In 1946, Eastern Airlines used the Columbia's food in a publicity stunt. To promote its new fast flight to Chicago (in just five hours and forty minutes!), the airline flew meals of Spanish bean soup, Trout Columbia, arroz con pollo, avocado pear salad, flan, and Cuban bread for Chicago's mayor and his staff. Head chef Sarapico cooked through the night to make his deadline. When the meals arrived in Chicago's City Hall, the mayor was out of town. "Somebody else had a good meal," Wilder observed. The mistake was not the Columbia's, so Wilder did not dwell on the subject.

A patron in St. Petersburg called the cashier one night after midnight with a desperate craving for arroz con pollo. When he asked if he had time to make it to the Columbia before it closed at 2, she replied, "It's up to you." Forty minutes later, he sauntered into the café with a smile and took his order home.

Not all desperate patrons could drive to satisfy their hunger. A New York man who spent his winters in Miami longed for the Columbia's food. With no other options, he called the restaurant from the Big Apple, and ordered twenty dishes each of arroz con pollo and paella one morning. At five that evening, a delivery man brought the food in large thermal containers from the airport. The incident inspired Casimiro to invest in more of them in hopes of catering to an increasingly national clientele.

By 1954, the Columbia had streamlined the process for special deliveries. A party in West Palm Beach just had to taste paella, and asked for Casimiro's help. Once the kitchen finished cooking the order, a taxi rushed it in insulated containers to a cargo officer at Tampa International Airport. Cuban bread and guava shells with cream cheese rounded out the meal, which the hostess of the party declared a success. Guests enjoyed the food so much with so little effort that she determined to throw another Columbia party.

Patio Problems

The Patio Room's most distinctive features also supplied the most vexing problems. The fountain required frequent maintenance and supervision. It once overflowed after its pipes became clogged. No one could find the shutoff valve to stop the flow of water, and a puddle spread over the entire Patio Room during dinner. Patrons coped with the event much more calmly than the waiters or management. They simply propped their feet on the bases of the tables and continued to dine. A plumber turned off the fountain and found the clog under the Patio Room floor, which would have to be torn up to get at the pipe. Casimiro deferred the repairs to late that summer when he could more readily close the Patio Room for several days.

When asked to shut off the fountain one night, a busboy mistakenly turned the pressure to maximum, spraying nearby guests. The patrons themselves sometimes provided their own hijinx: A woman captured fish with her napkin, toddlers fell in, and several children stripped naked to enjoy a bath together. Patrons littered the fountain with trash.

Tired of watching live plants and goldfish die, Casimiro employed plastic water lilies in eternal bloom. Casimiro complained to a nursery that the Patio's plants kept dying. He asked for hardier specimens. Patrons and busboys, it turned out, dumped unfinished drinks into planters, where countless cigarette and cigar butts resided. The nursery had to switch out the plants every six or eight weeks to ensure their survival. The plants in the patio required frequent replacement "because of too much alcohol and tobacco," Wilder wrote. "The nurseryman who cared for them says they are the most dissipated plants in Florida."

In pleasant weather, the Patio atrium provided unexcelled al fresco dining. But uncooperative weather could put a damper on things. One day a sudden thunderstorm sent Patio patrons running for cover. Workers could not close the retractable roof fast enough to save several tables of food and drink. Wilder noted, "There are friends who the minute they notice rain sprinkles call and warn us to 'cierra el techo'—shut the roof."

Management sometimes forgot to close it at the end of the night. The next morning, workers often found themselves mopping up the rain. On one cold winter night, the oversight killed about a hundred fish in the fountain.

The Hanging Gardens of Babylon were said to have retractable roofs, and Casimiro wanted to be able to close the skylight with the flip of a switch. Byron Bushnell, owner of a Tampa steel company, built the patio's double windows on rollers. An electric winch powered the contraption. Sometimes the cables got stuck, and temperature fluctuations cracked panes of glass so often that the Columbia's insurance carrier refused to pay for more.

By 1950, Casimiro had tolerated enough from the troublesome skylight. A heavy thunderstorm during the noon rush broke a pane. Waiters rushed their patrons to new tables away from the rain.

In 1951, Casimiro upgraded the Patio Room. New plastic windows came with none of the worries of the glass. He obtained Chinese cane chairs. He tore out the planters and paved some areas of the room. The new arrangements opened space for eight new tables, and no one missed the planters. Casimiro took pride in the room's renovation, but he had reached his wit's end about the roof. In the hottest days of summer, heat drove diners from the patio, and sudden rain continued to

The fountain in the Patio Room caused frequent headaches in the 1940s and 50s.

be a problem. The sliding windows closed for the last time that August. Air-conditioned comfort outweighed patrons' desire to dine in the open air.

For years, patrons avoided the Patio balcony. In the days when that room's roof remained open, the heat there made dining unpleasant. "So instead of shunning the balcony except in desperation, some Columbia guests now actually are asking for one of the 135 seats on the higher level," Wilder wrote. "It's comfortable, it's more secluded and quiet, and some patrons like to look over the railing and watch the diners below." Despite the comfortable temperature, waiters disliked the balcony's stairs. Casimiro installed a second-floor kitchenette for butter, coffee, soup, and other necessities.

Chacho

Early on the morning of May 13, 1953, seventy pounds of coffee in the Columbia's coffee mill caught fire, sending smoke into the intakes of the restaurant's air-conditioning. The coffee mill adjoined the restaurant on its west side. The kitchen personnel first noticed the pungent fumes, and cooks covered all the food in the kitchen with damp towels to protect it.

Employees dashed to the roof to find the coffee mill billowing black clouds. Waiters and bartenders watched from the sidewalk. An excited bystander ran to the emergency call box on the corner and opened the panel. Increasingly agitated at the lack of response, the man resorted to walk-

Evelio "Chacho" Hernandez, Casimiro Jr.'s youngest brother, abused the bottle, but made the best coffee in town.

Evelio and Gustavo Hernandez in 1968.

ing in circles and wailing. Wilder observed, "Somebody else walked over and found that in his excitement, he had opened the door all right but he had forgotten to pull the handle inside."

Once the call was made, three fire trucks arrived within two minutes. The firefighters made short work of the flaming coffee beans, but the building reeked of smoke. The restaurant fared better. Blowers provided by the fire department cleared the Columbia in a half hour, just in time for lunch service at eleven.

The full story was not told in the newspaper. Casimiro's brother Evelio (known affectionately as Chacho, short for friend, *muchacho*) probably had drunk too much again and burned the coffee beans. Everyone in the family had a Chacho story. A kind man with a tendency toward drunkenness, he could make the best coffee in Tampa. Casimiro tried to rein in his brother by locking up his liquor.

Chacho's slumbers and fires happened so often that the insurance company balked. It refused to insure the building unless management removed Chacho from the mill or built a fire wall around its entire roasting room. The family spent the money to build the fire wall, as Chacho's expertise was too valuable to do without.

Family friend and plumbing company owner Charlie Hero remembers Chacho's last coffee mill fire. "One day I was coming by [the mill] and I see a fire coming out! The bad thing is, he's on the floor! I drug him out to the sidewalk, or he would have died right there! I said, 'Run! Get out! Your coffee's burning!'

"Not long after that, he says, 'I'm going to quit drinking.' Every time he'd see me, 'Charlie, one month!'; 'Charlie, two months!' He quit completely. Cold turkey."

Chacho made a special blend for Adela, family, and close friends. The family missed his knowledge and skills after he passed in 1983. Charlie Hero remembers: "He had a

secret formula. I don't know what he did. Everybody used to come buy coffee for that reason. We would talk about it after he died. He should have had it written somewhere."

Charlie's wife, Melba, explains, "Adela would make the coffee. She taught me, she said, 'When the coffee is boiling, you let it come up [to a boil] one time, then let it go down. Let it come up the second time, let it go down. Let it come up the third time, then you take it out.' That was her special [way]."

Workers at the Columbia's Royal Palm bakery package Cuban crackers.

The Finest Bakery in Town

One morning the baker arrived late to the café with his tray of baked goods. Patrons were so impressed with the sight and smell, they snapped up the day's supply. After that, to improve sales, Casimiro asked the baker to deliver most of his goods while patrons sipped coffee in the café. Casimiro soon added a second display case to the café, moving a table to make room. Lack of space for more displays and increased demand forced the bakery to churn out three batches of sweets daily.

In its day, the Royal Palm was among the best in Florida.

In the late 1940s, customers ate five hundred yard-long loaves of Cuban bread every day, and the figure tripled during the winter season. Pedro "Perico" Martinez heated and cut the bread to order. By 1951, the Columbia's business demanded four shipments daily, each provided by a different bakery.

To accompany coffee and satisfy sweet teeth, the Columbia stocked pastries in the café. Besides the usual éclairs and guava turnovers, the restaurant supplied Gallegos—doughnut-shaped cream puffs. Pastry chefs rolled out the dough five times instead of three, making the Gallegos exceedingly flaky. Senoritas, a variation of the napoleon, held custard between layers of Spanish pastry crust.

Casimiro established the Columbia's own bakery in about 1950, hoping to produce the best bread in the world. But this was no normal Cuban bread. The ambitious pastry chef created something he called "Continental bread,"

drawing the best of baking practices from a variety of nations. Following an Italian custom, the bakers steamed the dough for twenty minutes, then dried it with a fan for ten more. In Cuban fashion, a strip of palmetto leaf formed a cleft along the top of each loaf, allowing steam to escape. Three feet long like a Cuban loaf, the width was closer to narrow French bread. The bakers dusted the bread with poppy seeds as was common in Jewish bakeries. The ovens turned out six loaves as an experiment, but demand soon ballooned to seventy-five loaves daily. The crust resembled that of Cuban bread, but the moist interior was more like Italian, with the benefit of olive oil.

The bakers experimented in other ways, working on a six-foot novelty loaf weighing ten pounds. It required the ingredients of twelve ordinary loaves of Cuban bread. Management thought patrons might like broad slices of bread instead of twelve-inch sections. They tried miniature loaves a foot long. Patrons never liked the variation for long, and the Cuban bread has changed little since. The bakery proved to be short-lived.

The Columbia found only two bakers qualified to make guava turnovers as baked in Cuba and Spain. So in 1956, the Columbia opened its own bakery, the Royal Palm, run by the restaurant's pastry chef. Located on the northwest corner of the city block, the business began with twenty-five or thirty pastries in its repertoire, displaying the delights at the store and in the café's case.

The raw pastry dough stuck to wood and slid on stainless steel, prompting Casimiro to buy an eleven-foot-long, three-hundred-pound slab of marble from Cuba's Isle of Pines. The pastry chef used his new counter well, creating pastries with sixteen tissue-thin layers of flaky dough.

Misguided and Supreme

A Menu of 1950s Favorites

Shivering Soup
Columbia Assorted (Antipasto)
Trout Sarapico
Harlequin Dessert

Some of the Columbia's food was rather astonishing. In

their idle time, Columbia chefs created new dishes, but some food conceived in the 1950s did not age well.

Take the chilled consommé, or "shivering soup." Flan molds held a rich broth with gelatin added. When ordered, the soup was dumped onto a plate and held its shape perfectly. You won't find shivering soup on the menu today, as such things are no longer popular or especially palatable.

The Columbia Assorted, an antipasto dish, would fare little better among today's patrons. Recommended for those with jaded appetites, it included a medley of seafood (including anchovies, oysters, and tuna) simmered in tomato sauce, Tabasco, and Worcestershire, then forced into a flan mold and baked with pimiento and olives. Turned out onto a plate, the mold was a centerpiece for an assortment of olives, pickled kingfish and shrimp, salami, and cheese.

Perhaps a better example of regrettable menu items is Trout Sarapico, named after Pijuan's successor. He mixed cream cheese, Roquefort, olives, pimiento, and truffles, and

Sarapico sometimes dished out dubious cuisine.

Adela

sandwiched the paste between trout filets. Topped with American cheese and lemons, the concoction was sprinkled with champagne and olive oil, then baked in a pouch of aluminum foil.

Management featured the Harlequin Dessert in the 1950s, a perfectly good custard ruined by watery canned fruit cocktail. One must wonder what master chef Pijuan would have thought of such misguided culinary energy.

Sarapico redeemed himself with the Columbia staple shrimp supreme, wrapped in bacon, battered, and fried. Simple and satisfying.

Showtime

Victory overseas brought mixed results at home. The cigar industry was all but dead in Ybor City. Fueled by postwar affluence and the GI Bill, the Latin Quarter's youngest residents flocked to the suburbs. Shopping malls drew business from downtown Tampa and Ybor City. Tampa faced an uncertain future, and so did the Columbia.

As it turned out, music, dancing, and celebration saved the Columbia from an ugly fate. Salvation came from a very unlikely source: Casimiro's daughter, Adela, the beautiful pianist. Adela had not been groomed as a successor for several reasons. First of all, she was female, and few women

Cesar

The power couple made time for family. Young Casey Gonzmart was followed by Richard (right).

ran businesses then, especially in Ybor City (although her granddaughters would one day learn differently). Second, her father nurtured her dreams to become a musician—an elegant pianist—not a restaurateur. But her destiny was bound to the Columbia.

It seems appropriate that Cesar Gonzmart's first professional engagement at age sixteen was as the Columbia orchestra's first violinist. Handsome, confident, and a fine violinist, he was one of a kind. A dreamer and schemer, he always made the most of what he had at any moment.

Cesar married Adela in 1946, forming one of the most handsome, glamorous, and talented couples Florida has ever seen. They went on tour with Cesar as performer and Adela as housewife, making time for their baby, Casey, who was born in 1948. Cesar's band played the finest halls and hotels of the day. He performed at the Plaza and Waldorf-Astoria hotels in New York City, the Tropicana in Cuba, the Copacabana in Brazil, and once performed for Argentine president Juan Perón and his wife, Eva.

A call from Casimiro in 1951 brought the homesick couple back to Tampa after years on the road. He had suffered a heart attack and found it difficult to keep up with his busi-

ness. Cesar learned that he had not just married a wonderful wife. He had married the Columbia as well, where family and business were entwined. In a troubled time, love and marriage saved the Columbia from Ybor City's complete decline.

Tradition dictated that Adela could not work directly in the business. Instead, she became a new public face for the restaurant and suggested new menu items. Cesar became the other public face, who was expected to learn the business inside and out. Casimiro enjoyed a less than perfect union with his new partner and son-in-law. Cesar had led orchestras but was lost in the kitchen. He brought passion, charm, and vision, but lacked practical business sense.

"Cesar is a great race horse," Casimiro was fond of saying, "but he needs a jockey to hold him back." Richard was

Adela still managed to be approachable despite her aura of glamor.

born in 1953, the same year Cesar became visible in Columbia operations.

Luis Diaz, Cesar's cousin, remembers the two men's opposing natures. "Casimiro was always amused by Cesar. Cesar was a guy, you had to judge him twice a week, because he was always a different man. Casimiro was amused because he was a bread and butter man, a real working man, and Cesar was a fancy guy, always flying. I find he was amused by, 'How in the devil did this guy have my daughter?' but Cesar was a charmer."

Cesar worked with Casimiro but kept a respectful distance, "so that Casimiro really never passed judgment on Cesar. It was unpleasant to have Casimiro always there. When Cesar came up with worthwhile ideas, Casimiro would be there to put the brakes on."

"Cesar had ideas 10 years ahead of his time. So many ideas in a time of bread and butter. It was hard to comprehend Cesar. He was a guy that got a dream and he didn't mind touching the corners that would help him to get to the dream. Cesar was always a flirt, a very successful flirt. Wonderful, wonderful individual."

Over the next few years of his apprenticeship, Cesar ran the gauntlet of the kitchen stations, enduring constant training and insults from workers who made the Columbia great before he had been born. "I felt I had to learn the business," Cesar admitted. "I had some very rough years." Cesar proved he had the patience to match his great ambition and claimed his rightful place in the Columbia's lineage. All of this while making $100 a week, augmented, no doubt, with money from music gigs.

He certainly proved his patience with his father-in-law. Sarapico became the Columbia's de facto head chef when Pijuan died in 1949. Pijuan's reputation was such—especially with Casimiro—that Sarapico was not openly celebrated as Pijuan's successor until 1961. When Cesar held

a press conference to announce Sarapico as the Columbia's new head chef, Casimiro did not hide his irritation.

Adela remembered, "My husband, Cesar, who had not been around during Pijuan's time, loved Sarapico. He and my father bought Sarapico a house and helped him educate his son and daughter. My daddy, however, held that the great Pijuan had no peer."

A dramatic photograph of the press conference tells two stories. "Cesar holds up two fingers indicating that the Columbia has boasted two great chefs. Sarapico accepts the praise. Look closely and you see Daddy making a face and holding up one finger. There was only one master chef at the Columbia Restaurant as far as Daddy was concerned."

With fresh leadership and talent, the Columbia faced a new era of challenges and triumphs. Adela was never far from the scene and gradually became more engaged in the business over the years.

While Cesar declares Vincenzo "Sarapico" Perez the Columbia's second great chef in a press conference, Casimiro objects, indicating there was only one, Pijuan. Perez was responsible for some regrettable recipes, such as Trout Sarapico, with olives, lemon, champagne, truffles, and American cheese. Bartender Pete Scaglione (at left) looks on with cool indifference.

An Unpleasant Memory

Adela took her infant son Casey off the road and home to Tampa when he was ill. As his condition worsened, she learned that the waiters had gone on strike at the Columbia. Casimiro enlisted his novice daughter to wait tables, the Columbia's first female server. She wore a tuxedo and caught on fast. When she could spare a moment, she played piano to entertain the customers. The whole family pitched in, even Carmen, Gloria, and her son, Casey.

Between her worry for Casey and her grueling schedule, Adela was exhausted. She could never forget an incident as she crossed the picket line to leave the restaurant on her way to visit Casey in the hospital.

Cesar toured with his band all over the Western Hemisphere. After settling in Tampa and working at the restaurant, his Continental Orchestra played two nightly shows six days a week for over twenty years.

"One of our most trusted waiters, a man who stayed with us thirty-five years, confronted me and sarcastically said, 'I guess you're good and tired now. That's how it feels to be a waiter.' Not a word about my child lying between life and death. This from a man I had known since I was a child. Oh, how it hurt. Even today I find it hard to be courteous to that man."

At age two, Casey complained about pains in his legs, and Adela was terrified he'd get polio. When the Salk vaccine became available, she rushed to inoculate Casey: "I think I was one of the first in Tampa," Adela said.

The Continental Orchestra

Shortly after Cesar and Adela's return, music took on a new importance at the restaurant. The young violinist looked forward to performing popular music again. In Havana, he grew tired of playing long symphonies to silent audiences. His friend and colleague, the composer Ernesto Lecuona, told Cesar he was too young and energetic to sit through symphonies year after year. "You're the type of person who's a performer," Lecuona said. After playing the Latin pop circuit for several years, Cesar couldn't have agreed more.

At the Columbia, Cesar's flash and finesse manifested themselves in many ways. His Continental Orchestra played popular American songs and set them to Latin beats. The familiar songs engaged listeners and dancers alike. Those who could not normally dance the Conga, Samba, or Mambo found it easier when moving to familiar tunes. Cesar recruited excellent musicians to form the house band, stealing them from prominent gigs across Florida. The orchestra's 1954 debut marked the first time that large-scale music and dancing returned to the Don Quixote since the war began in 1941.

Last-minute shuffling of the orchestra lineup took place just before opening night. Another mishap almost sabotaged the debut: The dancers could hardly lift their feet

Cesar lords over the Don Quixote Room dance floor from the stage.

Cesar had a knack for playing popular Americans songs with Latin beats. His mambo version of Dixie especially delighted audiences.

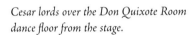

from the floor. Wilder wrote, "They practically had to bend over backwards in order to move their feet."

The night before, management had asked the porter to polish the floor to a fine gloss with the waxing machine. It had been so long since the Don Quixote's terrazzo floor had been polished that the porter mistakenly used the wax meant for tiles instead of the fine wax made for dance floors. The label to the tile wax claimed, "guaranteed non-skid," decidedly inappropriate for a dance floor.

A most unusual floor show ensued. While the perplexed patrons returned to their seats, every available staff member scrubbed the dance floor with mops, brushes, and brooms. After they quickly buffed the new application of wax, the band struck up with *Siboney*, and dancing resumed without impediment.

The dinner dancing was originally meant to increase business during the slack summer days, but it became much more.

Airwaves

By May 1954, Cesar and his Continental Orchestra appeared on a radio show Wednesday and Saturday nights from ten-thirty to eleven on WDAE radio. During one of the first broadcasts, the band became distraught when they could not hear themselves over the house speakers. It is especially important for singers to be able to hear their pitch. Knowing this, the featured singer waved his arms at the recording booth in near panic and indicated he could not hear. The monitor speakers had become unplugged, but the band soldiered on and gave a fine performance. They listened to a recording of the show afterward and were pleased.

Cesar increased his profile further on WFLA-TV's *Latin Quarter Review* program. Besides the backing of his Continental Orchestra, he relied on the accompaniment of two singers, two dancers, and his own wife, pianist "Adela Hernandez." At the time, the ads did not mention their marriage or Cesar's grooming as successor at the Columbia. Casimiro must have wanted to see Cesar succeed on his own merits, and if his training did not work out, no one would be too embarrassed.

With several degrees in music and years of experience as a conductor and touring musician, Cesar brought a new air of sophistication and brilliance to the Columbia's entertainment.

A consummate showman, Cesar played the audience when he wasn't making his violin sing. He made frequent appearances on radio across the country, and briefly had his own local television show, Latin Quarter Review.

When Cesar's show did not appear for several weeks, fans asked when he would return. Nor did his orchestra play in the Columbia. Instead, the Continental Orchestra played the Hotel Chase in St. Louis for two weeks. A radio station there featured the revue for several nights. Cesar and his band could travel freely and play select gigs across the country, but the Columbia would always be home base in their hearts.

In 1956, head chef Sarapico gave an unusual presentation while preparing arroz con pollo. He showed off his nimble knife work and said he could mambo, too. When the production crew played recorded mambo music, Sarapico happily danced and diced.

Arroz con Pollo

In Ybor City, no aspiring chef or restaurateur could expect to stay in business without serving excellent arroz con pollo. After her marriage, Adela wanted to turn out good food in the kitchen. Chicken and yellow rice is a very simple dish, but difficult to perfect. A humble version of paella, arroz con pollo has a magic all its own, with the saffron providing a yellow background for the savory chicken and colorful vegetables. Revered in the days when poultry was more expensive, the joyous meal matched the American South's tradition of Sunday fried chicken.

Enrique Neo Castro spent all of his time in the kitchen making arroz con pollo—ten to thirty pans daily. The large cazuela pans measured thirty-seven inches in diameter and held thirty orders each. The kitchen processed the all-important saffron. Columbia cooks toasted the fibers and ground them with a mortar and pestle. Infused into water or broth, saffron lends a subtle taste and distinctive yellow color. With chicken and vegetables, arroz con pollo is at once familiar and exotic to tourists, who have cherished millions of orders at the Columbia.

Casimiro was a romantic at heart, and he ordered a five-tiered wedding cake for the restaurant's fiftieth anniversary celebration. His wife, Carmen, the Columbia's great silent partner, cut the cake with Tampa Mayor Curtis Hixon standing by. Clearly, Casimiro does not enjoy the camera.

Fifty Years

When writing about the Columbia's fiftieth anniversary, a *Tribune* reporter marveled at Casimiro's reticence: "It's even hard to get an anecdote out of the modest Hernandez about his fifty years as a restaurateur. He says he likes to walk around unknown to anyone and find out what people really think about his establishment."

Casimiro saw the occasion in a very personal way. His father had founded the restaurant and safely navigated Prohibition. But Casimiro himself had faced the Great Depression and his father's heavy debts. When he agonized over whether to chart the Columbia into extravagant new directions with the Don Quixote Room in 1935, he turned to his wife, Carmen. She encouraged him to take the plunge despite the risks.

Casimiro also invited a crowd of couples celebrating their fiftieth wedding anniversaries that year and treated them to dinner at the Columbia. Cesar serenaded them into the night, although some seemed reluctant to dance.

Twenty years later, Casimiro turned to his beloved Carmen once again to celebrate the restaurant's golden anniversary. He unveiled a huge cake with five tiers. Together, husband and wife cut the first slice, as if renewing their vows to each other and the restaurant.

Abuelo Casimiro

Casimiro could be gruff on the exterior, but he had a heart of gold, especially for his grandchildren.

Casey Gonzmart: "My first memory is in his house on a Christmas morning. It begins with sitting at a kitchen table and then having a meal, and him being the oldest and the most revered person in the house.

"I remember him getting up and putting on his suit. He would never tie his tie at home; he would put his tie around his collar. He wore a lot of bow ties. It was always a bow tie. He would wear straw hats.

"He was very devoted to the restaurant, very important in the community. He belonged to a lot of organizations, and a lot of people counted on him.

"I recall riding with him in his car, probably a 1955 Cadillac. It was one of the first cars that had air-conditioning. I remember him driving slow. We only lived a mile away, and it seemed like it took forever to get here.

"I remember going to the beach with him one time. Doctor told him to go. We went to Clearwater Beach, and he never went on vacation, but it was for his health to go. I probably remember it because he never used to take time off."

Richard Gonzmart remembers grandfather Casimiro in an eventful visit as a child: "I remember my grandfather and going to his house; he wanted me to drink something. He gave me a shot glass full of Scotch, and I was drinking it. He smoked cigarettes all day long, and so he gave me a cigarette, and I'm running around my parents' house pre-

In his later years, Casimiro almost seemed content. The restless perfectionist had built his gourmet bastion and found his successor in Cesar.

tending I was a choo-choo train. My mother was not very amused by my grandfather's actions. Smoking a cigarette and drinking Scotch at five years old.

"I remember him taking me into his bathroom, and I asked him about shaving. He takes me in there, and I am standing on the chair. He has his electric razor and he's pretending he's shaving me. My mother walked in and got furious with him. I could remember that disillusionment when he said there weren't any blades in there. I really thought I was shaving. I guess he took the blades out."

An amazing businessman, only heart disease could slow down Casimiro in the 1950s.

Right: Casimiro in a happy place: Running the Columbia with his arm around his grandson Casey.

Luis Arrives

Cesar's younger cousin Luis, the manager of a Cuban rice farm, ran afoul of Batista's regime in 1953. General Fulgencio Batista took over Cuba's government during the 1930s, suspending democracy and personal freedoms.

Luis Diaz:"I did my little thing against Batista. I had an encounter with an officer and two soldiers, and that was the last of my great adventures in Cuba. They take me to a boat and I say, 'time for me to go.'

"So I wrote to Cesar and Adela. I asked them for the opportunity to come as a legal immigrant to this country, which they did immediately. Cesar being the effective person that he was and all his influence in Tampa, within three weeks I have an answer from him. 'I'm going to cover the papers, and the affidavits and the bonds, come over here and work.'

"Within three or fours weeks I left Cuba, everything clear. I came into this country on the 28th of March, 1953. I went to live in the rooming house, five dollars a week. Cesar and Adela after a few days put me to work at the Columbia Restaurant as a bus boy. It was perfection."

Luis had seen the Columbia when visiting with his father years before. The buzzing restaurant was always an impressive sight: "The waiters were the best in the world. Everybody looked like a million dollars. I was like everybody at 20, charming and trying to do my best with the ladies. I love ladies in Tampa. I thought they were the most beautiful girls, period. They were rounded, much nicer than the ones I left in Cuba. Voluptuous is the word. In Cuba everybody had to struggle, you know, [and] you don't put on extra ounces if you don't have extra food. In Tampa everyone, everybody was beautiful."

One of Luis's first assignments was to manage the Columbia's Royal Palm bakery. There he tasted "the most magnificent pastries and breads. He [Cesar] brought over pastry chefs from Cuba. It was the best pastry that Tampa has ever seen. Joaquim Noda was the perfect baker, and the other was Luis Belizantana. That man was a master. Those people were making pastry for the Columbia, and Cuban crackers and bread."

The bakery occupied the northwestern portion of the block, where the gift shop resides today. Luis Diaz: "It was retail. Very wonderful idea, that one of Cesar's. I'm telling you it was the best bakery Tampa has ever seen. There hasn't been anything close to that. Le cheap, le cheap, le cheap. The profits we made in there were astonishing."

The Flan-Eater

Luis worked in the restaurant as manager and found Casimiro and Cesar to be judicious bosses. He poured his efforts into the Columbia and became a model employee. But even Luis sometimes succumbed to his greatest

Luis Diaz, third from right, with family. He fled Batista's Cuba and found a new start at the Columbia with his cousin Cesar.

The flan-eater Luis Diaz was a good manager, but could not resist eating flan on the sly two or three times a day.

temptress—flan. "I love sweets," Luis confesses. "I don't get tired even if I tried to."

It is easy to see how he could be carried away by the Columbia's flan. It is rich yet delicate, an effortless taste of indulgence. Unlike some cloying custards, the Columbia's caramelized sauce never overpowers the creamy comfort of the finest flan.

Management prohibited employees from eating free dessert, but Luis could not help himself. He became proficient at eating flans in one gulp, especially the smaller lunch portions. When he picked up the tins of custard, he pressed the bottom to loosen it from the mold. He then brought the flan to his mouth, took off the lid, and ate it in one motion, like a shot of liquor. The entire operation may have taken two seconds.

Luis remembers, "I was a good worker but I had to stop for flan at least two or three times a day."

Casimiro caught Luis in the act, with flan in hand. "Casimiro saw me one time doing that. It was forbidden for the employees to eat custard." Luis apologized profusely in Casimiro's "majestic presence." He swore he would never do it again.

Instead of accepting the apology, Casimiro asked Luis to repeat his trick. "No," Luis remembers him saying, "I want you to do it again."

Luis responded that another flan might cost him his job.

Casimiro insisted, "I tell you to do it! I want to see how you do that."

"I took one flan," Luis recalls, "Press it on top . . . plop. He never saw anything like it. *This guy is fast.* He was proud of this feat. He didn't say anything about it, he didn't say anything, he just keep on walking. He was a tremendous man."

Out of respect for Casimiro, Luis never ate flan on the clock again.

The Recipes

Tapas

Cakes de Cangrejo (Crab Cakes)
Chicken "Chimichurri"
Chorizo Puffs
Croquetas de Langosta "Madrileño"
   (Lobster Croquettes)
Croquetas de Pollo (Chicken Croquettes)
Devil Crab Croquettes
Empanadas de Cangrejo (Crab Turnovers)
Garbanzo y Gambas "al Ajillo" (Garbanzos and Shrimp)
Langostinos "1905"
Mejillones y Chorizo "Andrés" (Mussels and Chorizo)
Queso Fundido (Spanish Fondue)
Scallops "Casimiro"
Shrimp "a la Plancha"
Shrimp and Crabmeat "Alcachofas"
Shrimp and Scallops "Santiago"
Tortilla Española

Soups

Black Bean Soup
Caldo Gallego (Turnip Greens Soup)
Gazpacho Andaluz (Chilled Gazpacho)
Spanish Bean Soup

Salads

Beefsteak Tomato Salad
Columbia's Original "1905" Salad
Ensalada de Carmorones y Uva
   (Shrimp Salad with Grapes)
Lula Mae Chopped Salad

Sandwiches

George's Burger
Mojo Chicken Sandwich
The Original Cuban Sandwich

Rice

Arroz con Maíz (Rice with Corn)
Arroz con Pollo (Rice with Chicken)
Arroz con Puerco (Rice with Pork)
Good Rice
Paella "Campesina"
Paella "Marenara"
Paella "Valenciana"

Meat

Boliche "Criollo" (Eye of Round Roast Beef)
Carne con Pappas (Beef Stew)
Filet Mignon "Chacho"
Filet Mignon "Columbia"
Roast Pork "a la Cubana" (Cuban Style)
Veal "Isabella"

Chicken

Pollo Cacerola (Chicken Casserole)

Mojito Chicken

Pollo "Champinion" (Chicken Parmesan Spanish Style)

Pollo "Riojana" (Chicken with Mushrooms)

Pollo Salteado (Chicken Cuban-Chinese Style)

Seafood

Camarones Rellenos con Cangrejo
    (Crab-stuffed Shrimp)

Cannelloni de Langosta (Lobster Cannelloni)

Lobster and Crab Enchilado

Mahimahi "Cayo Hueso"

Pompano en Papillot (1939)

Pompano en Papillot (2001)

Salmon "Nuevo Latino"

Sea Bass "Bilbao"

Shrimp Criollo

Snapper "Adelita"

Snapper "Alicante"

Snapper "Russian Style"

Sauces

Alicante Sauce

Catalana Sauce

Coroñesa Sauce

Mornay Sauce

Rioja Sauce

Desserts

Brazo Gitano "Cien Años"

Guava and Cream Cheese Empanadas (Turnovers)

Flan

Torrejas

White Chocolate Bread Pudding

Cocktails

Bloody Gazpacho

Café con Leche Martini

Cuban Manhattan

Margarita "Garrafon"

Mojito Pitcher

Sangre de Toro Sangria

Sangria de Cava

Silver Meteor

Spanish Flag

Tango Mango Daiquiri

The Recipes

The Columbia's cuisine was originally influenced by the rustic, simple food of northern Spain, especially the provinces of Asturias and Galicia. Influences from other parts of Spain, especially the sunny south, crept in steadily over the century, and still do. The Columbia has always been known as a Spanish restaurant, but the designation overlooks a deep connection to Cuba and the Caribbean. Spain may lord over the Columbia's paella, but Cuba claims its excellent black beans and white rice. Good drinks are indispensible for a fine dining experience. The Columbia's Spanish heritage demands excellent wine, and its Cuban roots favor cocktails.

Frequent trips to Spain provide managers and chefs a vital link to culinary developments there. When the Columbia reinvented itself in the 1990s, the kitchen's recipes were overhauled like every other aspect of the company. Many of the recipes come straight from Adela's family cookbook. Others, developed by chefs at the Columbia, reflect lighter, more contemporary trends in Latin cooking.

Note: You can use a mix of garlic powder, salt, and pepper in place of Columbia Seasoning. You may order Columbia Seasoning and Columbia Hot Sauce from the Columbia's website: www.columbiarestaurant.com/shop.asp.

Tapas

Spanish appetizers, known as tapas, are meant to be consumed with wine. Tapas are especially enjoyed while sipping an ice-cold Manzanilla or Fino sherry from the Jerez region of Spain. A glass of sangria is also a great accompaniment to tapas.

Cakes de Cangrejo (Crab Cakes)

The passion fruit and mustard aioli provides a twist on the typical garlic mayonnaise. It is also a great alternative to cocktail sauce.

3 eggs, beaten
2 teaspoons Worcestershire Sauce
6 tablespoons yellow mustard
7½ tablespoons mayonnaise
1 tablespoon lemon juice
1 tablespoon Old Bay seasoning
2 teaspoons parsley, chopped
½ cup ¼"-diced bread, crust removed
3 pounds crabmeat, preferably claw
Passion Fruit–Mustard Aioli (recipe below)

Mix eggs, Worcestershire Sauce, mustard, mayonnaise, lemon juice, Old Bay seasoning, parsley, and bread together well. Gently fold in the crabmeat. Chill mixture in refrigerator for at least 1 hour. Take ¼ cup of crab mixture and form into cake, repeating until all of the

mixture has been used. Serve with Passion Fruit–Mustard Aioli for garnish. Makes approximately 28 cakes.

Passion Fruit–Mustard Aioli

2 tablespoons egg yolks

2 teaspoons garlic, minced

1¼ tablespoons white vinegar

1½ tablespoons water

1 tablespoon yellow mustard

Pinch of salt

Pinch of white pepper

½ teaspoon lemon juice

¼ cup Spanish extra-virgin olive oil

¾ cup passion fruit pulp

1 tablespoon honey

In a small bowl, combine egg yolks, garlic, vinegar, water, mustard, salt, white pepper, and lemon juice. Whip together until mixture is slightly foamy. Gradually add oil in a thin stream, constantly whipping until oil is incorporated and mayonnaise thickens. Add passion fruit pulp and honey and combine well. Refrigerate until ready to serve.

Chicken "Chimichurri"

Richard developed this versatile sauce/marinade with Ybor chef Paco Duarte. It is a family favorite for the holidays and entertaining, especially for picky eaters. It has a nice kick without being fiery.

Wooden skewers

Water

4 boneless chicken breasts (or substitute beef tenderloin tips)

Chimichurri Sauce (recipe below)

Soak wooden skewers in water to prevent burning while cooking, for at least 1 hour.

Dice chicken breasts into 1-inch cubes. Place cubes on each skewer. Cover skewers with Chimichurri Sauce and marinate at least 1 hour. Grill or broil chicken skewers for 10 minutes, turning skewers and basting with sauce as they cook. Serves 4 to 6.

Chimichurri Sauce

1½ cups Spanish extra-virgin olive oil

2 tablespoons parsley

¾ cup red wine vinegar

2 teaspoons crushed red pepper

3 tablespoons Columbia Seasoning

1 cup tomato puree

2½ tablespoons paprika

2 teaspoons cumin

4 tablespoons oregano

6 tablespoons garlic

Chop all ingredients in a food processor, leaving sauce chunky. Refrigerate until use. Makes 4 cups.

Chorizo Puffs

On a trip to Spain with the management team, the family first encountered this appetizer at a large Spanish winery. After spending several days enduring mediocre food, they devoured this new favorite by the dozen. Richard's daughters, Lauren and Andrea, hungry and irritable, had argued earlier that day. These simple chorizo "puffs" brought immediate peace. Ideal finger food for cocktail parties.

Chorizo (Spanish sausage)
Pizza dough, store-bought

Roll out pizza dough to ¼" thickness. Cut dough into 1¾" rounds. Cut chorizo into ½"-thick pieces. Wrap chorizo pieces into balls with dough. Bake in 400° oven (convection preferably) for approximately 4 minutes, or until golden in color. Lightly brush with olive oil before serving.

Croquetas de Langosta "Madrileño" (Lobster Croquettes)

Croquettes continue to evolve at the Columbia. Andrea especially loved the seafood croquettes, which were eventually taken off the menu. This new version makes Andrea happy, indeed.

½ cup butter
1 cup Spanish onion, minced
½ cup flour
2 cups milk
1 pound lobster meat, claw and knuckle
2 eggs
2 tablespoons fresh lemon juice
1 tablespoon Columbia Seasoning
Bread crumbs for breading
Oil for frying
Lobster Sauce (recipe below)

Melt butter in sauté pan, then add onions and cook until translucent. Add ½ cup of flour; stir and cook for approximately 3 to 4 minutes. Add milk and combine well. Cut lobster into ¼" pieces; combine into flour and onion mixture and cook approximately 2 minutes. Scramble two eggs and add to mixture. Add lemon juice and Columbia Seasoning. Cook until mixture thickens, approximately 10 minutes. Cool mixture completely before forming croquetas.

To form croquetas, take ¼ cup of lobster mixture and roll into an egg-shaped ball. Bread each croqueta in the remaining ½ cup of flour, then in the egg wash (remaining egg combined with a splash of water), and then in the bread crumbs. Keep in refrigerator until ready to fry. Cook croquetas in 350° deep-fryer until golden brown, working in batches. Serve immediately with Lobster Sauce for dipping. Makes 15 croquetas. *Wine-Pairing Suggestion: Marqués de Caceres Rosé*

Lobster Sauce

1 cup Coroñesa Sauce (see p. 150)
¼ cup heavy cream

Combine Coroñesa Sauce with heavy cream, heat, and reduce slightly.

Croquetas de Pollo (Chicken Croquettes)

The Columbia first introduced chicken croquettes as a way to employ leftover chicken. They sell so well that the restaurant must now cook chicken to fulfill demand.

½ cup butter
1 cup Spanish onion, minced
½ cup flour
2 cups milk
3 cups cooked chicken, ¼" diced
2 eggs
2 tablespoons fresh lemon juice
1 tablespoon Columbia Seasoning
Bread crumbs
Oil for frying
Columbia Hot Sauce (may substitute another hot sauce)

Melt butter in sauté pan, then add onions and cook until translucent. Add ½ cup of flour, stir, and cook for approximately 3 to 4 minutes. Add milk and combine well. Add chicken, stir and cook for approximately 2 minutes. Scramble 2 eggs and add to mixture. Add lemon juice and Columbia Seasoning, and cook until mixture thickens, approximately 10 minutes. Cool mixture completely before forming croquetas.

To form croquetas, take ¾ ounce of mixture and roll into a small egg-shaped ball. Bread each croqueta first in the remaining ½ cup flour, then in egg wash (egg combined with a splash of water), and then in the bread crumbs. Keep in refrigerator until ready to fry. Cook croquetas in 350° deep-fryer until golden brown, working in batches. Serve immediately with Columbia Hot Sauce for dipping. Makes 24 croquetas.

Devil Crab Croquettes

Adela always liked to make these much smaller than typical Cuban deviled crabs. Columbia Hot Sauce makes this appetizer "hot as the devil."

Devil Crab Mix (recipe below)
Flour for breading
1 egg, beaten
Bread crumbs for breading
Lemon wedges
Oil for frying
Columbia Hot Sauce

To form croquettes, take ¾ ounce of mixture and roll into a small egg-shaped ball. Bread each croquette first in flour, then in egg wash (egg combined with a splash of water), and then in the bread crumbs. Keep in refrigerator until ready to fry. Cook croquettes in 350° deep-fryer until golden brown, working in batches. Serve immediately with lemon wedges and Columbia Hot Sauce for dipping. Makes 28 croquettes.

Devil Crab Mix

3 tablespoons extra-virgin olive oil
¼ cup garlic, minced
½ cup Spanish onion, finely diced
½ cup green pepper, finely diced
1½ pounds crabmeat
2 teaspoons chili powder
1½ teaspoons salt
1½ teaspoons black pepper
½ cup dry white wine
2 cups Catalana Sauce (see p. 150)
½ cup bread crumbs

Heat oil in large sauté pan. Add garlic, onions, and peppers, and cook until transparent. Add crabmeat, chili powder, salt, and pepper. Combine well. Add wine and reduce until most of the liquid has dissolved.

Add Catalana Sauce and bread crumbs and cook for 5 minutes. Refrigerate until use.

Empanadas de Cangrejo (Crab Turnovers)

This dish is inspired from Tampa's traditional crab enchilado (or chilau), which was often served over pasta. These empanadas are stuffed with the venerable crab mixture.

Crab Filling

1½ tablespoons Spanish extra-virgin olive oil
⅛ cup garlic, minced
¼ cup Spanish onions, thinly sliced
¼ cup green peppers, thinly sliced
12 ounces crabmeat
1½ teaspoons mild chili powder
1 teaspoon salt
1 teaspoon pepper
¼ cup dry white wine
1 cup Catalana Sauce (see p. 150)
¼ cup bread crumbs

Heat oil, add garlic, onions, and peppers, and sauté until translucent, being sure to not brown the garlic. Add the crabmeat, chili powder, salt, and pepper and mix well. Add white wine and reduce until most of the liquid is dissolved. Add Catalana Sauce and bread crumbs, and cook for 5 minutes. Chill thoroughly before making turnovers.

Pastry Dough

2 cups all-purpose flour
1 teaspoon salt
⅓ cup shortening with 1 tablespoon water (for glaze)
⅓ cup margarine
7 tablespoons ice water
1 egg, lightly beaten

Mix flour and salt. Add shortening and margarine and mix with a fork or pastry blender until mixture resembles coarse cornmeal. Add water, one tablespoon at a time, mixing lightly until dough leaves sides of bowl. Wrap in waxed paper and refrigerate for 30 minutes. Cut dough in half; roll with floured rolling pin into a 10-inch circle. Cut smaller circles with 4-inch round cutter. Combine leftover fragments and roll out again. Repeat with other half of dough.

Make turnovers, putting 1 tablespoon of filling in the center of each circle. Moisten edges with water and fold over. Using fork, crimp edges and prick top twice. Brush with egg-water mixture. Bake in a preheated oven at 400° for 15 minutes or until golden brown. Serve with Black Bean Salsa. Makes about 16 turnovers.

Roasted Corn and Black Bean Salsa

1¾ cup fresh tomatoes
⅓ cup red onion
1 cup black beans, cooked
2 tablespoons garlic, minced
1 cup frozen corn
2 tablespoons fresh lime juice
1 tablespoon cilantro, chopped
¼ cup Spanish extra-virgin olive oil

Dice tomatoes into ½" pieces and dice onions into ¼" pieces; place in a mixing bowl. Strain and rinse black beans and add to bowl. Roast corn in 400° oven for 20 minutes; cool and add. Add all other ingredients and toss well.

Garbanzo y Gambas "al Ajillo" (Garbanzos and Shrimp)

When Richard saw garbanzos simmered "al Ajillo" style with spinach in Spain, he immediately thought of the Columbia, which uses them prolifically in Spanish bean soup.

⅓ cup extra-virgin olive oil
¼ cup garlic, chopped finely
1 whole chili pepper
10 shrimp, 36–40-count
1 teaspoon parsley, chopped
⅓ cup garbanzo beans, cooked
½ teaspoon Columbia Seasoning
⅛ cup dry white wine
1 lemon

Heat oil and add garlic, cook until golden brown. Add chili pepper, shrimp, garbanzo beans, and Columbia Seasoning. Add white wine and sauté until shrimp are pink, approximately 1 minute. Add juice of half a lemon and add parsley. Place in serving dish and garnish with lemon wedges. Serves 2.

Langostinos "1905"

A brand-new hit, these jumbo grilled shrimp are put over the top by an emulsified version of the "1905" salad dressing.

4 shrimp, 8–10-count
Spanish extra-virgin olive oil
"1905" Sauce (recipe below)
Columbia Seasoning
Lemon wedge

Lightly brush shrimp with olive oil and season with Columbia Seasoning. Cook shrimp on grill until lightly browned on both sides and shrimp are cooked through—be careful to not overcook the shrimp. Before removing the shrimp from the grill, brush with "1905" Sauce and allow the sauce to melt on top of the shrimp. Remove the shrimp from the grill and serve with a side of the "1905" Sauce for dipping and a lemon wedge.

"1905" Sauce

"1905" Dressing (see p. 123)
Emulsify the "1905" Dressing with a handheld mixer until dressing thickens, approximately 3 to 5 minutes.

Mejillones y Chorizo "Andrés" (Mussels and Chorizo)

Cesar always wanted to put a special mussel dish on the menu, but never found the right recipe. After Cesar's death, the Columbia kitchen dedicated this dish to Andrés Sanchez, who made the restaurant's chorizo for years. His son, Bonifaso, remains a close friend to the Columbia family. Bonni, as he is known, recommended a mussel and chorizo combination, and this variation with spinach works quite well. A modern classic.

⅛ cup chorizo
½ cup fresh tomato
⅛ cup fresh spinach
⅓ cup extra-virgin olive oil
1 tablespoon garlic, finely chopped
⅛ cup celery, diced
½ cup Spanish onion, chopped into ¾" pieces
6 fresh basil leaves
1 whole chili pepper
½ teaspoon Columbia Seasoning
½ cup dry white wine
1 ounce lemon juice
12 mussels

Cut chorizo in ¼" slices on bias, chop tomatoes in 1" pieces, and chop spinach coarsely, removing stems.

Heat oil in sauté pan and add garlic, celery, and onion; cook until onions are transparent. Add chorizo, tomato, spinach, basil, chili pepper, and Columbia Seasoning; cook for approximately 4 minutes. Add wine, lemon juice, and mussels; cover and simmer until all mussels are open. Place mussels in serving bowl, removing any that have not opened, and serve immediately.
Serves 2.

Queso Fundido
(Spanish Fondue)

Tetilla cheese, soft and mild, is so named because it is often shaped like a woman's breast. When paired with acidic tomato sauce, the cheese provides a smooth comfort. The restaurant puts the cheese in the freezer for a few minutes before slicing it, which makes it easier to handle. Because tetilla can be difficult to find, Andrea suggests fresh mozzarella. Chef Jerry offers Monterey Jack as another substitute. When asked about this recipe, the Gonzmart ladies answered in spontaneous unison, "Yum."

4 cups Rioja Sauce (see p. 151)
Tetilla cheese, a semi-soft Spanish cheese with a mild, tangy flavor (or substitute fresh mozzarella or Monterey Jack)
1 loaf Cuban bread

Ladle warm Rioja Sauce into an ovenproof dish, and cover the entire surface with thin slices of cheese. Bake at 350° for 10 minutes, making sure not to brown the cheese. Cut Cuban bread diagonally into ½"-thick pieces and brush with olive oil and toast until golden brown. Serves 4 to 6.

Scallops "Casimiro"

When asked how this appetizer came to bear his grandfather's name, Richard said with a grin, "So we could sell 'em." Casimiro would have appreciated that. He also would have loved the buttery delight of his namesake. If possible, obtain larger scallops, which hold up well to cooking. The smaller scallops overcook quickly, so be mindful. The toasted Cuban bread crumbs are a nice touch.

¼ cup butter
2 small lemons
¼ cup Spanish extra-virgin olive oil
24 scallops, 10–20-count
1½ tablespoons Columbia Seasoning
4 tablespoons unseasoned bread crumbs

Melt butter over low heat in a small saucepan. Add the juice of 2 fresh-squeezed lemons and stir well. Keep warm until use.

Heat oil in a shallow saucepan large enough for all scallops. Dust scallops with Columbia Seasoning. Blanch scallops in hot oil for approximately 30 seconds. Place blanched scallops in ovenproof dish. The scallops can be covered and refrigerated until cooking time.

Preheat oven to 400°. Reseason top of scallops with Columbia Seasoning and spread bread crumbs evenly on top. Ladle lemon butter on top and bake for 10 minutes, or until scallops are brown on top and cooked through. Spray with white wine and serve immediately. Serves 4 to 6.

Shrimp "a la Plancha"

The achiote rub brings a little burn to these grilled shrimp.

32 shrimp, peeled with tail, 16–20-count
Wooden skewers
Achiote Marinade (recipe below)
Tobacco Carrots (recipe below)
2 lemons, cut into wedges
Salt and pepper to taste

Place 4 shrimp on each skewer and marinate at least 3 hours in Achiote Marinade. Cook on grill for approximately 1 minute on each side. Serve skewered shrimp on bed of Tobacco Carrots garnished with lemon wedges. Serves 4 to 6.

Wine-Pairing Suggestion: Martin Codax Albariño

Achiote Marinade

3 tablespoons achiote powder (available at most Latin supermarkets)
1½ cups orange juice
1 cup lime juice
2 teaspoons dried oregano
2 teaspoons ground cumin
1 tablespoon black pepper
¼ cup salt
1¼ cup garlic, minced
3 cups vegetable oil

Dissolve achiote powder in orange and lime juice. Add all ingredients, mix well. Refrigerate until use.

Tobacco Carrots

3 carrots, cleaned and peeled
Water
3 cups flour
½ cup Columbia Seasoning
2 cups oil for frying

Cut carrots into 3"- to 4"-long pieces, thinly sliced. Cover carrots with water until cooking time. Combine flour and Columbia Seasoning in a medium-sized bowl. Drain carrots and coat with seasoned flour. Deep-fry carrots until golden brown. Serve promptly.

Shrimp and Crabmeat "Alcachofas"

Created by Chef Craig in St. Augustine, this sublime seafood and artichoke blend is also served in the Pompano en Papillot. The positive reaction from the new pompano recipe was so strong that this rich dip is now served as an appetizer as well.

½ cup Spanish extra-virgin olive oil
½ cup Spanish onions, diced
½ cup green peppers, diced
1¼ cup shrimp, chopped coarsely
1 cup heavy cream
1 teaspoon dried oregano
¼ tablespoon black pepper
1½ teaspoons salt
2½ tablespoons bread crumbs
1 tablespoon mustard
¾ cup Romano cheese
3 eggs
¾ cup crabmeat, claw recommended
1 cup artichoke hearts, chopped coarsely
Cuban crackers

Heat oil and sauté onions and peppers until soft. Add shrimp and cook until pink. Add cream, oregano, pepper, salt, breadcrumbs, and mustard. Place 2 tablespoons of the cheese to the side and reserve for later; add the remaining cheese to the mixture. Cook for 5 minutes. Whip eggs and fold into mixture. Add crabmeat and artichoke hearts; blend well. Remove from heat and allow to cool so mixture will thicken. Ladle mixture into ovenproof casserole dish and sprinkle with remaining cheese. Bake in oven at 350° for 15 minutes. Serve with Cuban crackers.

Shrimp and Scallops "Santiago"

Chef Jerry created this special recipe for a wine dinner, and it quickly caught on. The shrimp and scallops are mixed with tangy sour apple, and bathed in a creamy Mornay sauce.

24 scallops, 10–20-count
8 4¾" casserole dishes
Stuffing (recipe below)
32 shrimp, 36–40-count
Mornay Sauce (see p. 151)
1 cup Manchego cheese, grated

Place 3 scallops in each of the casserole dishes and then top with ½ cup of stuffing. Place shrimp on top of stuffing. Ladle Mornay Sauce over shrimp and stuffing; then sprinkle 2 tablespoons of cheese on each. Bake in oven at 400° until golden brown on top. Serves 8.

Stuffing

¼ cup melted butter
¼ cup onions, chopped
3 ounces Granny Smith apples (⅜" dice)
½ cup milk, heated
1 egg yolk
Pinch of nutmeg
⅛ teaspoon Columbia Hot Sauce
1½ teaspoons dry white wine

Heat butter and sauté onions until transparent. Add ¼ cup flour and apples; stir to incorporate. Add hot milk, stirring to thicken. Beat together egg yolk, nutmeg, Columbia Hot Sauce, and white wine; add to apple mixture. Allow to cook approximately 10 minutes.

Tortilla Española

When in Madrid, the Gonzmarts seek out the Casa de Tortillas for the best Spanish omelet. When at home, they cook or go to the Columbia. The traditional version is simple and sublime—egg, potato, and onion—but the tortilla is open to improvisation. One of Richard's favorite variations includes chorizo, mushrooms, and peas. Ham and asparagus are also popular.

¼ cup diced potatoes
Vegetable oil for frying potatoes
4 eggs
¼ cup chopped chorizo
2 teaspoons green peas (cooked)
¼ cup sliced mushrooms
¼ cup olive oil

Deep-fry potatoes in vegetable oil. Drain and let cool. Beat eggs until frothy; then add all ingredients with the exception of the olive oil. Combine well.

Heat olive oil in 6-inch omelet pan. Add egg mixture, shaking pan and stirring. When eggs leave the sides of the pan, invert omelet onto a plate. Return to the pan and brown lightly on the other side. May be served hot or at room temperature. Serves 2.

Soups

Black Bean Soup

This classic fills you up fast. It is also a healthy vegetarian option. Arguably the national dish of Cuban Americans, black bean soup is both rustic and refined. Condiment preferences vary widely. Andrea favors diced tomato and onion, sprinkled with balsamic vinegar. Richard loves olive oil and vinegar. Hot sauce is also popular.

1 pound black beans, dried
2½ quarts water
2 medium onions, chopped fine
2 green peppers, cut in strips
½ cup olive oil
1 teaspoon oregano
1 bay leaf
½ teaspoon ground cumin
4 cloves garlic, minced
1 tablespoon salt
½ teaspoon black pepper
White rice, cooked
Chopped onions for garnish

Before washing the beans, spread on a flat surface and pick out broken beans and foreign particles. Wash beans thoroughly and soak overnight in 2 quarts of water.

Next day, pour beans and water into a 4-quart soup kettle; bring to a boil. Cover and cook over medium heat.

Meanwhile, in a skillet, sauté onions and green peppers in olive oil. Add crushed oregano, bay leaf, cumin, and garlic. When onions and peppers are light golden, add mixture to beans, stirring well. Add salt and pepper and cook slowly over low heat, covered, until beans are tender (at least 1 hour). Serve over white rice and top with chopped onions. Serves 4.

Caldo Gallego
(Turnip Greens Soup)

Richard remembers being told by his mother, Adela, that Caldo Gallego was "Giant's Soup." The turnip greens in this hearty soup were said to release the powers of Popeye. Traditionally, this soup was served on Sunday and is a meal in itself. To this day, the restaurants in Ybor and Sarasota cannot agree upon the best recipe. The competition is healthy: Both recipes are excellent. This recipe is served at the flagship restaurant in Ybor City.

1 pound great northern beans dried
2 quarts water
¼ pound salt pork, cut in pieces
1 pound ham hock
1 beef bone
½ pound beef chuck, cut in 2-inch pieces
1 onion, chopped
3 medium potatoes, peeled and quartered
2 turnips, peeled and quartered
2 cups turnip greens, coarsely chopped, thick stems removed
1 chorizo (Spanish sausage), sliced in thin rounds
Salt to taste

Soak beans overnight in water in a large pot. Next day, add salt pork, ham hock, beef bone, beef chuck, and onions. In same water, bring beans to a boil and skim off foam. Cover and simmer over low heat for about 2 hours, or until beans are almost tender. Add potatoes, turnips, and greens. Cook about 30 minutes or until potatoes are tender. Add chorizo. Let stand for 2 to 3 hours before serving. Heat and serve in large soup bowls. Serves 4.

Gazpacho Andaluz
(Chilled Gazpacho)

A classic summer soup from the south of Spain, this gazpacho is a sippable salad. It was introduced to the Columbia in the 1960s, when more influences from southern Spain became evident.

2 cups water
1 medium onion, finely chopped
3 ripe tomatoes, peeled, seeded, and chopped
1 cucumber, peeled and sliced
4 tablespoons white vinegar
2 teaspoons salt
3 cloves garlic, crushed
4 slices bread, cut in pieces
4 tablespoons olive oil
Garnish:
1 cucumber, diced
1 green pepper, diced
1 medium onion, finely chopped
1 tomato, finely chopped
1 cup croutons

Combine first nine ingredients and let stand for one hour. Purée in a blender and chill in refrigerator. Garnish and serve chilled in soup bowls. Serves 4.

The Columbia's soups (clockwise from the top): Caldo Gallego, Black Bean, Gazpacho Andaluz, and Spanish Bean.

Spanish Bean Soup

This is the soup that made the Columbia famous for food. The Columbia's founder, Casimiro Hernandez Sr., adapted his version from the heavy, multicourse cocido madrileño stew of Spain. His simplified version served elements of the original feast—meat, potatoes, and garbanzos—in one bowl. By the 1920s, newspapers boasted of Tampa's three great delights: sunshine, cigars, and soup. For a thicker soup, stew it longer.

½ pound garbanzo beans (chickpeas), dried
2 quarts water
1 tablespoon salt
1 ham bone
1 beef bone
¼ pound salt pork, finely diced
1 onion, finely chopped
2 potatoes, peeled and cut in quarters
½ teaspoon paprika
Pinch of saffron
Salt to taste
1 chorizo (Spanish sausage), sliced in thin rounds

Wash garbanzos. Soak overnight with 1 tablespoon salt in enough water to cover beans. Drain the salted water from the beans. Place beans in 4-quart soup kettle; add 2 quarts of water and the ham and beef bones. Cook for 45 minutes over low heat, skimming foam from the top. Fry salt pork slowly in a skillet. Add chopped onion and sauté lightly. Add to beans along with potatoes, paprika, and saffron. Add salt to taste. When potatoes are tender, remove from heat and add chorizo. Serve hot in deep soup bowls. Serves 4.

Salads

Beefsteak Tomato Salad

Cesar often ate simple salads of lettuce wedges and sliced tomatoes. This hearty salad adds flavor with Cabrales cheese, a tangy cheese made in northern Spain. High-quality tomatoes are essential.

1 large beefsteak tomato
1 large red onion, peeled
½ cup Cabrales cheese (or substitute gorgonzola or bleu cheese)
Sherry vinegar
Extra-virgin Spanish olive oil

Slice tomato into ¾"-thick pieces. Slice onion into ½"-thick pieces. Alternate tomato and onion on plate using 4 slices of tomato and 3 slices of onion. Place crumbled Cabrales cheese on top and serve with sherry vinegar and olive oil on the side as dressing.

Columbia's Original "1905" Salad™

In the 1970s, this flavorful salad was the Columbia's answer to the ubiquitous salad bar. Created by waiter Tony Noriega in the 1940s, it was adapted by the Columbia, eventually phasing out the use of black olives and celery. The Columbia kitchen designed a new dressing that features Worcestershire Sauce, lemon, and Parmesan cheese. When the president of Lea & Perrins heard that the Columbia was his biggest customer, he investigated and ate a "1905" salad. He soon discovered the salad's delights for himself.

4 cups iceberg lettuce, broken into 1½" × 1½" pieces
1 ripe tomato, cut into eighths
½ cup baked ham, julienned 2" × ⅛" (may substitute turkey or shrimp)
½ cup Swiss cheese, julienne 2" × ⅛"
½ cup pimiento-stuffed green Spanish olives
2 cups "1905" Dressing (see recipe)
¼ cup Romano cheese, grated
2 tablespoons Lea & Perrins Worcestershire Sauce®
1 lemon

Combine lettuce, tomato, ham, Swiss cheese, and olives in a large salad bowl. Before serving, add "1905" Dressing, Romano cheese, Worcestershire, and the juice of 1 lemon. Toss well and serve immediately. Makes 2 full salads or 4 side salads.

"1905" Dressing

½ cup extra-virgin Spanish olive oil
4 garlic cloves, minced
2 teaspoons dried oregano
⅛ cup white wine vinegar
Salt and pepper to taste

Mix olive oil, garlic, and oregano in a bowl. Stir in vinegar and season with salt and pepper. For best results, prepare 1 to 2 days in advance and refrigerate.

Ensalada de Camarones y Uva (Shrimp Salad with Grapes)

A summertime favorite that tastes far better than you might expect.

1½ tablespoons fresh lemon juice

¾ teaspoon sugar

¼ teaspoon cayenne pepper

½ teaspoon salt

3 tablespoons olive oil

1 large shallot, thinly sliced

¼ teaspoon mustard seeds

1 garlic clove, minced

1 pound medium shrimp, shelled and deveined

Salt and pepper

1 cup red seedless grapes

1 tablespoon chopped cilantro

In a bowl, combine the lemon juice with the sugar, cayenne pepper, and salt. In a large skillet, heat the thinly sliced shallot in the olive oil and cook over moderately low heat, stirring a few times, until browned and crisp, about 4 minutes. With a slotted spoon, transfer shallot to a plate. Add the mustard seeds to the skillet and cook over moderate heat until they just begin to pop, about 10 seconds. Add the garlic and shrimp, season with salt and pepper, and cook stirring, until opaque, about 3 minutes. Transfer the shrimp to a bowl and stir in the grapes, cilantro, lemon dressing, and half of the fried shallot. Sprinkle the remaining fried shallot on top of the salad and serve at once. Serves 4.

Lula Mae Chopped Salad

This fresh salad replaced an old version that once used canned vegetables. It was known as a "Spanish mixed salad" until the death of Lula Mae Tollaman, a treasured employee of nearly fifty years.

¼ cup iceberg lettuce

¼ cup Romaine lettuce

¼ cup celery

¼ cup carrots

¼ cup hearts of palm

¼ cup hard-boiled eggs, chopped

¼ cup artichoke hearts, cut in half

¼ cup tomato, ¼" dice

¼ cup cucumber, ¼" dice

2 white asparagus spears

⅓ cup favorite Caesar dressing

1 tablespoon Cabrales cheese

Chop both lettuces in equal parts, approximately 1½" by 1½" pieces. Slice celery, carrots, and hearts of palm on bias into ¼" thin pieces. Toss lettuce with celery and place onto a platter. In the following order, place these ingredients in rows onto the lettuce: egg, carrots, artichoke hearts, tomato, cucumber, and hearts of palm. Garnish with asparagus. Combine Caesar dressing and Cabrales cheese, stirring until cheese is smooth. Serve salad with dressing on the side.

George's Burger

Despite all the gourmet and comfort food at the Columbia, everyone craves a hamburger from time to time. Sometimes over the years, longtime manager George Guito cooked up burgers for coworkers. This big burger, served on crusty Cuban bread, is the real deal.

On the day Lauren told Andrea she was pregnant for the first time, they sat down to lunch at the restaurant. Andrea was amazed when Lauren ate two of George's burgers. Later that day, Lauren discovered that she was expecting twins.

1¼ pounds ground beef

Columbia Seasoning

2 slices of cheddar cheese

12" Cuban bread

Mayonnaise

Mustard

Catsup

Onion, thinly sliced

Tomato, sliced

Iceberg lettuce

Combine ground beef with 1 tablespoon of Columbia Seasoning. Shape beef into two 4" × 6" ovals. Cook burgers on grill to temperature; do not press burger while cooking. Place the cheese on the burger. Cut bread into two 6" pieces, and then cut in half; toast on grill. Spread mayonnaise on the top half of the bread and spread mustard and catsup on the bottom half of the bread. Then layer the onion, tomato, and lettuce onto the mustard and catsup. Place burger on lettuce and top with other half of bread.

Mojo Chicken Sandwich

There are a lot of chicken sandwiches out there, and this flavorful variation stands up with the best. For an easy shortcut, use store-bought mojo marinade.

6 ounces chicken breast
Mojo marinade
Columbia Seasoning
3 ounces roasted red peppers
1 slice Swiss cheese
6" Cuban bread, cut in half lengthwise
1 leaf of Romaine lettuce
2 slices of tomato, ¼" thick
2 ounces Olive Aioli
1 pickle spear

Pound chicken breast until it is approximately ¼" thick, and then marinate in mojo marinade for at least one hour. Remove chicken from the marinade and season with Columbia Seasoning; grill until brown on both sides and the chicken is cooked through. Before removing the chicken from the grill, place peppers on top of the chicken; then place the Swiss cheese on top of the chicken and peppers. Once the cheese is melted, remove the chicken from the grill and place on bottom half of the bread. Place the lettuce and tomato on top of the cheese. Spread the Olive Aioli on the top half of the bread and place on top of the sandwich. Place a toothpick in the center of the sandwich and cut in half diagonally. Place the sandwich cut side out on a platter and garnish with a pickle spear.

Olive Aoili

¼ cup egg yolks
4 teaspoons garlic, minced
2½ tablespoons white vinegar
3 tablespoons water
2 tablespoons yellow mustard
Pinch of salt
Pinch of white pepper
1 teaspoon lemon juice
½ cup Spanish extra-virgin olive oil
1 cup green olives, pitted

In a small bowl, combine the egg yolks, garlic, vinegar, water, mustard, salt, pepper, and lemon juice. Whip together until mixture is slightly foamy. Gradually add oil in a thin stream, constantly whipping until oil is incorporated and mayonnaise thickens. Finely chop the olives and combine well with the mayonnaise. Refrigerate until ready to serve.

The Original Cuban Sandwich

No mayo. No lettuce or tomato. No turkey. A true Tampa Cuban is layered from bottom to top: ham, roast pork, salami, Swiss cheese, pickles, and mustard. The better the quality of the ingredients, the better the sandwich. Good bread is essential, and La Segunda Central Bakery in Ybor City has supplied the Columbia for much of its history. The sandwich should not be overstuffed with ham, but carefully proportioned. Pressing the sandwich toasts the bread, melts the cheese, and renders the juices of the ingredients. Some prefer a "smashed Cuban," which is pressed heavily for a long time.

9" piece of Cuban bread
4 ounces smoked ham, thinly sliced
1½ ounces pork loin, thinly sliced
1 ounce salami, thinly sliced
1 ounce Swiss cheese
2 pickle chips
1 tablespoon yellow mustard

Cut Cuban bread in half lengthwise. Layer sliced meats and cheese in the following order: ham, pork, salami, and then cheese. Place pickle chips evenly on top. Spread mustard on top half of bread. Heat sandwich in press until crisp. Cut diagonally from corner to corner. Serves 1.

Wine-Pairing Suggestion: Torres Sangre de Toro

These rice dishes pair wonderfully with a bottle of red or white Spanish wine. If you prefer a red wine, Alidis Crianza or any of the Torres Sangre de Toro or Coronas wines are a wonderful complement. If you are looking for something lighter to pair with these heavier dishes, Torres Milmanda chardonnay makes a refreshing complement as well.

Arroz con Maíz
(Rice with Corn)

This beloved Gonzmart family favorite is satisfying, easy to make, and serves as a great accompaniment to grilled dishes.

8 slices bacon

1 large onion, chopped

2 15-ounce cans whole kernel corn, drained (or substitute 4 cups fresh corn, scraped from cob)

2 cups long-grain rice

4 cups liquid (combine liquid from canned corn and water)

2 teaspoons salt

Fry bacon until crisp. Drain and set aside. Sauté chopped onions in bacon grease. When onion is transparent, add corn, rice, liquid, and salt. Stir well, cover, and cook over low heat for 20 minutes. When ready to serve, garnish with crumbled bacon. This is a great side dish to serve with breaded steak, barbecued chicken, or ribs. Serves 6.

Arroz con Pollo
(Rice with Chicken)

During lunch, this dish is cooked in batches, Sarapico style, named after the Columbia's chef of the 1950s and 1960s. By night, it is made to order Valenciana style and baked in a traditional Spanish clay dish, or cazuela.

½ teaspoon saffron

4 cups chicken stock

½ cup Spanish extra-virgin olive oil

1 3-pound chicken, cut in quarters (may substitute 4 to 6 boneless chicken breasts)

2 large Spanish onions, chopped into eighths

1 large green pepper, chopped into eighths

2 medium tomatoes, chopped

2 garlic cloves, minced

½ tablespoon salt

1 whole bay leaf

2 cups long-grain rice

¼ cup dry white wine

½ cup small green peas, cooked

2 roasted red peppers, cut into strips

4 white asparagus tips

Using a mortar and pestle, pulverize the saffron to create a powder. In a small saucepan, heat chicken stock and add saffron. Allow saffron to dissolve; keep warm until use. In a large ovenproof casserole, heat olive oil on stove and cook chicken until skin is golden brown on both sides. Remove chicken and set aside. In same oil, sauté onion, green pepper, tomatoes, and garlic until onion is transparent. Scrape bottom of pan to loosen any chicken drippings. Add chicken stock, salt, bay leaf, and rice; stir well. Return chicken to pan. Bring mixture to a boil, then cover and bake in oven at 400° for approximately 20 minutes or until chicken and rice is done. Sprinkle with wine and garnish with peas, roasted red peppers, and asparagus tips. Serves 4 to 6.

Wine-Pairing Suggestion: Torres Gran Sangre de Toro

Arroz con Puerco
(Rice with Pork)

Richard is wild about pork and yellow rice, especially with hot sauce.

½ teaspoon saffron

4 cups chicken stock

½ cup Spanish extra-virgin olive oil

2 large Spanish onions, chopped into eighths

1 large green pepper, chopped into eighths

2 medium tomatoes, chopped

2 garlic cloves, minced

1 3-pound boneless pork tenderloin, cut into 1-inch cubes

½ tablespoon salt

1 whole bay leaf

2 cups long-grain rice

¼ cup dry white wine

½ cup small green peas, cooked

2 roasted red peppers, cut into strips

4 white asparagus tips

Using a mortar and pestle, pulverize the saffron to create a powder. In a small saucepan, heat chicken stock and add saffron. Allow saffron to dissolve; keep warm until use. In a large ovenproof casserole, heat olive oil and sauté onion, green pepper, tomatoes, and garlic until onion is transparent. Add pork, chicken stock, salt, bay leaf, rice, and stir well. Bring mixture to a boil, then cover and bake in oven at 400° for approximately 20 minutes, or until pork and rice is done. Sprinkle with wine and garnish with peas, roasted red peppers, and asparagus tips. Serves 4 to 6.

Good Rice

Adela often served baked chicken with white rice to her growing boys, but Richard didn't care for rice. Tampa's Latin community still eats a diet rich with rice: white, yellow, and fried. Adela created a rich and fragrant recipe of browned butter, chicken stock, rice, and fresh basil. When Richard tasted it, he declared it was "good rice." Whenever Adela cooked chicken, he asked if she would make the good rice, and she usually did. Like so many other dishes, this rich side dish has been passed down from Adela to the Columbia's kitchen. Incidentally, Richard also enjoys white rice today. In fact, he is very particular about the Columbia's rice.

1 stick butter

1 large onion, chopped

2 cups long-grain rice

4 cups chicken broth

½ cup parsley, chopped

½ cup fresh basil, chopped

Salt to taste

Melt butter and sauté onion until transparent. Add rice and stir constantly until it turns into a caramel color. Add chicken broth, then parsley, basil, and salt. Bring to a boil and lower flame. Cover and steam rice for 18 minutes. Fluff with a large two-tined fork. Serves 6 to 8.

Paella "Campesina"

The Columbia uses a blend of long-grain and Valenciana rice for its paella, and paella "campesina" emulates the varieties of inland Spain with meat and green beans. This is a perfect paella for those who don't care for seafood. This version was created to honor the Torres wine family and originally named to honor their home province of Catalonia. Today it is known as country-style campesina.

½ teaspoon saffron
4 cups chicken stock
¼ pound chorizo
¾ pound filet tenderloin tips
¾ pound boneless chicken breast
¾ pound boneless pork loin
1 cup Spanish extra-virgin olive oil
2 large Spanish onions, chopped into eighths
1 large green pepper, chopped into eighths
1 medium tomato, chopped
1 garlic clove, minced
1½ cups cut green beans, cooked
½ tablespoon salt
1 whole bay leaf
2 cups long-grain rice
¼ cup dry white wine
½ cup small green peas, cooked
2 roasted red peppers, cut into strips
4 white asparagus tips
Columbia Seasoning

Using a mortar and pestle, pulverize the saffron to create a powder. In a small saucepan, heat chicken stock and add saffron. Allow saffron to dissolve; keep warm until use. Cut chorizo in half lengthwise and ¼" on bias. Cut tenderloin, chicken, and pork into approximately 1" pieces.

In a large paella pan or large ovenproof casserole, heat olive oil on stove and sauté onion, green pepper, tomatoes, and garlic until onion is transparent. Add all of the meat and green beans to the pan, season with Columbia Seasoning, and cook until meat is lightly browned on all sides. Add chicken stock, salt, bay leaf, rice, and stir well. Bring mixture to a boil, then cover and bake in oven at 400° for approximately 20 minutes or until rice is done. Sprinkle with wine and garnish with peas, roasted red peppers, and asparagus tips. Serves 4 to 6.

Wine-Pairing Suggestion: Alidis Crianza

Paella "Marenara"

Marenara style, or "from the sea," this luxurious paella is for the seafood lover and emulates coastal Spanish recipes.

½ teaspoon saffron

4 cups chicken stock

½ pound grouper fillet

½ pound squid, tentacles and tubes

2 teaspoons Spanish extra-virgin olive oil

2 large Spanish onions, chopped into eighths

1 large green pepper, chopped into eighths

2 medium tomatoes, chopped

2 garlic cloves, minced

16 scallops, 10–20-count

¾ pound shrimp, 36–40-count

16 mussels

16 littleneck clams

8 shrimp, 10-count

2 tablespoons Columbia Seasoning

½ tablespoon salt

1 whole bay leaf

2 cups long-grain rice

¼ cup dry white wine

½ cup small green peas, cooked

2 roasted red peppers, cut into strips

4 white asparagus tips

Using a mortar and pestle, pulverize the saffron to create a powder. In a small saucepan, heat chicken stock and add saffron. Allow saffron to dissolve; keep warm until use. Cut the grouper into 4 equal pieces and cut the squid into ¾"-wide tubes.

In a large paella pan or large ovenproof casserole, heat olive oil on stove and sauté onion, green pepper, tomatoes, and garlic until onion is transparent. Add all of the seafood and season with Columbia Seasoning; sauté for approximately 1 minute. Add chicken stock, salt, bay leaf, rice, and stir well. Bring mixture to a boil, then cover and bake in oven at 400° for approximately 20 minutes or until rice is done. Sprinkle with wine and garnish with peas, roasted red peppers, and asparagus tips. Serves 4 to 6.

Wine-Pairing Suggestion: Torres Milmanda Chardonnay

Paella "Valenciana"

The Columbia's signature paella, this version balances seafood, pork, and chicken.

½ teaspoon saffron

4 cups chicken stock

½ pound grouper

½ pound squid, tentacles and tubes

1 pound boneless chicken breast

¾ pound boneless pork loin

½ cup Spanish extra-virgin olive oil

1 large Spanish onion, chopped into eighths

1 large green pepper, chopped into eighths

2 medium tomatoes, chopped

2 garlic cloves, minced

Columbia Seasoning

8 mussels

12 scallops, 10–20-count

8 littleneck clams

Paella "Marenara"

¾ pound shrimp, 36–40-count

½ tablespoon salt

1 whole bay leaf

2 cups long-grain rice

¼ cup dry white wine

½ cup small green peas, cooked

2 roasted red peppers, cut into strips

4 white asparagus tips

Using a mortar and pestle, pulverize the saffron to create a powder. In a small saucepan, heat chicken stock and add saffron. Allow saffron to dissolve; keep warm until use. Cut the grouper into 4 equal pieces. Cut the squid into ¾"-wide tubes. Cut the chicken and pork into approximately 1" pieces.

In a large paella pan or large ovenproof casserole, heat ½ cup olive oil on stove and sauté onion, green pepper, tomatoes, and garlic until onion is transparent. Add pork and chicken to the pan, season with 2 tablespoons Columbia Seasoning, and cook until meat is lightly browned on all sides. Add all of the seafood and sauté for 1 minute. Add chicken stock, salt, bay leaf, and rice; stir well. Bring mixture to a boil, then cover and bake in oven at 400° for approximately 20 minutes or until rice is done. Sprinkle with wine and garnish with peas, roasted red peppers, and asparagus tips. Serves 4 to 6.

Wine-Pairing Suggestion: Torres Gran Coronas

Boliche "Criollo" (Eye of Round Roast Beef)

Boliche is a Cuban blue-plate special, served at the Columbia with a rich gravy of beef juices puréed with braised vegetables. Leftovers are great on sandwiches.

3 pounds eye of round beef
3 whole chorizos (Spanish sausage)
½ pound smoked ham, cut in 1-inch pieces
¼ cup Spanish extra-virgin olive oil
1 tablespoon salt
2 teaspoons black pepper
2 tablespoons oregano
4 tablespoons paprika
3 large onions, sliced in half-moons
1 large green pepper, cut in strips
3 large onions, sliced in half-moons
6 cloves garlic, minced
3 cups beef broth
1 cup red wine
4 bay leaves

Pierce a hole (about 1 inch in diameter) through the length of the roast. Stuff with Spanish sausage and ham. Heat oil in a Dutch oven. Mix salt, pepper, oregano, and paprika and rub on outside of roast until it is well covered. Add onions, green peppers, and garlic. Brown boliche in Dutch oven. Add broth, red wine, and bay leaves. Cover. Cook over medium-low heat for approximately 2½ hours, turning several times. When done, remove from Dutch oven and process gravy in food processor until smooth. Cut boliche into ½-inch slices and pour gravy over them. Serve with white rice, black beans, and fried plantains. Serves 8.

Wine-Pairing Suggestion: Arzuaga Crianza from Ribera del Duero

Carne con Papas (Beef Stew)

Do not sell this beef stew short. It is wonderful, especially on cold nights.

1 pound tenderloin of beef tips, trimmed and cut in
    1-inch cubes
2 tablespoons olive oil
1 green pepper, chopped
1 onion, chopped
1 bay leaf
2 cloves garlic, minced
½ teaspoon sweet paprika
1 cup canned whole tomatoes, chopped
3 medium potatoes, peeled and cubes cut in
    1½-inch chunks
Pimiento or roasted red pepper strips and
    green peas (cooked)

Brown beef tips in oil. When half-cooked, add green pepper, onion, bay leaf, garlic, and paprika. Cook with tomatoes over medium heat for 15 minutes. Place potatoes with meat and tomato mixture in casserole dish and bake for 40 minutes at 350°. Decorate with peas and pimiento strips. Serves 3.

Wine-Pairing Suggestion: Montecillo Tinto from Rioja or any of the great full-bodied red wines from the Priorato region of Spain.

Filet Mignon "Chacho"

Who knew that a Spanish/Cuban restaurant in Florida would be become the nation's biggest consumer of fine Kentucky bourbon? The flambéed bourbon deepens the flavor of the demi-glace, mushrooms, and beef. Be sure to let the bourbon burn itself out; it will remove the alcohol flavor.

4 8-ounce filet mignons
Columbia Seasoning
4 ounces Booker Noe Bourbon (any bourbon may
   be substituted)
Chacho Sauce (recipe below)

Season filets with Columbia Seasoning. Before cooking filets, allow them to come to room temperature to ensure even cooking. Grill filets until desired temperature and place on individual plates. Ladle Chacho Sauce generously over each filet. Fill a tablespoon with approximately 1 ounce of Booker Noe bourbon and ignite. Pour flaming bourbon over the filet, allowing the flame to burn out. Repeat until all filets have been flambéed. Serves 4.

Wine-Pairing Suggestion: Torres Mas la Plana from Penedés

Chacho Sauce

¼ cup Spanish extra-virgin olive oil
¼ cup shallots, minced
1¼ cup button mushrooms, sliced
5 cups Alicante Sauce (see p. 150)

Heat oil and cook shallots until translucent. Add mushrooms and cook for approximately 3 minutes. Add Alicante Sauce and bring to a boil. Then simmer for 3 minutes. Keep warm until use, or if prepared in advance, refrigerate until use. Makes 5 cups.

Filet Mignon "Columbia"

This recipe has served as the Columbia's signature steak for over sixty years.

4 8-ounce filet mignons
4 strips of bacon, cooked
Columbia Seasoning
Columbia Sauce (recipe below)

Wrap filets with bacon, secure in place with a toothpick. Season filets with Columbia Seasoning and allow to come to room temperature before cooking. Grill filets until desired temperature and place on individual plates. Ladle sauce generously over filets and serve immediately. Serves 4.

Wine-Pairing Suggestion: Don Cesar Crianza from Ribera del Duero. Don Cesar is a private label wine only available at the Columbia Restaurant, but a fine Crianza from Bodegas Viña Mambrilla would be a fine substitute.

Columbia Sauce

3 tablespoons Spanish extra-virgin olive oil
1 tablespoon garlic, minced
⅓ cup Spanish onion, thinly sliced
⅓ cup green pepper, thinly sliced
6 ounces ham
2½ cups Alicante Sauce (see p. 150)
¾ cup fresh mushrooms, quartered
1 cup Catalana Sauce (see p. 150)
⅓ cup red wine
1 tablespoon Worcestershire Sauce

Heat oil and brown garlic. Add onions and peppers to oil and garlic. Julienne ham into 2″ × ⅛″ pieces and add. Add Alicante Sauce, mushrooms, Catalana Sauce, red wine, and Worcestershire; simmer for 10 minutes. Keep warm until use, or if preparing in advance, refrigerate until use. Makes 6½ cups.

Roast Pork "a la Cubana" (Cuban Style)

Traditional mojo pork is a Cuban necessity on Christmas Eve, but it is delicious any time of year, with rice and vegetables or on sandwiches.

3½ teaspoons Spanish extra-virgin olive oil
⅓ cup fresh lemon juice
1 whole bay leaf
2 teaspoons garlic powder
½ teaspoon dried oregano
¼ cup fresh garlic, minced
⅓ cup white vinegar
2 cups water
2 pork tenderloins, ¾ to 1 pound each
Salt and pepper to taste
½ teaspoon paprika

Combine the olive oil, lemon juice, bay leaf, garlic powder, oregano, fresh garlic, vinegar, and water to create a marinade for the tenderloins.

Place tenderloins in pan and cover with marinade, then season tenderloins generously with salt and pepper and sprinkle with paprika. Cover and refrigerate tenderloins allowing them to marinate overnight.

Place tenderloins in baking dish, pouring the remaining marinade over meat. Roast tenderloins at 400° for approximately 30 to 45 minutes, or until cooked through. Slice tenderloins before serving with marinade on the side. Serves 8.

Wine-Pairing Suggestion: Torres Sangre de Toro

Veal "Isabella"

Named after Queen Isabella of Spain, this extravagant dish is a real indulgence. The creamy béarnaise sauce, spiked with sherry vinegar, complements the crabmeat and browned veal wonderfully. Be careful not to overcook the crab. Top the cooked meat with lump crab. When adding the crab, leave it lumped, and top with hot béarnaise sauce.

2 pounds veal scaloppini
Salt and pepper
Flour
Butter
12 ounces lump crabmeat
Sherry Béarnaise Sauce

Cut veal into 8 medallions and season well with salt and pepper. Dredge veal pieces into flour, shaking off any excess. Melt approximately 1 tablespoon of butter in frying pan. Once butter has melted, place veal in pan and cook on both sides until golden brown. Place veal onto a platter and place equal amounts of crabmeat on each medallion, trying not to break up the lumps. Ladle the Sherry Béarnaise Sauce on top of crabmeat and serve immediately. Serves 4.

Wine-Pairing Suggestion: Marimar Torres Pinot Noir from California or Torres Atrium from Spain

Sherry Béarnaise Sauce

2¼ teaspoons shallots, chopped
3 whole black peppercorns
1½ tablespoons dried tarragon
3 tablespoons Spanish sherry vinegar
1½ teaspoons dry white wine
1 tablespoon water
3½ tablespoons egg yolks
¾ cup clarified butter
¼ teaspoon salt

Combine shallots, peppercorns, half of the tarragon, and vinegar; reduce to evaporate liquid. Remove from heat. Add wine and water and strain liquid to remove any solids. Combine liquid and egg yolks in a stainless steel bowl and cook over a double-boiler, whipping until mixture forms ribbons. Remove from heat and slowly add the butter, whipping constantly. Add remaining tarragon and salt. Hold at room temperature until ready to serve.

Chicken

Pollo Cacerola (Chicken Casserole)

This rustic chicken casserole is a comforting family favorite and often appears as a daily special.

10 pieces quartered chicken (5 breasts and 5 thighs)
1 tablespoon salt
1 tablespoon black pepper
⅓ cup Spanish extra-virgin olive oil
1 pound Spanish onions, sliced into ¼" pieces
3 tablespoons fresh garlic, minced
¾ cup ham, diced into ½" pieces
1 cup fresh mushrooms, quartered
3 teaspoons dried oregano
1 cup red wine
2 pints Alicante Sauce (see p. 150)
1 whole potato, peeled and diced into 1" cubes, parboiled

Preheat oven to 400°. Season chicken with salt and pepper. Pour olive oil into an oven-proof pot and heat over medium-high heat. Place chicken in pot and cook until golden brown on both sides; remove chicken and place to the side. In the same pot, add onions and garlic; sauté until translucent. Add ham, mushrooms, diced potato, oregano, red wine, and Alicante Sauce, bring to a boil. Return chicken to the pot and coat well with the sauce. Cover and bake in oven for 20 minutes or until chicken is cooked thoroughly. Serves 6 to 8.

Wine-Pairing Suggestion: Cuné Viña Real Crianza from Rioja

Mojito Chicken

Wake up your chicken with mint, lime, rum, and mojo. Just before cooking, roll the chicken in a sweet mojito glaze. Grill this dish if possible, as it heightens all of the flavors.

1 whole chicken (approximately 3 to 4 pounds), cut into quarters
Mojito Marinade (recipe below)
Mojito Glaze (see p. 139)

Place chicken in a pan and top with the Mojito Marinade, making sure chicken is covered well with marinade. Allow chicken to marinate at least 4 hours before cooking.

Remove chicken from marinade and drench with Mojito Glaze. Bake in a 350° oven for approximately 20 to 30 minutes or until chicken is cooked through. An alternative cooking method would be to cook the chicken on an outdoor grill. Serves 4.

Wine-Pairing Suggestion: Algareiro Albariño from Rías Baixas or Miguel Torres Santa Digna Cabernet Sauvignon Rosé from Chilé

Mojito Marinade

1 quart mojo marinade (store-bought)
½ cup fresh lime juice
3 ounces fresh mint, chopped
¼ cup Columbia Seasoning
3 cups Spanish extra-virgin olive oil

Combine all ingredients and mix well.

Mojito Glaze

1 cup sugar
1 tablespoon Bacardi Superior Rum (or any light rum)
½ cup water
⅛ cup fresh mint, whole
½ cup fresh lime juice

Combine all ingredients in a small pan and bring to a rapid boil. Lower heat and simmer for approximately 10 minutes, until it has the consistency of syrup. Remove mint.

Pollo "Champinion" (Chicken with Mushrooms)

This dish takes grilled chicken from the backyard to the fancy bistro. Mushroom lovers, rejoice! The rich and fragrant Amontillado Sauce elevates a simple chicken and mushroom dish to luxurious heights.

8 cups chicken stock
¾ cup fresh lemon juice
2½ tablespoons Columbia Seasoning
3 tablespoons fresh garlic, chopped
8 chicken breasts, boneless and skinless (approximately 6 ounces each)
4 portabello mushroom caps (3"–4" in diameter)
Amontillado Sauce (recipe below)

Combine the chicken stock, lemon juice, Columbia Seasoning, and garlic to create a marinade. Allow chicken to marinate overnight if possible. Cook chicken on grill. Right before the chicken is finished, place the mushrooms on the grill and cook on both sides until grill marks are evident. Once the chicken and the mush-rooms are finished cooking, remove from the grill and slice the mushrooms diagonally into ¼" pieces (approximately 5 slices). Place two chicken breasts onto each individual plate and place the sliced mushroom caps on top. Finish with ladling the Amontillado Sauce over the chicken breasts and mushroom slices. Serves 4 to 6.

Wine-Pairing Suggestion: Campillo Blanco from Rioja

Amontillado Sauce

5 cups Alicante Sauce (see p. 150)
½ cup Spanish amontillado sherry

In a large saucepan over moderate heat, combine the Alicante Sauce with the sherry, stirring until fully incorporated. Keep warm until ready to use or refrigerate for future use.

Pollo "Riojana" (Chicken Parmesan Spanish Style)

From the 1940s until the 1980s, the Columbia reserved a whole section of its menu for Italian favorites. When chicken Parmesan was discontinued, regular customers complained. The kitchen created this Spanish variation of the Italian-American classic, topped with tetilla cheese.

8 chicken breasts, boneless and skinless (approximately 6 ounces each)
Columbia Seasoning
1 egg
Flour
4 cups bread crumbs
Spanish extra-virgin olive oil
Rioja Sauce (see p. 151)
8 ounces Spanish tetilla cheese

Evenly pound chicken breasts and season with Columbia Seasoning. Whisk egg with a splash of water to make an egg wash. Bread chicken breasts in flour, then egg wash, and then bread crumbs. Coat the bottom of a large frying pan with olive oil and warm over medium-high heat. Cook chicken until done, browning on both sides. Place chicken breasts on a rimmed cookie sheet, top with Rioja Sauce and tetilla cheese. Place under broiler until cheese has melted. Serves 4 to 6.

Wine-Pairing Suggestion: Faustino VII from Rioja

Pollo Salteado (Chicken Cuban-Chinese Style)

This Cuban preparation was originally inspired by the influx of Chinese workers who replaced the slaves in the late 1800s. Their stir-fry techniques inspired the Cubans to try their hand at fried rice and stir-fries of their own: Cuban-Chinese sautés, or salteado.

½ cup Spanish extra-virgin olive oil
2 teaspoons garlic, chopped
¼ cup chorizo (Spanish sausage)
1½ pounds boneless chicken breast, cut into 1" pieces (or substitute pork, tenderloin tips, or shrimp)
2 tablespoons Columbia Seasoning
½ cup mushrooms, quartered
1 large green pepper, cut into ¼" slices
1 Spanish onion, cut into ¼" slices
½ cup potatoes diced into ½" pieces, preblanched
½ cup red wine
1½ cups Alicante Sauce (see p. 150)

Heat oil and sauté garlic until golden brown. Cut chorizo in half lengthwise and cut diagonally into ¼" pieces. Add chorizo and chicken and season with Columbia Seasoning; sauté approximately 30 seconds. Add mushrooms, green pepper, onions, and potatoes; sauté for 1 minute. Add red wine and cook for approximately 1 more minute. Add sauce and heat through. Serves 4.

Wine-Pairing Suggestion: Pesquera Tinto from Ribera del Duero

Seafood

Wine suggestions: An Albariño from the Rías Baixas region would be a fine complement to any of the seafood dishes. Any of the food-driven chardonnays from Penedés are good choices as well. If you are feeling adventurous, pair your dish with a light red, such as a pinot noir from California—you will be pleasantly surprised at how well it complements the heavier seafood dishes.

Camarones Rellenos con Cangrejo (Crab-stuffed Shrimp)

Imagine jumbo shrimp stuffed with crab cake, topped with lemon butter, and baked to perfection. This dish is a tribute to Jesse Gonzalez, who supplied the Columbia's shrimp for years. The restaurant still does business with Gonzalez at a different company—Marpesca, run by a Greek family based in Panama.

1 cup butter
6 whole lemons
16 shrimp, peeled and deveined, 10-count
Columbia Seasoning
8 Crab Cakes (see p. 107)
2 cups water

Preheat oven to 400°. Melt butter over low heat in small sauce pan. Add juice of 4 fresh-squeezed lemons and stir well; keep warm until use. Butterfly shrimp and season well with Columbia Seasoning. Fill each shrimp with half a crab cake. Place shrimp in an oven-proof baking dish with water, and ladle 2 tablespoons of lemon butter on top of each stuffed shrimp. Bake in oven until golden brown on top, approximately 20 minutes. Place four shrimp on each plate and ladle remaining lemon butter on top. Serve immediately, garnished with lemon wedges. Serves 4.

Cannelloni de Langosta (Lobster Cannelloni)

Pasta and cannelloni aren't exclusive to Italy. These lobster-stuffed delights were inspired by a 130-year-old recipe from Barcelona.

1 pound lobster meat
3 cups ricotta cheese
2 eggs
½ cup bread crumbs
½ cup Romano cheese, grated
½ teaspoon salt
½ teaspoon black pepper
½ teaspoon oregano
½ teaspoon dried basil
Frozen pasta sheets (may be substituted with manicotti tubes)
Mornay-Coroñesa Sauce (see p. 142)
1 cup Manchego cheese, grated

To make the lobster filling, drain lobster meat thoroughly and dice into ¼" pieces. Add ricotta cheese, eggs, bread crumbs, Romano cheese, salt, pepper, oregano, and basil. Mix well and refrigerate until ready to use.

Pipe approximately ½ cup of lobster filling along the side of each pasta sheet. Roll pasta sheet to form cannelloni and then cut in half, creating two cannelloni rolls. Repeat process until all lobster filling is used.

Ladle Mornay-Coroñesa Sauce into the bottom of a 10" × 15" baking dish, enough to cover the bottom. Place cannelloni rolls into the baking dish and coat with a thin layer of sauce on top. Bake in 400° oven for approximately 20 minutes or until heated through. Serve with remaining sauce and Manchego cheese for garnish. Serves 6.

Wine-Pairing Suggestion: Torres Fransola Sauvignon Blanc

Mornay-Coroñesa Sauce

1¼ cups Coroñesa Sauce (see p. 150)
¼ cup amontillado sherry
1 cup Mornay Sauce (see p. 151)

Combine the Coroñesa Sauce with the sherry and heat in saucepan until warm. Add to Mornay Sauce. If not using immediately, cool until ready to use and reheat over low heat.

Lobster and Crab Enchilado

This old-time Tampa favorite dates back to the early 1900s, when crabs were plentiful in Tampa Bay. In enchilada (or chilau, as the Crackers called it), Sicilian pasta was sauced with a Spanish/Cuban seafood and sofrito mixture. This variation calls for a crab sauce over browned lobster and linguini.

4 ounces Spanish extra-virgin olive oil
2 pounds lobster meat
1 tablespoon Columbia Seasoning
1 cup dry white wine
Enchilado Sauce (recipe below)
2 pounds linguini, cooked

1 tablespoon fresh parsley, chopped
Romano cheese, grated

Heat oil in large sauté pan. Season lobster with Columbia Seasoning and add to the pan; brown in oil on both sides. Deglaze pan with white wine. Reduce the liquid to half. Add 2 cups of Enchilado Sauce; cook lobster through. Toss cooked linguini with ¼ cup of Enchilado Sauce and place linguini in four individual pasta bowls. Arrange lobster meat on top of each mound of linguini, dividing equally. Ladle the remainder of the Enchilado Sauce over lobster and garnish with parsley and Romano cheese. Serves 4.

Wine-Pairing Suggestion: Dehesa la Granja, Alejandro Fernandez

Enchilado Sauce

3 tablespoons Spanish extra-virgin olive oil
⅛ cup garlic, minced
¾ cup Spanish onion, julienned
¼ dry white wine
4 cups Catalana Sauce (see p. 150)
½ teaspoon salt
1½ teaspoons black pepper
1 whole bay leaf
4 cups water
¾ cup crabmeat, claw preferably
1½ tablespoons Columbia Hot Sauce
½ teaspoon Columbia Seasoning
1½ teaspoons paprika

Heat oil in large saucepan and lightly brown garlic. Sauté onions until transparent. Deglaze pan with white wine. Purée Catalana Sauce and add to saucepan. Add salt, pepper, and bay leaf; bring to a boil. Add water and bring to a boil once again. Add crabmeat, Columbia Hot Sauce, Columbia Seasoning, and paprika; simmer for 10 minutes. Keep warm until use, or prepare ahead and store in the refrigerator.

Mahimahi "Cayo Hueso"

"Cayo Hueso," the original Spanish name for Key West, means "Bone Isle," but there is nothing skeletal about this bright tropical dish. The citrus of the mojo cooks and marinates the onions and fish. Feel free to use store-bought mojo as a shortcut.

4 8-ounce fillets of mahimahi
8 cups mojo marinade (store-bought)
1½ cups onion, sliced very thinly
Columbia Seasoning
2 limes, cut into wedges

Marinate mahi fillets in 6 cups of mojo marinade for at least 4 hours for the best results. Place onions in the remaining mojo marinade and let sit until onions soften. Season fillets with Columbia Seasoning and grill for approximately 15 minutes, turning when necessary. Place fillets on individual plates and top with 1 tablespoon of marinated onions. Garnish with lime wedges and the remaining marinated onions. Serves 4.

Pompano en Papillot

In the restaurant industry, it is sometimes necessary to revise recipes to keep up with the times. In 2001, Adela insisted that the pompano recipe remain the same, but it sold poorly. The new creamy crab and artichoke recipe made the dish a favorite once again, launching it into the Columbia's top five entrees. Both are good recipes, but Columbia patrons strongly favor the 2001 version.

1939 Version

¼ pound butter
1 onion, chopped fine
1 cup flour
1 pint milk, heated
2 eggs
Dash of nutmeg
Dash of Columbia Hot Sauce
1 ounce dry white wine
Salt and pepper
½ pound shrimp, cooked and chopped
½ pound crawfish, cooked and chopped
4 8-ounce fillets of pompano
Columbia Seasoning
Parchment paper (4 pieces, each approximately 11"×17")

Melt butter in skillet. Sauté onion until transparent, approximately 5 minutes. Add flour and stir until it forms a ball with butter and onion. Add hot milk and stir until mixture becomes a thick sauce. Beat eggs with nutmeg, Columbia Hot Sauce, and wine. Fold into cream sauce; add salt and pepper to taste. Add shrimp and crawfish and mix thoroughly.

Season pompano fillets with Columbia Seasoning. Working one sheet at a time, brush half of the parchment paper with melted butter and spread ⅛ of the cream sauce on top. Place the seasoned fillet on top of the sauce and then spread another ⅛ of sauce on top of the fillet. Fold paper over (corner to corner); crimp edges to form half circle and close pouch. Once all four pouches have been formed, place on baking sheet and cook in 400° oven for approximately 20 to 30 minutes. Once fish is cooked through, remove from baking sheet and place on individual plates. Use sharp knife to cut pouches open. Serves 4.

2001 Version

¼ pound butter
1¾ pounds fresh pompano fillet
Columbia Seasoning
2½ cups shrimp, Crabmeat Artichoke Mix (see p. 118)
Lemon
Parchment paper (4 pieces, each approximately 11"×17")

Melt butter. Cut the pompano into 8 equal fillets and season with Columbia Seasoning. Working one sheet at a time, brush half of the parchment paper with melted butter and place seasoned fillet on top. Layer approximately ¾ cup of shrimp, crabmeat, and artichoke mix on top of the fillet. Place second fillet on mix and top with 2 tablespoons of butter. Fold paper over (corner to corner), crimp edges to form half circle, and close pouch. Once all four pouches have been formed, place on baking sheet and cook in 400° oven for approximately 20 to 30 minutes. Once fish is cooked through, remove from baking sheet and place on individual plates. Use sharp knife to cut pouches open. Serves 4.

Wine-Pairing Suggestion: Torres Mas Borras Pinot Noir, Spain

Salmon "Nuevo Latino"

Another creation of Chef Jerry. Salmon was not popular in old Tampa, where local fish varieties reigned. These days, one can find salmon everywhere—why not at the Columbia? Chef Jerry's preparation features a mango-mint salsa.

3 cups Spanish extra-virgin olive oil
1 cup shallots, finely chopped
1½ cups garlic, finely chopped
¼ cup fresh parsley, chopped
¼ cup Columbia Seasoning
4 salmon fillets (approximately 8 ounces each)
Mango-Mint Salsa (recipe below)
Tobacco Carrots (see p. 117)

Combine olive oil, shallots, garlic, parsley, and Columbia Seasoning; marinate salmon fillets in olive oil marinade for at least 1 hour.

Grill salmon, flipping as needed until it is cooked thoroughly. Place grilled salmon on platter. Serve carrots on the side with Mango-Mint Salsa. Serve immediately. Serves 4.

Mango-Mint Salsa

1¼ cups ripe tomatoes
½ cup red onion
1 cup mango
⅛ cup scallions
1 tablespoon fresh lime juice
1 tablespoon garlic, finely chopped
1½ teaspoons cilantro, chopped
1½ tablespoons mint, chopped
1 tablespoon Spanish extra-virgin olive oil
¼ teaspoon of salt

Dice tomatoes in approximately ½" pieces, and place in mixing bowl. Dice onion into ¼" pieces; add. Dice mango into ½" pieces; add. Chop scallions in small pieces; add. Add all other ingredients, toss well, and refrigerate until use.

Sea Bass "Bilbao"

Inspired by the cookery of northern Spain, this dish is healthy and clean. You can precook the potatoes, assemble the recipe ahead of time, and impress company without breaking a sweat.

2 potatoes
Columbia Seasoning
1 large tomato
1 Spanish onion
1 pound fresh sea bass fillets
Spanish extra-virgin olive oil
Dry white wine
Lemon

In boiling water, blanch potatoes until fork tender and then drain. Peel potatoes and slice diagonally across into ⅜" pieces. In a baking dish large enough for the fish to fit in one layer, place potatoes and season with Columbia Seasoning. Cut tomato into ¼" slices (approximately 6 slices) and layer on potatoes; season with Columbia Seasoning. Thinly slice onion and layer 4 to 5 slices on tomato. Place sea bass fillets on onion and top with approximately ⅓ cup of olive oil evenly distributed, 2 tablespoons of wine, and the juice of one lemon. Season with Columbia Seasoning. Bake at 400° for approximately 20 minutes or fish is cooked through. Garnish with lemon wedges. Serves 2.

Wine-Pairing Suggestion: Jean Leon Chardonnay, Spain

Shrimp Criollo

This shrimp variation adds sweet notes of fried plantains and hot paprika.

1 ripe plantain
Vegetable oil for frying
1 cup Spanish extra-virgin olive oil
4 teaspoons garlic, finely chopped
¾ cup green pepper, julienned
¾ cup Spanish onion, julienned
1 whole bay leave
32 shrimp, peeled with tail on, 21–25-count
1 tablespoon Columbia Seasoning
2 teaspoons picante (hot) paprika

1 cup tomatoes, ½" dice
¾ cup potatoes, ½" dice and preblanched
1½ cups Martini & Rossi dry vermouth (may be substituted with any dry vermouth)
1 tablespoon fresh parsley, chopped

To prepare plantain, slice diagonally about ½ inch thick. Fry in oil over medium heat, turning to brown on both sides. Drain on paper towel until ready to use.

Heat olive oil in sauté pan, add garlic, peppers, onions, and bay leaf. Cook until garlic is golden brown. Add shrimp and Columbia Seasoning, sauté for 30 seconds. Add paprika, tomatoes, potatoes, and 1 cup fried plantains; sauté to thoroughly heat. Deglaze the pan with vermouth; do not reduce, but allow to heat thoroughly. Garnish with parsley. Serves 4.

Snapper "Adelita"

In 2005, Chef Carolyn White helped Richard develop this recipe, which originally featured Ketel One vodka in the sauce. Neutral spirits in the commercial kitchen are a terrible temptation for workers, so the restaurant uses clam juice instead. Feel free to substitute white wine or chicken broth. Hearts of artichokes and hearts of palm raise the dinner entrée to new heights.

1 cup Spanish extra-virgin olive oil

½ cup Spanish onion, diced

4 hearts of palm

1 15-ounce can artichoke hearts

½ cup sun-dried tomatoes

½ teaspoon crushed red pepper flakes

½ teaspoon dried oregano

1 cup clam juice

4 snapper fillets, boneless (approximately 8 ounces each)

Columbia Seasoning

Flour

Heat ½ cup of olive oil in sauté pan and add onions. Cut hearts of palm in ½" pieces diagonally, quarter the artichoke hearts, and julienne the sun-dried tomatoes; add to pan. Then add the crushed red pepper and oregano, and sauté for approximately 1 minute. Add clam juice and simmer for 1 minute. Use immediately or keep at room temperature to reheat when ready to use.

Season snapper fillets with Columbia Seasoning and then dredge into flour, shaking off any excess. Heat olive oil in pan over medium-high heat and cook fillets on both sides until golden brown. Place cooked fish on platter with vegetable mixture on top; serve immediately. Serves 4.

Wine-Pairing Suggestion: Torres Viña Esmeralda, Penedés

Snapper "Alicante"

Some food theorists don't think that a beef-based sauce can work with seafood. Over the years, millions of Columbia patrons have disagreed. This classic is one of the Columbia's signature dishes.

8 shrimp, peeled with tail on, 10-count
4 slices cooked bacon
4 cups Spanish extra-virgin olive oil
1 cup lemon juice
½ cup garlic, finely chopped
Columbia Seasoning
4 cups flour
4 eggs, beaten
1 eggplant
2 cups bread crumbs
2 Spanish onions, cut into ¼" slices
4 7-ounce fillets of snapper, boneless
2 green peppers, cut into ¼" slices
6 cups Alicante Sauce (see p. 150)
Dry white wine
¼ cup almonds, lightly toasted in the oven
1 lemon, sliced thinly

Wrap shrimp with ½ slice of bacon and secure with a toothpick. Combine 2 cups extra-virgin olive oil, lemon juice, garlic, and 2 tablespoons of Columbia Seasoning to create marinade. Marinate shrimp for 2 to 3 hours. Combine flour with 6 tablespoons of Columbia Seasoning. Beat eggs in a small bowl. Batter shrimp in the following order: seasoned flour, egg, and then seasoned flour again. Peel and slice eggplant into 1" slices. Batter eggplant in the following order: seasoned flour, beaten egg, and then bread crumbs. Keep refrigerated until cooking time.

Preheat oven to 550°. Place eight slices of onion on the bottom of a shallow casserole dish. Season fish with Columbia Seasoning and place on top of onions. Lay two slices of green pepper on top of each fillet, and then top with Alicante Sauce. Bake in oven for approximately 20 minutes.

While fish is cooking, deep-fry the breaded eggplant and shrimp at 350° in 2 cups of extra-virgin olive oil until golden brown. Remove toothpicks from shrimp. Remove fish from oven when cooked through and splash with white wine and top with toasted almonds. Garnish with shrimp, eggplant, and lemon wheels. Serves 4.

Wine-Pairing Suggestion: Montecillo Crianza, Spain

Snapper "Russian Style"

Originally made with trout and then merluza, sales of this dish have doubled since the restaurant began using snapper.

10 eggs
4 tablespoons fresh parsley, chopped
6 whole lemons
¾ cup butter
2 cups flour
¾ cup Columbia Seasoning
4 8-ounce fillets of snapper, boneless (or any white fish)
4 cups bread crumbs
Pimiento strips for garnishing

Hard-boil 5 eggs and let cool. Finely chop hard-boiled eggs and combine with parsley. Thinly slice one whole lemon into ⅛" slices. Refrigerate above items until serving time. Melt butter over low heat in a small saucepan. Add the juice of 4 fresh-squeezed lemons and stir well; keep warm until use.

Combine flour and Columbia Seasoning in a medium-sized bowl; mix well. Beat one egg with ⅛ cup of water. Bread the fish in the following order: seasoned flour, then egg, and then bread crumbs. Coat the bottom of a large saucepan with lemon butter and cook the fish on medium-high heat until golden brown, approximately 5 minutes on each side. Place fish on a platter and garnish each fillet with 2 lemon wheels, egg mixture, and 2 pimiento strips. Top with the remaining lemon butter and serve immediately. Serves 4.

Wine-Pairing Suggestion: Adelita Chardonnay. Adelita Chardonnay is a private label wine only available at the Columbia Restaurant. A fine substitute would be any of the Jean Lean Chardonnays from Spain.

Sauces

Alicante Sauce

2 tablespoons unsalted butter
¾ cup olive oil
2 onions, chopped
2 stalks celery, chopped
2 carrots, chopped
2 bay leaves
1 teaspoon thyme
½ cup flour
2 cups tomato puree
5 peppercorns
14 cups beef stock
¼ cup parsley, coarsely chopped
½ cup Madeira wine
4 tablespoons heavy cream
⅓ cup white wine
Salt to taste

Melt butter and olive oil in sauce pan. Saute onions, celery, carrots, bay leaves, and thyme. Add flour and cook mixture over medium heat until flour is lightly brown. Add tomato puree, peppercorns, 8 cups of beef stock, and parsley. Cook over low heat, covered for 2 hours. Add rest of the beef stock and Madeira wine. Simmer until reduced by one third. Strain sauce. Add heavy cream and white wine. Season with salt to taste. Makes approximately 5 cups.

Catalana Sauce

4 Spanish onions, chopped
4 green peppers, cut into strips
½ cup Spanish extra-virgin olive oil
4 garlic cloves, finely minced
1 28-ounce can crushed tomatoes
1 28-ounce can tomato sauce
2 bay leaves
1 teaspoon sugar
1 quart of water
Salt and pepper to taste

Sauté onions and green peppers in olive oil. Add garlic, tomatoes, and tomato sauce. Add bay leaves, sugar, and water. Cook over medium heat for 1 hour. Add salt and pepper. Makes about 2 quarts.

Coroñesa Sauce

½ cup unsalted butter
2 tablespoons Spanish extra-virgin olive oil
1 Spanish onion, chopped
1 small stalk of celery, chopped
1 carrot, scraped and chopped
3 garlic cloves, finely minced
8 ounces canned tomato sauce
2 blue crabs, shelled and cut up in small pieces
    (approximately 4 ounces)
½ teaspoon paprika
1 teaspoon tarragon
1 tablespoon flour
1 quart of water
¼ cup dry white wine
2 tablespoons Spanish brandy

1 teaspoon Pernod
1 teaspoon salt
½ teaspoon white pepper

Melt butter and olive oil in large saucepan. Sauté onion, celery, carrot, and garlic. Add tomato sauce, crab, paprika, tarragon, and flour. Stir well and add water. Boil gently for 30 minutes. Strain through a fine sieve. Return to pot and add wine, brandy, Pernod, salt, and pepper. Makes about 4 cups.

Mornay Sauce

2½ tablespoons unsalted butter
3 tablespoons flour
2 cups heavy cream
1 ounce Manchego cheese, shredded
1 ounce Romano cheese, grated
1 bay leaf
¼ cup dry white wine
¼ teaspoon Columbia Seasoning
Dash of nutmeg

Melt butter and add flour to create roux. Cook for approximately 1 minute without browning. Add cream gradually to dissolve roux. Add cheeses, bay leaf, and white wine. Stir until smooth and bring to a simmer. Add Columbia seasoning and nutmeg. Continue cooking on medium-low heat until the sauce thickens. Strain before using. Makes 2¼ cups.

Rioja Sauce

¼ cup Spanish extra-virgin olive oil
¼ cup garlic, minced
1 cup red wine

2 tablespoons tomato puree
1 28-ounce can crushed tomatoes
2 tablespoons capers
1¼ cups green olives
3 tablespoons fresh basil, chopped
1¼ teaspoons Columbia Seasoning

Heat oil and lightly brown garlic. Add red wine and reduce by one-quarter. Add tomatoes and simmer for 10 minutes. Add remaining ingredients and combine well. Refrigerate until use. Makes approximately 5 cups.

Desserts

Brazo Gitano "Cien Años"

Adela added meringue to this traditional Spanish jelly roll. To celebrate the Columbia's centennial, strawberry sauce was added as a topping, then flambéed in Kirschwasser brandy.

15 eggs, separated
1¼ cups granulated sugar
1¼ cups cake flour
4 cups Crema Catalana (see p. 153)
3 cups syrup (see p. 152)
Strawberry jam or preserves
Meringue (see p. 153)
3 pounds fresh strawberries
¾ cup Kirschwasser, or any other cherry brandy
¾ cup grain alcohol

In a large mixing bowl, beat egg whites with an electric mixer at high speed for 2 minutes. Add egg yolks one at a time. Then add sugar slowly. On low speed, gradually add flour. Bake in wax-paper-lined jelly-roll pan (11" × 16" × 1") at 400° for 12 to 14 minutes. Sprinkle cloth kitchen towel with sugar. When cake is done, immediately invert on towel. Remove wax paper. Evenly spread cake with Crema Catalana filling. Roll up lengthwise like a jelly roll. Place on an ovenproof serving tray. Soak cake slowly with syrup. Cover completely with meringue and bake at 425° for 6 to 8 minutes or until meringue is lightly browned.

To prepare the strawberries, remove hulls and cut large berries in quarters and small berries in half. Coat strawberries with strawberry jam and place to the side until ready to serve. Combine Kirschwasser and grain alcohol in a small fire-safe pitcher. When ready to serve, pour strawberries evenly over cake. Light alcohol mixture on fire and pour evenly over cake and strawberries. Once flames dissipate, cut cake crosswise as you would a jelly roll.

Syrup

2 cups water
2 cups granulated sugar
1 strip of lemon peel
1 cup dry Spanish sherry

Boil water, sugar, and lemon peel for 10 minutes. Add sherry and remove lemon peel.

Meringue

5 egg whites
¼ teaspoon cream of tartar
1 cup granulated sugar

Combine egg whites and cream of tartar. Beat with electric mixer until soft peaks form. Start adding sugar very gradually and beat until stiff.

Crema Catalana

Browning the top with the broiler makes this presentation special.

4 egg yolks
½ cup sugar
¼ cup cornstarch
2 cups milk
½ teaspoon salt
1 strip of lemon peel
1 strip of orange peel
1 cinnamon stick
1 tablespoon vanilla extract

Beat egg yolks lightly in stainless steel or any nonstick saucepan. Add sugar; beat well with wire whisk. Add cornstarch and milk; mix thoroughly. Add salt, lemon peel, orange peel, and cinnamon stick. Blend well and cook over medium heat, stirring constantly. When custard thickens, cook for 1 minute, stirring. Remove from heat; add vanilla extract; remove cinnamon stick and orange and lemon peels; and cool (in individual ovenproof ramekins or ovenproof serving dish). Sprinkle with sugar and place directly under broiler until sugar caramelizes. Serves 4 to 6.

Wine-Pairing Suggestion: Torres Malvesia de Oro

Guava and Cream Cheese Empanadas (Turnovers)

These empanadas will make you forget all about apple pie. A favorite on Valentine's Day.

24 frozen 3½" empanada shells
1 egg
Water
Guava Paste (recipe below)
3 cups cream cheese
Whipped cream

Defrost the empanada shells in advance. Combine egg and a splash of water in a bowl to make an egg wash. Brush edges of shells with the egg wash. Place 1 teaspoon of Guava Paste and 1 teaspoon of cream cheese in middle of each shell. Pull top over to form a half circle; using fork, crimp edges closed. Deep-fry at 350° until golden brown (approximately 3 minutes). Serve immediately, garnished with whipped cream. Makes 24 empanadas.

Wine-Pairing Suggestion: East India Solera sherry

Guava Paste

3 cups guava marmalade
½ cup cornstarch
½ cup water

Bring guava marmalade to a boil. Combine cornstarch and water and mix well. Add mixture to guava marmalade. Remove from heat and chill.

Flan

Anyone can make this variation of flan with superb results. Just don't boil the milk.

1¼ cups whole milk
1 8-ounce can sweetened condensed milk
1 strip lemon peel (¼" wide)
1 whole cinnamon stick
5 eggs
2 tablespoons granulated sugar
1 teaspoon vanilla extract
Pinch of salt
Caramelized sugar (recipe below)

Combine whole milk and condensed milk with lemon peel and cinnamon stick in a heavy saucepan; scald. Beat eggs and add sugar, vanilla extract, and salt in a medium-sized mixing bowl, blending well. Add milk mixture gradually, straining the lemon peel and cinnamon stick. Pour into six 4-ounce ovenproof custard cups with caramelized sugar in bottom (see below). Place cups in hot water (2 inches deep) and bake in preheated oven at 300° for 40 minutes. Never let water boil or custard will be filled with holes. Remove from pan and cool in refrigerator. To serve, unmold by pressing edges of custard with spoon to break away from cup, then turning upside down. Spoon caramelized sugar from bottom of cup over top of each custard. Serves 6.

Caramelized Sugar

¼ cup sugar
1 tablespoon water

Place sugar and water in small skillet. Cook over medium heat, stirring constantly until sugar is a golden brown color. Pour immediately into six 4-ounce ovenproof custard cups, approximately 1 teaspoon in each.

Torrejas

This cream-filled delicacy is great for dessert or a decadent breakfast.

16 slices of Cuban bread, 1" thick
2 cups milk
⅓ cup granulated sugar
1 cinnamon stick
2 teaspoons lemon peel
Oil for frying
Crema Catalana (see recipe on p. 153)
Sugar and ground cinnamon, combined
Caramel-Sherry Sauce (recipe below)
4 eggs

Slice day-old Cuban bread diagonally into 1" pieces. Cut each slice to make a pocket for the filling. Dip bread in beaten eggs. Place slices of bread in a single layer in a pan. Bring milk, sugar, cinnamon, and lemon peel to a boil. Simmer for 1 minute. Discard cinnamon stick and lemon peel. Pour evenly over bread and soak for 2 minutes. Transfer bread to dry pan and let sit for at least 2 hours.

Heat oil in sauté pan. Dip bread slices in lightly beaten eggs and then fry until golden, turning once. Drain well. Pipe Crema Catalana in warm fried bread. Lightly dust with cinnamon sugar. Drizzle toast with Caramel-Sherry Sauce. Serves 4.

Wine-Pairing Suggestion: Osborne LBV Port 1990

Caramel-Sherry Sauce

1 cup caramel
8 tablespoons Don PX Spanish sherry

Combine ingredients and mix together.

White Chocolate Bread Pudding

A perfectly good bread pudding drowned in canned fruit cocktail graced the menu of Cesar's age. It was his idea of a way to use leftover Cuban bread. Richard upgraded the recipe in the 1990s, and began by asking Brennan's of New Orleans for their recipe, which he passed on to the Columbia kitchen. This new version of bread pudding, developed by Chef Jerry, is among the very best, rich with white chocolate, topped with sweet rum sauce, and sprinkled with chocolate shavings. Today, the Columbia must order fresh bread to fulfill demand. Easy to make and richly rewarding.

6 cups heavy cream
2 cups milk
1 cup sugar
¼ cup vanilla extract
28 ounces white chocolate, cut into small pieces (approximately 3½ cups)
4 eggs
2 cups egg yolks (approximately 12 eggs)
18 ounces Cuban bread (preferably 1–2 days old)
White Chocolate Rum Sauce (recipe below)

Heat cream, milk, sugar, and vanilla over medium heat in a large saucepan. When hot, remove from heat and add 2½ cups of the white chocolate. Stir until melted. Combine eggs and yolks in a large bowl. Slowly add the cream mixture into the eggs, whipping as you pour.

Cut the bread into ½ inch slices and place in a large bowl. Pour mixture over bread; press bread to absorb mix and allow bread to become soggy. Let cool for 15 minutes.

Add the remaining cup of white chocolate, stir (do

not let the chocolate melt). Pour mixture evenly in a 10" × 12" baking pan and cover with foil. Bake in a 350° oven for 1 hour. Remove foil and continue to bake for an additional hour until set and golden brown. Remove from oven and cool thoroughly before cutting.

Slice bread pudding into individual portions and place on a cookie sheet. Bake in 350° oven until crispy and heated through. Top with White Chocolate Rum Sauce and serve immediately. Serves 8.

Wine-Pairing Suggestion: Torres Jaime I Brandy

White Chocolate Rum Sauce

½ cup heavy cream
8 ounces white chocolate, cut into small pieces
¼ cup Light Bacardi rum

Bring cream to a boil in a small pan. Take off heat and add chocolate. Stir until smooth and melted. Add rum and stir. Keep warm until ready to serve.

 **Cocktails**

Bloody Gazpacho

Be sure to make these fresh. Mix prepared ahead of time does not store well.

1¼ ounces Ketel One vodka
Gazpacho Soup (see p. 120)
Tabasco Bloody Mary Mix
Pickled vegetables

Fill glass with ice and add vodka. Add 1 part Gazpacho Soup and 1 part Bloody Mary mix to fill glass. Garnish with pickled vegetables.

Café con Leche Martini

This drink is the delicious brainchild of Barry Strauss, longtime Columbia bartender. The Van Gogh vodka is not cheap, but it makes preparation a snap.

3 ounces Van Gogh Double Espresso Vodka
1 ounce Godiva Caramel Liqueur
3 espresso beans for garnish

Fill martini glass with ice and water to chill. Then fill martini shaker with ice, add vodka and liqueur, and shake vigorously. Discard ice water from glass and strain the vodka and liqueur from the shaker. Garnish with espresso beans.

The Columbia's signature cocktails (left to right); Margarita "Garrafon," Bloody Gazpacho, Mojito, and Café con Leche Martini.

Cuban Manhattan

3 ounces Bacardi 8-year-old rum
½ ounce sweet vermouth
Splash of bitters
1 cherry

Fill martini glass with ice and water to chill. Then fill martini shaker with ice; add rum, vermouth, and bitters; shake vigorously. Discard ice water from glass and strain ingredients from shaker into the glass. Garnish with a cherry.

Margarita "Garrafon"

Garrafon was a Columbia bartender—his nickname means "loudspeaker"—for almost fifty years. Torres brandy and orange liqueur are indulgences. To put the drink into the stratosphere, use Petron tequila.

1¼ ounces Cuervo Especial Gold
¼ ounce Gran Torres Liqueur (or substitute any orange liqueur)
¼ ounce Torres 5 brandy (or substitute any Spanish brandy)
Sweet and sour mix
Lime, sliced

Fill glass with ice and combine the tequila, liqueur, and brandy. Add sweet and sour mix to fill remainder of glass. Garnish with a lime slice.

Mojito Pitcher

Why make just one? Mint-infused simple syrup makes the preparation and consistency especially easy.

7 ounces Bacardi Superior Rum (or any light rum)
1¾ cups sparkling water
1 tablespoon fresh mint, packed tightly
Juice of 2 limes
Mint Simple Syrup (recipe below)

Fill pitcher with ice and add all ingredients. Stir well. Serve in glasses garnished with mint sprigs and lime slices.

Mint Simple Syrup

¾ cup granulated sugar
¾ cup hot water
1 tablespoon fresh mint, packed tightly

Mix sugar with hot water and add mint. Boil water for 10 minutes, stirring to dissolve sugar. Strain to remove mint; chill before using.

Sangre de Toro Sangria

This libation became the rage at the Columbia in the 1960s. The twenty-first-century version is the best. The use of Torres brandy elevates this drink to extravagance. Miguel Torres is rightfully proud of his fine brandy. When he first heard the Columbia was using it in sangria, he was not especially pleased. But when he discovered that the customers consumed 150 cases every month, he was delighted. Who can argue with success?

Simple Syrup (see below)
1 orange
1 lime
1 375 ml bottle of Sangre de Toro wine (or any other red Rioja wine)
1 ounce Torres 5 brandy (or substitute any Spanish brandy)
Splash of lemon-lime soda
Cherries for garnish

Simple Syrup

To make simple syrup, combine one part water to one part sugar in small saucepan. Bring to a boil, stirring to dissolve sugar. Chill before use.

Cut orange and lime in half. Fill large pitcher with ice and combine the wine, brandy, lemon-lime soda, the juice of half of an orange, and the juice of half of a lime. Stir. Add Simple Syrup to obtain desired sweetness. Slice remaining orange and lime into thin slices. Garnish glasses with orange, lime, and cherry.

Sangria de Cava

This sparkling white sangria is great for a fancy brunch.

Simple Syrup (see p. 159)
1 375ml bottle of Cava (or any sparkling wine)
1 orange
1 lime
¼ ounce Torres 5 brandy (or any Spanish brandy)
¼ ounce Gran Torres liqueur (or any orange liqueur)
Splash of lemon-lime soda
Cherries for garnish

Cut orange and lime in half. Fill large pitcher with ice and combine the wine, brandy, liqueur, lemon-lime soda, the juice of half of an orange, and the juice of half of a lime. Stir. Add Simple Syrup to obtain desired sweetness. Slice remaining orange and lime into thin slices. Garnish glasses with orange, lime, and cherry.

Silver Meteor

Named after the famous railroad line, connecting New York City to Miami, of the same name.

½ ounce Bacardi light rum
½ ounce Gran Torres liqueur
Splash of cava (sparkling wine)
Orange slice and mint to garnish

In a champagne flute, pour the rum and liqueur. Top off glass with cava. Serve with a slice of orange and a sprig of mint as garnish.

Spanish Flag

Impressive but exacting, the Spanish Flag has been involved in many memorable accidents at the Columbia. A waiter once spilled a flaming drink on a beautiful lady, who immediately tore off her blouse. Cesar comforted her by offering his coat and telling her she had nothing to be embarrassed about.

1 ounce grenadine
1 ounce Licor 43
Splash of Bacardi 151

In a small cordial glass, layer the grenadine, Licor 43, and Bacardi 151, with the grenadine on the bottom and the Bacardi 151 on the top. Serve flaming.

Tango Mango Daiquiri

While on a cruise, Richard and Melanie enjoyed blended mango drinks. They enjoyed them so much that their memories are a little fuzzy. The Columbia's version is just as hard to put down.

1¼ ounces Bacardi Limon Rum
4 ounces mango fruit pulp purée
Lime for garnish

Combine ice, rum, and mango in a blender; blend until smooth. Pour into glass and garnish with a lime wheel.

Menus

Andrea Gonzmart has assembled several themed menus to help you plan your next Spanish feast.

Sunday Brunch

This is a great combination of the sweet and the savory. This menu is light enough to be a late breakfast, but filling enough to be an early lunch. Greet your guests with a Bloody Gazpacho, a classic with a Spanish twist, and then toast to another beautiful day with a bubbly Spanish cava.

- *Shrimp Salad with Grapes*
- *Tortilla Española*
- *Torrejas*
- *Guava and Cream Cheese Empanadas (Turnovers)*

Suggested Wine: Codorniu Cuvée Raventos Cava
Suggested Cocktail: Bloody Gazpacho

Summer Barbecue

What better way is there to spend a warm summer afternoon than with friends and family? You get a chance to light up the grill and cool down with this chilled soup and icy cocktails.

- *Chilled Gazpacho Andaluz Soup*
- *Chicken "Chimichurri"*
- *Shrimp "a la Plancha"*
- *George's Burger*
- *Mojito Chicken*
- *Rice with Corn*
- *Flan*

Suggested Wines:
   Blanco: Torres Viña Esmeralda
   Rosé: Miguel Torres Santa Digna Cabernet Rosé
Suggested Cocktails: Mojitos; Tango Mango Daiquiri

Christmas Eve Dinner

Christmas Eve, or Noche Buena, was the most important family night of the year in Ybor City. Homes were filled with both familiar aromas and familiar laughter of loved ones gathering together. This rich menu is festive and traditional.

· *Empanadas de Cangrejo*

Suggested Wine: Torres Gran Viña Sol

· *Beefsteak Tomato Salad*
· *Black Bean Soup*
· *Roast Pork "a la Cubana"(Cuban Style)*
· *Good Rice*

Suggested Wine: Torres Sangre de Toro

· *Crema Catalana (see recipe on p. 153)*

Suggested Cocktail: Traditional Spanish Cider

Winter Menu

This savory menu will keep you warm during the chilly winter months.

· *Mejillones y Chorizo "Andrés"(Mussels and Chorizo)*

Suggested Wine: Bodegas Mauro Tudela Crianza

· *Caldo Gallego (Turnip Greens Soup)*
· *Carne con Papas*

Suggested Wine: Montecillo Tinto from Rioja or any of the great full-bodied red wines from the Priorato region of Spain

· *White Chocolate Bread Pudding*

Tapas Party

Tapas, or appetizers served with wine, are a centuries-old tradition from Spain. A perfect excuse for friends to gather!

- *Queso Fundido (Spanish Fondue)*
- *Croquetas, a selection of:*
  - *Chicken*
  - *Lobster*
  - *Devil Crab*
- *Scallops "Casimiro"*
- *Shrimp and Crabmeat Alcachofas*

Suggested Wines:
*   White: Nerolla Xarello*
*   Red: Faustino VII*
Suggested Cocktails: Sangre de Toro Sangria (red);
*   Sangria de Cava (sparkling)*

Wine Dinner with Friends

Rather than hosting another regular dinner with friends, take it up a notch and pair each course with a different wine. Everyone is sure to be impressed.

- *Shrimps and Scallops "Santiago"*

Suggested Wine: Lagar de Cervera Albariño, Rioja Alta

- *The Columbia's Original "1905" Salad*

Suggested Wine: Faustino V Rosado

- *Paella "Campesina"*

Suggested Wine: Torres Gran Coronas Mas la Plana

- *Brazo Gitano "Cien Años"*

After-Dinner Drink: Osborne LBV Port 1990

Romantic Dinner for Two

He can handle the appetizer on the grill outside while she prepares for a romantic dinner for the two in the kitchen. The pompano pouches can be made earlier that day and then slipped into the oven right before the shrimp go on the grill. This menu allows a couple to spend time with each other and not too much time in the kitchen.

- *Langostinos "1905"*

Suggested Wine: Torres Milmanda Chardonnay

- *Lula Mae Chopped Salad*
- *Pompano en Papillot*

Suggested Wine: Torres Mas Borras Pinot Noir
After-Dinner Drink: Café con Leche Martini for her; 1905 Martini for him

The 3rd Generation, 1956–1979

The second half of the Columbia's history begins at the top. By the late 1950s, the Columbia reached a zenith of entertainment and cuisine. Perched at a new high, the new owner and dreamer, Cesar Gonzmart, found opportunities for a Columbia beleaguered by problems in the surrounding community. Through civic engagement, expansion, promotion, and sheer bravado, Cesar guided the Columbia through some of the restaurant's most difficult years yet. He cut costs where he could and sought new revenue. First, his Siboney Room became a new venue for the Latin American entertainment circuit. Second, Cesar boldly gambled on a Sarasota location. His two sons, Casey and Richard, took their places in an expanding Columbia empire.

By the mid-1950s, Cesar Gonzmart made the Columbia his stage. With his orchestra he threw fiestas six nights a week and invited the public to join him.

The 3rd Generation, 1956–1979

The Gonzmart family joined many others in opting to leave Ybor City in favor of the suburbs and upscale neighborhoods. When the family moved to Davis Islands in 1954, they brought a few Ybor City traditions with them, including livestock. Richard, the younger Gonzmart son, eventually collected a flock of eighty noisy chickens, goats, and other animals. He looked after the Gonzmart menagerie when he wasn't tearing up the yard in front-lot football games. When neighbors complained of farm noises in their exclusive neighborhood, the Gonzmarts threw a block party barbeque. "Everyone came out to eat," Richard said. "But none of us in the family could touch those birds."

 ## A New Dream

"I am an artist, perhaps a dreamer," Cesar told the press. "I don't see things in a cold-blooded business eye." The Columbia's prince sold himself short on one count, for he became a shrewd and daring businessman after taking the restaurant's helm. He also added to the restaurant's collection of art depicting Don Quixote, another visionary of sorts.

Ybor City sank into disrepair in the decades after the war, and Interstate 4 tore a swath through its heart. If Cesar married the Columbia with his vows to Adela, the Columbia Restaurant had always been wed to Ybor City.

Cesar had a strategy to snatch victory from the jaws of progress—boost musical entertainment at the restaurant. The violinist had a vital part to play in the Columbia's orchestra, acting as manager, spokesman, political ambassador, and seductive artist.

Showmanship became the order of the day. Inspired by the lavish restaurants founded in Miami's Cuban community, Cesar introduced strolling accordion and violin players. Then he led a section of strolling violins himself, but he was only getting started. He hosted a local television show called *The Latin Quarter Review* with his orchestra. Adela

played her own piano solos on the airwaves. In order to provide the scale of entertainment that Cesar envisioned at the restaurant itself, more space would be needed.

Cesar suggested the addition of a three-hundred-seat showroom with a stage. As his old friends died off, an aging Casimiro didn't see opportunities in decaying Ybor City. Yet the old man must have seen his own flair in the plan, having taken a similar chance with the Don Quixote Room decades before.

So Casimiro observed the restaurant's fiftieth anniversary in yet another way—he chose to expand again. Together with Cesar, Casimiro announced his plans to the press. The Siboney Room required a $140,000 investment, much of it to acquire the Bambi Bakery next door. Expenses included $25,000 to commission eight murals from Cuban artist Teok Carrasco. Cesar wanted the murals to depict the idyllic lives of Cuba's Siboney Indians, but the painter balked. Spanish soldiers and diseases had annihilated the entire tribe. "Cesar didn't want to know that," Carrasco said. "He wanted pictures of Spanish and Indians in a friendly intercourse, smoking together and such."

As a musician, it never occurred to Cesar that painting took time. When Carrasco said he would need two months to do the job, Cesar protested that he could not wait that long. He invited the muralist to hang canvas in the dining room and paint in the bustling restaurant. Patrons liked

When the artist could not finish the murals in time for the Siboney Room's debut, Cesar opened it anyway. The Cuban artist Teok Carrasco often painted while patrons dined. With the Columbia's fringe benefits, at least the artist would not starve. At Cesar's request, the murals offered a serene depiction of Siboney Indians, with no whiff of the invading Spanish.

to watch him at work, and Carrasco enjoyed the audience. He certainly enjoyed the fringe benefits. "I was having a great time in Tampa . . . and the food at the Columbia was superb." It would be hard to blame Carrasco if he did drag his feet and slow his brush.

The Siboney accommodated four hundred more diners and a stage fit for the Continental Orchestra. That the remodeling was news at all is evidence of how high the Columbia rose. The restaurant became a real economic engine in Ybor City, grossing more than $3 million annually in the late 1950s.

With the stage complete in 1956, the Siboney exuded a glamour rarely seen in Ybor City. The Don Quixote Room answered the dreams of the 1930s. The Siboney fulfilled the impulse for variety shows, fiery flamenco, comedy, romance, and star power.

Then Cesar filled the stage, bringing in talent from the Latin music circuit. Some of the musicians and dancers stayed on for many seasons. Cesar brought the nonstop entertainment of Havana and Las Vegas to Ybor City like no one else could. He built his own orchestra and flamenco troupe and presided over the scene, mingled with customers, told jokes, and kissed the hands of the ladies. When he stepped onto the stage, the restaurateur became a fun-loving maestro. He possessed unmistakable magnetism on and off the stage, and became the natural center of attention. He became the Desi Arnaz to Adela's Lucille Ball—they were a power couple who invited the public to join their marvelous party at the Columbia.

The public responded. While the rest of Ybor City slid into the shadows of neglect, the Columbia became a destination unto itself, a dazzling nightly gala that rivaled television's most glamorous events.

Coming-Out Party

The series of events opening the Siboney was indicative of Cesar's grand sense of gesture. It is also evidence that

ERNESTO LECUONA
World Famous Pianist Composer

Cuban composer Ernesto Lecuona wrote the popular song "Siboney," and christened the Columbia's new room of the same name with a thrilling performance.

Cesar exercised more control. The room, after all, was his brainchild. While Casimiro cautioned against rash extravagance, Cesar took his first major risk in the restaurant business, and he liked the taste. Many more followed over the years.

In declining health, Casimiro slowly ceded more control to his successor. He maintained a firm grip on the kitchen and supplies while Cesar looked after the entertainment, publicity, and merchandising.

Management called the new dining room the "Siboney" as a tribute to the extinct Native American tribe of Cuba. The name also honored the island's composer Ernesto Lecuona, who wrote the famous song of the same name. When Lecuona played a few nights at the Centro Asturiano Theatre in 1954, he agreed to hold an informal late-night "long-hair jam session," a romp in the room named in his honor. Such sessions gave the musicians the opportunity to play for their own enjoyment, and they often brought more passion to those appearances, than they displayed in more formal settings.

As a coming-out party for the new Siboney Room, the revue from Havana's La Tropicana played for the first three months of 1955. Management imported a Cuban peasant—a *guajiro*—to thatch a roof for the bandstand. Most impressively, Lecuona presented the Columbia with the original manuscript of his song "Siboney." The document remained in a glass case for the viewing public.

While Cesar flaunted his antiques and orchestra, Casimiro loved to recount how he obtained a perfectly good grand piano for a mere fifty dollars during the Great Depression. A local man bought the piano for his daughter. He grew so disgusted when she refused to play it that he hastily sold the piece to Casimiro at the bargain price.

Little did he know then that a world-famous composer would play his greatest song on the piano twenty years later.

A crowd packed the Siboney to watch Lecuona play with his own band and a few locals. By the end of his intimate performance, a crowd stretching into the other dining rooms gave Lecuona a standing ovation.

The many spectators that night may have tried the Columbia's media noche (midnight) sandwich before they left the restaurant. For many years, Havana residents enjoyed small sandwiches on soft egg bread after emerging from concerts and the cinema late at night. The Columbia featured this sandwich with the patron's choice of fillings, though it usually was filled with the same ingredients as a Tampa Cuban sandwich.

"You Win . . . Dancing Returns"

Several months into the band's summer stint, the Siboney received an acoustic makeover to improve the sound of the band. "As usual around the Columbia, when somebody gets an idea it has to be done in a big hurry," Wilder observed. Eighty-three yards of golden velvet drapes lined the walls to absorb the sound. Management installed fiberglass padding above the bandstand, reinforced with new beams and ribs. Sound-absorbent tiles replaced the entire ceiling. Scheduled to last two days, the makeover lasted two weeks.

On August 21, 1954, Wilder announced the end of dancing season at the Columbia. Casimiro planned to employ the orchestra during the lean summer months, then phase them out to make room for winter's crowds. "That's when the trouble started," Wilder wrote.

"People kept coming in from Clearwater and St. Petersburg, from Sarasota and Bartow—from all around—complaining because they had driven to the Columbia expecting to find the orchestra." So many patrons returned to the restaurant wearing their dancing shoes that management could no longer turn them away. Letters arrived asking for the orchestra's return, one in the form of a petition bearing forty signatures.

On October 2, Wilder's column read, "You win . . . dancing returns to the Columbia tonight. Surprised? Well, so are we at the Columbia, sort of." With the winter season imminent, management thought fast, arranging the Siboney to accommodate additional guests *and* the stage. Cesar made use of the time off in his own way—he traveled to Havana to obtain arrangements for new Cuban songs. The new material would come in handy during the orchestra's long sets, which started at 9:30 P.M. and ended at 1 A.M. on Fridays and 2:30 on Saturdays.

Siboney

The restaurant swirled with activity in the weeks leading up to New Year's Eve 1955. Workers struggled to complete the room in time for the big party. Once they succeeded, Casimiro faced a new struggle—to find an unengaged orchestra at the last minute. The finished Siboney Room meant that a second band would be needed for the Don Quixote Room. Cesar and his band played double duty that night, alternating sets between the two dining rooms. Leaving nothing to chance, Casimiro reserved an orchestra a year in advance for the next New Year's Eve.

Just as the Columbia served Latin food for American tastes, Cesar specialized in playing familiar pop songs with Latin rhythms. Sometimes the results were most striking. Cesar's rendition of "Dixie" surprised and delighted listeners when it debuted, and became a favorite in Cesar's repertoire. A naval officer let out a long rebel yell when he heard the mambo version of his hallowed song. "It was as if he were cheering the blending of the cultures of the Deep South and Old Havana," Wilder mused.

The Siboney Room evoked other varieties of passion and romance. In the first year after opening, patrons held at least seven weddings in the hall, which also hosted a countless number of dates, proposals, and romantic encounters. Wedding events became so common that management refused them after Christmas to make room for the height of dancing season.

From the beginning, the Siboney was Cesar's pet project. Casimiro allowed the budget that Cesar proposed, but it proved too little for the grand scheme. Casimiro granted another $18,000 for the project, but refused to budge beyond that. Although the room had been in use for two years, Cesar did not have the money to complete the stage.

Cesar needed more space, and proposed to buy an adjoining building and tear down the shared wall. Casimiro would not hear of such extravagance—they had spent too much already, he warned. Finally, a sympathetic Carmen personally loaned Cesar an additional $35,000 to finish his dream. His kind mother-in-law was just as unflaggingly supportive of her husband, Casimiro, twenty-five years before. The Columbia occupied most of the block, sharing it only with its own coffee mill.

By all accounts, the dream was a lavish one, boasting two fountains and a plethora of sculptures, paintings, tapestries, and antiques. The bronze works dated to the sixteenth century. The stained glass dated back three centuries to the early days of Spanish settlement in Cuba. The stage, finally finished, featured an alcove in the wall for the grand piano and ample space for large orchestras. Just as they did for the Patio, the designer Iva de Minicis drew up the architectural plans. Even with the generous stage and décor, the latest renovation made room for sixty more patrons.

The reopening party on New Year's Eve 1957 required special reservations, and Cesar played two shows from eight-thirty that night until one-thirty in the morning. Management also announced a new season of the *Latin Quarter Review* television show that year.

Buyout

Together, Casimiro and Cesar made a wise and momentous decision. They bought Lawrence's shares of the restaurant. Neither of his sons worked in the restaurant full-time. They sold their shares in 1956 for $500,000, leaving Casimiro and Cesar with full ownership. A hundred

GRAND OPENING
MONDAY NIGHT

Columbia Restaurant

PROUDLY ANNOUNCES
THE OPENING OF IT'S FABULOUS
NEW
Siboney Dining Room

Shows at 9 P.M. and 12 P.M.
with
CESAR GONZMART
and his
Continental Orchestra
featuring
the songs of CORINA

12/30/55

SARITA ESCARPINTER
Cuban Soprano

**RAUL
and
EVA
REYES**
America's
Rhumba
"One"
Dance

2/18/56

OPENING SATURDAY
in the
COLUMBIA RESTAURANT'S
fabulous new
SIBONEY DINING ROOM
SHOWTIME 9 P.M. and 12 P.M.

★ **MARQUEZ SISTERS**   STARS OF TV and RADIO, STAGE and SCREEN

HELD OVER BY POPULAR DEMAND
★ **DORITA ORTIZ** and **MARTIN VARGAS**
FLAMENCO DANCE TEAM DIRECT FROM SPAIN
WITH
★ **CAESAR GONZMART**
and his **CONTINENTAL ORCHESTRA**

8 DINING ROOMS
for your convenience

Columbia
GEM OF SPANISH RESTAURANTS

Internationally famous
since 1905
in the heart of Tampa's Latin Quarter
FREE PARKING—for reservation call 4-2311

In 1956, the Siboney Room became the Columbia's new showcase for Cesar's orchestra and the Columbia's cuisine.

Tampans, most of them loyal customers, bought bonds to finance the deal.

Some patrons celebrated the news. Bill Abbott of the *Tampa Tribune* wrote to Casimiro: "The Columbia is one of Tampa's finest assets, and I am sure its excellence would suffer under any other management. Therefore, many of your friends are glad the present management is being continued."

The Columbia required good management and harmonious ownership, but the halcyon days would not last long.

 ## New Challenges

As business began to wane in Ybor City, Cesar sought out new opportunities for the Columbia. He opened a Columbia in Orlando's airport in 1953. The new restaurant opened to success, but it did not last long.

Casey Gonzmart: "We had been there long before Disney and long before anything else, when Orlando was a landlocked orange grove city that had no connection with tourism, compared to many of our coastal cities and other famous places like Cypress Gardens and so forth. So, we were there first."

Casimiro discouraged the risks and unknowns associated with a venture outside Tampa, and his fears proved well founded. Rumor had it that local politicians wanted a locally owned eatery in the airport, not a Spanish restaurant from Tampa.

Luis Diaz provided a different reason for the failure in Orlando. "Pilferage. Some of the well-trusted men that we used to have working for us there, they were cleaning. They were not supervised. They really broke that trust."

Casimiro, being biased, he just look upon the [financial] numbers of the Columbia Restaurant and said, 'Close it!'

"I went there for the closing in the truck. We loaded everything and brought it to Tampa. That was the first venture of Cesar in the restaurant business. He lacked the wisdom of the control. To him everybody was wonderful. And it was not the case. It was a misstep."

Problems with theft were not unique to Orlando. Charlie Hero, owner of the Columbia's preferred plumbing company, once overheard a revealing conversation. An employee butchered about 100 chickens and set aside the chicken necks, which the restaurant could sell. He then stole sixty of the birds. When management collected the necks, it discovered the theft. Forty chickens and one hundred necks did not add up.

You are cordially invited
to attend a
Gala Pre-Opening Dinner
Friday, December eighth
Nineteen hundred and sixty-seven
at the
Columbia Restaurant
Orlando, Florida
in the
Cherry Plaza Hotel
at eight o'clock p. m.

Regrets only
Please call { Tampa 251-1067
Orlando 241-3311

Black Tie

Sarasota seemed a world apart from Tampa in the 1950s. The beach town was almost abandoned every summer. Three attempts to open restaurants in Orlando failed over the years.

Other employees routinely stole the Columbia blind. The most popular method was carrying items to the roof, wrapping it in plastic or paper, and throwing it into the dumpster behind the restaurant. Accomplices picked up the packages at arranged times. Charlie remembers, "Somebody [was] in cahoots. They would get the whole filet, the lobsters, the ham, whatever. I didn't know this was going on here all the time. Somebody told Cesar." Years later, Richard bricked off the door to the roof, ending the problem.

Aggressive expansion plans opened restaurants, but could not always sustain them. Orlando proved to be a tough nut to crack. Cesar would try and fail to open a Columbia

there two more times over the next twenty-five years. Another location on Tampa's Rocky Point closed after a short tenure. Only Sarasota survived.

The Sarasota Gamble

Humbled but not discouraged, Cesar prepared for a new adventure. Sarasota seemed like a strange choice for the location of a fine restaurant. Wealthy snowbirds roosted in the beach town by winter. Few people remained during the summer months. An eerie skeleton of an aborted Ringling Hotel from the 1920s stood against the sky.

Beer distributor Jerry Cigarran counted Cesar among his friends. He told Cesar of his exclusive restaurant on Lido Beach nearby. Cigarran could not afford the taste and tabs of his friends, who were his only customers, and closed.

Joe Hamilton, another friend, needed an anchor for his development on St. Armands Circle. He offered Cesar a generous long-term lease. After another wrangle with an aging Casimiro, Don Quixote charged into a new escapade.

Luis Diaz: "Cesar kept on dreaming. Eighty or 90 percent of the people that hear we're opening in Sarasota told him that he was insane. It was a mistake that in twenty years paid for itself one thousand times. We bought a place that wasn't popular and we were losing money. I was continuously making trips twice every week to Sarasota. I couldn't see any future in Sarasota because I didn't have the vision of Cesar. Sarasota at the time was nothing."

Casey Gonzmart: "In Florida in general and in Sarasota at the time, it's extremely seasonal. The highway system was just coming into play, air-conditioning was still a new phenomenon, jet aircraft had just begun to fly to shortened distances. There was nothing to do in many cities of Florida like Sarasota. Unless you went there in the winter season, when there might be some shows or activities, there were no social opportunities beyond that. After Easter, as the few residents went back up north, so did all the activity. So you really only had a short span.

"There were many businesses—not ours—but many businesses that only operated during the winter months. They would cater to these wealthy people, and after that, the local people had nowhere to go, because many of the restaurants and even the retail clothing stores would board themselves up for the entire summer. So we went down with a different philosophy and a different attitude and signed a long lease."

Sarasota Herald-Tribune   Sunday, July 19, 1959—9

LEASE CLUB HERE—Casimiro Hernandez, Jr., shown signing papers, with Cesar Gonzmart, standing, have leased the Club Jora here for 50 years. It will be operated under the name Columbia Restaurant similar to the Tampa operations of the firm. Mrs. Nancy H. Watkins, seated, represented Jora, Inc. Key personnel will be brought here from Tampa.

The Columbia on St. Armands Circle opened in 1959. It was an outpost on the tourist frontier. Casey described the Sarasota of yesteryear as "physically, ethnically and psychologically another world from Ybor City." Management imported workers from Tampa to open the restaurant. Over time, Cesar recruited workers from Cuba to staff it. Only a few locals could cut it in the Spanish "kitchen madhouse."

Spanish ingredients and foods could not be obtained at any store near Sarasota. "Weird products," Casey says, "like garbanzo beans and black beans and Spanish sausage." Those edibles were as foreign as moon rocks in Sarasota. Ethnic food distributors wouldn't waste their time hauling supplies to backwaters and deserted beaches. Every day, workers at the Columbia in Ybor loaded a flatbed truck with exotic ingredients and coffee for their sister restaurant to the south.

George Guito took that ride countless times. In the days before the Sunshine Skyway Bridge, George drove by way of Gibsonton and Rubonia. "They would get in this truck," Casey says, "and go down U.S. 41, which wasn't that developed in those days, and supply the restaurant as if it were an outpost somewhere out west. If you took the donkey trail and it was in the winter season, you probably took forever to come and go." Workers at the Sarasota restaurant spent many an hour waiting for the daily truck to arrive. The tenuous supply line kept the restaurant alive.

Richard, who was five or six at the time, remembers those early years. When he visited with his father, they stayed in a spartan apartment above the restaurant. Richard also remembers that little happened on St. Armands Circle. Sarasota was a ghost town for half the year. The restaurant struggled with no real plan. But it could count on one blessing: cheap rent that was based upon a percentage of the restaurant's sales. Hamilton had offered to sell the

In 1959, the Columbia's new location in Sarasota seemed destined for failure. It was Casimiro's last gamble—and one of Cesar's first. It paid off handsomely.

A young Richard Gonzmart at the piano with his mother, Adela.

a brisk pace—the large, busy Columbia was quite a chore to clean.

George came from a humble background and remembers his youthful fascination with Cesar and the Columbia. "Every day, Mr. Gonzmart would come and tell me how was I doing, and that's the way I became friendly with him. I was really amazed with coming into a place this size and beautiful as it is. Besides that, the gentleman that's in charge of the whole operation, he's performing here nightly, and he's going through the tables. It was really amazing."

The young man had never met someone so respected and connected. George marveled at the celebrities of the day passing through: Bob Hope, Marilyn Monroe, Frank Sinatra, and Carol Burnett. "We've had kings here. We've had queens here. People coming here from all parts of the world."

property for a mere $240,000 in 1960, but Cesar didn't have the capital or Casimiro's consent. Today the Columbia pays $50,000 a month in rent. The restaurant struggled into the 1970s with scant success and no direction.

From Cleaning the Castle to Running It

Born and reared in Tampa, George "Chiquito" Guito (GEE-toe) got a job at the Ybor Columbia in 1961–62 at age fifteen. He came from a poor and hardworking family; his father worked as a cigar maker by day and a janitor by night. His mother cleaned in a hospital. After finding himself in some trouble, George came to the Columbia referred by a friend. Cesar thought George too young to be scrubbing floors, but the teen insisted he needed the work and asked for a chance. George was as old as Cesar's son Casey. Over the years, he became as close to the family as one of its own.

The manager could pay George only thirty-five dollars a week, but he graciously accepted. It was fifteen dollars more than his mother's wage. He worked six days a week at

Street tough George Guito matured into a reliable employee under Cesar Gonzmart's wing.

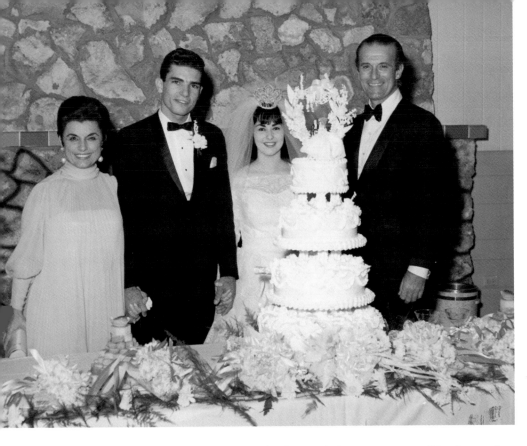

When George got married, Cesar paid for the honeymoon.

What impressed George most was the free meals for employees. To a fifteen-year-old who had gone hungry, having access to the ingredients of the cooking line was a godsend. "I said, 'Man!' I was really amazed."

George clearly saw Cesar as the center of everything. "It was all Mr. Gonzmart." There was no general manager or chief of operations. His two assistants bore the title of maître d'. He arrived to work at about noon each day and left after midnight, after his two concert sets and a late dinner.

Some thought Cesar could be demanding but George saw a dedicated businessman, a devoted artist, and a caring person. "Once you got to know Mr. Gonzmart, if you would take care of his place, he would do anything for you, help you out in any way. People that were working here, he was always asking them about the family and if they needed something."

He often sat hungry locals down in the café and told the waiters he'd pay the bill. He gave countless loans, knowing they would go unpaid.

George became a busboy before long and worked odd jobs at the restaurant. Cesar returned his loyalty and found a way to reward George and the restaurant. He sent George to butcher school and paid the bills. "I think the name of the school was Tampa Butchering Professional Meat Cutting Association," George said. He became a certified butcher and worked with the Columbia's meat and poultry. No longer a troubled Ybor boy, he gained a respectable career and brighter future.

He became part of the restaurant family in other ways. George soon got to know the Gonzmart-Hernandez clan well. Casey and Richard became his new brothers, and the family gathered every Sunday at the Gonzmart home. Carmen Hernandez, Casimiro's wife, did not drive. When

The Columbia's butchery allowed the kitchen to buy whole sides of beef and carve its own steaks. Here, Chef Sarapico displays fresh cuts.

George never forgot a lesson Cesar taught him, "I tried to talk intelligent to most of these people. Mr. Gonzmart always used to say, 'If you talk intelligently, you sound intelligent. If you talk dumb, you sound dumb.'"

Back in the kitchen, George worked with Chef Sarapico. He enjoyed his job, cutting beef tenderloins into filets, carving and trimming rib eyes, sirloins, and round steak. The Columbia's menu was huge at the time, ballooning to more than twenty-five pages. That variety of dishes required many different cuts of meat.

George also remembers the earthy recipes and fresh seafood. Blue crabs were cheap and plentiful. The kitchen simmered tripe, ox tails and pig feet, red beans and rice. A Cuban dish called *congri* filled patrons with black beans, rice, and pork.

Sarapico left after an illness, and George assumed more control in the kitchen. He became a jack-of-all-trades at the restaurant. George can cook dishes that no one else can remember, such as those named above. He is, in many ways, the Columbia's collective memory.

"I know the kitchen inside and out. I can do anything that has to be done. I can cook. I can order the stuff. I can do basically anything." In George Guito, Cesar gained a hard worker as loyal as a son. The Columbia's struggle to stay afloat called upon all of George's loyalty and know-how, and he delivered.

George scratched together thirty-five dollars to buy a 1950 Plymouth, management often enlisted him to drive Carmen home from the restaurant.

George Guito: "I would take her home and she would give me five dollars. Back then, five dollars was a lot of money. Then she would tell me, 'Oh, come in and have something to drink and eat.' They were really nice people."

He spent every Christmas with the Gonzmarts. When George got married, Cesar paid for the wedding reception at the Columbia. He then offered George the use of his credit card and El Dorado Cadillac, telling him to take them to Miami for his honeymoon.

George Guito: "It was weird! I went to Miami [for our honeymoon] and every place I would go, 'Mr. Gonzmart is taking care of it.' He sent me to a bunch of places in Miami that were famous and are probably still famous today. You always watch, and you always try to learn different stuff."

Trumphant Cesar

A serious heart attack in 1960 gave notice of Casimiro's declining health. He lived to see his restaurant recognized twice by *Holiday* magazine. Casimiro died in July 1962, days after being honored by the publication. He was at the Mayo Clinic in Minnesota awaiting a lung operation days before his seventieth birthday. He suffered a heart attack while joking about the upcoming procedure. Like Pijuan before him, Casimiro was an irreplaceable asset.

By the 1960s, the Columbia caught national attention. Holiday *Magazine's awards made Casimiro (3rd from right) and manager Pete Deemer (center) especially proud.*

The Columbia soldiered on without him under Cesar's leadership. His style was different in almost every way: He showboated for the press and public, focused on entertainment over food, and brought his own sense of whimsy to the restaurant. After several years of running the restaurant by himself, Cesar seemed more self-assured than Casimiro had ever been. It was all part of the character that circumstances called on him to play.

In 1968, he pondered his cufflinks. "I design jewelry, for myself, and my wife. We love diamonds. These cufflinks each hold a perfect 3-carat blue white diamond which sits in a fishtail mounting of 18-carat gold. The gold pattern is my design," he beamed. He updated his wardrobe with the most elegant European styles from boutiques in Miami and Palm Beach. He also doted on his antique Napoleon clock and new 47-foot yacht, the *Miss Columbia*.

Still, the Columbia remained his favorite subject. When investors moved the Spanish Pavilion from the New York World's Fair brick by brick to St. Louis, they asked Cesar

to run the five planned restaurants inside. The venture never materialized, but Cesar had his hands full in Ybor City. He introduced two new shows nightly, one in Spanish and one in worldly French.

Cesar may have sounded like a playboy, but he worked long days and nights. Cesar typically drank orange juice in the morning. His only daytime snack was an occasional sandwich of green olives in Cuban bread. Between his onstage performances each evening, he enjoyed a large, leisurely dinner. He couldn't have rushed if he had wanted to, such was the constant stream of fans, friends, and well-wishers. He rose from his chair dozens of times, interrupting his meal for each guest, and always took care to kiss the hands of the ladies and flirt. He managed to be gracious, elegant, and suave, all in a night's work.

In 1968, he was in top form, one of the most enthusiastic businessmen in Ybor City. Only enthusiasm—"the show must go on"—could ensure repeat customers. Cesar did not kid when he said, "I'm always on, every day, seven days a week, every hour of every day." His restaurant drew a million visitors a year for dinner alone.

"To watch Gonzmart work is to watch the complete and total showman," an entertainment journalist noted. "Some find Gonzmart's antics, his overwhelming manners, and his enthusiasm on and off the stage less than amusing. Gonzmart the entrepreneur finds them only one thing: successful. The sweet smell of success comes from hard work." The writer described Cesar as "confident, since that is the nicest way to sum up the energy, ham, drive, gall and ambition that make up a complete showman. There are so few total showmen because there are so very few who can summon all of those qualities and keep them constant."

Cesar's charms worked wonders on a pianist who had been let go from the Columbia Sarasota after two weeks on the job. She traveled to Ybor City and went to Cesar, demanding an explanation. Cesar calmed her and sat her down for cocktails and dinner. She watched his show that night in

Cesar and Adela hold court at the Columbia.

the Siboney, which also featured stomping flamenco dancers. The once disgruntled pianist left mollified, carrying home a signed album of Cesar's music.

Richard Gonzmart remembers countless nights at the Siboney, where his parents held court and walked the thin line between work and play: "Every Saturday was a celebration of life. It seemed like just routine to me. Everybody did it. The women would dress up in their finest gowns and chiffon and sequined dresses and gentlemen in tuxedos or black suits."

Cesar and Adela's dramatic entrances to the Siboney always impressed Richard's wife, Melanie. "They were like movie stars. When they entered that room . . . I could see her breezing through, head held high, telling everybody 'hello.' It gave me goose bumps because she was just so cool."

Cesar's favorite place: Female fans lavish him with attention.

They always proceeded to the same table in front of the stage, laden with pre-ordered appetizers and a small bar. "You'd go there and you'd have buckets of ice and bottles of whiskey," Richard says, "bottles of VO, Cutty Sark, or J&B. Everybody would serve themselves. I thought everybody lived that way. I thought everybody dressed up on Saturday nights, outrageous, and drank."

Cesar and Adela's gang of twelve or so became their court, Ybor City's Rat Pack. Such was their clique's hedonism that they would sometimes start the party all over again at a friend's house the next morning with brunch and Bloody Marys. The friends outdid one another in the kitchen, always striving to be the best. With too much to do, Cesar and Adela sometimes skipped those bubbly Sunday brunches.

Dressed to kill, Cesar and Adela spent every Saturday night gathered with friends in the Siboney Room. Their celebrations of life lasted late into the night, and sometimes began again the next morning.

Cesar was a co-founder of the Krewe of the Knights of Sant' Yago, a social group involved Latinos with Tampa's elitist Gasparilla culture.

Left: Tampa's Fiesta Days promoted its Latin culture, and the Columbia contributed her fair share of charm.

Right: An incurable ham, Cesar made the most of status as King of Sant' Yago.

Below: Cesar and fellow krewe member Henry Fernandez at Ybor City's night parade.

"The King's Party"
El Rey of Sant' Yago
Cesar Gonzmart
and his wife, Adela,
request the pleasure of your company
for a
Cocktail Buffet
Sunday, December 22, 1974
four o'clock in the afternoon
Columbia Restaurant
Tampa, Florida
REGRETS ONLY: 248-4961

Cesar helped found the Krewe of the Knights of Sant' Yago, a krewe inspired by Gasparilla associated with Spanish culture. It was important to Cesar that Tampa's Latin community assert itself in public events like Gasparilla. Ever since Ybor City's founding, there had been a constant—if invisible—tension between Tampa's Latins and Anglos. It took a player with the social and commercial ambitions of Cesar to thrust Latin culture directly into Tampa's annual bacchanal. Cesar's krewe could assert the city's Latin presence in ways that Casimiro's old parade floats could not. The annual coronation of the club's elected king and queen was always a grand, gaudy spectacle. The night parade in Ybor City became the krewe's main event every year.

Adela turned on all of her charm when throwing the Latin Quarter Gala every October at the Columbia. As trumpeted in the newspapers, the black-tie event opened the "social season." Mrs. Cesar Gonzmart and other Las Damas of Sant' Yago members presided. Beginning with cocktail hour, the evening culminated with a lavish Columbia dinner and floor show.

Showmanship

Cesar's relentless showmanship and engagement with the community kept the Columbia alive during Ybor's decline. The Columbia encouraged performances and romantic demonstrations. Cesar made the entire restaurant a stage. "Cesar really built up the business," waiter Joe Roman remembers. "He came in as a general manager, with his band and his music around the tables. A lot of people, you hear, 'Oh come on, let's go to the Columbia.' Cesar would play for twenty, twenty-five minutes by himself, and people would love it."

One of Cesar's ensembles specialized in tableside serenades, with an accordion, horns, and, of course, violins. Cesar claims that business doubled in the years after he introduced the floor show, a boast to be taken with a grain of salt.

Cesar partnered with Miami nightclubs to form a Latin entertainment circuit in Florida. "Tampa was always a humble city," Luis Diaz said, but there was nothing humble about the acts Cesar booked in the Siboney. Cuban jazz floor shows, Mexican mariachi bands, flamenco dancers, burlesque acts, and even ice skaters graced the stage with the help of special coolers. "It was the best thing that ever happened to Tampa," Luis said. "The Columbia Restaurant was standing room only."

Joe Roman: "We had a couple that used to sing on the balcony right here. She would stand on one side, and he would stand on the other. They would start singing, and they would meet in the middle."

Joe's favorite house singer, a Mr. Alvarez-Mera, often performed on the balcony and fancied his flask of brandy. The Cuban impresario sang beautifully, even after imbibing too much. He took to wearing sunglasses to performances, which Cesar would not tolerate. Joe hated to see him go: "He was a beautiful person. He could sing, what a voice. Wonderful! I never forget that man."

The Miami and Tampa's entertainment circuit welcomed artists from all over Latin America. In the days before the arts had a strong presence in Tampa, the Columbia showcased culture that would never have come to town otherwise.

The comedian Carol Burnett appeared to be taken with Cesar's charms. A shameless flirt, he loved to kiss the hands of the ladies and flash his wolfish smile.

Cesar did not stop impressing the ladies with his nightly shows until the mid-1980s.

Unexpectedly, Joe began singing with the band one night in 1962. Cesar struck up the band to start a set, and Joe took up the lyric. "It so happened that I was standing there, and Cesar was coming to the bar, and they came out to play." Joe began to sing, "*I left my heart. . .*"

Cesar loved the spontaneity. "Right Joe, sing it!" he urged.

Joe obliged. "*I left my heart in San Francisco, high on a hill, it calls to me. . .*" He always admired Cesar's showmanship— "That's where I learned," he says—and loved to demonstrate his own.

"I made some money with that too, because a lot of waiters would say, 'Joe, that table over there wants to sing.' 'Would you sing something for my girl here?' I used to enjoy it very much. I would come out with a tray and they were playing something, and I just go on there, right there. In a big room with that voice. That's a hell of a room."

Beginning in 1970, Joe performed sleight of hand "magic" tricks tableside, another way to entertain customers. He used a rubber dummy finger in a trick involving sangria. He appeared to trickle a little of the punch into a cloth napkin, but he caught it in the finger and left the napkin free of wine stains.

One of Joe's tricks required a bottle of wine. Whatever the customer ordered, he said, "I'm glad you order this bottle of wine, because my wine, you can put a fifty-cent piece in it." His gag half dollar impressed many a patron. Bound

Waiters such as Joe Roman (center) became part of the Columbia's entertainment as well. Joe sang in Cesar's show and performed magic tricks.

Ladies seated with Cesar playing. Joe Roman serves the VIPs to the left.

by a rubber band around its edge, the coin could fold into bottles and snap back into shape. Joe did the impossible every night and hoped for bigger tips. It was also a great way to sell wine.

Looking back, he says of the gag half dollar:"I'm going to buy it again. I tell you the truth. I am waiting to buy the tricks again."

Luis Leaves

In the mid-1960s, Luis Diaz became manager of the Columbia in Ybor City. Looking sharp in a tuxedo, he greeted customers in the dining rooms, but his employment did not last. One night in 1966, Cesar and Adela took their dinner with friends in the restaurant, enjoying another celebration of life. "He was having a very good night with Adela and friends," Luis said. When Luis asked the waiters to close a nearby dining room, Cesar took umbrage at his tone.

Luis remembers Cesar's outburst:"'You are acting like you are the owner of the restaurant. You're not the owner of the restaurant.' He decides to override my orders," Luis recalls. "I told the waiter, 'Leave everything the way I tell you to.' He [Cesar] was very angry because I wasn't paying attention to him. He was a customer at that time. I took offense in the fact that he broke my orders." Cesar had impulsively confronted Luis in front of the waiters and customers. Luis felt "cold anger, which is the worst anger."

Luis thought: "Tomorrow he is going to realize that he is wrong. But I'm going to leave." Luis looked Cesar in the face and said softly, "I am leaving this place."

On his way out, Luis saw the old maître d' Pepin, who said:"Wait a minute. If you are going to leave tonight never to come back, God bless you. But if you leave and your cousin is going to call you tomorrow and you are going to come back, you take it like a man, and it is forgotten tomorrow."

His jobs at the Columbia gave Luis a new beginning in a new country. Though he left the restaurant in 1966 after an argument with Cesar, his connection with the Columbia remained—he became a very successful wine salesman.

Cesar and Adela visited with Generalissimo Francisco Franco, longtime dictator of Spain, but the publicity brought mixed reactions in Tampa. Many Spanish families could not dismiss the fascist's brutal excesses during the Spanish Civil War. On the other hand, the visit began a close relationship between the Columbia and Spain that is stronger than ever today.

"No, Perpinga," Luis said, calling the mâitre d' by his nickname. "I'm leaving not to come back."

He went home and had a drink and long conversation with his wife, Helen.

Cesar phoned the next day. He apologized and asked Luis to return. "That was a bad moment that I had." Cesar implored, "Luisito, I wish you the very best of life. I want you to come to work for me. I want you and I to get old together."

Luis accepted the apology but wanted to try something different.

He said tenderly to Cesar, "I won't have any hate in my life. I love you to death. You are the one that has brought me to this country. You have given me all kinds of opportunities. So let's remain friends, and we are going to do very well together." The next Monday, Luis landed a job at a wine company. By all accounts, he and the Columbia did quite well together.

Franco

In 1965, some especially distinguished guests investigated the Columbia, by then a mecca for tourists. Cesar and the Columbia did not disappoint when the Spanish ministers of government and tourism paid a delightful visit. The Columbia became the subject of the tourism minister's report to Generalissimo Francisco Franco, the Spanish dictator. Long in years and the recipient of hard-won international respect, Franco was intrigued by the palatial outpost of Spanish culture in Tampa. It seemed fitting that the

Columbia kept Iberian traditions alive in Spain's former colony La Florida.

Franco invited Cesar and Adela to visit him at his palace. After traveling to Spain with sons Richard and Casey, they waited in line to see El Jefe. A *Time/Life* correspondent stood in line in front of the Gonzmarts. Franco met with the man for a mere ten minutes. Cesar wondered to Adela, "If he was only given ten minutes, how long will we be given? Two minutes?"

Cesar and Adela sat with Franco for a half hour. The old man peppered them with questions about restaurant and family. Cesar spoke at length about his ambitious plans for the Columbia. Franco talked about Spanish history, literature, and music, especially Zarzuela operettas. Cesar presented the elder statesman with a key to Tampa, boxes of cigars, and a transfer from Tampa's long-defunct streetcar line. In gratitude for promoting tourism in Spain, Franco bestowed the *Merito Turistico* medallion upon Cesar. The journey was a fine publicity stunt, despite some hard feelings toward Franco still lingering in Spanish Republican Ybor City.

Richard Gonzmart: "My mom and dad were so nervous. I had never seen him nervous like that. They had to dress in tails and use the proper formal Spanish language. In Tampa we speak Spanglish. I'm there in the hotel room watching TV, and there's my father and mother with Franco."

The entire family attended a banquet in a palace outside Madrid as the honored guests. Richard continues: "My mother was telling us—I'm 12, Casey is 17—she says 'Now don't make any faces. Whatever they put in front of you, eat. Don't say anything.'

"We're trying to be proper. We are sitting next to children, and we're given what looks like linguini and garlic. It tastes good. A little girl tells us in Spanish, 'Look closely, you can see the eyes and the mouth.' They were baby eels. My

brother gets sick. My father and my mother said, 'You've got to eat the whole thing.' My brother gets violently ill the rest of the night in a palace. Whenever I see the baby eels, my brother still can't eat them, and I *can't wait* to eat them. I kept on eating."

Casey's illness lasted well into the next day, through the family's train ride to Barcelona.

The Red Carpet

The Columbia garnered awards from a variety of influential sources. Starting in 1961, *Holiday* magazine honored the restaurant with top rankings. Year after year in *Florida Trend* magazine, readers' polls placed the Columbia among the top 10 restaurants in Florida. Cesar soon began lobbying for the publication's annual awards ceremony to be held at the Columbia. In 1968, Cesar said, "I finally convinced them that they should see Tampa before holding a meeting in Europe." Diverting the event from Europe in favor of Tampa took serious nerve. In the midst of the demolition and upheaval of urban renewal, Tampa was not the ideal showcase. But the Columbia was.

After a week-long tour of Florida, the owners of the finest restaurants across the country gathered for several magical days in Cesar's palace. For the next three days, Cesar pulled out every stop he knew and then some. The honored guests arrived on two chartered coaches. Local guests in formal wear lined the street in front of the

SIXTH GALA DINNER

Honoring Recipients

of the

Holiday Magazine Awards

FOR DINING DISTINCTION

COLUMBIA RESTAURANT

7th AVENUE from 21st to 22nd STREET

TAMPA'S LATIN QUARTER

Eight o'clock
OCTOBER 25th 1968

Above: *In 1968, Cesar rolled out the Columbia's red carpet for a who's who of culinary dignitaries during Holiday magazine's annual restaurant awards ceremonies. Cesar was instrumental in bringing the event to Florida. The celebrations at the Columbia lasted three days, and Cesar gave a welcome fit for royalty.*

Right: *Joe Roman (left) prepares to pour champagne as part of the Holiday festivities.*

Cesar and Adela hosted over one hundred of the best restaurateurs in the country, and they schmoozed with every one of them. Cesar created a special stage show featuring songs in Spanish, English, and French..

restaurant to greet the visitors. Staff unrolled a red carpet to the bus, and the entire cast serenaded the guests, kicking off an evening inspired by the "grandeur of Spain."

Guests enjoyed a champagne reception by the Patio's murmuring fountain. After a tour of the restaurant, the party mingled on the Patio's balcony. They took dinner in the Siboney Room. Cesar proudly wore his Spanish medallion on a ribbon around his neck, the one conferred on him by Franco. Adela could not have looked more radiant in her "elegant soft gold, beaded chiffon gown and matching coat," a reporter noted.

Instead of cluttering the evening with speeches and self-congratulations, Cesar and company presented two very brief introductions. Mayor Dick Greco greeted officials from *Holiday* magazine. The seven-course dinner included

four wine pairings. Cesar exuded class and charm. He only introduced one person, none other than his mother-in-law, Carmen, the Columbia's great silent partner.

The concert that night included a cast with new costumes "singing and dancing as if they were auditioning for the job." Cesar's violin took center stage in a set of international music pulled from former Columbia revues. With Adela, Cesar basked in a standing ovation by the country's best restaurateurs and journalists. As a performer, he worked the crowd like never before.

Many of the visitors wrote gushing letters afterward. The Columbia did far more than to lavish guests with great food, drink, and entertainment. Cesar and company made them feel *special*. Cesar set a new standard for *Holiday* award dinners that year.

After the festivities, many of the award-winning restaurateurs wrote letters of thanks and praise for the Columbia's food, atmosphere, and hospitality.

Honored Restaurants
&
Restaurateurs

AU PETIT JEAN
Mr. Stephen Crane
Miss Cheryl Crane
Nicky Blair
Louis R. Baranello

LA RUE
Mr. and Mrs. Orlando Figini

THE WINDSOR
Mr. Ben Dimsdale
Mr. Hans U. Hiltpold

GALLATIN'S
Mr. and Mrs. Gallatin Powers

LUBACH'S
Mr. and Mrs. R. C. A. Lubach

AMELIO'S
Mrs. Inez Pacini

THE BLUE FOX
Mr. and Mrs. Piero Fassio

DOROS
Mr. and Mrs. Don Dianda

ERNIE'S
Mr. and Mrs. Roland Gotti

KAN'S
Mr. and Mrs. John Kan

L'ETOILE
Mr. and Mrs. Claude Rouas

LE TRIANON
Mr. and Mrs. James Coulot

L'ORANGERIE
Mr. and Mrs. Pierre Dupart

YAMATO
Mr. and Mrs. Joe Ishizaki

ONDINE
Mr. and Mrs. Alfred Roblin

THE QUORUM
Mr. and Mrs. Pierre Wolfe
Mr. and Mrs. Heinz Gerstle

LE CORDON BLEU
Mr. and Mrs. Harold Kane Kaufman

LE DOME OF THE FOUR SEASONS
Mr. and Mrs. Calvin Haughland

JOE'S STONE CRAB RESTAURANT
Mr. and Mrs. Jesse Weiss
Mr. and Mrs. Irwin Sawitz

CHESLER'S
Mr. Hylan Chesler

LE PARISIEN
Mr. and Mrs. Claude Nicollet

THE BUCCANNEER INN
Mr. and Mrs. Herbert P. Field
Mr. and Mrs. Marvin Ghermann

PETITE MARMITE
Mr. and Mrs. C. Pucillo

COLUMBIA
Mr. and Mrs. Cesar Gonzmart

MICHEL'S
Mr. and Mrs. John Barkhorn

BIGG'S
CAFE DE PARIS
L'EPUISETTE
Mr. and Mrs. Ray Castro

BLACKHAWK
Mr. and Mrs. Don Roth

DON THE BEACHCOMBER
Mr. J. Weiss

MAXIM'S DE PARIS
Miss Nancy Goldberg

CAFE JOHNELL
Mr. and Mrs. John Spillson
Mr. and Mrs. Harold Rehrer
Miss Ann Colone

KING COLE
Mr. and Mrs. Max Comisar

BRENNAN'S
Mr. and Mrs. Owen Brennan, Jr.
Mrs. Owen Brennan, Sr.
Miss Adelaide Brennan

CARIBBEAN ROOM
Mr. and Mrs. Alfred Aschaffenburg
Pontchartrain Hotel

MASSON'S RESTAURANT FRANCAS
Mr. and Mrs. Ernest Masson

CHESAPEAKE
Mr. and Mrs. Phillip Friedman
Mr. and Mrs. Alfred L. Freud

ANTHONY'S PIER 4
Mr. and Mrs. Anthony Athanas

JIMMY'S HARBOURSIDE
Mr. and Mrs. James Doulos

HUGO'S LIGHTHOUSE
Mr. John C. Carzis
Mr. Nicholas Kamarinopoulos

LONDON CHOP HOUSE
Mr. and Mrs. Lester Gruber

WIN SCHULER'S
Mr. and Mrs. Win Schuler
Hans and Nancy Schuler

CHARLIE'S CAFE EXCEPTIONALE
Mrs. Charles W. Saunders
Mr. and Mrs. Alfred Mahlke

CONTINENTAL ROSEWOOD ROOM
Mr. and Mrs. H. R. Bell
Mr. and Mrs. Jacques Loth
Northstar Inn

THE BLUE HORSE
Mr. and Mrs. Clifford Warling
Mr. and Mrs. David Speer

MATTERHORN ROOM
Nelle O. Palmer
Lowell Inn

CAFE CHAUVERON
Mr. and Mrs. Albert Kaiser

CLOS NORMAND
Mr. and Mrs. Maurice Bertrand

FORUM OF THE 12 CAESARS
Mr. and Mrs. Paulus C. Kovi

FOUR SEASONS
Mr. Harvey Daniels

GAGE & TOLLNER
Mr. and Mrs. Edward S. Dewey

GLOUCESTER HOUSE
Mr. Edmund Lillys

LA POTINIERE DE SOIR
Mr. and Mrs. Albert Forgelle

RAINBOW ROOM
Mr. and Mrs. Brian Daly

"21" CLUB
Mr. and Mrs. Jerry Berns

GOURMET
Mr. and Mrs. Henri J. Guglielmi

MAISONETTE
Mr. and Mrs. Lee Comisar

LE MONT
Mr. and Mrs. James A. Blandi
Mr. Frank Blandi

JUSTINE'S
Mr. and Mrs. Dayton Smith

MARIO'S
Mrs. Christine Vaccaro

OLD WARSAW
Mr. and Mrs. Stanislaw Slawik

MAXIM'S
Mr. and Mrs. Camilla Bermann

CANLIS' CHARCOAL BROILER
Mr. Peter Canlis

THE CROWN
Mr. and Mrs. Milton J. Arps

FRENCHY'S
Mr. and Mrs. Paul La Points

KARL RATZSCH
Mr. and Mrs. Karl Ratzsch

DRAKE HOTEL
Mr. and Mrs. Roy Cowdrey

Honored Guests

Mr. and Mrs. Silas Spitzer   ---   Mr. Caskey Stinnett
The Honorable Mayor and Mrs. Dick Greco
The Honorable Congressman and Mrs. Sam Gibbons

Los Vinos...

Mum's Cordon Rouge - 1962
Manzanilla La Gitana Sherry

Cepa de Oro Chablis
Reserva - 1962

Viña Pomal
Reserva - 1952

Arias Spanish Champagne Cider

☆☆☆☆☆☆☆☆

Los Licores...

Anis del Mono
Cuarenta y tres
501 Brandy

Of the sixty-seven restaurants honored in 1968, only twenty-three remain in business today. Few are still owned by the same family forty years later. Longevity is rare in the restaurant industry, even at the very top. The celebrations of 1968 soon gave way to tough times in Ybor City and the Columbia.

All of the guests could see the Columbia was special, too. While federal bulldozers had leveled much of Ybor City, the gem still stood among the ruins. The unlucky age of "urban renewal" had just begun.

 ## Rediscovery

At a young age, Richard learned about the restaurant from the very best. "I can recall my earliest recollection of the Columbia and the events that began my education and love of the food service industry. It was the summer of 1956."

Richard remembers watching the fish being delivered, packed in shaved ice. He was just three years old. When he heard the truck park behind the restaurant, he ran to the walk-in refrigerator to watch the delivery.

"I walked inside only to be looking eye-to-eye with a huge fresh Gulf of Mexico red snapper covered with flaked ice." Fascinated, Richard cautiously approached it. He poked the fish to see if it would move.

Casimiro watched his grandson with great interest. He crouched in front of him to give him his first lesson in being a restaurateur. "Look into the eyes to see if they're clear," the old man explained softly. "That's how you can tell if the fish is fresh. Touch the skin to see that it is firm, not sticky. Look inside the mouth at the gills to be sure they're bright in color."

Casimiro granted Richard the title of unofficial fish inspector. The young appointee took the honor seriously and evaluated shipments before they could be served. "I felt so grown up, and here I was nothing but a baby and being taught my first lesson by the man I had such respect for. I cannot explain, but I was kind of scared by his presence. He was the boss, and everyone knew it.

"Every visit to the Columbia would have me scurrying to the kitchen where Chef Manuel Trujillo, the best grill man I have ever had the pleasure to work with, would tell me 'Ricardo, there are big fish today,' or 'Too late today, we have already cleaned the fish.' How I looked forward to checking to be sure the fish were fresh just as my grandfather had instructed."

His grandfather reminded Richard that people came to the Columbia only because the food was always good. He became angry with one of the chefs for making the Spanish bean soup too salty. The chef pleaded, "But Don Casimiro, I can fix it by adding water." Casimiro responded by dumping the entire sixty-gallon batch.

Richard asked his grandfather why he wouldn't let the chef save the soup. "The answer," Richard recalls, "made sense even to a child." Today, it is almost a cliché because it is so true. "You are only as good as your last meal." The Columbia survived because people liked the food time after time.

That afternoon, Richard said, "made a big difference in my life. I had one life and one chance to be a success. I wanted to be just like my grandfather, so smart, so imposing, yet so kind to this small boy who was trekking through this bustling kitchen.

"I had all the confidence in the world, walking through the kitchen that summer of 1956. Everyone was so kind and explaining their trade to me. I could not wait to be old enough to cook. In time, when I was twelve years old, my apprenticeship at the Columbia kitchen would begin."

The Reluctant Heir

Cesar and Adela sometimes worried that the extravagant gifts they gave their sons would spoil them. They tried to instill a strong work ethic through jobs at the restaurant and studies on their own. Most of all, they treated their

Young Casey, right, and Richard were often overshadowed by the Columbia. Richard became the restaurant's unofficial fish inspector at age five.

sons equally, giving them the same resources and opportunities to follow their dreams.

Casey was always close to his mother, Adela, and grandmother, Carmen. Cesar spent all his energy on the restaurant.

Casey Gonzmart: "All I heard while I was growing up was the importance of this place called the Columbia." He remembers summers the most, when the family rented a beach house, and Cesar could take a few scattered days with his wife and children. As a teen, Casey spent summer vacations in the kitchen learning the stations. Casimiro's seasoned kitchen staff schooled the boy in the arts of cooking.

At sixteen, Casey graduated from Jesuit High School in Tampa, and Cesar took him to Europe to attend culinary school. Once alone, the young man felt like a small fish in the ocean. He was on his own: enrolled, armed with a credit card, and ready to adapt. He quickly made new friends and ate in the finest French restaurants. He studied cooking in Switzerland but stalled out in Spain, spending more time with his girlfriend than his classmates.

In the summer of 1968, when he was fifteen, Richard visited Casey and enrolled in culinary courses. During some time off, the Gonzmart brothers took an improvised vacation. They hopped a mail plane to the Balearic Islands in the Mediterranean Sea. "A thirty-nine-dollar flight to Palma Mallorca on a DC-3," Richard remembers. They arrived during the height of tourist season, and every hotel was full.

Richard Gonzmart: "We got to Palma Mallorca at about five in the morning. We didn't know where we were going, so the taxicab driver took us to the beach. All of the hotels were full, and I remember just lying on the lounge chair on the beach trying to sleep, just hurting. We were on a very

The pressure of living up to Cesar's standards and the Columbia's demands was daunting. Both brothers played vital roles when called upon.

tight budget. We got a hotel for eight dollars a night. We had hot dogs for thirty cents, went out to the discos. It was neat.

"My brother had lost his Rolex that summer in Tampa. We were water-skiing in the bay, we were in our boat, and my dad was in his yacht. We were supposed to meet my dad, and my dad yells, 'Where the hell have you all been?!' He is yelling at me, and my brother says he can't get much madder."

"Where have you been?" Cesar demanded.

"I lost my Rolex. We're looking for it," Casey responded.

Cesar said he should have bought Casey a clock to hang around his neck.

Richard Gonzmart: "Then my dad buys my brother a Timex watch, and now we're in Palma Mallorca. We got back from the beach, and my brother says, 'I lost my watch. We've got to go back.' So I've got to put on my cold bathing suit. We're walking down the beach, we're talking. We see a gentleman, start talking to him and he's from America. He says, 'Are you from the States? If you ever go to Florida, the best paella in the world is at the Columbia restaurant, Tampa. Probably never heard of it.'

"That's when I realized: I am in Spain, and somebody is telling me that my family makes the best paella. He didn't know who we were. We told him we were the owners, and he said, 'Yeah, yeah, right.' It made us realize how famous the Columbia was.

"I always thought that to be a part of the Columbia was special," Richard says.

Casey found his Timex, and the episode is one of Richard's treasured memories.

Soon after, Casey quit school and spent all of his money entertaining a girlfriend. Cesar grudgingly gave him more money to finish his training, and Casey came home with a chef's skills and better street sense. He concluded his education in time to meet another challenge far from home.

Touchdown

During his summers off, Richard rotated through the kitchen stations. He struggled in the classroom, unaware that he was dyslexic. His keen and active mind was easily distracted, a common trait in much of his family.

In high school, he squeezed by in his studies and shone on the gridiron. He and his friends had torn up the Gonzmart family lawn for years playing ball. Richard became the star running back of Jesuit High School's football team. At six feet two inches and 215 pounds, Richard was capable of explosive speed. He cleared the 100-yard dash in 9.9 seconds.

At first, Richard's teammates at Jesuit High would go into games thinking, "We're going to get our asses kicked." Shocked by their initial victories, they would say, "We had no business beating these guys." With an excellent coaching staff and Richard's speed, however, Jesuit's football team made short work of competition. Tampa Catholic considered Richard such a threat that the students there burned him in effigy.

Richard found new confidence playing football. In 1969, he also found a girl named Melanie Heiny—she was fourteen, and he was sixteen. They danced once at a school party, but both were too shy to speak. Although he did not know Melanie, he helped her gain a position on the cheerleading team. Today, Richard insists that Melanie had such looks and personality that she didn't need his help. She marveled at his athleticism and good looks. "He was the fastest boy in town."

One day after cheerleading practice, Melanie was calling her mother on a public telephone. When Richard drove by with some friends and saw her, he said he would like to meet her some time. His friend replied, "C'mon, get out of the car!" He loudly introduced the two.

"He left me there," Richard says. "I was such a dork." She told Richard that her cousin would be celebrating her bridal shower at the Columbia. In his best suit, he sat alone, waiting at table 92 beside the famous fountain. "Dressed up in a suit trying to look Joe Cool, sixteen years old. My dad came and told me how beautiful she was, how beautiful her mother was."

"His dad [Cesar] looked me up and down," Melanie said, "like I was a horse."

Young Richard Gonzmart found new confidence in football at Jesuit High School.

Richard and Melanie had eyes for one another from the outset, and fell in love.

Cesar and Adela got lost on the way to Richard's impressive game against Palmetto High. "I scored an 80- or 90-yard touchdown in the first play of the game. The second play was 60 yards. I was throwing up, couldn't play the rest of the game." His parents, who arrived in formal finery, missed Richard's entire show.

Born in Tampa during the 1950s, Melanie Heiny is a true Tampa hybrid, with her Cracker father and mother of Sicilian and Asturian descent. Her mother rejected an arranged Sicilian marriage and chose instead to attend a university in New Orleans. There, she found a husband of her choosing, a Cracker through and through. "My father, who was a major cracker, had to acclimate to these crazy Latinos, and he did it well," Melanie says.

Melanie Gonzmart: "I remember being a cheerleader, watching these two people show up at the football game. Cesar's in his tuxedo because they're going to the restaurant. Adela is dressed to the nines. Like she always said, 'Don't just walk into a room, make an entrance.' I said to myself, 'If those were my parents I would be embarrassed, but I think these people are very cool.' We all knew that they were so busy, but they would stay and watch their son and then go to the restaurant."

Richard gave his parents plenty of action. As the star player, he led Jesuit to many improbable victories. "I remember my dad was proud of those achievements. He was a musician. He was never allowed to be an athlete. So I think he was living through me."

At Jesuit, Richard also found his love, Melanie Heiny (third from left). 1970

Suddenly, Cesar saw Richard going pro on the gridiron instead of in the restaurant. Colleges and universities all over the country courted him with scholarships and incentives. "I was being recruited by all these schools. The coaches from the University of Minnesota and from Michigan State were trying to convince me I should go to play football. I had all these scholarships." Paid tuition seemed too good to be true, at least to Cesar.

Closer to home, the University of Tampa and Florida State University sent letters to Richard. At seventeen, UT announced his presence at a game during halftime in front of forty thousand people. He stood on the field beside one of the team's most promising new recruits and was clearly their next prospect.

Only his grades held him back from the top tier. Michigan State looked at his marks and suggested he study physical education instead of hospitality.

After thinking about his options, Richard said to Cesar, "Dad, let me ask you this question: Do you want me to be a football player or a restaurateur?"

Richard and Melanie on their first date (above) and before their senior prom (below).

Cesar said, "That's a stupid question!" He assumed Richard would play football in college.

To Richard, it was serious. He saw too many athletes lose their sense of fun in the college routine. The pressure put him into a strange position: disappointing his father by wanting to run the Columbia instead of chasing his football ambitions.

His counselor at Jesuit High, Father Kelly, gave him books and brochures from every major hospitality program in the country. After careful consideration, Richard selected the one at the University of Denver.

Richard quit football and went to Denver. Richard Gonzmart: "I can't tell you that I got a lot out of college. I could tell you everything I got in a few minutes. Never count how many hours you work in a week. It means you're not happy, and you're going to think you're underpaid. If you have to count the hours it means you're not satisfied. Don't drink with your customers; you could become an alcoholic. So I don't drink at the restaurant.

"It's okay to make a mistake as long as you don't commit the same mistake twice. It means don't be afraid, and don't commit the same mistakes. I always tell people I make more mistakes than anybody. And you learn from the mistakes other people make."

Richard found it difficult to apply any of his education to the Columbia. Cesar created the kind of business people didn't teach in school. "The Columbia Restaurant was its own monster. You couldn't change it. What they teach you in books is not necessarily the real world. Those things I learned."

Richard didn't dwell in Denver for long. Thoughts of his high school flame Melanie dating other men became unbearable. When he left Tampa and Melanie left for Florida State shortly afterward, they had agreed to see other people. He found his heart could not live with their pact. "I told him all about my dating, which drove him crazy," Melanie recalled with a grin.

Cesar knew how his son felt and encouraged him to marry his first love.

Melanie Gonzmart: "When Cesar saw how very happy we were together, I think he feared that if Richard went away that I would find someone else and Richard would as well. Maybe he liked me more than I thought at that moment. I don't think Richard felt that he could go to his father and say, 'I want to get married.' Cesar knew we were pining for each other when he was in Denver. When Richard came back, he saw all the letters that I wrote him every day, hundreds and hundreds of letters. At least I came from a Hispanic family. I knew their customs: They should take care of their man and always support them."

Cesar himself understood romance. "You're going to be miserable," he told Richard. "I think you should get married now. Don't wait until you come back. You'll be lonely and unhappy. Get married now, and we'll help you."

The vivacious beauty had studied art for less than a year before Richard flew into Tallahassee to see her in the fall of 1972. She agreed to marry him then and there. When Melanie returned to Tampa for Christmas, he proposed at the Columbia, at table 92 in the Patio Room beside the fountain where they sat on their first date.

Richard and Melanie married at the restaurant in September 1973. The size of the wedding overwhelmed the eighteen-year-old bride. The marriage was the first among Cesar's sons, making the celebration especially joyous.

Their honeymoon occurred just before Richard was due to begin culinary school in Madrid. "What a dream come true," Richard recalls, "Cesar's going to put me on the payroll and give me a check. And then he gave me the Ameri-

can Express card. Our two-week honeymoon in Spain was with the Torres [wine] family during the harvest at the end of September. It was wonderful.

"We planned around September because it was slow time and school was going to start in Spain. So now I'm getting a hotel room, I'm getting a check, I'm going to school, and come back to my wife, who cooks and so forth. I finish my

Richard and Melanie were married in 1973. The wedding seemed overwhelming to Melanie, a feeling she would get to know well in Columbia's shadow.

vacation, and we're tired of eating out. My dad is asking where we are eating, and I'm tired."

While Richard learned the ways of a chef, Melanie learned Spanish, more so she could survive her new family than her time in Spain.

After a year in Spain, Richard completed his studies and considered his next move. "In front of the Columbia in the parking lot, in space number 5, on the east side of the parking lot," Richard remembers a life-changing conversation with Cesar.

Cesar asked, "Are you finished with your education?"

"I'm finished," his son replied. "I'm ready to go to work."

"You're done? You sure?" Cesar asked.

With his mind racing, Richard only managed to say, "Yep."

"Well," Cesar pronounced, "get ready to work long, long hours." Richard's stomach sank.

As he toiled in the kitchen during the following days, he thought, "I'm now an adult." A month later, he expressed interest in a fine graduate program in Madrid.

Cesar said with some satisfaction, "I gave you a chance, and you blew it; it's over."

Whatever misgivings Richard had then about joining the working world, he remains deeply thankful to his father for his wonderful marriage. "I thank my dad for giving us that year of being able to have the foundation for a great marriage."

Richard and Melanie's honeymoon in Spain took place just before he entered culinary school in Madrid.

Although Richard attended culinary and hospitality school, his most important lessons were learned on the job.

The Walled City

The 1965 visit with Franco provided Cesar with a new burst of inspiration. Ybor City needed more than fine dining to make it a popular destination. He had visions of several nightclubs, all providing different music; a six-floor "Spanish-style castle motel"; townhouses and bachelor apartments; a wax museum; and painters and artisans in the streets. Of course, all of those things cost money that

Cesar didn't have. He hoped to court Spanish money, any money, to fund his ambitions.

Cesar also knew his dreams could not become a reality by relying on others. He erected 100 signs in the Tampa area urging people to "Visit Tampa's Latin Quarter, courtesy the Columbia Restaurant." The signs belied that the Columbia was one of Ybor City's only surviving attractions.

In 1965—the same year of the Franco visit—officials announced the beginning of a federal program called urban renewal in Tampa. The newspapers trumpeted the creation of a "gleaming new and modern Latin Quarter." According to the plan, federal funding cleared away old buildings and private capital redeveloped Ybor City. Officials faced the challenge of clearing away blight while preserving the Latin Quarter's unique qualities.

Cesar increased his engagement in civic affairs to assist redevelopment in Tampa. Over the coming years, he became Ybor City's spokesman as well as the Columbia's. At that point, one could not survive without the other. He promoted Ybor City so aggressively that the Optimists Club named him Outstanding Citizen of the Year in 1965, and he was only warming up.

Originally opened in 1890, Las Novedades remained the Columbia's greatest competitor. Manuel Garcia Jr., son of the former Columbia partner, ran the fine Spanish restaurant a few blocks away. Shrinking Ybor City did not have room enough for both. When Cesar partnered with manufactured-home builder Jim Walter to redevelop Ybor City, he found a new opportunity, and took down his nemesis. Garcia, the rigid Spanish owner of Las Novedades, could not compete with Cesar's flair for romantic promotion.

With a half million dollars supplied by Walter, Las Novedades became the property of the Columbia restaurant in 1970. The Garcia family began a successful Burger King franchise in Orlando. Cesar kept Las Novedades open for about a year, with Casey as manager. Without the capital or customers to sustain both restaurants, Cesar closed his new acquisition in 1971. The closing of Las Novedades left the Columbia in command of Ybor City's tourist trade. The Spanish Park Restaurant, opened in 1932 a few blocks away, was the only remaining competitor. But Ybor City was not the prize it once was: The few remaining residents were too poor or too old to cavort in the Siboney Room.

Cesar had reason to gloat when he bragged of the Columbia outliving Las Novedades: "I think perhaps my flair for showmanship was one reason we were able to remain in business and they were not. We came in with a very elaborate musical production, of which I was the star. And violins dealt them a mortal blow. It destroyed them. Have you seen me perform? I persuaded my dear friend Jim Walter . . . to save it from becoming a lost landmark."

In Tampa, only Las Novedades could match the Columbia in ambience and cuisine. The restaurant was run by Casimiro's former partners, the Garcia family. In 1970, Cesar bought the restaurant with the help of home builder Jim Walter.

He also dwelled on his well-crafted business deals. "I paid zero for the buildings and the business, and I owned 50 percent, which we leased for $1 million. Jim Walter took tax losses on his 50 percent, leaving me with 100 percent of the profit. Then I sold the lease and property for $350,000, including $100,000 in cash. I retained the Las Novedades corporation, which gave me a tax advantage for losses incurred in the past, plus we held the name."

Cesar found enthusiastic partners to support his most ambitious plan yet. After bidding on land cleared by urban renewal, they planned a Spanish walled city, teeming with artists and artisans, entertainment, dining, music, and dancing. At various times, Cesar talked about opening a hotel, bachelor apartments, and European-style nightclubs.

They pondered a variety of focal point attractions, finally agreeing upon Portuguese—or "bloodless"—bullfighting. With the support of state politicians, Cesar finessed a bill into the state legislature making such exhibitions legal. Mayor Dick Greco marveled at the restaurateur's flair with politicians and secretaries alike. Luis Diaz keenly remembers Tampa's fast and loose politics: "In Tampa, you could do anything at that time. If you had friends, you find a way to get things done." For those concerned about the plans for bullfighting, Gonzmart offered comfort. "The attraction will offer much more than bulls," he said. "It will have the air of a Spanish rodeo or fiesta, with much singing and dancing, and will be family oriented." The bullfighting ring was set to open in October 1971, to coincide with the grand opening of Walt Disney World in Lake Buena Vista.

Plans for the walled city grew from fifteen acres to twenty-five, and costs skyrocketed. Opposition to the bullfighting plans increased as well. An untested bull went berserk during a bullfighting exhibition in Bradenton, broke out of the ring, and charged at the audience. The spectacle of police shooting the bull did not endear their new law to the legislature, and it was repealed. Without the central attraction, Cesar's dream of a walled city crumbled. His erstwhile partners scattered.

The race horse had dreamed too big, but there would be greater opportunities. The rest of Florida beckoned.

New Start in Sarasota

Casey received an earnest call from Cesar one day in 1971. Shortly thereafter, he visited his parents, who sat him down and explained that the general manager of the Sarasota Columbia had been fired. He'd been stealing food from the company and giving it to another restaurant where he was a partner.

Cesar explained that they needed Casey in Sarasota to manage the restaurant. "I asked them when," Casey remembered, "and they said, 'Tomorrow.'"

Having just returned from school overseas in 1970, he was more interested in catching up with friends than in managing an underperforming restaurant in a backwater. "I had gone to school in Europe for several years and came back to Tampa. I didn't want to go someplace that had no connections, no friends, and my instinct was to stay where I was comfortable, back home," Casey said.

After a brief stint as manager of Las Novedades, Casey stabilized the Sarasota location. It soon grew into one of the company's crown jewels.

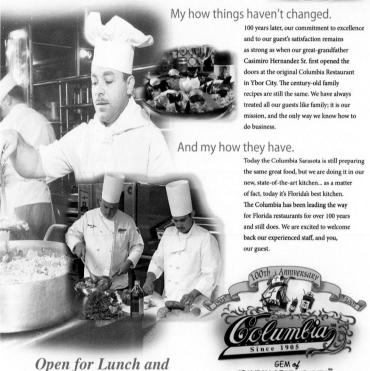

"I'm a lucky guy," Casey says. "I've always been a lucky guy. The timing was such where things started flowing." He could be thankful that the Columbia paid only a minimum rent not based upon the square footage it occupied. He retained a "good crew," many of whom had fled Castro's Cuba. Casey also recognized a "nucleus of local customers" who could be relied on for business most of the year. Sarasota showed increasing promise over the course of the 1970s.

"Almost like the Columbia of Ybor City, all the things that had given us the success in Tampa were just beginning to grow there. It just was sixty years later than Ybor City."

Although Casey attributes his success in Sarasota to his good luck, Luis Diaz insists: "'Til Casey took over, Sarasota was a horse gone wild. By the time that Casey took it over, the place was starting to behave like a business. Casey gave that place a tremendous shine. It became ever so nice. Casey was responsible for the great success of Sarasota."

Luis had left the Columbia just a few years before and was delighted to do business with them as a wine dealer. "It was so fantastic," Luis said. Casey must have thought so, too. Some Sarasota sand crept into his shoes. The reluctant savior of the Columbia Sarasota built up his outpost for the next twenty years.

Slump

All the talk about Las Novedades could not conceal the fact that the Columbia itself was struggling to survive. During the summer of 1970, Cesar closed the restaurant's doors for lunch. Not enough workers counted Ybor City as home to support the lunch trade.

As the 1970s wore on, Cesar began to question the results of urban renewal. The program gave no incentives for businessmen to take risks in Ybor City. As the head of Ybor's largest business, Cesar did not seek greener pastures. He invested in the Columbia and took risks of his own. Cesar

He agreed to take over operations in Sarasota but refused to stay indefinitely. Sarasota may as well have been the surface of the moon. He lived at the Sheraton Sandcastle for months, straightened out the restaurant, and got a feel for the clientele. He found a restaurant "in limbo" because of the feast-or-famine seasonal flow of business. One of Adela's old gift shops gathered cobwebs and dust on the property. Entire dining rooms remained devoid of furniture and customers. A pessimist would have thought the Columbia at Sarasota doomed.

Jr., the son from his first marriage, joined him in refurbishing Ybor properties.

Even Cesar, the eternal optimist, acknowledged how difficult those years were. "Yes, the Columbia suffered when Ybor City suffered. That's when we put in the entertainment. We had to attract the tourists because the Tampa people would not come to Ybor City."

The food quality fell, and prices remained high. Casimiro's legacy of tight management unraveled in the 1970s. In 1980, Richard publicly admitted that the food had suffered as a result of the business slump. Even George Guito, a man as loyal as they come, admits, "Possibly, one time, it slipped away a little bit."

"There were a few years here where the quality did go down," Joe Roman says. "Thank God it went up again. Sometimes you would bring a dish out and the customer would say, 'This dish doesn't taste. . .' What can you do? Take the dish and try and serve them something else. In those years things were bad, and the freezers and coolers weren't freezing the right way. They didn't have the money to buy the new."

The Columbia was in danger of becoming known as a tourist trap. The awards that Casimiro and Cesar had been so proud of stopped coming in. The most bitter blow was the loss of *Florida Trend* magazine's Golden Spoon Award. The spoons had come reliably every year until 1973, when the publication changed the award rules. A reader poll determined the results before then.

New guidelines in 1973 allowed two Golden Spoons: critic's choice and people's choice. That year, only the readers awarded the Columbia. The critic did not. From the next year on, only the critic chose winners. It seemed the magic had left for good—for the next thirty years, the Columbia did not garner a single Golden Spoon.

When Richard joined the restaurant operations in 1974,

By the 1970s, Ybor City had been vivisected by highways and decimated through urban renewal. The government cleared a great deal of land, but private developers failed to build anything new. Ybor City has yet to fully recover.

he could see not all was going as planned. "We won for seventeen years or so, and all of a sudden we didn't win it. My dad was devastated. I remember the hurt in his eyes. He did not receive the *Holiday* magazine award. We lost it, and my dad was devastated, bitching at [*Florida Trend* critic] Robert Tolf and 'What did he know?' The truth is, we had slipped. I took a picture of Robert Tolf on TV's *Mystery Diner*, and I put it in the kitchen."

"Cesar was the only person alive—I'll say it today with the utmost respect—that could've kept the Columbia alive through his showmanship. He had to make sacrifices in the quality of food. Maybe it wasn't the right thing. It harmed our reputation. But we got people in, and the restaurant survived."

Melanie remembers when the family acknowledged their fall from the grace of critics. "The Golden Spoons, I remember taking them down from a display in the restaurant. We put them away because they had lost it. Because it became a giant gap, okay? We had all these Golden Spoons and then nothing. Because his father had lost it. We had gotten really bad."

Cesar did not serve mediocre food because he wanted to. The legendary Columbia operated on a thin dime. Cesar's ultimate goal became survival during the 1960s and 1970s. He coped with uncertainty and risk just as his Columbia forebears had done: He improvised. He cut corners wherever he could, and the quality of employees and products sank accordingly.

If Cesar had been too idealistic, he might have closed up at any time because he couldn't replicate Pijuan's cooking with scant money. Not even Casimiro's business genius could have conquered the stark balance sheet. Only Don Quixote could have taken on such odds with such self-assurance. He believed, and it became true.

The Columbia's maestro did not conduct business in an ordinary way. He operated in Cesar World, where inside connections with sometimes questionable company ensured survival. In 1968, state legislative investigators called upon Cesar to testify about organized crime in Tampa. He acknowledged mob boss Santo Trafficante as a frequent customer but claimed to know nothing of his activities. Cesar's testimony was harmless, unconvincing, and understandable. Certain powers—like the IRS or the mob—were too strong to challenge.

Escapades

The Gonzmarts always have treated travel abroad as a form of homework for restaurateurs. The entire family made memories on vacation. While taking Casey to culinary school in France, the Gonzmarts dined in a fine Parisian restaurant. Cesar received a menu with no prices. The waiter had mistakenly given Adela the menu intended for the man at the table, the only one complete with prices.

In an expansive mood, Cesar ordered with gusto. "We want two dozen oysters!"

Looking at the steep prices, Adela said, "We don't want oysters."

Cesar insisted, over Adela's objections.

"I remember when that bill came," Richard said. "My dad's like, 'Oh, man.' Those are memories."

They visited a Hungarian restaurant in Paris, where Cesar and Casey drank too much champagne. A tipsy Cesar took

Occasionally, Cesar and Adela would take their sons on vacation. On this occasion, they were dropping Casey off to begin culinary school in Switzerland and Spain.

With a keen memory and sense of direction, Adela made an excellent navigator.

up the violin with the house band. After returning to his table, he told the family that the violin was out of tune.

"Why didn't you tune it?" Adela asked.

"Because I'm too drunk!"

Out of all their friends, Cesar and Adela most liked to travel with Charlie and Melba Hero. Charlie's father, Hermino, was best man at Casimiro's wedding. His plumbing company had served the Columbia for decades. Cesar was never offstage, even at home. Vacations proved most beneficial when he surrounded himself with good friends like the Heros and he could relax.

Charlie Hero: "You had to know Cesar when you went out on a trip. He'd always tell me, 'Charlie if you've got five good friends, you're lucky.' And it's true! Because when we went traveling, he had his hair down. Forget about the business and all, we enjoyed! We saw, we took pictures, and we bought things."

Adela especially liked to shop for antiques and art. She possessed an incredible memory. "She was like an encyclopedia," Charlie recalls, memorizing directions, addresses, names and numbers without fail. She had a keen sense of where to find the best deals. Charlie Hero: "She really was the navigator. Whatever she wanted, he gave her. Wherever she wanted to go, we went."

Charlie remembers a 1970s trip to Spain and Germany. "We were driving down this road in Spain, just getting

With close friends like Charlie and Melba Hero, Cesar and Adela could have fun virtually anywhere.

Although thoroughly enjoyable, many of the trips overseas gave Cesar and Adela ideas for the Columbia. Here, they visit the inner sanctum of the Torres winery, a valued partner for many years.

For sport, Charlie Hero and Cesar Gonzmart competed to pay the restaurant bill, employing subterfuge if necessary.

dark, you know? We passed by a place that had all kinds of displays outside where they sell all kinds of memorabilia and Spanish goods.

"So we stopped there. All the stuff that we buy, they had it there, but a lot cheaper. We started buying stuff. The owner got to know us, very happy. He had his own little dungeon, where he had his wine. [laughs] He took us in there, he said, 'Look, look, you bought enough!'

The marathon shopping sprees could be quite tiring. Charlie Hero corrals packages (above), and Cesar gets comfortable while waiting for Adela to finish shopping (below).

"Don't buy anymore," Melba remembers the proprietor saying, "Come and drink with me!"

Charlie enjoyed Cesar's rascality. Near the Pyrenees Mountains and the French border, Cesar wanted to see an exclusive eighteenth-century hotel for himself. While inside, he was so enraptured with a display of royal Spanish portraits that he proceeded to film them with his motion-picture camera.

A hotel employee saw the scene and said, "What are you doing here? You're not in the hotel."

Cesar replied, "No, we're just looking."

The inquisitor insisted, "Sir! If you're not in the hotel, you don't belong here." He then escorted the Gonzmarts and Heros out of the rarefied hotel.

Charlie joked to Cesar, "Man, I've been thrown out of better places than this!"

Cesar quipped back, "Not me!"

They also explored an exclusive resort and casino in Berchtesgaden, Germany. Hitler had once used his residence there as his retreat, but not Cesar. When he whimsically asked how much a room cost, the concierge snootily replied, "Sir, if you have to ask, you can't afford it."

The nightly sporting contest featured the restaurant bill. Cesar and Charlie competed for the honor of paying, going to great lengths and feats of treachery to do so.

Charlie would sneak over to the waiter and say, "Make sure I get the bill."

Cesar responded by taking the waiter aside, demanding: "You give him the bill, you're fired!"

Adela admires some hand-painted tile in Spain. In the following years, Cesar and Adela bought enough tile to clad the Columbia in beautiful colors and the brushwork of Seville.

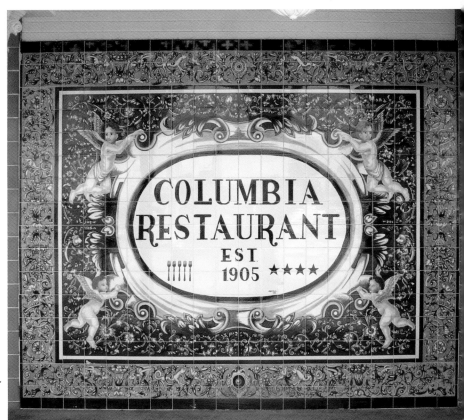

The colorful Spanish tiles brought splashes of beauty to what had been a rather bland exterior.

Photo By Rob/Harris

 ## Reinvention

Joseph Cusimano placed the first hand-painted tile on the restaurant's outer wall in 1973. The beautification project was especially dramatic in declining Ybor City. The Gonzmart family had accumulated a vast collection of hand-painted Spanish tile. Some of the tiles came from the storeroom of the old Las Novedades.

For more than a decade, Cesar employed aging Sergio Mesa as the Columbia's artist. Mesa's salary paid for his studio, living expenses, and prolific smoking habit. Meals at the Columbia came free. He painted copies of Spanish classics and various original works on canvas, vases, and tile.

"I find that I can't stay at my painting easel for too long anymore," Mesa said. "It tires me out. If Cesar weren't so nice, I wouldn't mind staying home once in a while. But he never docks me a day when I don't come to work, so I feel an obligation to be here."

When Cesar and Adela vacationed in Seville, they fell in love with the colorful tiles produced there. The most magnificent showcase was the Hotel King Alfonso. In 1978,

Cesar spent $160,000 to cover most of the restaurant's exterior with imported tile painted in Seville.

Disaster almost struck during the installation. The back of the tiles, which bore instructions for the proper arrangement, had been mislabeled. Shortly after the tile setters went to work, they discovered the error. Thankfully, the mortar had not yet dried, and workers pried the tiles loose to have them washed and rearranged.

In 1981, Cesar and Adela commissioned local artist Richard Sorrentino to create some of the large tile murals on the restaurant's exterior. Years before, the young man had been happy painting with oils. A friend asked Sorrentino to paint some tiles for a bathroom, and he soon preferred to work with tile.

Sorrentino found steady work when the Columbia approached him to paint pieces as large as seven by three feet. The artist drew inspiration from library books and the Columbia itself. "I approach the tile work for the Columbia as a restoration project," he said. "I try to keep the flavor of what is already there rather than to impose my own ideas. As time goes on, I fall more in love with the brushwork of the old painters of Seville . . . their unique brush strokes, their colors."

Cesar shared his infectious enthusiasm with a journalist on the sidewalk outside the restaurant. He compared two depictions of vases on either side of a doorway. "Stand back here," he said, and turned his back to Seventh Avenue. "Now they look the same. But look. They are not the same. Each vase is full of different flowers. Why? Because if they were the same it would not be art; it would be reproduction. Anything worth doing is worth doing right."

The "1905" Salad

Every year, Tony Noriega Jr. performs a ceremony to honor his late father. He wears his father's jacket and union badge and dines at the Columbia. He always orders his father's

Adapted from Tony Noriega's recipe, the Columbia's "1905 salad" has become a true classic.

salad. Today, it is known as the "1905" Salad, but it began at midnight in Tony Sr.'s kitchen after a long evening at work.

Hungry for a hearty salad, Tony raided his refrigerator for ingredients: lettuce, onion, pepper, ham, Swiss cheese, Parmesan cheese, tomato, olives, lemon juice, and vinegar. He waited tables at a different restaurant then, and made a version tableside for special customers.

Tony worked as a waiter at the Columbia in the 1940s, when Casimiro first offered the "Tony" Salad as a special and his creation was perfected. The salad's flavors reflect Tony's Spanish and Italian ancestry and appealed to patrons in his hometown of Ybor City.

The dish grew in popularity when he left the Columbia to start his own restaurant, Tony's, off of Dale Mabry Highway, in the 1950s. His creation became part of Tampa's Latin menu. The popular Seabreeze Restaurant adopted the recipe. It became so symbolic of Tampa's Latin roots that Cesar renamed it the "1905" Salad as the Columbia's seventy-fifth anniversary approached in the 1970s.

In a genuine effort to help dissident Cubans, Cesar and hundreds of Tampeños became ensnared in the legalities of the Mariel Boatlift. (Photos courtesy of Florida State Archives and U.S. Coast Guard)

Tony was proud of his salad's illustrious career and never resented the imitations he saw around town. He made a living selling them. Tony's restaurant is long gone, but his timeless creation lives on as one of the Columbia's signature dishes. The dressing of oil, vinegar, Romano cheese, and Worcestershire sauce is a Columbia original. It is so popular that the Columbia is the biggest restaurant consumer of Lea & Perrins in the country.

Lighter, more colorful cocktails became popular in the 1970s and 80s. Only a beverage as colorful and pleasing as sangria could do justice to the Columbia's atmosphere. The flavor of full-bodied, sweet Rioja wine mingles with the acidic bite of lemon and orange. The sweetness of cherry and sugar slightly mask the punch of Spanish brandy. The concoction is intriguing, complex, and so balanced that it defies improvement. For many tourists and suburbanites, dinner, entertainment, and a glass of sangria at the Siboney room are worth the journey, however far. Mixed to order tableside, sangria is one of the Columbia's signature libations.

The Cuban mojito cocktail is a fresh delight that can cool the attitudes of the toughest customers. This perfect summer cocktail combines light rum, club soda, mint, simple syrup and lime. The mojito functions only if it is balanced properly.

Mariel

In April 1980, the flood of Cuban refugees continued for several weeks from the port of Mariel. Cubans fled in a desperate flotilla, and Fidel Castro let them go. Family members in the United States suddenly saw hope for relatives still living under the Communist yoke. A desperate boatlift ensued, often undertaken by shrimp trawlers and fishing boats of questionable seaworthiness.

Tampa already was home to thousands of post-Castro refugees who staged loud demonstrations nightly around MacFarlane Park in West Tampa, Ybor's sister Latin quarter. Throngs of Cubans denounced Castro. Caravans of cars wound through the neighborhoods to rally support for Mariel's oppressed. The political fervor ran so high it concerned Tampa's older Cuban immigrants. The city's Latin community united to offer food, shelter, and jobs to 1,000 refugees.

Moved to take action, Cesar announced that he planned to charter a ship to bring dissident Cubans safely to Florida. The response on the part of Tampa's recent Cuban refugees was overwhelming. They thronged the Columbia with their life savings in hand. Many nights of fund-raising proved to be "hectic," as Cesar described it. Tampa's struggling *Nuevo Cubanos* invested more than $400,000 into the venture. "People are coming in with fistfuls of bills," Cesar told a reporter. "The response has been so tremendous." Adela thought Cesar's enterprise was a disaster in the making, a serious risk in the midst of the Columbia's own business struggles. Having been born in Cuba with family still there, Cesar thought the venture a worthy gamble.

Cesar himself threw in tens of thousands of dollars of his own money to bring Cubans to freedom, a heavy investment with no certainty of success. But it was a risk worth taking for Cesar and about 1,500 other Tampa Cubans.

When a former band mate called Cesar to buy passage for twenty-seven relatives, he asked how much it would cost. "To you," Cesar replied reassuringly, "nothing." The band mate insisted on paying his way: $210 per person.

Cesar chartered *Anaqua*, a one-time banana boat, to evacuate as many people as possible. He also hired the small Panamanian liner *Rio Indio* for $340,000, hoping to shuttle two thousand people to Key West. Tampa's Cubans funneled all of their hopes and passions into the *Anaqua* and *Rio Indio*. Adela was furious that her husband had gambled on such a grand scale.

Cesar aroused hope where little existed, but hope can be more painful than despair. He begged the Red Cross for a doctor and supplies for his vessels, which it denied. When the *Anaqua* was about to embark, a freighter crashed into a piling of the Sunshine Skyway bridge, causing it to collapse and clutter the channel. On the second embarkation, the Coast Guard did not permit the *Anaqua* to set out, citing safety regulations. Hundreds of Cuban investors crowded the Columbia, desperate for good news. Cesar allayed their fears: He had a new plan.

The Panamanian liner *Rio Indio* looked promising and could carry far more people. The Cuban Port Authority had already granted the vessel permission to dock. The ship could ferry about fifteen thousand refuges during its month of service.

Success seemed certain until a thunderbolt came from Washington on May 14—President Jimmy Carter ordered the boatlift to end after forty-four thousand refugees swarmed Florida's shores. The incident allowed the Cuban dictator Fidel Castro to rid himself of political prisoners and undesirables while straining resources in the Unites States.

President Carter's statement ended the boatlift. Most people foretold failure for Cesar's evacuation efforts, but he insisted he'd find a way. He faced a tense, worried, and unruly gathering of investors at the Columbia. Some asked for refunds, but the money was already tied up in chartering the vessels.

Cesar left aboard *Rio Indio* for Cuba without taking a delegation of Tampeños, and the investors started to panic. He instead paid for the delegation to travel to Grand Cayman by air and board the *Rio Indio* there. He hoped to dodge any U.S. jurisdiction by embarking from a foreign port. The ploy did not work. No other nation volunteered to accept any refugees taken aboard.

Rio Indio docked at Mariel harbor. A Cuban officer halted the loading operation as it began. Unbeknownst to Cesar, the U.S. government had pressured Panama to revoke the ship's charter, prohibiting trade of any kind. Cesar fruitlessly sought a charter from another country—"any flag that's available," he said—and even looked for another ship. The vessel was useless without international cooperation, and the venture was a complete loss. The *Rio Indio* alone cost $340,000. Together with the *Anaqua* and travel expenses, little remained of the approximately $420,000 Cesar had raised. He gave $80,000 back to investors.

"What can I tell you?" a disappointed Cesar said. "After struggling since the beginning of May, I don't know how I continue. I feel very sad. Only God and Fidel Castro have the ultimate word on whether people will leave Cuba."

The investors took out their rage on Cesar and the Columbia. Unable to retrieve their relatives, they demanded their money back. Some blamed Cesar for the failure ultimately caused by a breakdown of international relations. Whenever he came to the restaurant, people hounded him, women clutched him, and onlookers hurled rumors and threats. Some said they'd burn the Columbia down, or eat meals and refuse to pay.

During the initial excitement of the venture, Cesar gave Richard's home phone number to Hispanic radio stations. At home with her daughters, Melanie coped with incessant telephone calls, and every voice cried in Spanish.

In a business slump himself, Cesar couldn't hope to pay everyone back. Rumors swirled that he had raised more than $600,000 and pocketed some of it. He claimed to have lost $82,000 of his own money in the venture. Richard said to the press: "My father has lost 25 pounds and countless nights of sleep over this." He also lost the confidence of Tampa's *Nuevo Cubanos*.

A lawsuit filed by Cesar's old band mate ground on for the next two years. Testifying in court, Cesar said, "I felt completely destroyed that I couldn't help these people who wanted so desperately to get their families out." He presented documentary evidence that he had spent the money on chartering the ships. The judge cleared Cesar of any wrongdoing.

Looking back, he said: "For the first time in my life, I felt completely defeated. I was extremely depressed for three months. The Mariel boat problem was one of my Don Quixote episodes." He vowed to avoid politics in the future. Don Quixote may have fallen from his horse, but he rode again.

The 4th Generation, 1980–2005

Richard and Casey took on new responsibilities by the 1980s. In Sarasota, Casey's restaurant came into its own with the growth of the city. After Richard opened two successful gourmet nightclubs at the Ybor location, he helped Cesar aggressively expand his empire across Florida: St. Augustine, Harbour Island in Tampa, St. Petersburg, and Sand Key in Clearwater. At its heart, however, "Cesar World" was deeply troubled. After Cesar's death, Richard faced the Columbia's greatest crisis.

The 4th Generation, 1980–2005

 ## Tapas

Every upgrade in the 1970s reminded all that the Columbia would not give up on Ybor City. In 1976, management renovated the café and marketed tapas for the first time. The newspapers tried to use terms that Americans could understand, such as "barhopping" and "pub-crawling," which did not quite capture the spirit of tapas. In Spanish cities, small plates of food accompany friends, wine, and conversation, often lasting late into the night. It is no wonder Spaniards take siestas every afternoon.

The new café boasted a menu of fifteen tapas, including fried squid, stuffed potatoes, and Cuban tamales. Adela looked after the plants, art, and antiques adorning the reborn café. She stocked the room with a Victorian buffet, stained glass, a palm tree, and models of galleons. The facelift beautified the café, but did nothing to better utilize the Columbia's oldest room. That achievement was left for the next generation of the Gonzmart dynasty.

The Café Reborn

Late in 1978, Richard Gonzmart saw a great jazz concert while traveling in New Jersey. The music brought visions of the Columbia hopping to a new beat for a younger set. Today, he admits the selfishness of his idea. Tampa's

Family visits to Spain inspired the Columbia during the 1970s, from new tapas-style appetizers to hand-painted tile.

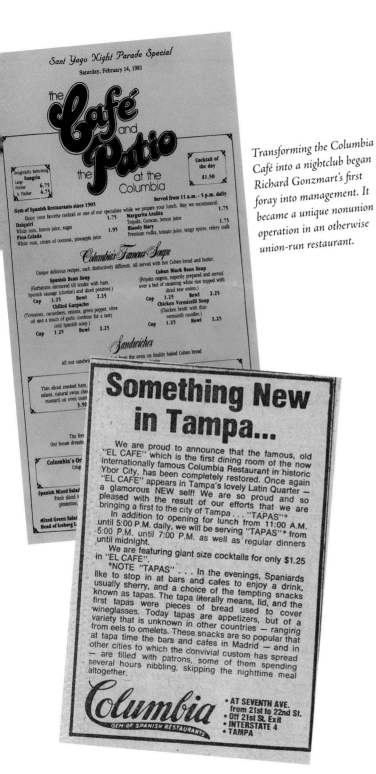

Transforming the Columbia Café into a nightclub began Richard Gonzmart's first foray into management. It became a unique nonunion operation in an otherwise union-run restaurant.

younger adults, his contemporaries, had few hip places to go to besides the bubblegum disco joints. Ybor City remained desolate except for the El Goya Lounge, a gay club down Seventh Avenue housed in the old Las Novedades building.

The 1970s had changed America's cultural landscape, and Cesar's floor show could not leap over the generation gap. While the Columbia carried a brisk dinner trade, no customers ate in the café, which management viewed as a room used only for lunch. Richard envisioned a classy nightclub with fine food, beverage, and music, where young professionals could mingle and celebrate life in their own way. According to Richard, the café had "always been one of my favorite rooms in the restaurant. It hurt me not to see it being used at nighttime."

He obtained permission from Cesar to treat the remodeled Café as a separate eatery. He could experiment with the business on a small scale and try his hand at being a real restaurateur. The Café represented Richard's first opportunity to fly. "He let me do it," Richard remembered, "but I could tell he didn't think it would work. He told my mother he thought it was going to be a fiasco."

Melanie Gonzmart was excited by Richard's ideas. "To me, my husband has always been very ahead of the times. He could foresee the trends. He knew the Columbia had to make a change. We couldn't stay where we were, with this huge menu and old rude waiters."

"That was the time of the union," Melanie reminds us.

The Café offered a new way of doing business. Richard's project was always unique as a nonunion room within a union restaurant. It employed its own servers, bartenders, and chefs. When Richard hired female servers in scant uniforms, they endured relentless sexual harassment from the Columbia's kitchen crew. He intervened several times before the old guard backed down.

INVOICE

The Columbia Restaurant is proud to announce a new addition to Tampa's night life

Warehouse *at the Columbia*

2117 East 7th Avenue

Tampa's only true jazz club
Featuring
"TAPESTRY"
Monday thru Saturday, 9 p.m. - 2 a.m.
Please join us for our grand opening
Thursday evening, February 12th at 9 p.m.
for a champagne celebration.

At its height, Richard's Café and Warehouse became Tampa's most popular clubs for young professional singles.

As this hand-drawn greeting card illustrates, Richard's nonunion operation included female waitresses.

Hasta la vista! See you Soon!

Richard took advantage of the opportunity to update the food and beverages in the Café. The Columbia's food had suffered during the prolonged business slump, so Richard put his culinary and marketing knowledge to work.

Richard Gonzmart: "I thought, hey, I want to get the top dollar spenders in Tampa. We served our famous Australian lobster tails for $14.95; the rest were selling them for $29.95. We sold it. I was selling Dom Perignon for $44 a bottle, which was a lot, but people had money. The restaurants were charging $90 to $95. We were the largest user of Dom Perignon in the state of Florida. Moet et Chandon was not happy, because we were making all the other restaurants look like they were thieves.

"My strategy was like the grocery stores during Thanksgiving. They offered turkey cheaper than I could buy it. It's a lost deal, but they sold you the cranberry sauce. They sold you the vegetables, the salad and so forth. So my idea was just get them in. Because I figured they would have a couple drinks. And all my wine was priced different and different strategy, two or four dollars it would cost. It was getting people to drink and get a certain clientele."

The Café opened to immediate success, garnering rave reviews and offering the "rocking jazz beat" that Richard loved so much. A restaurant critic found that the Café's steak "rivaled that of Bern's," referring to Tampa's famous steakhouse, and that she could not stop tasting her husband's Greek red snapper. "With the prices we're charging," Richard told the critic, "other restaurateurs tell me I'm crazy." The cost of the critic's meal, including two cocktails, a bottle of wine, and her husband's dinner, was a mere $25. The food wowed another critic who attended a jazz brunch at the Café. "My Shrimp Rockefeller melted in my mouth."

Richard shocked the community in 1980 when his Café won the *Tampa Tribune's* annual Cuban Sandwich contest in a landslide. One of his secrets: baking the ham with the bone in. He used the leftover bones for Spanish Bean soup.

A reporter marveled at the Café's success more than a year after it opened: "It is more than a success. [On weekends] the crowd of young adults is shoulder to shoulder and spills over into the other dining rooms and the adjacent bar."

Richard remembers the active dating scene at the Café. "The guys would go there to meet the girls. They'd have two Scotches so they would have the courage to go talk to a girl. A guy came in, and he said to hold this table for him every night. If he didn't come, just charge him. We would get the table all ready. We were serving Dom Perignon left and right. That brought beautiful women. It brought the men. So that had a solid run for about four years."

Richard sought good musical acts when he traveled. He found a band called Street Beat and brought it to the Café. He marketed the band, using radio, mail, television, and fliers. He ran a series of savvy teasers promoting "Street Beat on Broadway," referring to the old name for Seventh Avenue. He kept Tampa guessing.

"Nobody knew what it was, and it was really commercial saying, 'Street Beat straight from New York City featuring Joey Mangione.' I never said it was Chuck Mangione's brother, but everybody assumed it was Chuck Mangione. Everybody turned and said, 'That's Chuck Mangione's brother.' 'Really? I don't know. Is it?' His name was Mangiove, not Mangione. It was my marketing ploy. Then somebody came in that knew Chuck Mangione's brother, whose name is Gap Mangione, and he said, 'That's not Gap!' And I said, 'Who said it was?'" The public responded in droves, and Richard later brought Gap Mangione himself to exploit the publicity.

Publicity was not a problem for long. Melanie Gonzmart: "The band came, and the music started, and we started getting these huge lines, huge lines, because basically there was nowhere to go like that in Tampa. We really were a destination. We are like, 'Oh my goodness, this is really working.'" Richard tried to seat people in La Fonda, which today is part of the Café, but customers could not see the band. Richard needed to expand. The long lines meant lost money.

Richard convinced Cesar to break down the wall separating the Café from the La Fonda, uniting the restaurant's two oldest rooms and doubling the size of his maverick nightclub.

Jazz in the Warehouse

While visiting Orlando on December 30, 1979, Richard saw an excellent jazz fusion band named Tapestry playing at Valentine's, a jazz club. He *had* to hire them. "When are you available?" he asked.

"The second week of February," they replied.

"Well, what do you know," Richard said with a grin. "That's when I'm going to have an opening in my club." The band was too large for the Café; in fact, Richard had no club at all. When they asked the name of his club, he thought fast. "The Warehouse," he said.

Richard spent the first six weeks of 1979 turning the shabby warehouse behind the restaurant into a swanky lounge. With a small budget and no construction permits, he enlisted trusted friends to build the club and keep it a secret. Richard didn't think Cesar would approve of his impulsive gamble. He also wanted to do it on his own.

George Guito remembers scavenging building materials from the ruins of Ybor City. "Richard and myself had gone over and borrowed a bunch of old wood, and we built the warehouse, converted it over to being a lounge. We made the walls ourselves, and we got this old-type wood and we put it up against the walls."

They lifted wood for the bar and tables from a bowling alley that had burned down. Richard paid a Tarpon Springs sawmill for worn, hole-ridden cedar for the interior walls. They found an old bell and mounted it over the bar to celebrate big tips.

The Warehouse also featured décor and knicknacks from the Columbia's storied past: Discarded porcelain lamps, pushcarts, streetlamps, and antique wooden posts. "This club means a lot to me," Richard said at the time. "Being able to use all this old stuff I found in this room when it was a warehouse for the restaurant."

Melanie recalls unexpected visitors at the club three weeks before opening night. "In walk these four gentlemen and they go, 'Hi, we're Tapestry.'" The Warehouse was still in shambles.

Dumbfounded, Richard replied, "Oh yeah, I hired you." He thought up some quick lies: He had fired the last band; he was renovating his club. Finally he confessed that no club yet existed, but it would by the time of their gig. "We'll be ready!" he promised.

When a contract inspector saw the activity in the Warehouse, he asked for Richard's permit. Richard explained the he was merely "fixing up." He fondly recalls, "I was telling him the truth."

The clandestine club could not be kept from Cesar forever. When he saw a newly installed air conditioner outside the Warehouse, he asked his son, "Since when does a warehouse need air-conditioning?" One must still admire Richard's stealth—Cesar did not discover the night club until the week before it was set to open, and Richard had already installed two bathrooms.

A week before opening night, torrential rains flooded the Warehouse. Richard remembers the storms well. "The roof was not sound, and I had eight inches of water in the back of the club. I had to puncture a hole in it so it would drain out. This was the old driveway, so it was at a pitch.

"A story came out about the band because this writer for the *Tampa Tribune* knew who they were. I was excited. Tapestry was coming to Ybor City. This came out before we opened, and so the building inspector came back all pissed off and said, 'I'm going to red-tag you. You can't do anything else.' And I said, 'We're finished.'"

Melanie Gonzmart remembers the importance of Cesar's influence. "Those were the good old days: We start pulling strings and my father-in-law now was in the whole mix. Needless to say, everything worked out fine, and we opened."

Instead of preventing the Warehouse's completion, Cesar hastened it. Whatever he thought of the idea, too much had been invested in Richard's dream to turn back. "He gave me enough rope so I couldn't hang myself," Richard says. "My toes were touching the ground. I couldn't totally destroy everything."

He had created a unique space blending trendy chic, Spanish art, and kicking jazz. That first night, Tapestry left the *Tampa Tribune's* music critic amazed. "High voltage riffs … so tight they squeak. There is simply not a more exciting band playing on a continuous basis in Tampa. Jazz never sounded so good, or sounded in such classy digs as it does at the Warehouse at the Columbia." Bandleader, flutist, and scat singer David Philbrick impressed everyone who saw him. Even Cesar acknowledged his incredible musicianship. The rest of the band were not slouches, either.

A day after opening the Warehouse to great acclaim, Richard told a reporter: "The Café has been very gratifying, and it showed people that it is safe and desirable to come to Ybor City at night for entertainment. The jazz club is something I'm doing for myself; it's me. It's something I've been wanting to do for seven years."

The 85-seat Warehouse brought crowds from day one, and the entertainment was always excellent. Richard used his relationships with radio DJs and concert promoters to get backstage at all the major shows. He always invited the artists to party at the Warehouse and Café, Tampa's most happening night spot. On various occasions, Kenny Loggins, George Benson, Little Milton, Dave Mason, Al Jarreau, and members of Chicago joined the house band for impromptu performances.

His club became so successful that crowds lined up as if it were Studio 54, the notoriously popular New York disco. "It was like three or four years of having a line," Richard said. "We were standing outside and it was like, 'You can come in, and you can come in.' It got to the point that the whole restaurant was full. People just wanted to be in it all over the place." He started to charge a two-dollar cover in an attempt to thin the crowd. Even so, the Warehouse served six hundred to seven hundred customers on good nights.

Richard also offered incentives, such as club memberships and backstage passes for special customers. Club members could run tabs, and some took advantage of the practice. Melanie recalled, "One guy in particular I can think of has never paid us. Hollywood. We call him Hollywood."

Trendiness brought more than deadbeats named Hollywood. Cocaine was practically a national obsession in those years. It permeated the atmosphere of all popular clubs.

"It got so bad," Melanie says, "because this was the early '80s. I would say '82, '83, it got really bad. The cocaine, the cocaine, the cocaine. We would go around the corner to the Patio, we would see people's plates and lines of cocaine. Behind bushes and stuff, all the nooks and crannies."

The sheriff called Richard to inform him that undercover officers had witnessed drug activity in the Columbia. Management responded by hiring security officers and spotters to keep tabs on patrons' activities. After the Columbia closed, it was off-limits to Café and Warehouse patrons, but the drug seemed irrepressible.

Cesar never cared for all the noise and drugs in his restaurant, but he saw the crowds, the kind of crowds he had attracted in the 1950s: young, successful, and a little wild. Impressed with his son's handiwork, he was proud and probably a little jealous.

Richard Gonzmart: "He used to be amazed at how many people would come in. It was packed and people dancing, and he would just stand there in his suit and tuxedo, arms crossed."

Seventy-five Years

The Columbia celebrated its seventy-fifth anniversary in 1980 by declaring "1905 Day" in September, offering food at yesteryear's prices. People lined up along the block and across the street.

Richard experienced a profound moment as he came out of the restroom and saw his parents in the Patio. Behind the bustling scene, Cesar and Adela told Richard how proud he should be of "what we accomplished, overcoming so many obstacles."

"The one hundredth will be great," Richard said, but his parents looked at him as if they knew they wouldn't be there. Old photographs flashed through Richard's mind. Casimiro had missed the seventy-fifth celebration. "It struck me so solid," he remembers. His parents would not live to see the centennial celebration in 2005. "I realized that every quarter century, the generations change."

When Richard and Melanie visited San Francisco in 1980, Cesar and Adela gave the young couple an assignment to visit all the notable restaurants in the area. Richard soon discovered that the number of restaurants exceeded the days of their visit.

Thank — you
for making our
75th Anniversary
Celebration a success!

In 1980, the Columbia threw a seventy-fifth anniversary fiesta not to be forgotten. Every September, the Ybor restaurant celebrates its birthday with yesteryear's prices. The public always responds with enthusiasm.

Due to the great turnout, the Columbia Restaurant, the largest Spanish restaurant in the world, could not accommodate all of you at one time. We thank-you for your patience in waiting to be seated and we hope that our fine food at yesterday's prices was worth waiting for.

We at the Columbia Restaurant would like to express our gratitude to you by having a special anniversary menu which will be available to you for the next 30 days -- still at yesterday's prices.

Columbia Restaurant's 75th Anniversary Celebration

October 10th, 11th & 12th
10 a.m. until closing

**Featuring
Throughout the Weekend**

• Old-Time Street Vendors
• Food Prices of Yesterday
• Continuous Outdoor Entertainment

**Saturday - Oct. 11th
"BACK TO YBOR CITY DAYS"**

• Juried Art Show
• Outdoor Flamenco Review
• Honorary Presentation

Sunday - Oct. 12th

• Jazz Brunch In The Cafe (11 a.m. - 4 p.m.)
• More Outdoor Entertainment

Located In Historic Ybor City On Seventh Avenue

Columbia
GEM OF SPANISH RESTAURANTS

2117 East 7th
248-4961

A visit from a Spanish prince added further pomp to the celebrations.

While his parents beamed with pride during the Columbia's seventy-fifth anniversary celebrations, Richard had a stark realization: They wouldn't live to see the centennial.

Richard Gonzmart: "We're getting down to the end and there's not enough days left. And I'm telling Melanie, 'We're out of time.' We started doubling up. We started eating a lunch at 11, a lunch at 3 or 4, and then dinner at 8 or 9. Chocolate soufflés everywhere. We get to the second meal, we can't really eat. But we eat this food and then we'd get to the third meal, I say, 'How're we going to eat?'"

They do not remember gaining any new trade secrets, but Richard and Melanie put on ten pounds each in as many days.

Melanie Gonzmart: "The last thing we want to do is disappoint his parents."

The Rise of Sarasota

Empty lots and shell roads. Lonely summer beaches and abandoned shacks. The old ruin of the Ringling Hotel warned against hubris. The Columbia stood in St. Armands Circle, surrounded by empty lots of shells and weeds.

Casey recognized a complete lack of entertainment in Sarasota. With Cesar's violin still ringing in his ears, Casey sought out music of his own. "We thought of flamenco and things like that. The history of the Columbia in Ybor City hadn't been dancers, it had been orchestras, bands that played for the customers to dance. So in another strange way, history kind of repeated itself, because rather than trying to have performances, we started very small with just a single entertainer." The entertainment evolved into duos and trios. Much as Cesar had years before, the bands mixed pop music with Latin beats.

The customers wanted to dance, so Casey remodeled and set up disco balls and strobe lights. Trios and ensembles serenaded diners with what Casey describes as "a live sound with modern music, a Latin beat. One number might be an American disco song, next one would be a song sung in Spanish with conga drums, and people liked that. At nine each evening, the venerable Columbia became a trendy disco called The Patio. "Some people would go to The Patio at night and not know it was the Columbia Restaurant."

Casey cultivated more than disco balls and good food. He operated with complete autonomy: He and his staff

Under Casey's keen leadership, the Sarasota location became enmeshed into the community and catered to sun-loving tourists.

created the recipes, implemented management decisions, and remodeled at will. His chef Frank Lorenzo came from Cuba. Known as Guantánamo, Frank had served there with the Navy. Casey Gonzmart: "We had our own recipes. It had the same name, but it was made like Frank Lorenzo would make it. He made a great beef stew."

Casey wanted to further adapt the restaurant to Sarasota's social climate. By the mid-1980s, music was lowered in priority at Sarasota. Inspired by his travels, Casey made a special effort to feature fresh seafood. He created an oyster bar and took advantage of great stone crab suppliers. Fresh crabs beckoned pedestrians from a large window's ice display. Casey's Stone Crab Corner took advantage of that crab's season: October 15 through May 15, a perfect match for the inundation of tourists.

Casey Gonzmart: "All of a sudden, that took off. When you're living here and you're on a roll, you think you're invincible. We became the place to eat stone crab, not just the place to have a Cuban sandwich or the place to have paella, but we were the place that people came and danced at night until three in the morning. We were the place that people came and had seafood at the bar or at the table. Great food prepared by a wonderful chef. The timing was incredible.

"You have opportunity and you act on it. We didn't always ask [Cesar] for permission. It was almost, you ask for forgiveness sometimes because we weren't doing that great everywhere. It may not have been the right choice. From a standpoint of your intuition and your heart, you knew it was worth it to roll the dice."

Casey's keen observation of Sarasota's clientele over the years served the Columbia well. The reluctant errand boy became his own man in Sarasota. "My three older children were born in Sarasota, and then I just embraced it, my friendships."

Spring training by Major League Baseball teams provided new opportunities. The Chicago White Sox trained in Sarasota then. "We became great friends with the owners of the team, with the players. They came to hang out. My son Casey became the bat boy in spring training for the Chicago White Sox. They would have all their parties at the Columbia." Like his grandfather Casimiro, Casey developed a passion for baseball.

Also like Casimiro, Casey relentlessly experimented with his restaurant. "We always wanted to do something; we never settled down. I never grew up, actually. We called it dancing as fast as you can. It wasn't dancing, it was working. We just called it dancing, always trying to move faster."

"We would get complimented in the winter time, because people come in on a cold night, and we would sit them at the table, and the seat was warm. 'That's what we like about this place, we can come in here, we're cold, we can sit down, and get warm.' The reason the seat was warm is because the other person had just gotten up, and we wouldn't take a second to sit the next four people down. That's what we kept doing. We kept trying to overperform by doing the next thing."

Tourists came by the thousands from Germany and the British Isles. Europe discovered Florida's affordable delights. Best of all, they usually took their long vacations over the summer, when snowbirds nested in their northern homes.

The Europeans wanted badly to dine al fresco in the dog days of Florida summer. Mystified but determined to provide outdoor seating, Casey ran into an immediate obstacle. A county code made it illegal for a restaurant to serve food outside. The misguided officials who thought it up assumed any food taken out of doors would be "contaminated." County officials then amended the measure by allowing the Columbia to serve covered dishes. By uncovering their own food, patrons became legally responsible for the risk of contamination. No one familiar with Florida's bizarre politics would be surprised at this story, and Casey used the covers. "It's a ridiculous story," he admits. Laws to curb the dangers of dining outdoors have since relaxed.

In an effort to cash in on outdoor dining, Casey proposed renovations to the landlord. The Columbia would pay for the improvements, and the landlord would own them. Despite those conditions, the landlord denied the proposal. Al fresco dining waited until a new investor bought the property and immediately approved the plans. By then, Casey had outgrown his original plan and gave it a complete makeover.

"Over ten years, yes, the blueprints were faded already. Good things happen sometimes, because in those ten years we had evolved. When I opened those blueprints again, what I had envisioned ten years before wasn't the best idea, you know. There were other things, different improvements that could be done.

"We only put seven tables outside. Home run. Everybody wanted to sit outside. Even though the biggest thing to happen to the Columbia in Ybor City was inventing air-conditioning, the most important thing to happen in Sarasota was sitting outside in the hot sun. I don't know why, but the Europeans love it." Today, more than half of the Sarasota restaurant consists of outdoor seating.

The Columbia's Sarasota colony took more than thirty years to blossom, and today it is a pillar of the Columbia empire. "Yes, we may have made a mistake, or we may have jumped the gun," Casey says of the Sarasota experiment. "We had good intuition, and even though it took awhile, we never would have had the opportunity had someone not had the foresight. Even when things weren't obvious."

Expansion

In 1960, Cesar and Adela took the family on a vacation to Quebec in his 1959 Cadillac Sedan DeVille. They wanted to visit the most historic cities on the east coast. Pedro Menéndez de Avilés founded St. Augustine, America's oldest city, in 1565 after destroying a French colony nearby. The family stopped in St. Augustine on the first day of their vacation.

Richard Gonzmart: "Upon arriving in the city limits, we were ready for lunch when my dad came upon a city policeman. He told my mom, 'Adela, he is sure to be able to tell us where the best Spanish restaurant is in the city.'"

Without hesitation, the patrolman replied, "Mister, if you drive 189 miles down south to Tampa you will find the best Spanish restaurant. It is called the Columbia.'"

Cesar dreamed of opening a restaurant in St. Augustine some day. He fantasized about the company surviving long enough to become the nation's oldest restaurant in its oldest city. The glorious epics of history entranced him.

Cesar scribbled on the back of a business card and handed it to the patrolman. His next visit to the Columbia was on Cesar Gonzmart.

"Keep on sending everyone down to the Columbia," Cesar said. He promised to build a restaurant in St. Augustine some day.

In 1981, a Mr. Cole dined at the Ybor Columbia. He represented a man named Lawrence Lewis. He introduced himself to Richard and explained that he wanted to bring the Columbia to St. Augustine. Cesar had heard many unrealistic proposals before, and he never took them seriously. Richard had never heard of Lewis, but he told Cesar about the visitor's idea. Cesar let Mr. Cole wait for two or three hours.

GALA GRAND OPENING CELEBRATION
JUNE 29 & 30, 1983

In his own way, Cesar "discovered" St. Augustine, opening a restaurant there in 1983. With Richard's hard work, Cesar realized his dream of opening Florida's oldest restaurant in America's oldest city.

Richard Gonzmart: "My dad kind of blows it off. I said, 'This gentleman is still waiting for you.' My dad said, 'Oh God, I forgot.' He's still there. 'He's sitting at table 10 in the Don Quixote,' I tell my dad. So we start talking to the guy. So many other people always said they had a deal for restaurants, and usually it wasn't true. My dad really doesn't believe him, figuring this is just another guy full of hot air."

But Lewis was no lightweight. He was an heir to the Florida railroad baron Henry Flagler, Cole explained, and controlled the foundation named after his famous great uncle. And Lewis wanted the best Spanish restaurant to open in St. Augustine.

Cesar liked the idea of opening a restaurant in the historic district, but had to beg off the idea for lack of funds. Unless Lewis could offer incentives, Cesar could not consider the deal. "No problem," Cole answered.

Several months passed.

Hugh Culverhouse, a respected tax attorney and owner of the NFL Tampa Bay Buccaneers, a team in the National Football League, called Cesar to set up a meeting with Lewis. It took place at the University Club, which overlooks Tampa in a prominent skyscraper.

The expansion to St. Augustine rekindled Cesar's Don Quixote imagination and tested Richard's resolve.

Lewis talked so nonchalantly about building a Columbia that the family became unnerved. Richard: "We looked at one another wondering, 'Who is this person? Is he for real?' Honestly, we began to question if he was just a dreamer or a nut, for that matter."

During a short break in the meeting, Culverhouse discreetly took Cesar aside and said, "Mr. Lewis has *a lot of money*. He's my best client." Florida's oldest restaurant in the nation's oldest city seemed to be within his grasp.

Once Lewis decided upon the Columbia in St. Augustine, he did everything in his power to make it happen. He was indeed kind to the Columbia: He built the restaurant, which could seat seven hundred, charged no rent until the restaurant profited, and asked little compensation for his trouble. Best of all, the Gonzmarts would have an option to buy the property and building for the original purchase price within ten years. "It was a Cesar deal if there ever was one," Richard remembers. Historic St. George Street—part living museum, part shopping mall—was just what Cesar had in mind for Ybor City in the 1970s. It seems

fitting he would find a new home in St. Augustine, redeveloping a historic district.

The Gonzmarts unwittingly stepped into St. Augustine's hotly contested politics of preservation. The city's Historic Architecture Review Board monitored the design and construction of the new restaurant. The board disliked large buildings because historic St. Augustine had few like the proposed 23,000-square-foot restaurant. So the Columbia hired local architect Craig Thorn to design a facility that looked like several different buildings from the outside. Some bemoaned the "Florida boomtime Spanish" design of the St. George Street development. Inside, the Columbia St. Augustine pays homage to the original, with the same intriguing fountain.

Crash Banquet

Cesar took Casey to Mexico to purchase antiques and fixtures for the latest edition of the Columbia. Richard stayed behind in Tampa to keep an eye on operations. An important banquet for fledgling airline Air Florida was scheduled at the Ybor restaurant that Friday. As Richard helped prepare the restaurant for the 500-person event, he got a call. The Sarasota restaurant's kitchen had caught fire.

Richard rushed to Sarasota in his new red Porsche 944. There, city officials insisted on closing for two weeks to repair the kitchen.

"I said, 'No, we're not,'" Richard remembers. The kitchen may have burned, but the prep kitchen remained untouched. He devised a limited menu to sustain the restaurant while repairs commenced.

Then he got back into his Porsche, bound for Tampa. A police officer on the circle flagged him down and said, "That car must go really fast."

"Sure it does," Richard said.

Richard Gonzmart: "I'm going back to Tampa on [U.S.] 41, and I'm hurling. I've got to get there. I feel this pressure. I'm going before the Ringling School of Art, a pickup truck is crossing 41 and stops in the middle. I'm not wearing my seat belt. I brace my arms so that I'm prepared. I hit him broadside, hit the windshield. My car is totaled." At 70 miles an hour, Richard slammed into the pickup truck. "That's when I believed that Porsche was a great car. I lived without wearing a seat belt.

"Then I called the dining room manager, Emilio Quadra, to get me. He and the police wanted to take me to the hospital; I said 'I have to go to the Columbia.' This is the dedication or the craziness I had. I said, 'No, I can't go to the hospital. I have to go to the Columbia.' On the way back to Tampa, I'm fainting, fading. Bad shape. I tell Mr. Quadra, 'You have to take me to the Porsche dealership,' and I bought another car.

"When I got home, I wasn't able to do anything. Then they did brain scans. Of course, I had a serious concussion."

Days later, wearing a neck brace, Richard drove to open the St. Augustine location in his brand-new Porsche. Air Florida went bankrupt. The six first-class tickets to Madrid they promised as payment for the banquet never materialized.

Anxiety

The St. Augustine venture was where Richard says he obtained his master's degree in business. The seasoned entrepreneur and one-time football star felt the pressure.

Construction began in July 1982. He told Melanie he'd be gone to St. Augustine only a few days. There, he assembled a staff and management team for the restaurant, which was slated to open in May or June 1983. Richard trained the staff, but the general contractor fell behind in the construction schedule. Each day of delay cost the company.

Finally, Richard announced a grand opening party on the Fourth of July, St. Augustine's biggest weekend of business. Hugh Culverhouse and other notables attended the VIP event. Adela took Melanie aside and said, "I've done the seating, I'm going to put you next to Mr. Culverhouse."

Richard coped with chaos at home while Cesar and Casey took a relaxing business trip to Mexico.

After he opened the St. Augustine restaurant, Richard bordered on a nervous breakdown. He suffered from panic attacks before the medical profession had a name for them.

Intimidated at having to sit beside such an important guest, Melanie begged off. "I can't do this, Mom, I just can't."

Melanie Gonzmart: "I am a kid, *okay?* I am 28. I'm like, 'Please, Mom, don't do this to me.' She goes, 'Look, shut up. You can do this, Melanie. Who the hell am I going to put next to him?' Then I realize this guy is like everybody else. I mean, he was *schmoozing* me. He was a very sweet guy."

Cesar, Adela, and the Heros booked hotel rooms to spend opening weekend in St. Augustine. Charlie Hero, who came on the pretext of helping to celebrate, picked up parts at the hardware store. In the coming days, he resolved all the plumbing issues, including the fountain centerpiece, which Charlie remembers "had to be complete!"

Adela did much more than seat guests. She rolled up her sleeves and set to work in the kitchen. While making the picadillo, she found the kitchen short on beef. She dispatched Charlie to the grocery store to buy forty pounds of ground beef. She also showed Richard's kitchen crew

how to make one of her specialties: *brazo gitano*, or "gypsy's arm," a rolled cake studded with fruit that resembles the bejeweled arms of Gypsies. Today, the Columbia's version is covered in meringue, flambéed with Kirchwasser and topped with a luscious strawberry sauce.

The opening party went smoothly, and the restaurant performed well. Perhaps the extra days of training had paid off. Still, the delay brought heavy financial losses, and much of the spending was on credit. The community response fell short of expectations. Some locals were irritated that Columbia employees had the gall to speak Spanish. Some hissed, "Speak American, boy!" St. Augustine was still a staunchly conservative Southern town with a handful of traffic lights.

Determined to get the restaurant off to a good start, Richard asked Melanie to live there and bring the children. They spent that summer in a condominium, and Richard realized how relaxing it was to be out of his father's shadow. He loved Cesar dearly, but often felt stifled expectations. He also enjoyed the anonymity of living in a new town.

There was some stress. His management team did not get along. The young employees often engaged in drug use and theft. In August, Richard decided to stay in St. Augustine for as long as another year. Melanie moved to St. Augustine and enrolled their daughters Lauren, six, and Andrea, four, in school there. It took two years for Richard to resolve the internal issues at the restaurant.

One day, he took an espresso break, overlooking the courtyard. "I started getting very anxious, and I didn't understand that feeling. I thought I was having a heart attack. Then, that next night, I was not feeling comfortable. The next morning, I wake up having the same feeling. I don't tell my wife. I drive myself to the hospital. They put me in cardiac care. My blood pressure was through the roof. The mind is so strong. My mind had checked me out. I was in CCU for five days, and then I went home."

The tough opening of the St. Augustine location is where Richard likes to think he earned his master's degree in business.

Melanie Gonzmart: "Richard was always a success. He was a tremendous player, and he'd always been successful. He had severe anxiety and stress coming at him from all angles—the combination of the lack of sales, my father-in-law, his feeling of poor performance. He was very overweight. I missed him so terribly when he worked, so I'm sure that I contributed. And he just broke down, that was it."

Richard Gonzmart: "I was convinced I was dying. I did not know I was hyperventilating. I could not leave my house.

This went on and on. Melanie would say, 'Let me drive you to work.' We'd go about three or four blocks—I'd say, 'Just take me back.' I couldn't breathe. I couldn't take it.

"This is the most difficult time for me. I went there, opened this restaurant, had challenges, corrected it, and when I corrected it my mind said, 'Okay, checking out.' A breakdown of some sort. You have to rebound back, can't check out. That is where you gain your strength. My mind is set that when it gets tough, when it's challenging, that's the best.

"To say that I don't ever suffer from panic attacks would be a lie. I eventually learned how to deal with it. You stop breathing, creating a lack of oxygen to the brain which causes light-headedness. You feel a sense of fatality, the worst feeling in the world. I talk to people that have had it. I will sit there to make them understand, 'Hey, it is okay. I've the pain right now. But I can deal with that.'"

Richard suffered from panic attacks before the medical profession had a name for them. Cesar thought he suffered from a weak will, but his problem was genuine. He saw a psychologist, who identified the sources of his anxiety. Through bio-feedback therapy, Richard gained a measure of control. He learned to change the rhythm of his breathing.

He remembers seeing a movie with his family in St. Augustine. When he saw a scene in which a son confronted his father, Richard suffered a panic attack. He left the theater with his embarrassed family, but with a new insight. The episodes stemmed from his strained relationship with Cesar.

Richard Gonzmart: "I realized it had to do with my father. Ashamed or embarrassed that maybe I failed him. My fear was always that I wasn't making my father happy, because I truly admired my dad. To me, Cesar was larger than God. My dad admired me and appreciated me, but I just

It took strong women like Adela to raise a family in the shadow of the Columbia.

never wanted to disappoint him. This was a two-year-long struggle."

Cesar beckoned Richard back to Tampa, asking him to run the Columbia's new commissary, and to help open a restaurant at Harbour Island. Richard Gonzmart: "I'm feeling this pressure. I didn't want to get involved. I couldn't handle it."

Cesar probably sensed that he was part of his son's problems. Melanie Gonzmart: "Cesar wrote him a very beautiful letter, which I still have. 'You're my son, I love you.' I'm sure he knew he had been very hard on Richard, and he had. It's a very beautiful letter."

Richard returned to Tampa in 1985, uncomfortable in Cesar World. Therapy with a counselor provided Richard with more insight and peace of mind. He found fulfillment and approval in his work and became a whiz at opening restaurants over the next few years. Richard's hard work

and attention to detail secured the Columbia's new outpost in St. Augustine.

Richard Gonzmart: "My dad wanted to buy the land across the street [in 1987], and my brother and I convinced him that we should wait to see how the business would go. This proved to be a mistake, as we had agreed we would pay the appraised value. Of course, when we decided to purchase, the appraised value had significantly increased due to the new world-famous Columbia Restaurant! Go figure: We had been our best and worst enemy. We bought the property anyway, at an increased value of 40 percent."

The logic of Lawrence Lewis's lavish incentives suddenly made sense. The Gonzmarts bought the Columbia St. Augustine for $2.4 million. They saved about 40 percent— $1 million—because they purchased the building for the original value.

Domestic Demands

The Columbia demanded an incredible amount of time and effort. Every owner found it difficult to have a life outside the restaurant: Casimiro poured his entire livelihood into the business; Casimiro Jr. slept in his office or leaning on the register. Cesar ran the restaurant by day and entertained patrons by night. His sons rarely saw him for extended periods outside the restaurant.

Nurturing a marriage and children and running the Columbia were possible only with strong women running the household. If Casimiro Jr. obsessed about the restaurant, his wife, Carmen, loved their family just as strongly. Adela, the independent classical pianist, reinvented herself as housewife, cook, and grand dame of the Columbia.

Richard and Melanie adapted to the roles in which they were cast by the business and family. He picked up bread in the morning, opened the restaurant, and stayed until closing. Being the son and co-owner did not grant Richard any breaks; it forced him to work harder than a wage-earner. Without the leadership of hired managers, the Gonzmarts shouldered the Columbia's demands on their own. As the restaurant expanded into new cities, so did the burden on the family.

The family grew as well. Melanie gave birth to Lauren in 1976 and Andrea in 1979. She knew the business required a good deal of the family's time. She soon found herself shocked at how little time remained in the men's lives.

"I said to Richard, 'I don't see you all week. You work horrific hours,' because sometimes he'd go early in the morning, and then he'd close at night. That is the restaurant business. I don't remember him eating at home with us for dinner during the week ever, *ever*. We didn't have the management team that we have now, so therefore he closed. Cesar played violin every night, except Sunday."

Melanie did not realize how much the family cared for her—especially Adela—until the death of her father. "Once my father passed away, they were there for me in a heartbeat. He died very early in the morning, and by the time I got home from the hospital they were waiting for me, and they scooped me up and they took care of me.

"From then on," Melanie remembers, "things really changed." She found a new acceptance of her life, of the demanding business. "I think I grew up, and I was able to accept what they were doing, they were doing it out of their love. They took care of me, they took care of my mom."

Adela could see her big heart in Melanie, and they soon became the best of friends. "Even when Richard would give me trouble I would call her and complain," Melanie says. "She'd say, 'My son's a pain.'"

Children presented their own demands. One difficult lunch at the Columbia stands out in Lauren's mind: "I was with my grandmother, my mother, my sister, and I didn't want to go. I was probably three years old, having a fit.

I wanted to eat at McDonald's, and we were in the car. I didn't like the food at the Columbia. My mother is trying to be a good mother and tell me no, I have to eat at the Columbia because that's our restaurant and we need to like that food. My grandmother said, 'Just get her McDonald's, and we'll take it to the restaurant.'

"That was the one and only time that I was allowed—I can still remember the table we sat at in the Café. I was still kind of nasty even though I got my McDonald's, and I sat there and ate. My mother was not happy with me, but because my grandmother was there, she allowed it to occur."

If Melanie missed her husband during the week, Lauren missed both of her parents on weekend nights. "Our parents went out literally every Friday and Saturday night," Lauren said. "We would go pick out our TV dinners. He would bring home McDonald's or Burger King, come to pick up Mom so he could just go back to the restaurant again. 'We're sorry we're leaving you… and I'm sorry I haven't seen you all day because I've been working. Here's your McDonald's.'

"I was like, 'Why do you have to go?' They would try to explain, 'This is the business we're in, we have to entertain, and we have to be there.' As a child you don't understand that. Now as an adult, looking back, I can understand. It was that kind of business. It was appropriate for that time in their life and for the business.

"It was a larger-than-life thing, because we would sit there in the bathroom and watch our mother. She'd get very glamorous and her hair and her curlers. She would come out with these beautiful outfits. It was very exciting. Meanwhile, we would be sitting on the bed watching *Dance Fever*, we'd watch the *Solid Gold* dancers, we'd watch *Happy Days*. The same routine every Friday and Saturday night."

Melanie relished the opportunity to let loose and talk to adults for a change.

The family's move to St. Augustine allowed them to spend more time together. The Gonzmarts found a closed social scene in St. Augustine, a city ruled by Crackers, not Spaniards. Melanie missed Adela's help with the girls. The new restaurant was small enough—and initially slow enough—to allow quality visits with Richard in the afternoon. Every day after school, Melanie took the girls to the restaurant. The young ones found friends and played in a small park across the street.

Andrea Gonzmart: "Nothing ever happened there."

Lauren Gonzmart: "My mother hated it. I thought it was a cool place to grow up as children. We lived right on the beach. You could ride your cars on the beach. I was a six-year-old with my own surfboard. We lived in a nice little place."

Best of all, Lauren and Andrea spent much more time with their parents than before.

The family returned from St. Augustine in 1985. Richard had tried to sell his Tampa home because he once planned

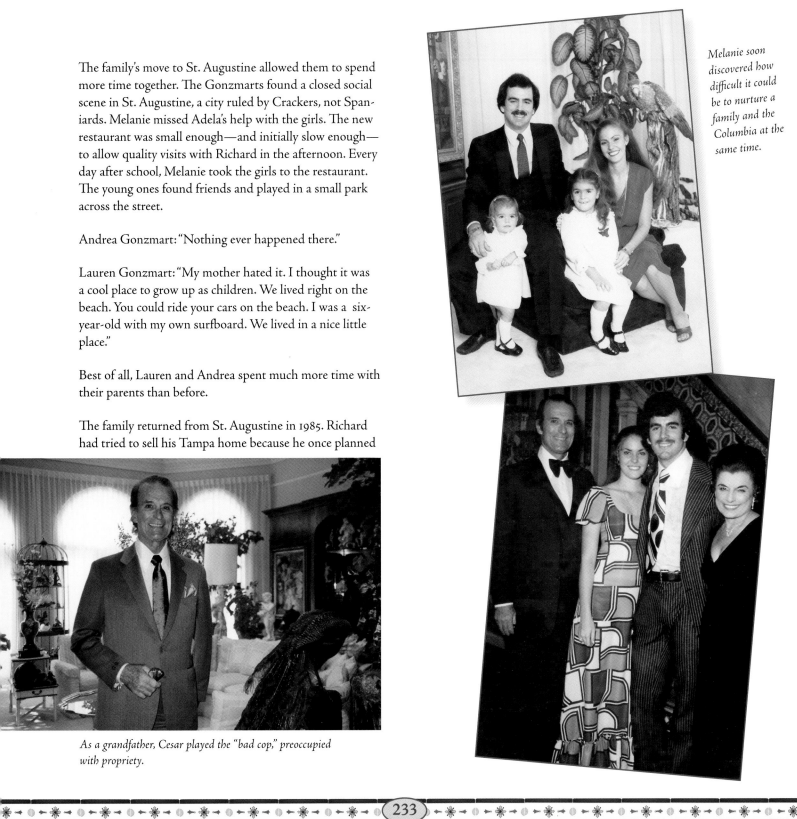

Melanie soon discovered how difficult it could be to nurture a family and the Columbia at the same time.

As a grandfather, Cesar played the "bad cop," preoccupied with propriety.

Adela indulged her grandchildren, but Cesar was often too formal to be as much fun.

on building one in St. Augustine. His home in the Tampa neighborhood Lago Vista went unsold, so the family moved back in.

"Our house [in Tampa] is empty and we move back in," Melanie remembers. "The children get back to school where they are supposed to."

Lauren had grown into the Columbia. She could even visit without a McDonald's Happy Meal. She gained a new appreciation for her grandfather Cesar when she attended his show with grandmother Adela.

"I am sure I had seen him perform before that, but I guess this is the first real 'Wow!' moment, where he's on the stage doing the "Yellow Rose of Texas." He's in his glory and just enjoying it, and the crowd is enjoying him. I really appreciated it at that point. I was old enough to really go, 'Wow, this is my grandfather, and he can perform and play this violin.' I can again remember the table we were sitting at, ringside at the Siboney Room. I just thought it was so cool."

By the time Lauren and Andrea were old enough to go out, Adela took them to dinner every weekend at the Siboney. Lauren: "We would go for the show. We'd probably fall asleep. We'd end up sleeping on the chairs."

Andrea: "Or they used to put us in my grandfather's office. It had a nice couch and a big TV. It was awesome. We'd fall asleep, and they didn't have to worry about us. We would stay all night."

Lauren and Andrea remember how much fun their grandmother Adela was, and how serious Cesar seemed. He didn't even own any casual wear, except for the time he wore a guayabarra shirt to Disney World.

Lauren: "Always dressed to a 'T.' He was either like Hugh Hefner in his pajamas, or he was decked out in his beautiful suits."

Andrea: "You never saw him wearing anything but those two things. I remember eating breakfast at their kitchen table, and he would sit there and talk in Spanish about us! And you could not understand him."

Lauren: "I had already kind of started to figure out what they were saying. We would go there, and eat a bagel or a bowl of cereal. He would sit there and criticize and go [makes fast Spanish sounds], telling my grandmother, 'They should be eating eggs and ham and bacon! What kind of breakfast is this? This isn't going to give them their energy.'"

Andrea: "She's giving us café con leche, and we're six years old."

Lauren: "He was just so prim and proper and wanted everything so perfect and by the book. You have to put up this appearance and maintain it at all times. You don't do certain things and you *do* do certain things."

Lauren especially remembers one night at her grandparents' when a friend spent the night. Adela and Andrea went to sleep by midnight, and Cesar came home shortly after. What he found in his kitchen shocked and outraged him.

"I was probably eight or nine years old. We're sitting there in her kitchen on the floor," Lauren said of herself and her friend. "She [Adela] had this candy cabinet where she had all of these little miniature candy bars and she had a bar refrigerator full of Sunkist and Coke, every kind of sugary soda you can imagine. We didn't have this at home. We weren't allowed that kind of soda.

"So he comes home and it's like midnight and we're watching *Saturday Night Live* or something. And my grandmother is asleep. Candy wrappers all over the floor. Empty soda cans all over.

"He was so mad. I will never forget his little speech. 'Girls, there are things that are right, and there are things that are wrong, and this is very wrong. I don't know what you girls think you're doing.'"

She laughs about it now, but she was surprised at the time.

"He was so flabbergasted that these little girls had just consumed all this sugar."

Clearly, Cesar played the bad cop, and Adela just the opposite.

"With my grandmother it was anything goes, you know?" Lauren says. "Every time we were with her, we'd go shopping."

Andrea: "She would take us to get burgers and I mean it was always fun, fun, fun."

Lauren: "Yes, it was always Toys 'R' Us, get whatever you want, as much as you want. We would go buy shoes and clothes, and it was like a new wardrobe every time we were with her. She just loved to do that stuff with us."

Harbour Island

Even with the Columbia as a tenant, the upscale development at Tampa's Harbour Island struggled after opening in 1985. Parker's Lighthouse, the other large restaurant there, failed, and several other shops left in the first year. It had space for fifty stores, and ten shut their doors in the last two months of 1986. Cesar expressed some disappointment in his fellow tenants: "We were given a beautiful building, beautiful parking, and a spectacular location. The merchants have missed the pass. They had the enthusiasm, but they lacked the knowledge, the capital, and the quality."

Cesar was not spooked easily, and thought the situation would turn around, especially when the Tampa Convention Center opened across the Hillsborough River. He finally got the checkered floors he always wanted. Casimiro had forbidden them when they built the Siboney Room. Cesar got his wish when he renovated the Harbour Island space.

Back in Ybor City, Richard and Cesar installed a commissary beside the kitchen to prepare soups and sauces for Harbour Island two miles away. They shipped the product to the restaurant in iced bags. It was never frozen. Management installed an expensive chiller to cool the bags in bulk.

The Gonzmarts opened a bar next to the Harbour Island Columbia. They had recently developed the new concept after being inspired by a daiquiri bar in Miami's Bayside development. "They're just serving frozen daiquiris in a clear plastic cup," Richard recalls. "Ice coming down from a Plexiglas tube." It seemed so easy—and so profitable. Premixed slush took all the skill out of tending bar, and people loved the sweet icy drinks.

Columbia

GEM
OF SPANISH RESTAURANTS
SINCE 1905

LOCATED ON BEAUTIFUL HARBOR ISLAND

Explore the cuisine of old world Spain. Savor our traditional dishes…authentically prepared from fine, fresh ingredients…and served with a courtly flair.

So set your course for an adventure in fine dining and try us the next time you'd like to discover something really special.

Bring this card when you dine at The Columbia Restaurant and receive a pitcher of our house beverage.

Columbia Restaurant, 1008 The Market on Harbor Island, Tampa, FL 33602   (813) 229-2992

3084

The American Express® Card
is always welcome…
Don't leave home without it.®

© American Express Travel Related Services Co., Inc., 1985

AMERICAN EXPRESS
3712 95006
C F FROST

The Harbour Island location made a splash during Gasparilla festivities.

The Gonzmarts created their own breezy daiquiri concept. While meeting with their architect, Norman Staehr, in Orlando, Cesar and his sons debated what to call it. Cesar and Richard had favorite names but could not agree upon which.

Richard Gonzmart: "My dad and I were fighting back and forth. My brother barks out, 'I don't care if ya'll want to call it Cha-Cha Mambo Coconuts!'"

Cesar and Richard looked at one another with wide eyes. "What a great name!" Even the architect liked it.

Casey could scarcely believe his ears. "You guys are crazy!" he said.

They shortened the name to Cha Cha Coconuts, and a new business was born. In a small space—only 1,400 square feet—they built the bar beside the Columbia. Featuring the slushy daiquiris, appetizers, sandwiches, and light entrées, Cha Cha Coconuts provided people with a funky Caribbean feel.

The extremely tight kitchen space for the bar at Harbour Island dictated a limited menu. The Harbour Island kitchen space was a mere eight by four feet. To conserve space and money, the Columbia shared restrooms with the bar. Richard Gonzmart: "The walls were painted on the Cha Cha Coconuts side so that the door blended right in. On the Columbia side it was mirrored on the door." The facilities also shared the same food and liquor licenses.

Then the Gonzmart flair for the dramatic came to the fore. The family wanted to be open in time for the Gasparilla invasion in February, one of the busiest days for Tampa's bars. Harbour Island is in the epicenter of the party, with plenty of docking opportunities for yachts and party boats. Low on time and money, Richard finished the facility, but could not obtain the certificate of occupancy. The inspections—electric, plumbing, health, etc.— involved too much time from too many government agencies.

Like a band of guerilla fighters, Richard and his crew unofficially opened Cha Cha Coconuts for Gasparilla and brought in $40,000 that day without selling a crumb of food.

The next day, the fire marshal walked in and told Richard, "You guys were open. I was here." Richard denied it, and gestured toward the empty bar. No liquor or mess could be found. The Gonzmarts had dodged a bullet. Most importantly, they made enough money to fully renovate Cha Cha Coconuts and complete their Harbour Island project.

Richard Gonzmart: "Cesar was very proud. He was very, very proud." The Columbia's bold expansion helped restore confidence in the Harbour Island development.

The Fifth Generation

Young Lauren pined for her father, Richard, and became curious about what he did all day at the restaurant. Sometimes, she and her sister, Andrea, still wonder what Richard does in his blinding rush of frenetic activity and meetings.

Lauren: "I would start telling him, 'I want to go to work with you.' By the time I was ten I was working in the [Ybor City] office. He would let me go one day a week for half of a day. We'd get up early, he would take me to the produce market, we'd go in, he would check the food into the kitchen. He would go through his daily routine, show me things, check on things and then by lunchtime, my mother would come pick me up and take me home.

"So that was my first way of getting introduced into what he did, how he did it, why he did it. Because it did con-

sume so much of him that I wanted to understand. What was it that he was doing and why was it taking so much time? I thought it was cool. I wanted to keep going back.

"I wanted to make money as a little girl. At ten, after probably driving him crazy enough, he told me, 'Fine, you can come to work.' I would ride to work in the morning with him, go in the office, and it was very cramped. They were all very patient and tolerant of me, and they'd give me like a gigantic stack of invoices and they'd make me file every single one of them and make me do copies. Whatever they needed.

As the Gonzmart sisters grew up, they took odd jobs at the Columbia. Left to right: Lauren, Melanie, Richard, and Andrea.

Young Andrea Gonzmart, far right, danced in the Ballet Folklorico troupe, which showcased the traditional culture of Ybor City's Latin immigrants.

"When I was twelve, I was well-spoken enough and had enough of a presentation that I could start seating people and greeting. I was able to make the move to become a real hostess and manage the dining room, judging how to run it and seat the tables. By the time I was fifteen or sixteen, when I was in high school, I was still working there on the weekends and definitely during the summer. I was able to be more a supervisor and be able to do the manager-in-training stuff."

Andrea, on the other hand, had no interest in working. "I think they *made me* go to work at 10 [laughs]. I would be like, 'Please fire me. I'm done!' I didn't want to work. I was just happy that he went to work and came home. I would file. I hostessed for awhile, and he'd fire me. I'd go back to work the next summer. In high school, I did cashiering. I don't know how they trusted me with that.

"There used to be this cashier booth in the kitchen that literally every single transaction, every single server had to go through the cashier. Oh, and God forbid if you made a mistake." The booth Andrea remembers dated back to Casimiro Jr.'s kitchen secretaries, or checkers.

Andrea found she liked dancing far more than running a cash register. "I was always into the piano, ballet, tap dancing, all the girly-girl stuff. Lauren and I started taking Flamenco lessons together. I kept on doing it, and that's when I did my big debut at the restaurant."

Adela had helped found a dance troupe called Ballet Folklorico, which featured dances to represent Ybor City's diverse ethnic heritage. Andrea joined as the group's youngest member. "I was definitely the performer and the ham out of the group."

The distinctive Pier in then-sleepy St. Petersburg badly needed improvements during the mid-1980s. The Columbia renovated the space and added a Cha Cha Coconuts bar and grill on the roof, which hosted live music.

"The leader of the troupe at the time was Gisela, who created a dance just for me. I danced with the dancers, and then I did my own solo. I think I was only ten when that happened. It was kind of sad because I did it, and then it was like, 'Okay, you did it.' [My parents] were like, 'Okay, you're done with your flamenco!' I did the first big production, and then that was it. It wasn't an option to continue, and I kept on doing my ballet and my tap and my piano."

The Pier

Quick on the heels of the Harbour Island achievement, Cesar jumped at a new opportunity. He opened a Columbia in St. Petersburg's Pier, a five-story mini-mall and en-

tertainment center built a quarter mile off the downtown coast. If the old Pier's architecture seemed dated since its construction in 1973, the view from the fourth floor certainly did not. The city hired Bay Plaza Development Group to coordinate the rebirth of downtown, and its top attraction, the Pier. The Kansas City firm began renovation of the aging pier in December 1986.

Cesar had always considered St. Petersburg an aged "sleeping giant" with huge potential. He thought the city "a little timid and a little complacent" in the past. In the late 1980s, local government committed millions to fund improvements in downtown St. Petersburg, which was "on the threshold of a tremendous boom," Cesar told the city council. Under construction, Tropicana Field would be home base to the Tampa Bay Rays baseball team. The city renovated the Bayfront Center. Recent investment at the time totaled more than $200 million.

The next July, Bay Plaza approached the Gonzmarts and showed them The Pier's stunning view of St. Petersburg and Tampa Bay. Mayor Robert Ulrich and Bay Plaza master planner Neil Elsey courted the Gonzmart family. After the grand tour, an enthusiastic discussion yielded a burst of inspiration and enthusiasm. As the sunset burned gold and orange, Cesar caught the Don Quixote gleam in his eye.

The entire project required a tenant to lease a good deal of space. Bay Plaza and the city kept quiet about the negotiations with the Columbia, but Cesar could not contain himself. "That major tenant is us," he told a reporter. "We've been talking every day." He became so excited by the prospect that he convinced Phil Alessi, the owner of a fine Tampa bakery, to buy into the project. Together, they invested in 80 percent of The Pier's floor space.

"I was really selling him," Cesar said.

"That guy's a hell of a salesman," Alessi admitted.

"I'm a very enthusiastic person, and I am constantly selling," Cesar said. "He and I together will just make this thing explode."

Bay Plaza and Cesar Gonzmart had much to discuss. Bay Plaza pushed a ten-year lease, but Cesar wanted fifty. "Ten years goes by very fast," he explained. In November 1987,

the City Council approved a ten-year lease that could be expanded to fifty. The Columbia became the anchor attraction at the Pier. St. Petersburg offered early rent breaks to allow Cesar to recoup some of his invested money.

An interesting clause proposed for the lease gave voters the chance to oust the Columbia in twenty years if displeased with its presence. The clause was not included, and as of this writing, the Columbia at the Pier does a fine business.

The restaurant space required serious renovation. Too many walls and sunscreens blocked the glorious waterfront view, so management moved multiple walls, an office, a storage room, and the gift shop. The remodeling opened up the space, let in the natural light, and completely reinvented The Pier's fourth floor. A new cooking-exhaust system freed up valuable space in the kitchen.

The Gonzmarts opened a 12,000-square-foot Columbia Restaurant, Cha Cha Coconuts, and a catering operation in the Pier, requiring a $4 million investment. The caterer could service parties on the third floor, local venues, and boaters, who could order from telephones at the docks.

Cesar pitched it as a "gastronomic Disney World." City Councilman Ron Mason compared The Pier's signing of the Columbia with the Tampa Bay Buccaneers signing of quarterback Vinny Testaverde. Not a very flattering comparison for the Columbia, as it turned out.

Richard thinks the Columbia's opening in the remodeled space "sent flares into the air for other developers to see." Richard Gonzmart: "I remember watching live television broadcasts from the old building on Channel 38. The Saturday evening show would feature senior citizens singing songs from the Pier. I knew the Columbia would change that image."

Through careful menu planning, a tiny kitchen at the Pier could serve a 14,000-square-foot space. Cha Cha Coconuts opened on The Pier's roof with a concert by the Atlanta Rhythm Section. About two thousand attended, and the crowds—filled with beer and daiquiris—were too much for the restrooms. Male revelers took to the stairwells to answer nature's call. For much of the evening, the stairs became "the river of yellow falls," Richard says. "It was a mess."

Initially, business lagged behind expectations. Bay Plaza left town, and so did all of the company's assurances. Early disappointment could not scare off the Gonzmarts so easily. They had stuck by locations in Ybor City and Sarasota after much worse. St. Petersburg leaders continued to invest in their downtown, and over the next twenty years, hip cafés and bars replaced retirees' green benches, those public fixtures that identified St. Petersburg with the elderly. Major League Baseball replaced shuffleboard. The Salvador Dali Museum brought Spanish surrealism in 1982. Amid the new bustle of St. Petersburg, the Columbia at the Pier offered a taste of Spain.

The Columbia certainly changed The Pier's image. Richard collaborated with radio stations to hold "Low Dough Shows" at The Pier, selling concert tickets for two or three dollars. Richard could afford to sustain the low ticket prices because he made so much on drinks. The Pier hosted successful jazz festivals.

Favorites of the 1980s—such as the Romantics and Rick Springfield—played to capacity audiences. Richard was shocked to see so many women throwing their panties at Springfield, who hadn't written a hit song for years. A rough crowd of bikers turned out for Steppenwolf. Richard had never seen the campy cult film *Rocky Horror Picture Show* and was wholly unprepared when an army of people dressed outrageously as characters from the movie crowded into a Meat Loaf concert. Despite the scandalous distractions, he impressed Richard with the quality of his energetic set.

Richard once provided a mini-scandal of his own. While Tampa's raucous Guavaween festival took hold in Ybor City, he held concerts at The Pier during the weekend before Halloween. He dubbed the event "Pier-O-Ween." Disk jockey Mason Dixon became a valued concert partner. Together, they made a racket in a still-sleepy St. Petersburg. Dressed as an Indian with a headdress and loincloth, Richard amused the audience by lifting his leg to reveal a chorizo dangling from his loincloth.

A woman in the audience demanded that the barbaric man be thrown out. The bouncers could not evict Richard from his own restaurant. In fact, he yanked the sausage from under his loincloth and placed it on the woman's table as a spiteful gift.

Richard Gonzmart: "Mason Dixon will always remember that. He would talk about it on the radio. 'Richard the Indian and his loincloth.' I was just having fun, and this woman was really furious. Mason happened to be there, and he laughed his ass off."

Cesar would never have pulled such a stunt, but Richard was entertaining an altogether different generation. Sinatra and Stravinsky had long ago been replaced by Steppenwolf and Springfield.

Triathlon

Cesar may have been larger than life, but he was never an accomplished athlete. Richard had given up a college football career for the Columbia. When he put on weight in the 1980s, Cesar suggested he engage in athletics again.

"I am 265 pounds," Richard remembers; "I'm starting to ride a bicycle and I hear about this thing called a triathlon. And I say 'I can never win, never want to.'" Still, Richard trained with determination. By the time he opened the location in St. Petersburg in 1988, Richard had worked himself into peak physical form and never took the elevator. Instead, he raced it up the Pier's five floors and won.

By the late 1980s, Richard whipped himself into shape by training for grueling triathlons. He once placed third in a national contest, and had the honor of being trounced by Lance Armstrong.

"In 1988, we're in Miami Beach for a triathlon. I start getting a little quicker. I bought Melanie a new Jaguar. I had bought myself a new bicycle, a Kestrel. I bought these roof racks for her car, and we'd do the Miami Beach triathlon. I won my division. I tell Melanie, I tell the kids, 'We're going to go celebrate! We're going to go to Bal Harbor. We're going to buy everybody something.'

"So now we can't find any place to park the car. So I said, 'We'll go up to the garage.'"

None of them thought of Richard's bike as they drove under a low pipe into the garage. The collision ripped it up and tore a hole in the roof of the Jaguar.

Melanie says, "I'm going, 'My car!' He is going, 'My bike!'"

"It was a four-thousand-dollar bike," Richard recalls.

In a later race, Richard and most of his division were trounced by an unknown seventeen-year-old named Lance Armstrong.

In 1990, Richard placed in a nationwide triathlon against all odds. The night before, his car ran out of gas on a lonely, swampy stretch of Interstate 75 known as Alligator Alley. He rode his bike for many miles to get gas, and did not check into his hotel until four-thirty that morning. They had given his room away. He raced at six and had one of the best runs of his life. He took third nationally.

By then, Richard wanted to inject team spirit into what is a very individual competition. Richard ran in Team Cha Cha Coconuts. Their greatest rival: Team Chicken, sponsored by a poultry distributor. Cha Cha's T-shirts featured an illustrated coconut eating a chicken sandwich, with the chicken's head peeking out from the bun. Team Chicken got upset at the T-shirts—and got beat at the race. Team Cha Cha Coconuts won the state championship for the next three years.

Richard sponsored athletes to compete in international events. In Cancún, he swam through twelve-foot waves and ran through flooded streets. He saw used condoms floating in the water as he sloshed through. At water stops attendants offered only Coca-Cola.

For the past twenty years, Richard has supported triathlon competitions with more than his money. He's supplied his enthusiasm and energy and insists: "Camaraderie and relationships are what life is about." Richard prefers marathons these days. Always comfortable as a sprinter,

In 1989, the new Clearwater–Sand Key location endured a rough beginning. The restaurant quickly became a success.

Richard found long-distance running an agony. But he found triathlons to be too fiercely competitive for his tastes, and Richard's weight was never a serious issue again.

Sand Key

Jim Garris met Casey Gonzmart while working in a Sarasota hotel's restaurant. He mentioned Casey when he applied as assistant manager of a new Columbia on beachfront property at Clearwater's Sand Key.

When the restaurant opened in December 1989, a bitter winter sent temperatures plummeting in Florida. After the grand opening, the restaurant lost power. Demand for energy was so high that the state's power grid struggled to carry all the power. Amid a general "brown out," management closed the restaurant for several days to wait for temperatures to rise.

After the bumpy premiere, the restaurant successfully opened, but it took some time before it brought in the expected crowds. The Columbia's smallest restaurant came at a price. Richard Gonzmart observed: "That probably wasn't

the best deal. Rent was too high. Now we've operated long enough—we have a great deal."

When the general manager left a couple years later, Garris took over the position. When management planned to open a restaurant in Daytona Beach, he became the restaurant's first divisional manager, a position that coordinated operations between the company's restaurants.

Neither the new position nor the new restaurants would last long. Business was good, but long-simmering problems were about to boil over. The Columbia's biggest crisis was at hand.

Cesar World

By 1992, the Columbia had expanded across Florida, but fundamental problems mounted beneath the surface. Cesar's confidence and showmanship helped the Columbia to survive the lean 1960s and 1970s. As it turned out, Cesar's bravado also concealed the company's woes. Cesar's seemingly carefree world was about to come to an abrupt end. His shifty network of debt slid into an avalanche with his last breath in 1992. A close inspection of Cesar's influence on the business is necessary to make sense of the crisis that followed his death.

When Cesar described himself as an artist and dreamer, he told the truth. He learned to be an effective businessman through trial and error. Ultimately, he approached the problems of running a restaurant as a band leader. He was the main attraction, and unless everyone played their roles, his would be diminished.

He liked to visit his restaurants with family in tow. One of his favorite little nooks was the new restaurant in Clearwater's Sand Key, where Jim Garris applied for a position. After being interviewed, Garris had to pass muster with Cesar.

Jim Garris: "I remember having to interview with Cesar before I got the job, up on the balcony here over the Patio. He, of course, always left an impression. I think he was trying to feel me out as to what kind of person I was. I listened to a lot of his ideas: the family, the tradition, the fine dining portion of it, and the relationships that they had. It was only about fifteen or twenty minutes."

Garris got the position and served on the Sand Key location's opening crew. Cesar often visited with other family members to check on operations there. Sand Key's chef at the time, Guillermo Galera, was among Cesar's favorites. Galera always made Cesar and family something special. During these regular visits, Cesar scrutinized operations and gave encouragement.

Cesar insisted on strict loyalty to the restaurant. He went many years without hiring managers and tied most of their powers to himself, which preserved some control but greatly decreased efficiency. A branch restaurant might not see Cesar for days or even weeks. It might operate for months with minimal input from him. When he did come, the staff did not always like what he had to say—or how he said it. His predecessor, Casimiro, was infamous for yelling at his employees when they served lousy food. Cesar rightly did the same, except he did it in front of the customers, which is usually embarrassing for everyone involved.

The two sides of Cesar Gonzmart. When he died, the Columbia ceased to function properly. A financial crisis followed.

Jim Garris: "He would dress me down in the dining room for having a matchbook underneath the table leg. I'd get it right there in front of everybody. He came by on Easter and one of our specials was ham. The chef, anticipating how many reservations we had, cut some of the ham ahead of time and put it in a pan. They were serving the ham out of the steam table onto the plates. The ham dinners were selling like crazy.

"He [Cesar] went nuts when he came in there and saw that we weren't carving it to order. He stopped everything in the kitchen, and it really ruined our Easter Day because we got way behind. No food came out of the kitchen until Cesar was through telling everybody the way he wanted it. And he was right, we should have been carving it to order probably, but I guess the chef took the liberties of trying to speed the process and keep the tables turning and everything.

"That is a day I will not forget."

Garris thought the company's operations were haphazard and inefficient: "It was really a mom-and-pop operation. We didn't have recipes. We got our linen from Ybor City. We got our produce from Ybor City. We got our soups and sauces from Ybor City. So that's how in lieu of not having recipes, that's how they kept things consistent in the Bay area. In Sarasota, Casey oversaw all that and kept that the way he thought it should be. St. Augustine was another animal, too."

Each restaurant worked with its own recipes of varying quality. With no center besides Cesar himself, what would happen to the Columbia when he left? No one knew.

Commingling

Cesar treated the Columbia like a small family business in a sense: His family's financial fortunes were utterly tied to the restaurant. Cesar rarely took home a paycheck. In his later days, he made two hundred dollars weekly, anything to avoid income tax.

Richard Gonzmart: "I remember a dishwasher coming to see him one time about a raise and [Cesar said], 'How much do you make?'

"When the employee answered, [Cesar] said, 'Well, you make more money than I do.' The poor guy, my dad threw him for a loop. The guy's like, 'How do I get a Rolls Royce or my day in the sun?'"

Cesar had mixed the family's debts with the Columbia's. The restaurant's credit cards paid for vacations with Adela, antique hunting, splurges on art, and lavish gifts. Credit also paid for mortgage payments and electric bills. "Eventually," Richard recalls, "my brother, my dad, and I owed money to the company. I told my dad, 'We need to make a reasonable salary and live within our means, otherwise it doesn't work.' My brother owed over $1 million to the company."

Like a jazz musician, Cesar took spontaneous risks, relying on his companions to improvise. In mid-conversation with customers and colleagues, he came up with new pitches and stories, discreetly asking Adela, Casey, or Richard to play along for the audience. Melanie Gonzmart remembers: "I wished he would tell me what he was going to say, so I could say the same thing. Whatever he says, I say the same thing. I mean if people do question [him], it's like [an] *attack*. There were certain things I was not supposed to know or talk about."

Cesar could also be overzealous in his promotion of the Columbia. His family heard him give higher and higher income figures to reporters. Richard: "Cesar would give out numbers where he wished he was in sales." In 1986, *Restaurants & Institutions* named the top one hundred independent restaurants in the Unites States. The Columbia in Ybor City ranked twentieth with annual sales of $7.5 million and over 515,000 customers annually. No one in

Cesar and Adela celebrate Gasparilla with Charlie and Melba Hero shortly before Cesar became ill with cancer.

the operation believed the hype, but they didn't know the real numbers, either.

Richard: "Cesar would provide whatever numbers he wanted. Nobody ever believed the numbers. None of the bankers believed it, but it was a different world, hand shakes. One day my dad announced that we sold so many millions of dollars in the company. The IRS read this in the papers. They're coming down on us and they're nailing us with numbers that weren't true.

"My dad would be one that would tell stories. I think he got to the point where he believed the stories. Cesar World. My dad lived in Cesar World. Sometimes I tell people, 'Hey, I live in Cesar World.' We laugh about it, and Cesar World was great, but it had to change."

Cesar lorded over his chief financial officer and the Columbia's financial ledger, feeding him numbers and keeping him in the dark about the big picture.

A rare photograph of Cesar being still. While awake, he seemed to be in perpetual motion.

Richard Gonzmart: "Cesar hired the kind of people he could control. Only Cesar knew the real numbers. When my dad died, it was probably his time because the world had changed. My dad did not believe in paying professional managers. He didn't believe in paying salaries. It's because my dad did business different. I'm not putting it down, but he did things that nobody else could have done to keep the restaurant alive.

"Banking had changed, computers brought information and he wouldn't present it. Only he knew what was really going on, and nobody else did. He no longer could control what was happening. He lost control. That's why I say his body then checked out."

Casey: "His guts held the Columbia together."

A Dying Wish

Cesar was an avid fisherman, and spent many afternoons in the sun. In 1992, his case of skin cancer turned into something far worse. When it spread to his pancreas, his condition quickly declined.

Richard fostered the creation of Cesar's own wine, to become a Columbia specialty. Naturally, he asked Luis Diaz to find the best.

The original Don Cesar was a 1982 vintage from Rioja. Cesar was sick in the hospital when his label premiered. When Richard brought a sample case to Cesar's hospital room, the maestro autographed bottles for the nurses from his sick bed. In the sketch of Cesar on the label by artist Leroy Neiman, his eyebrows arch as if sighing with his violin, conjuring the romance of music and wine. Cesar didn't drink wine very much, but loved his label.

Knowing his time was short, Cesar had a dying wish for an old friend. He insisted that George Guito, whom he had practically raised as his own, become manager of the Ybor City Columbia. George attained the position when the Columbia as a company was in complete disarray. Cesar's restless energy and power kept the operation buzzing. When he "checked out," so did his Columbia empire.

George had difficulties managing the deteriorating restaurant, but without him, it may have fallen apart completely. No one else possessed George's institutional memory. Jim Garris began working with George after Cesar's death.

Jim Garris: "Having him here has been a blessing. Oftentimes, Richard would call George and say, 'Remember when we used to do it this way or that way?' George would get back in the kitchen and whip it up the way he remembers, and we'd break down the recipe. He's a gold mine, the mayor of Ybor City in my eyes."

Elegy

Like Don Quixote, Cesar could seem delusional, but where do dreams begin and delusions end?

Melanie Gonzmart: "In Cesar World, Cesar truly, truly believed every bit of it. He was a dreamer. If he hadn't dreamed, where would we be?"

Tribune photograph by JAY CONNER

Man of the Year

Cesar Gonzmart salutes family and friends Saturday after being honored as Man of the Year at the 1992 Tampa Hispanic Heritage Inc. dinner. The dinner, at the Harbour Island Hotel ballroom, was the official opening of the group's annual events.

Cesar was not too ill to accept an award as the Hispanic Heritage's Man of the Year in 1992. A showman to the end.

750 ml Product of Spain Alc 12% by vol

DON CESAR

LeRoy Neiman
Tampa

RIOJA
DENOMINACION DE ORIGEN CALIFICADA

Red Wine
Reserva 1985

THIS EXQUISITE WINE FROM RIOJA, SPAIN HAS BEEN SPECIALLY SELECTED FOR THE COLUMBIA RESTAURANTS IN FLORIDA, USA.
PRODUCED AND BOTTLED BY
BODEGAS HEREDAD DE BAROJA, S.A.
ELVILLAR, SPAIN
CONTAINS SULFITES

Cesar adored Disney World more than his children did. Melanie: "Cesar was the kind of guy who'd go, 'Look at this, look at these telephones!' He was in awe of every electronic thing and when we got to Disney, he drove us crazy, '*Look!*' He just could not believe the possibilities in the world to come. As worldly as he was, he was truly kind of childish. He was always in awe. He always impressed me because *I* looked at *him* with such awe. He was so incredible."

Richard: "He was a Don Quixote. Something inspires people to do great things. I think that dad was inspired by that, by that impossible greatness. That inspires me as well, because if you dream it, you can accomplish it.

"I'm very protective of Cesar. I get very angry because people don't remember what he did. Not only was he a restaurateur, he was a showman, but he was a caring person.

Artist Leroy Neiman provided the sketch for Cesar's wine label.

Cesar's passing was especially tough for Richard, who could not imagine the Columbia without him.

Only Cesar could have made the Columbia survive. Only Cesar, through whatever method it was, made it survive. My dad today would be so proud to see the sales in the Columbia and where we are realizing the potential."

No one can deny that Cesar, despite his faults and eccentricities, was a shrewd and instinctive entrepreneur. Casey became ensconced in Sarasota, but Richard had served a long, successful, and sometimes trying tutelage under his unconventional father.

Richard Gonzmart: "My brother says he never worked a day with my father as an adult. I tell him, he doesn't know what he missed. Cesar was always difficult and demanding. He was different; he was an artist. My dad would look at a contract—he knew exactly where to look and to question. He understood so much.

"He would ask me if I've read a certain article in the business section. I said, 'No,' and he would give me hell. He would tell me how history was so important from high school on up. When I said I didn't like history, he says, 'That's the most important subject you have.'

"I said, 'Why?'

"He said, 'Because history continues to repeat itself.' I didn't understand that in high school, didn't understand that in college." Richard remembers seeing a restaurant ad once that read, "History Repeats Itself Beautifully." "Then I realized that history repeats itself, beautiful or ugly. We can learn."

Once, Cesar wanted to buy a small lot near the Ybor Columbia to use for parking. Business was not good, and Richard advised, "We'll never need that." After Cesar's death, Richard kicked himself for not snapping up the property when they had the chance. "The property went up to $90,000 or $110,000," Richard remembers. "Because of us. It made me feel good, but it also made me feel stupid."

Hail Cesar

Running became a way for Richard to honor his father and take his advice to exercise. First, he preferred the individual competition of triathlons, but marathons became a spiritual exercise, an act of prayer. Running became therapy. The day Cesar passed, December 9, 1992, Richard prayed the rosary twenty times as he ran as many miles. "I said, 'God take him. He had suffered too much and it was very difficult.' I said I would never ever complain."

Immediately after Cesar's death, Richard channeled his energy and emotions into the Los Angeles Marathon. "On March 7, 1993, the day after Cesar's birthday, I did the L.A. marathon and the Lord was testing me." Temperatures were 88 degrees at ten that morning, climbing to 107 degrees by noon. Although Richard was in excellent shape, he began to collapse after clearing fifteen miles.

"I was picking up unwrapped candies on the ground, eating them; at mile 20 they wanted to pull me off the course. I was in the john having diarrhea and throwing up, blisters everywhere, the last six miles I threw up, totally dehy-

drated. I never complained. It was the Lord testing me. He took my dad. I wore a shirt saying 'Hail Cesar.' When I was suffering and feeling the worst, the Lord blessed me by somebody shouting, 'Hail Cesar!' That's what kept me going. I didn't run again for nine years or so. So I hate marathons. They're the hardest thing in the world to do."

To Richard, triathlons were always about individual competition and excellence. He found marathons most gratifying when dedicated to others. Pain and difficulty makes running—and philanthropy—more meaningful. "Now I run marathons dedicated to those who are suffering from cancer, that died from cancer. I live to fulfill my dad's dreams and to honor his memory. This has nothing to do with the restaurant business, but it has to do with being a family business and the passion."

The Olive Sandwich

Cesar World consisted of a state of denial that allowed adherents peace of mind. Anything could be taken care of his way. But not forever. The Columbia's biggest challenge came tumbling down after Cesar died. Nothing in the restaurant's or family's history could have prepared it for such a calamity.

Richard did not bear the burden alone for long. He assembled a team to deliver the Columbia—and his family—from the jaws of defeat. His mother, Adela, and brother, Casey, supported him, but the company needed a genuine leader. With a restless determination reminiscent of his grandfather Casimiro Jr., Richard Gonzmart wrote the next page of the Columbia's history.

A year after Cesar passed away, Richard visited his grave. He brought along Cesar's favorite snack—Spanish olives tucked into split Cuban bread. Richard wanted to eat one at the grave as a tribute to his father. He even considered adding it to the Columbia's menu.

Richard: "My dad loved his olive sandwich. On the anni-

While he mourned Cesar, running became therapy for Richard, an act of prayer.

During the Columbia's biggest crisis, the financial outlook was bleak for Adela and her sons.

versary of my dad's death, I made an olive sandwich and I didn't taste it until I went out there. I started eating it and I said, 'Dad, this is terrible!' Every time I eat it I say, 'Dad, why did you eat this!?' And I ate it.

"I said, 'Dad, I can't eat it anymore.' I just sat there with it. Forget about the olive sandwich. It's not going on the menu. The bread pudding can go, but not the olive sandwich."

Richard could not go back to Cesar World. He found the taste too bitter. He determined to find his own way.

 ## In the Red

The Gonzmart brothers hired a manager in Sarasota so Casey could move back to Tampa to work in the corporate office for the first time. Adela was left to be the Columbia's king-maker, but could not treat her sons unequally. She named Casey and Richard co-presidents according to Cesar's wishes, an unusual and impractical solution. In the

throes of a divorce and personal crisis, Casey withdrew. To a large extent, Richard took responsibility for Columbia's crisis alone.

No one knew how much the company made or owed. Before long, it became apparent that the restaurant—and the family—were passing into a serious crisis. The company did not have enough money to operate.

The worst threat came from the company's chief financial officer (CFO), who didn't seem to know how anything functioned. Richard Gonzmart: "My CFO couldn't get a profit and loss statement for six months from any of my restaurants." No one could hope to run a company with no information. Worse yet, the CFO had avoided paying sales tax to pay bills and buy time. Richard: "It comes out in the paper that we owe the state of Florida $280,000 sales tax. The bank finds out, I find out. I have got to go meet with the state of Florida. That's a theft, they're going to put me in jail."

A financial threat came from within the family as well. Casey's personal and financial affairs were in disarray, preventing his full involvement with the restaurant's recovery.

Financial troubleshooter Leigh Sanders (left) helped the Gonzmarts retrieve the company from disaster. As the new Chief Financial Officer, Dennis Fedorovich emphasized fiscal discipline and integrity.

Casey's bitter divorce almost ensnared the company itself. Because Casey's finances were so commingled with the restaurant's, it was all legally up for grabs. A disadvantageous settlement could have ruined the company. When all parties discovered the Columbia's heavy debts, the divorce proceeded without involving the company.

The Saviors

In the midst of the crisis, Richard moved the company out of his father's cramped upstairs office, where all the restaurant's distractions beckoned from outside the door. The new corporate office moved in across Twenty-first Street above the old Cha Cha Coconuts.

To provide some guidance for the company's upper management, the Columbia's accounting firm asked the Gonzmart brothers a series of questions. The test helped appraise their aptitudes and work preferences. The corporate shuffle took place in 1994: As eldest son, Casey became chairman of the board, while Richard assumed the daily duties of president, and Adela became director of operations.

As the new president, Richard went to work on damage control for the family and company, but soon realized he needed help. He sought out an expert to make sense of the family's situation. An accounting firm contacted the turnaround expert Leigh Sanders with news that the Columbia needed advice. Well known in the business community, Sanders became the Columbia's troubleshooter. His connections and credibility with banks certainly helped the company's recovery.

The business guru specialized, then and now, in strategic management, crisis management, and business valuation and analysis. For close Columbia associates, Leigh Sanders is better known as one of the company's saviors.

In September 1994, Sanders met with Richard, Casey, and Adela to assess the business. He immediately recognized "a situation that was painful and difficult, and you don't stare at it for very long. They were real people accustomed to acting responsibly if they knew what the circumstances were."

Leigh understood that Cesar had not prepared his family or the company to continue without him. Sanders had seen the same scenario elsewhere, where the owner wanted to protect the family but endangered it instead. He sized up Adela as "an extremely strong woman. That was clear to me from the way she was asking questions."

Sanders had never seen a restaurant run quite like the Columbia at the time. Richard and Casey had been observers of the business, in some respects, instead of partners. With no managers, most of the day-to-day power was delegated to the chefs. No centralized authority or coordination existed besides the family's whims. The cooks essentially ran the business out of the kitchen without fully realizing it.

"Each chef was his own kingdom," Sanders remembers. "Cesar gave them enormous sway, but no guidance for managing cost or quality." The restaurant lost money on many of the dishes. The Columbia simply gave away the 1905 salad with every entrée, without charge. The lavish fistfuls of expensive imported olives became a heavy expense with no compensation.

Sanders saw weaknesses in the Columbia's management. Cesar's scattershot approach did not create or share long-term goals for the business or employees. The Columbia retained a loyal following despite some mediocre food. The restaurant's expansion across Florida had been dictated by opportunity rather than a long-term strategy. In many ways, the Columbia did not truly compete as a business. It lost money as a matter of routine, and increasing volume became the only way to make more money. Management relied on the name and reputation for survival.

Leigh came up with six business principles to salvage the restaurant from ruin. Any recovery would be successful only if embraced by upper management. Because the restaurant lost so much money in the course of operations, Sanders sought to control cost and revenue. A new bonus structure encouraged employees through rewards. The company introduced managers to enforce standards and coordinate operations. Through reinvesting, the company could maintain the Ybor Columbia's dilapidated facility.

> SIX BUSINESS PRINCIPLES
> *by Leigh Sanders*
>
> Assist or resist an outcome
> Control cost and revenue
> Encourage employees through rewards
> Introduce managers
> Manage debts
> Manage facilities

It took a truly gifted money man to fulfill Leigh's fifth principle: *Manage debts*. If Sanders found management a mess, Dennis Fedorovich, the Columbia's new CFO, confronted a genuine challenge. When he interviewed for the job with Richard, he had worked for several large corporations. In search of a new challenge and the chance to make a real difference in a smaller business, his wish was granted.

Dennis Fedorovich: "I talked to Richard initially. I certainly remember that day. It was the end of the day, five or six o'clock. I just remember him being exhausted before we sat down. I don't know if he was tired physically or mentally or what, but we talked for a while. He had a lot of papers and he was trying to show me some things, but he didn't have faith in the information. He was frustrated.

"Richard still mentions something that I said to him in my interview about the need for integrity. One thing you can't take away is integrity. I knew about the Columbia, knew what it was, knew about the Gonzmart family. I knew there was some distress once I got here, the need to be organized and to get a better feel for what's really going on in the business."

Dennis remembers a conversation with George Guito shortly after his arrival. "It was about May or June and we were going into summer, which is traditionally the slow time. He was saying, 'We never make money at this time

In 1993, the company opened three adjacent restaurants in Daytona Beach: the Columbia, Cha Cha Coconuts, and Mangiare's, the family's new Italian concept.

of year.' Basically, what they tried to do was maximize as much as they could during seasons, and try not to lose it all during the off-season.

"I said, 'There's no reason why we can't make money here twelve months out of the year. Let's just remember this conversation because there will be a time when, twelve months out of the year, you will make money.' That certainly has happened. I remind him [George] of it a lot. Yeah, *a lot*."

Daytona (A Beach Too Far)

Before Richard could tackle the Columbia's fundamental problems, he sacrificed the company's most innovative development to slow the bleeding funds. Management had already squandered scarce resources by investing in other restaurant concepts and chains. Cha Cha Coconuts and an Italian concept created by the family, called Mangiare's, siphoned money away from the struggling Columbia.

Cesar's last gambit brought three adjacent restaurants—the Columbia, Cha Cha Coconuts, and Mangiare's—

to Daytona Beach in 1992. In better days, the development could have been a genuine innovation: All three restaurants shared infrastructure, kitchen space, and supplies, even employees.

Jim Garris remembers Richard's plans for the restaurant trio. "We were going to operate it like a hotel without any rooms. Like we were one big building and there were three different restaurants in there."

Opening weekend for all three restaurants brought all the stress one would expect. As an opening manager, Jim Garris felt the strain, and Melanie could see it. Jim Garris: "I'll never forget one thing that resonates with me about Melanie. I was in Daytona, and in the madness of opening three restaurants at one time, all in the same week and everything.

"We [the opening crew] were living there in Daytona. I had been there four and a half weeks, and I hadn't been home. We had opened up the restaurant and they [Richard and Melanie] had come over to see the grand opening.

"I saw Richard and Melanie at the door and went over to give Richard a handshake and Melanie a hug. She looked right at me and said, 'When was the last time you've been home to see your wife and kids?' I'm breaking up a little bit about this.

"'I haven't been home in about four and a half weeks.' She looked right at Richard and she goes, 'Send his ass home tomorrow!' and I was home tomorrow. Melanie is a sweetheart."

While he worked at the ill-fated Daytona location, Jim Garris saw the Columbia rise and fall in a matter of months. "My dad wanted to do Daytona Beach," Richard says. "We opened three restaurants with no chef in place." Cesar's death and its aftermath revealed a Columbia in deep trouble.

While assessing the company's sad state, Leigh Sanders immediately identified the large Daytona development as an unnecessary burden. It lost almost $1 million every year due to high rent and lack of company control. The long-term lease would have bled the company dry. Leigh maneuvered the company out of the contract in 1996, and Richard gave the orders to shut down Cesar's final dream.

Financing

New CFO Dennis Fedorovich had always wanted a tough challenge at work. He found it at the Columbia. "I don't think anybody really knew [how bad it was] until I was here for a couple of months. I needed to try to get my hands around everything financial here, and the records were such that that was not an easy task. In the meantime, while it's taking a little bit of time, the company continues to operate—or to not operate. Things needed to be done pretty quickly.

"The company was bleeding from a financial standpoint. Cash flow was not sufficient to cover normal business activity, whether it's paying vendors, paying banks, things like that. So we had to quickly get a hold of our cash flow."

In Cesar World, the Columbia borrowed money to fund routine operations, leaving the company with losses—plus interest. Sanders and Fedorovich suggested that the only way out of the crisis was for Richard to be honest with the business community.

Dennis Fedorovich: "I think that is really where the Columbia name and the Gonzmart family name served to benefit their business. Through both of those names, and through what they did for the ninety years up until that, they essentially built equity in the community."

Richard Gonzmart: "If you're having bad times and you tell people the truth, they will probably support you and help you. If you're lying to them, they will not. I worked with Lynn Culbreath at the bank. She had worked in the past with my dad, but she didn't trust my dad. She didn't trust any of the numbers. We went there with information and the first time, she wanted to show us the door."

Dennis Fedorovich: "I remember going into Lynn Culbreath's office and being not-so-gently escorted out, 'Come back to us in three months or six months when you have a plan.'

"She was at Barnett Bank and basically met with us as a courtesy at that time. We told her, 'Okay, we will come back. In three months, we're going to have a plan, and tell you how we've dented in the plan.' That's what started it—it was conversations like that."

Richard: "She assisted me with a loan to help me get through. That's where I started building my credibility. Now Lynn is one of our best friends."

Other banks fell in behind the Columbia. Richard hired a company to audit the business in 1994. Only then did the extent of the company's debt become apparent. Dennis Fedorovich: "The longer I was here, that initial time period, the worse it got, and the worse off the company really was. Certainly, when I took the job, I didn't think it was that bad. But I don't think Richard or anybody thought it was that bad, either. The deficit of the company, the negative net worth, was in the millions." Determined to right the situation, Richard refused to entertain thoughts of bankruptcy.

As Richard left the house the morning of a meeting with state tax officials, he told his wife: "Melanie, I'm going to meet with sales tax people. I haven't told you because I didn't want to bother you, but if I get arrested…." The company paid off the tax debt over the next three years.

Dennis gave first priority toward funding current operations and increasing efficiency. Virtually every remaining dollar paid down the company's debts. Richard asked his mother, Adela, to sell off a few antiques, jewelry, or art, but she could not let go of her memories. Melanie Gonzmart: "Every bracelet and ring meant something and someplace. That someone was always the same: Cesar. She refused to sell off anything."

Instead, Adela mortgaged her home to provide cash during the crisis, and the company gathered more funds by selling some of the shares of Cha Cha Coconuts to a private investor. These new funds provided a welcome boost in debt payments.

The Columbia owed the largest debt to Henry Lee food distributors.

Richard Gonzmart: "I had gone down to see Henry Lee's Ed Sterling, the son of the founder of this food service. We owed him and were way behind. I said, 'Ed, I want to meet with you.' I fly down with Leigh Sanders. They know the situation is way behind. They're waiting to hear me say, 'I'm going to pay pennies on the dollar [and declare bankruptcy].'" Instead, Richard vowed to pay off the debt in three years.

Richard and Casey only collected their salaries and eliminated their debts to the company. Dennis Fedorovich: "The first time I did a budget, they kept calling it a crystal ball. I was trying to explain to them the difference. A crystal ball is just hoping and wishing. Richard never lost sight of where he wanted the company to be. I think there was an incredible amount of weight on his shoulders to not be the generation that messed it up."

As he watched the company's improved performance, Leigh Sanders also saw Richard emerge as a genuine leader. "Richard was too emotional [at first]—he fired a bunch of people in a short amount of time. He came out a mature leader when he had been an observer. That's why the business survived. Because Richard decided to tell the truth when it was difficult to do so. *He* did it. My job was to remind him how to fix it."

Richard also recognizes the company's financial struggle as his moment of truth, personally and professionally. Of Leigh Sanders, Richard says, "He gave me the confidence to be that leader."

Closing Harbour Island

During the upheaval at Daytona, Richard had to decide which staff to retain and where to put them after the closing. Jim Garris went to Ybor City. "I knew things really started to go bad," Garris remembers, "when they hired Leigh Sanders and busted me back down into a position." Garris found the company's flagship nightmarish, with the massive, crumbling building and strange Cesar World management.

On his deathbed, Cesar had asked that stalwart George Guito be made general manager of Ybor City. There was little chance that George could tame what Cesar could not. George grew up in Cesar's unusual business, and knew nothing else. He found dealing with the workers, waiters, and cooks challenging. The essential arrangement of the restaurant remained the same, with most of the management coming from the kitchen.

Jim Garris worked in Ybor City and had never seen anything like it, a restaurant that ran itself. Eight or nine months into Jim's Ybor stint, Richard called him for an important meeting.

"I'd like you to go over to Harbour Island and take the restaurant over as the general manager," Richard said. "I've got some problems there, and I want you to straighten them out." Garris was relieved to get away from the dim, sprawling Ybor flagship and bask in the sunny atmosphere of Harbour Island. Before long, he turned around the Columbia's performance there.

Melanie Gonzmart has fond memories of the scenic location. "Harbour Island was so much fun. I loved Cha Cha

Curt Gaither (top left), Jim Garris (right) and George Guito (lower left) helped the Gonzmarts retrieve the company from disaster.

great, we had a good following, but we realized we had to focus on what was going to be a success for us."

When the opportunity to renew the lease came in 1995, Richard decided to withdraw from Harbour Island. The development had failed to retain enough retail shops, and redevelopment in downtown Tampa lagged. The new convention center was fraught with delays. The landlord would not provide funds for upgrades, nor would it allow outdoor music in the evening. Richard hoped that the flagship Columbia would absorb the Harbor Island location's traffic.

Jim Garris remembers the day he heard the news of the impending closing. "I was probably there for about eight or nine months when I got another serious call from Richard. We had been discussing a new concept over there on Harbour Island. I was working on some menu ideas and different strategies. I had come prepared to speak with him and Leigh about the new concept.

"When I go into the conference room in the corporate offices across the street, he and Leigh are sitting there. I had all my stuff with me, and I started spreading out."

Richard stopped Jim: "Wait a minute. We have to talk with you about something. I wanted to let you know something before it gets out in the public. I wanted to give you an opportunity in case you don't want to stay with us any longer. We're going to close Harbour Island."

Jim's heart dropped.

Richard continued, "I also have a proposal for you. I would like to have you go back over to Ybor City and get it straightened out."

Jim could not forget the disorderly ruin of the flagship Columbia.

Coconuts, where we had outdoor seating, which Tampa really didn't have, per se. We'd do music. Of course, Gasparilla was incredible, it happened right in front of us. So I have wonderful memories of Harbour Island."

Larger forces disrupted Jim's humming restaurant in 1995. Richard recalls the difficult choices he made: "It was doing

Jim Garris: "I looked right at him and I said, 'First of all, before we go any further, if I go over there, I'm going to be in charge.' They agreed to that. Then they talked to me about a bonus structure. That was the first thing that Leigh brought into the company, one of the things that turned this place upside down was having the managers buy in and have a piece of the pie."

Richard and Leigh planned a new bonus structure for managers and employees. Bonus pay rewarded good sales and profits. Until then, the Columbia's relationship with management and employees had been shaped by the union's shop stewards and strikes. The family coped by granting major concessions only when the union prodded. But the union's heyday was long past, and wages were mediocre.

Richard introduced the bonus plan, and some employees had never heard of such a thing. The proposal piqued the interest of Jim Garris.

Despite the bonus plan, Jim admits, "It was a struggle coming over. A grandiose plan was not thrown out. Just go over there, work with George and get the place straightened out because we want to absorb all of the business that we are going to lose when we close Harbour Island.

"We were closing Harbour Island in two weeks. So my immediate task after that meeting, I supervised the closing of the restaurant."

When he came to Ybor City, a face-off over policy began between George Guito and Jim Garris, the outsider.

George Guito tells the story rather mildly: "We brought other managers in here to work with me, and we started controlling the restaurant—Richard was here day and night."

Jim Garris, however, describes an intense struggle to change policy. "There were many times when George and I never really got physical with each other, but often times got very pissed. I would talk about doing it one way and then when I would leave it, would go the other way, or it would change back. I used to hear that happening between Richard and Cesar back in the day, too."

Jim remembers, "[I managed the restaurant] in everybody's eyes, but George. But he's a great guy. He and I have really grown up together in the last ten years. Reluctantly, George has learned a lot from me. You can't be here all the time. You can't be everywhere and work 24/7. God bless George, he was here from sun up to sun down. He didn't start taking a regular day off until about five years ago. But it took me five years to get him to take a day off. He thought something was going to happen while he was gone. But now he loves it. He loves taking his day off, which is good."

The entire way the Columbia did business was about to radically change.

Breaking the Union

Before management could change kitchen and dining room policy, it had to contend with the union one last time.

Curt Gaither had seen unions bring down famous restaurants like Mama Leone's in New York, where he once worked. When a union moved into the restaurant, wages shot up. "They got to a point where the labor cost was out of control. For a restaurant doing that kind of volume and needing the staff that it did, it couldn't support the labor costs required by the union. Unfortunately, up there, the union was the thing that put them out of business."

By the 1990s, the union at the Columbia—for cooks, waiters, and bartenders—had seen better days. Most of the new employees did not join the union, especially once the new bonus structure went into effect. If the chefs could devise delicious, efficient recipes, they received a share of the profits. The chefs' wages almost doubled as a result, according to Leigh Sanders.

Joe Roman remembers the union's decline: "We got a lot of people from Puerto Rico, Guatemala, all those places. They come in and they don't want to join the union. You can't do nothing about it, it's open shop. You have to let them work. With twelve dollars, his family will eat all month in Puerto Rico and Guatemala. So, the union started going down. The members of the union died out."

When Jim Garris returned to Ybor City as Director of Operations, he quickly identified an obstacle for major reforms. "The union was the biggest issue we had here. Basically, they ran the restaurant. The managers didn't run the restaurant. You can go into a dining room and tell a waiter, 'You left your tray over there against the wall. Can you take it back to the kitchen?' [Waiter:] 'It's not my job, it's the bus boy's job.' You can tell them, 'Take that back to the kitchen or you're going to have to leave.' He'd call the shop steward, and ten minutes later I'm dealing with him. So one of the biggest things that we did—and I don't know whether or not I should say this, but I'm going to—we broke the union, basically.

"Richard did that by meeting with some of the guys that were in charge and saying, 'We want to try to make this restaurant better, work with us. The union's going away, we have new management.' I think a lot of employees felt they had needed representation to protect their jobs. After a couple of years, the staff began to see that I wasn't going away. We brought new managers, a couple guys I had worked with before. We were firm and fair. We were writing people up, having meetings with people saying, 'Hey look, this happened last night. Why did you do this and that?' Whereas before, those things didn't happen. There was no 'Let's sit down and talk about it.' It was 'Okay, *you're fired*, get out of here.'

"I think after awhile, when they saw that the management style was changing, there was less need for a union. Then it became a problem paying dues every month for nothing. The union disappeared. When that happened, we were able to incorporate more handbooks, company policies, this is the way we do it. Before, guys did whatever they wanted to do service-wise."

There is no one better to provide perspective on this issue than Joe Roman, veteran waiter of over fifty-five years. "We used to make eighteen dollars a week. The waiters today can make two hundred dollars a day. So, they're well protected today, but in my day, it wasn't like that."

In 1996, the union governing waiters, cooks, and bartenders broke. For the first time, the Columbia could hire women into those positions.

 ## Bread and Family

In Tampa, good Cuban bread is a treasured art, one that is not taken lightly or mastered easily. Outside of Tampa, poor Cuban bread became the company's most distressing problem. "When I came to work for Columbia," Curt Gaither remembers, "I didn't know the rice from the beans, to be honest with you. I did know that what we were baking wasn't good bread compared to anything I have had anywhere else. It was as bad on Tuesday, but different. And it was as bad on Wednesday, but different again." In Ybor City, the local bread was always good, but at the other locations, quality varied drastically."

Gaither helped implement systemwide changes in the Columbia's food, and consistent Cuban bread became his first priority. To this day, Gaither thinks the most fundamental improvement at the restaurants was in the bread—it came delivered fresh or frozen from the same bakery in Ybor City to ensure quality and consistency. La Segunda Central bakery in Ybor City was the most obvious choice for the job.

The Moré family's brick ovens at La Segunda had supplied the Ybor restaurant's bread since the bakery opened in 1915. Juan Moré brought the recipe to Tampa from Cuba and founded the bakery. Originally named La Primera (or The First), the bakery burned down in the 1950s, replaced by La Segunda (The Second) on Fifteenth Street. When Interstate 4 tore a swath through Ybor City in the 1960s, La Segunda moved to its present location on Fifteenth Street. All the while, they supplied the Columbia's bread. Several generations of the Columbia have tried to run their own bakeries. Cesar and Casimiro Jr. both started excellent bakeries, but they didn't last. La Segunda did, and today it makes some of the best Cuban bread in the world.

"We have always had a good rapport with the Hernandez and Gonzmart families," Tony Moré observes. "We have had a long relationship through the years and have seen many changes in both our businesses."

Today, brothers Tony and Raymond keep their family's tradition alive by baking some of the best Cuban bread known to man. A warm length of the Morés' Cuban bread with a cup of café con leche at the Columbia is one of life's most simple and satisfying pleasures. The thin, delicately flaky crust gives way to a fluffy interior that invites a dunk of coffee, swath of butter, or smear of sauce.

Tampa tradition calls for a strip of palmetto leaf to crown the yard-long loaves. The leaf helps the loaf to split along its top and spread out. "We have a supplier who goes out, climbs the trees, picks the leaves, cleans them, and brings them to us," Raymond said. The leaves, and baking, set Tampa's bread apart from Miami Cuban bread. Miami bread is softer and less delicate.

"We have had a wonderful, long-term relationship," Tony said of the Columbia. "Everything went smooth until the Gonzmarts decided to open more restaurants. Customers started saying the bread wasn't as good as in Ybor City. The family was committed to being the best, just as their customers expected."

Curt Gaither remembers the Moré brothers' surprise when Richard asked them to supply the entire Columbia system. "They, a small family bakery, were not prepared to do that. They didn't have the baking facilities, the freezer, the staffing, and so forth. They did it. Their business has grown phenomenally. It certainly was the right move for them." The breakthrough in frozen bread brought La Segunda new clients—such as Beef O' Brady's—that stretch across the southeastern United States and beyond.

"We worked hard to come up with the right formula," Raymond said. "But bread is delicate and doesn't travel well. After years of trying, we threw our hands in the air and said, 'It is the Ybor water, that is the secret!'"

Curt Gaither senses some intangible secret behind La Segunda's bread. "It's definitely the bakery in Tampa. The water, the altitude, the guy who slides it in the oven. I don't know exactly what it is, but even buying it in the grocery store of another brand, it's different. Kind of like bagels in New York." Until La Segunda can open bakeries beside every Columbia, this arrangement yields the finest results.

"The best compliment I ever had was when Adela called after tasting the bread in Celebration," said Raymond. "She told me it was just as good as it is in Ybor."

Today, La Segunda is much like the Columbia: They are both thriving businesses with honored pasts. Neither has become a relic.

Basic Training

In 1994, Lauren Gonzmart, Richard's eldest daughter, worked in the restaurant full-time. Then age eighteen, she attended a year at the University of South Florida and worked as a supervisor in Ybor City. She moved to Virginia for two years as a new bride. She returned to Tampa in May 1997, just as Andrea graduated high school. Lauren enrolled at USF again and worked hard to support her husband, who was engaged in full-time studies of his own.

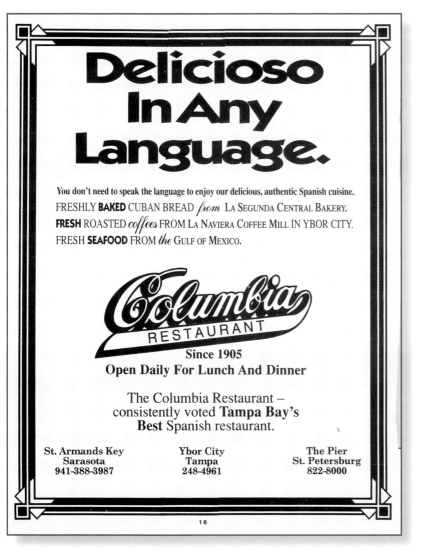
The reinvention of the Columbia began with its Cuban bread. By partnering with La Segunda Central Bakery in Ybor City, the Columbia can offer the best Cuban bread, fresh in every restaurant.

Lauren Gonzmart: "They started me out in Clearwater–Sand Key. I did that with Curt Gaither for awhile. My dad was like, 'This is the guy I want you to work with. If you're going to learn from anyone, it's going to be from him.' He was the best boss I could have ever hoped for. He still is. He's just a wonderful guy, a wealth of knowledge and experience.

"[Sand Key is] a very good teaching restaurant because it's smaller. You will learn to manage it because, a lot of times, you're the only one there. The kitchen, the orders, the deliveries, the food, the front door, the back door. Who's running out the door to smoke? Who's not showing up?

"You get every possible scenario thrown at you, but luckily on a very small scale. It was kind of like a *Reader's Digest* version. It's very condensed. You're learning how to deal with the computer, updating prices, changing specials, opening and closing the restaurant, and scheduling people. Everything I needed to learn, I learned in that little restaurant with Curt teaching me. What to look for, how to deal with customers, with complaints, how to make those judgments. It was new people, new customers, new opportunities, new servers to train. But it's a long day. It can burn you out and burn you up."

Feeling Goofy

Calls from people claiming to represent Disney World did not impress Richard. In 1996, he heard from a party that wanted him to open a Columbia Restaurant in Celebration, Disney's upscale planned community.

"So many people always said, 'We're with Disney World and we have a project for you.' They'd call and call. Finally, I went to Kissimmee. I introduced myself and they took me to a room called the Goofy Conference Room. That's about how I felt, because I wasn't prepared for a real serious group."

Richard returned to Tampa convinced that despite recent setbacks, the company should open a restaurant in Celebration. Like his Columbia ancestors, Richard snapped at opportunities as they presented themselves. His closest associates dissuaded him from taking any chances—they had just pulled out of Daytona to cut costs. He rolled the dice anyway.

"We started negotiating. They really wanted us, they didn't want a chain. It got to a point they were flying me first-class to New York to meet Robert Stern, who's on the board of directors of Disney. He's one of the leading architects in the country [and] for all of Celebration."

Through tough negotiations, Richard won some valuable concessions and complete confidence in the project. The facility itself, designed by premiere restaurant designer Morris Nathanson, dazzled.

Management transferred Lauren Gonzmart to Celebration as a manager. "Curt and my dad really wanted me to experience that," she says. "My dad told me, 'Look, this is your chance. We're opening a restaurant. I don't know when you'll have another chance to be a part of this and see it and understand it.' I was thrilled that he would think I was capable to do something like that."

The chef hired to open Celebration became difficult. Scoffing at the recipe for the "1905" salad, he refused to serve iceberg lettuce. He changed other recipes at will, ignoring management's desire for consistency within the company. On the day of a "test run" of the restaurant, the chef could not get food out of the kitchen. Richard made it plain that the chef's attitude and performance was unacceptable.

Richard brought the Columbia to Celebration, a private Disney town, in 1997.

Although many advised against it, the Columbia Celebration was a coup for Richard. The design emulated the original in Ybor, but it has a feel all its own. During the course of planning and opening the restaurant, Richard and his management team reinvented the Columbia.

The Columbia still maintains a flamenco troupe and various entertainments, but great food defines the experience.

The chef walked the day before opening in a bid to win his own fiefdom in Celebration, where chefs would call the shots. Richard had seen enough of those days. The chef did not come to work on the second day of the test run, but the restaurant went on without him. On the third day, the chef called to negotiate for his position. "He walked, thinking I would cave in," Richard said. Instead he promoted a promising sous chef, Geraldo Bayona.

The chef-swapping episode was all part of Lauren's learning at Celebration. "

"I was a manager. I went in as a part of this whole opening team. It was very hard to find people to work. It's a tough town to find people in the service industry. They can't afford to live there. I stayed on six months past the opening to make sure they were stable. As time went on, they kind of weaned me out to get me back to Tampa, because it was a haul. I'm twenty-one years old doing all this. I'm trying to figure out how to be an adult."

Luis Diaz: "Celebration was Richard's baby. A lot of people criticized the fact that Richard was going to Celebration, that it was a dream, that it was Disney World. Merchants in Orlando thought it wasn't such a good idea. The Columbia became a winner, a high-class winner. [For] all the real estate people trying to sell their wares, the Columbia was an ideal place for business. They sell high-class wine. Every seventy- or one-hundred-dollar bottle of wine go like crazy over there. So, the Columbia fit like a glove once in Celebration. That was Richard's doing. Richard was the one behind the idea of it all."

Richard Gonzmart: "It's been a tremendous success. Everybody in my family and the company didn't agree with me, but I felt I had to go with my gut feelings. I felt in Disney World, the pulse of what was happening in Florida. Anything Disney was involved with would be a success. I said, 'How could we fail?' I didn't want to put a Columbia in a tourist-oriented location. I wanted to put it in something where residents would come, and still would have allure to the tourists. It is two or three miles from the Disney gates.

"Cesar is smiling. When Disney was coming to Orlando, he wanted so bad to be with Disney."

Reinventing the Columbia

Celebration presented a chance to begin the restaurant afresh, outside of Cesar World. Ironically, to survive, the Columbia had to once again escape its own methods and traditions, borne of necessity and often dysfunctional.

After stints in Sarasota and Sand Key, Curt Gaither went to Celebration as general manager. With Richard and his coworkers, Gaither helped reinvent the restaurant. New employees received training in basic policies and procedures. Curt upgraded all of the tableware, scrutinizing every saucer, spoon, and sugar caddy.

The uniforms changed to a more casual look for every restaurant except Ybor City, where tradition demands tuxedo-like suits. "There was a time when we had different uniforms in each restaurant," Gaither said. "Here in Ybor City, they've always worn the black and white, the tuxedo kind of a look. Some of the restaurants' waiters just wore a vest. Some just wore a black tie. When we opened Celebration, we took it back to the look they had when it was just a café, of the white apron, more of a bistro look. That's what we do in all the other restaurants. Being a little bit more casual, being friendly."

In slow increments, Gaither implemented the changes restaurant by restaurant. About eighteen months after opening Celebration, Richard promoted Curt to director of operations. The happy result is a company that gets more attention, and a president that has a personal life again.

"What Curt has done for me is give me my husband back," Melanie beams.

Jerry and Celebration

Richard recognized the need for steady leadership in the kitchen. Curt Gaither worked with a new chef, Geraldo Bayona, to methodically reconstruct every recipe. "We were making the changes for the Celebration opening," Gaither said.

Geraldo Bayona, or Chef Jerry, may not have known about the great Pijuan. He probably didn't know he was cooking in the footsteps of both Casimiro Sr. and Jr.'s inspired cuisine. Richard wisely recruited Jerry as a chef to open Celebration. Disciplined and imaginative, Jerry knew how to lead a Spanish kitchen. Jim Garris admits, "We really need Latin influence in the back of the house. It's hard to be a white guy and run that place back there."

Corporate Chef Geraldo Bayona—or Chef Jerry—gave a fresh perspective in the kitchen. He began as the chef at Celebration and was soon promoted.

Jerry's guava-glazed lamb ribs are a wonderful choice for tapas.

Jerry can only laugh today that he majored in computer programming after high school. He couldn't stay still in the classroom and realized he had already chosen his profession. "I was always working in a restaurant before that [college] and I always enjoyed it. Everyone always said that I had my heart into that when I was doing it."

Jerry worked with European chefs at fine restaurants and went on to the Florida Culinary Institute in West Palm Beach. He became a journeyman chef for hire, drifting through many kitchens after his graduation in 1985.

"You're hooked then," Jerry said. "It's that whole pace in the kitchen, the fast pace, thinking on your feet—it's so lively, and that's what makes it so fun to me. Cooking and designing products, working with all these different foods, learning. You just can't explain sometimes, because it's just so much enjoyment from mixing everything up. And making people happy, of course."

Jerry worked in a restaurant on Florida's east coast when a new opportunity arose. "The chef got offered a position at the [Columbia] restaurant Celebration, when they were going to open up and they wanted me to come with him as a sous chef. I started in Celebration. We actually opened up Celebration, he left, and two months later I became the chef there.

"What I knew about the Columbia was, that they had a big old restaurant in Tampa, it was a city block long! I remember before I even came there that I had nightmares thinking about how Celebration would be, because I was used to working in smaller restaurants. You hear a restaurant that's 1,500 square feet you're just like, 'Oh, my God!'"

A wedding reception in Ybor forced Jerry to confront his nightmares. He saw the Ybor City kitchen for himself. When asked of his impression of that disorganized workplace back then, he replied, "Definitely appalled." There was no air-conditioning in the back of the house.

"Before I went to Celebration, they didn't want me training over here [in Ybor City] because they thought I might get too scared. That's why I trained in St. Pete." The chef there showed Jerry the ropes. Curt Gaither became one of Jerry's most important mentors. Today, the chef credits Curt with helping him attain his present status.

The Columbia Celebration opened in 1997, and Jerry lived nearby on the outskirts of Orlando. Jerry became corporate chef in 2006. For new chefs, he offers this advice: "You need to keep your calm, because your people will know that you're under control, and that will make them worry less. Make sure you delegate. Know what is going on, and make sure you have all your key people, especially when you have those big functions, having it all organized. Organization is key to running a big kitchen."

Jerry is decidedly a twenty-first-century chef, ordering supplies online, creating spreadsheets for his records, and keeping the kitchen more organized than ever before. He designed the kitchens in Celebration and West Palm Beach. He designed the renovated Sarasota kitchen, and plans on putting his own design touches on the new Ybor City kitchen.

In a short time, Jerry recognized the Columbia's unique qualities. "The big difference is the family orientation it has," he said. "A lot of restaurants, they are so corporate, everything is this way. Yes, we have our standards, but having family input makes it so much more enjoyable to work here."

The Next Generation of Cuisine

"I've always worked with Caribbean food," Jerry observes. "I'm Puerto Rican myself—mom's cooking. The most experience I have would be Spanish cooking."

Coming from the Northeast, Curt Gaither admitted that he "didn't know the rice from the beans" when he first arrived at the Columbia. Jerry, however, recognized many of the influences on the menu when he took the job: "Cuba, Spain, and some influence from the Caribbean. They [the Columbia] made their own cuisine, you can actually say. It evolved into what we make. We have the richness of the Spaniards, those [northern] regions up there. The freshness of the Caribbean, a lot of the fresh fruits, and all the vegetables they use over there."

Unable to adequately define the cuisine, he says, "It's just good. The garlic. We use a lot of demi-glace and stocks, and that makes it the richer food, and we use cream and butter. Comfort food.

"Like any chef coming into a new location I was like, 'Oh my God, I can't believe they do that,' or 'I can do that better.' When I was at Celebration, we actually started standardizing the recipes for all the locations. They had recipes, but we said, 'We need to standardize *all* the recipes.'

In between 1995 and 2000, the Columbia's recipes were standardized and improved after suffering through tough times. The Cuban Combination. Clockwise from top: boliche, yucca, roast pork, empanada, with black beans and rice at the center.

"A tourist might come once a year, they don't know how something should really taste. For them, it's probably good, but it wasn't at its best. But a regular customer who comes here twice a week, or once a month, they want to come back and have the same product they had the other time. This way they don't say, 'What's up with that? Well, I don't want to go to that location, I'm going to go to *this* location.' I really wouldn't want to hear that."

Curt Gaither: "We took a look at the presentation of the food, the recipes. We went through the menu and decided what could be made better. It needed an upgrade. We put so much on ourselves to get better, and Richard presses that as well. Sometimes we have to stop and look where we came from. It's gotten better and better everyday, every year, and when you look around the restaurant, even if you go look around Ybor City, it's the same restaurant, but it's not the same restaurant.

"At that time, we had six chefs that would all tell you they made the best boliche. In some cases they were good, but

they were very inconsistent. I could ask someone for a recipe and he would reach in his pocket and take out a crumpled piece of paper in Spanish. There was no way we were going to nail down the consistency of the restaurants like that. Jerry was a big part of that. [We] worked on implementing the recipes.

"We took what was being made in the restaurant, say in Ybor City, and one thing we constantly did was go back to Adela's notebook. If I could get a buck for every time Richard said, 'Check my mom's book.' We would make the recipe and make it in a batch and document what we put in, have a tasting with the family and whoever was to be involved.

"Richard was always there: Casey, Lauren, Andrea, whoever was going to be involved. And good, bad, different, we'd make an adjustment, make it again, make it again. When we finally got what we thought was best, that became the recipe.

"At that point, it was implemented in all the restaurants. So when we run a good special, we'll document the recipe, take some pictures, and add it to the book. We change the menu with the same process. The book was one small binder when we started; it's now three full books.

A recipe's efficiency was also scrutinized. Knowing how much a dish cost helped determine portions and prices. Andrea Gonzmart gathered information from Jerry to calculate every recipe's ingredients, cost, and yield. She then put the information into a central database, from which the Columbia's recipe books were derived. Andrea developed a keen sense of taste and scent as a result.

"We started making recipe books up," Jerry says, "writing down all the recipes in our own formats, passing [them] out to all the chefs in all the different locations, and that's when everything started getting more consistent.

"We made all the recipes, I think it was the first chef's

meeting they *ever* had [laughs]. That's when we brought out the books and we had a training session about some recipes; to present them here the way they were in the recipe book. So everybody saw what we wanted, and we all went back to our locations and did our recipes."

The revised recipes and procedures delivered consistently superior food at every location. Arroz con pollo received a much-needed makeover, according to Curt Gaither. "We know that the chicken and rice is best when it comes out of the oven. It's worth explaining to the guest, it may take a little longer, but it's going to be dynamite when it comes out. When they order the chicken and rice, it's going to be totally different than what they got years ago. Something that was baked in a big batch and sat around and waited. It was a big deal when we [changed] it. It was a big adjustment for some of the servers that had been here for a long time. Now, all of a sudden, they've got to wait for an item that was normally just, 'Pick it up and go.' Response from the guests has been great."

Chef Jerry: "We did make the yellow rice more consistent in every location by making sofrito. Basically they [in Ybor] measure everything out, and all they [in the other restaurants] have to do is add water to it, and it makes the rice good." Jerry brews a lively sofrito: "Onions, peppers, lots of garlic, white wine, saffron and coloring, bay leaves, all the seasonings, and tomatoes. Just add water to it and it comes out to the flavor that we want. So they can't mess it up! I would say, it's probably one of our biggest improvements in all the areas food-wise."

"Some of the recipes were re-created or revised," Curt Gaither says. "The pompano en papillot was an item from the '40s. It was a time to use canned vegetables. It wasn't uncommon to get canned string beans or canned fruit salad. No one can really do that now and be successful. The stuffing was basically a roux with very little seafood in it. Flour, butter, and a stuffing. Whereas now it's made with artichokes, spinach, crab. It's really a much better filling. So the item is still there and we refer to it as an item

revisited from the '40s. I think we make changes when they're necessary with the times."

Chef Jerry: "The staples will never change. The boliche, the roast pork, and Merluza. Those things will actually never change."

 ## Family Spirits

In 1996, Richard spoke about cigars at a nightclub convention in Las Vegas. Booker Noe, then sixty-eight, the grandson of Jim Beam, was scheduled to speak about his family's livelihood, bourbon. Noe introduced a line of some of the finest bourbons in the world, including Booker's, Knob Creek, Baker's, Basil Hayden, and a variety of other Jim Beam products. Richard was scheduled to speak after the bourbon heir. Richard decided to attend Noe's talk that morning, a seminar on small-batch bourbon.

Richard found himself facing five glasses of bourbon at ten in the morning when Booker reminded his audience, "It's five o'clock in the evening somewhere."

Richard became familiar with Booker Noe's bourbon during multiple visits to his estate.

Richard: "So I started drinking this bourbon anywhere from 90 up to 127 proof. And I'm friggin' lit. And I go to my presentation, I thought it was flawless. I thought it was the best."

Richard was so enthused about bourbon that he secured dinner with Booker Noe that night. "I sat there, nervously waiting like a groupie."

In an effort to calm down, Richard ordered a cocktail, thoughtlessly calling for a vodka martini. At six feet seven inches and all of 300 pounds, Booker was a massive presence. For Richard's associates, the unthinkable happened—he fell silent. "I could not find the words to speak."

A few glasses of Booker's amber elixir restored Richard's speech, perhaps too much for his own comfort: "I had dinner with him that night. I started to drink with Booker, and you can't drink with Booker." Today, Richard's memory of the meal is dim.

When the phone woke him at eleven the next morning, Richard had a hangover and the distinct feeling that he'd said or done something foolish the night before. Jim Beam's national account manager was on the line to say he'd made

arrangements for Richard and Melanie to visit Kentucky and select the Columbia's barrel of bourbon, equivalent to more than fifty cases.

"What the hell is a Cuban going to do with a freaking barrel of bourbon?" Richard wondered.

Richard visited Jim Beam's estate in Bardstown to see Booker and select his barrel of bourbon. Richard and Melanie arrived at four in the afternoon ready to talk whiskey. But Booker had other plans. They sat down to drink Kentucky tea, bourbon and water over ice.

Booker explained that people used coffee and tea to flavor their water, so why not bourbon? Then Booker asked Melanie, "Little lady, how many cubes for you?" He referred to ice cubes, not sugar. Richard suggested, "One cube, because they drink it neat, straight. You put an ice cube in it which dilutes it, because it melts right away."

"It sure did taste better than the water back home," Richard admits.

"Let's work tomorrow," Booker said. "How about if we go home and see what's cooking?"

A sumptuous southern feast awaited them: real Kentucky-fried chicken, collard greens, country ham, corn pudding,

One of Booker's massive bourbon rack houses.

As a tribute to his uncle Evelio, Richard named the Columbia's best-selling steak after him. It is topped with mushroom demi-glace and flambéed in Booker Noe bourbon.

black-eyed peas, and corn bread. Richard ate three helpings, then sat back with Booker to enjoy cigars, conversation, and more bourbon.

"I was in heaven," Richard said. He also admits, "I got drunk again."

"The next morning arrived too quickly for me," Richard remembers. "At eight in the morning I go out to meet his son Freddy in rack-house C. They call the buildings where they put the bourbon 'rack-houses.' Rack-house C was his favorite. He liked the way it faced the south and it's twelve stories high. They have probably thousands of barrels, but he likes the middle rack. The higher it is, the more evaporation on the bourbon it is; the lower, the less evaporation. The middle, he said, is perfect. He took five barrels out for me."

One by one, Richard sampled the barrels, sipping from brandy snifters. "They went left to right, right to left. Freddy told me it was the breakfast of champions. Here it was, 8:00 A.M., drinking bourbon right out of the barrel! I said, 'Man, I'm freaking drunk again! They all tasted good! I'll take the middle one.'

"Booker gave me a smoked ham to take home. I go to the airport totally annihilated. I put my ham through the baggage check. They said, 'What is that?' I said, 'It's a ham from Booker Noe!'"

Richard's trip to Bardstown was a distinct pleasure, but one question still vexed him: "What the hell is a Cuban going to do with a freaking barrel of bourbon?"

Richard's family provided inspiration. Evelio (Chacho), youngest of the Hernandez brothers, had run the Columbia coffee mill for over thirty years. Kind and warm-hearted, Chacho's love of bourbon sometimes surpassed his love of coffee. He roasted some of the best coffee known to man, but burned countless batches while drinking or passed out.

Richard remembers learning how to roast coffee from Chacho. "In the summer of 1970, he taught me how to carefully watch the coffee beans as they roasted in our 1926 Hobart Coffee Roaster. He would talk all about the old times in the business and of his military service." Chacho loved to tell people about the time he sent his mother a photograph of himself knee-deep in Alaskan snow, clad only in his underwear.

Chacho developed such a love of bourbon—especially mixed with Coca-Cola—that his brothers tried to keep him from it. He took to sneaking away from the roasting coffee to drink at the Lido bar down the street. He sometimes didn't make it back in less than twenty-five minutes, roughly when Cuban coffee is finished roasting. Entire batches of Columbia coffee beans often burned up, and the coffee mill itself caught fire, threatening the restaurant.

Richard: "The standing joke in Ybor was when the smoke would bellow through the roof, 'Casimiro must have caught Evelio at the Lido bar.' In memory of my loving great uncle and the meeting of Booker Noe, I created the filet mignon 'Chacho,' for his fun-loving spirit and lust for life."

A grilled filet mignon steak is topped with a mushroom demi-glace, then flambéed tableside with Booker Noe bourbon. The dish, and interest in the bourbon, brought sales that drained Richard's barrel. "We didn't only go through that barrel," Richard says. "We go through about three or four barrels a year. We're one of the largest users of Booker Noe in the world.

"I've been to Booker's house three times to pick the barrels, every time I've gotten drunk, and every time I've picked the

middle barrel. I say, 'Look, I'm not going back any more, just pick the middle barrel.'"

Chacho passed away in 1983, Booker in 2004. "I am a better person for having known them."

Solvency

The threat of financial ruin lingered over the Columbia for several years after Cesar's death. "These were the most difficult times," Richard confides. "We took major salary cuts. I was able to pay off our attorneys. We owed a bunch of money to the landlord in Sarasota. I talked to them, made those payments, paid off [food distributor] Henry Lee. They didn't think I would pay them off in full. I paid off everybody. That's where I gained the respect of the business community.

"One bank called me, they wanted my business. I said, 'You had the opportunity three years ago when I went there. I was shown the door.' Everybody wants a winner, but you want to be with somebody that's there in the tough times. People that switch for a nickel, when you have a problem, nobody is going be there for you. Those were the difficult times, facing the State of Florida, facing jail. I had to protect my mom, protect everything."

Food distributor Henry Lee stood by the Columbia and gave Richard three years to pay off the Columbia's heavy debt. Dennis Fedorovich: "I had mentioned to [Richard] that we were getting ready to make the final payment. I suggested, 'Why don't we just go down and hand them the last check [in person]?' They were part of sustaining the legacy here."

Richard wanted to thank Ed Sterling, the president at Henry Lee. "I called him. I was going to fly down to meet him, thank him and give him his check. I say, 'I would like to meet with you.' They're like, 'What the hell is happening? He's going to tell me that he can't pay!' They're waiting for some bad news. I gave them the last check. I said, 'I want to thank you very much for your faith and your trust in me.' That's where I gained the strength. I realized the power of truth."

Dennis remembers some additional milestones in the Columbia's remarkable turnaround story. "The first time that we were able to provide any kind of dividend payment to the owners, to Richard and Casey, was one of the top moments. I remember having a conversation with Casey in 1996 or so. I told Casey that there will come a time when the company will be able to pay dividends to them. They both understood that you can't pay dividends until you pay back that debt."

Casey said he didn't expect another dividend payment in his lifetime. But Dennis assured him that the company would soon be solvent. In 2001, the CFO proudly handed Casey his first dividend check in years. Richard

and Casey's fiscal discipline made the dramatic recovery possible.

With the debts paid off or under control, the company could plan for the future. Major repairs and renovations to the Ybor flagship began with the kitchen in 2000. Renovations proceeded in the other locations. Functionally and cosmetically, the company was virtually reborn.

Rebuilding

The Gonzmart brothers supervised a multimillion-dollar effort to preserve and upgrade the Columbia's original location in Ybor City. They replaced the Don Quixote Room's roof and installed new air-conditioning. Artifacts from the early days of chilled air lay abandoned on the roof for decades. Mike Charles, owner of the Columbia's climate control experts, C.G.M., called Richard after he'd found a relic. The serial number on an antiquated air hammer included only two digits.

Richard explained, "Mike, in 1935 it was left up there, how many places had air-conditioning?" They joked that the piece belongs in a museum, and it probably does.

A dramatic incident in 1998 illustrated how badly the building needed repairs. The roof had fallen into disrepair and retained water. Rain flowed through a small hole in the roof and gathered on the drop ceiling of the restaurant's commissary. A veritable swimming pool gathered during a heavy storm in the late 1990s when the ceiling broke. The ceiling of the commissary collapsed, releasing a filthy torrent onto the soup and sauce stations there. The waters did not crest until they flooded the Patio and Siboney rooms. It took the laundry room more than six months to recover. Thankfully, the commissary no longer served the entire company, and the Ybor location could manage its own soups and sauces.

Standing in the new Andalusia Room, Jim Garris can point out much of the restaurant's recent renovations. He

The vital new kitchen boasted air-conditioning for the first time in 95 years.

reminisces about the archaic switchboard system governing the restaurant's phone lines. He still brightens when he thinks about replacing the old electric systems and drop ceilings.

Jim Garris: "The roofs and the air-conditioning were a project, because all of the air-conditioning was breaking down. They were band-aided together.

"Ybor City was a wreck at that point in time. The building was falling apart. We had leaks everywhere, ceilings were coming in, the kitchen was falling apart, and there was no money to fix it. There was hardly even any money to buy glassware and things like that. It was crazy. So we were band-aiding everything up, and continued to struggle with building problems."

Beginning in 2000, vital kitchen improvements beautified the restaurant and boosted employee morale. The new kitchen, nearly a city block long, signaled that the Columbia was on the rise in dramatic fashion. Before renovation, the kitchen occupied only 1,500 feet. One could fit several small restaurants in the Columbia's new 5,000-square-foot kitchen. The project brightened spirits and improved the food at a cost exceeding $2 million.

It is hard to believe that the chefs could produce at all in the old, cramped kitchen, which was not even air-conditioned. The brothers Gonzmart worked with Chef Paco Duarte to design the new kitchen. The vast kitchen boasted twenty-first century technology. A blast chiller could drop the temperature of bagged soup and sauces to below 40 degrees in under ninety minutes, banishing any

The opening of the new Ybor kitchen in 2001 marked a great milestone in the Columbia's history. Family members of three generations passed an Olympic-style torch from the old kitchen to the new..

bacteria. The bagged product could be saved or shipped off site. Jerry's sofrito could stay fresh without losing flavor in a freezer. Huge sixty-gallon steam kettles warmed batches of vegetable stock, the base of the Columbia's sauces. Fresh fish went straight into a special cooler.

An industrial water extractor could suck food, liquid, trash, even cardboard boxes through a pipe and separate solids from liquids. The remaining damp pulp weighed a fraction of normal garbage, reducing volume by 85 percent, which saved money and allowed the dirty water to be re-cycled. In 2001, when the *Tampa Tribune* columnist Steve Otto wanted to escape the Pacific rim, French, and new fusion restaurants cropping up all over town, he came to the Columbia for a 1905 salad. Richard gushed about the new kitchen. Otto thought it unusual that anyone could get "excited over garbage. I couldn't get that excited over a waste disposal system." Nonetheless, Otto appreciated Richard's passion for his family legacy.

The gleaming new kitchen was constructed by Ken Schwartz, great-grandson to Louis Wohl, the designer of

Casimiro's 1935 kitchen. Despite all the impressive technol-ogy, one feature made the workers happiest of all: air-con-ditioning. If only Pijuan could have seen the new kitchen. The old master chef would have respected Richard's stand against the microwave oven.

To celebrate the opening of the new kitchen and attract the attention of the press, the company held a "passing of the torch" ceremony. Andrea lit an Olympic-style torch from the stove of the old kitchen—originally installed in 1935—and passed it to Adela in the new kitchen. Adela, in turn, passed the torch to Casey's oldest son, Casey Jr., who

When workers remodeled the Café, they found business cards bearing messages from Cesar, who had passed away years before.

Jim Garris remembers renovating the Café. "We tore the roof off, put a new roof on it, put new A/C in it, took out the interior ceilings, put in a new drop ceiling, put a new bar in the Café. We actually hoisted that [top] piece [of the bar] from Cuba from the rafters while the [base]was being built. They brought the bottom part in, set it underneath and lowered that back down on top. Then we had an artist come in and re-antique that and make it look old again.

"Then we went to the Don Quixote and redid the roof, new air-conditioning, and redid the ceiling on the inside."

George Guito remembers changing the Don Quixote Room from a dark dinner club to a brightened haven for lunch. "We took the Don Quixote and fixed it all up and made it brighter in the daytime. More people would come at daytime, because a lot of people, especially lunch business, want to be where there is a little daylight. We changed all the colors in that particular room."

While renovating the Don Quixote Room, Richard called a lighting expert to refurbish its elaborate chandelier. The majestic fixture once graced Miami's Eden Roc Hotel in 1956. The hotel closed in the 1970s, when Cesar and Adela bought the chandelier for three thousand dollars at an auction. Many of the prisms had cracked over the years, often because of repeated blows from the flamenco dancers' fans.

Fixing up the antique, with its 465 prisms, would be an arduous and expensive task. James Blocker, the lighting expert hired by the company, was awestruck by the artistry of the piece. "It's unique unto itself." He shocked Richard by assessing the chandelier's value at $250,000. A little research revealed that a French craftsman had fashioned the piece in the 1800s. It had taken him two years.

Refurbishing the fixture took some time and about fifteen thousand dollars. Workers washed each prism in hot water to melt off years of candle wax. At seven feet wide, the chandelier could not fit through the door, so Blocker

lit a stove in the new kitchen. The kitchen of the 1930s gave way to the twenty-first century. The ceremony was one of Adela's last public appearances.

Richard and company then renovated each dining room in turn, beginning with the Café. While workers rearranged the structure, the walls literally talked back on occasion. The old side door from the Café to Twenty-second Street had been boarded up for over thirty years. A key was still in the door lock when it was discovered in 2002 with one of Cesar's business cards taped to the door. On the front, it read, "This door was closed August 6, 1979, at the same time as all the windows." When removed from the door, a new message was revealed on the back of the card. "I hope you all are happy, and I love you and wish you well."

"It was like he was speaking from somewhere else," Casey Gonzmart said at the time. "I look at it every day." Richard and company found several other cards from Cesar around the place.

After the new kitchen opened, the old kitchen space was converted into the Andalucia Room and the adjoining Familia de Casimiro Room.

dismantled it and polished the brass. Today, the chandelier is still the room's centerpiece.

Management thought of the Columbia's makeover as preservation rather than renovation. They scraped down paint to find original colors. The Siboney Room morphed from a supper club to a banquet room, with movable walls to allow flexibility in the size of events. When crews ripped out the carpet, the original imported Cuban tile, first laid in 1955, was exposed.

Each room received a makeover until none remained. Fresh renovations produced the King's Room, formerly the

Vista Hermosa, in the late 1980s. La Familia de Casimiro Room seats twenty-four, the Andalucia seats eighty-eight—the company completed both in 2004. The world-class wine cellar appeared in 2005. The interior designer Morris Nathanson used materials imported from Spain.

George Guito: "Now we're constantly changing, upkeeping it. It's a constant battle. It takes a huge investment. Richard and Casey have done what a lot of people never thought that they were going to do."

By 2000, Richard reined in an aggressive expansion campaign that relied on new restaurant concepts to focus on existing restaurants. He gave up Cesar's dream of owning thirty eateries. An influx of high-end eateries into Tampa and Florida forced the company to focus on quality. The Gonzmarts increased staff by 20 percent. Despite the national economic downturn after the terrorist attacks of September 11, 2001, the Columbia's earnings increased between 2000 and 2002 (8 percent), and again the next year (11 percent).

Jim Garris: "The rest is history, basically. We rebuilt this building and it rebuilt the company. We have DSL in most of the rooms, and people wouldn't suspect it, but we're ready for the future now and continue to do as much business as we can. This is a living, breathing animal."

The renovation project took four years and $4 million and increased seating by 200 to 1,700. "We will never wear the place out," Richard said. "We'll just keep reinvesting. We're just the caretakers for this generation."

Lauren's Gifts

In the mid-1990s, cigars fell back into popularity with celebrities and the well-heeled. Richard responded by found-

Every room of the Columbia Ybor City was renovated between 1995 and 2005.

Photo By Rob/Harris

The Gonzmart family restored the Columbia with the sensibilities of curators.

working at Sand Key and waiting for Celebration to open, she stocked the store and ran the cash register.

In 1998, the company hired a manager to run the Columbia's new gift shops, who did not perform as expected. Lauren wanted to settle down in Tampa and start a family. She was interested in trying something different. After a little prodding from Lauren and Melanie, Richard gave Lauren control of the company's retail division.

When she surveyed her operations upon taking control in 1998, she was not impressed. "I don't want to call it 'rinky dinky,' but it was. We were selling whatever cigars we could get our hands on, which weren't necessarily very good." However, the Columbia carried a good house brand cigar, Gonzalez y Martinez, which is still available."

The company capitalized on the cigar craze of the 1990s. Andrea even appeared in *Cigar Aficionado* magazine smoking a cigar at age seventeen. Richard bought out a small gift store adjacent to the Columbia's own gift shop, the final piece of the city block to be acquired by the company. This allowed the removal of the wall between the two gift shops,

ing his own cigar company, Gonzalez y Martinez, housing it in a small retail space in the Ybor restaurant. Casimiro Sr. began the Columbia's first retail efforts, opening a package store that sold cigars, beer, wine, and spirits. Junior expanded offerings to include postcards, souvenirs, and packaged food products like canned soup. Adela opened a couple of shops called Adela's Gifts in Rocky Point and Sarasota, selling fine trinkets, jewelry, and keepsakes. Cesar marketed frozen food and sangria mix. But the Columbia had been without a discrete retail space outside the liquor store.

The gift shop opened in 1997 to exploit the growing popularity of cigars, and Lauren was its first employee. Finished

creating more space. Richard had seen trends come and go, and had no plans for the retail division beyond the cigar company. The gift shops made 90 percent of their revenue from cigars alone.

Lauren had free-standing gift shops in Ybor, Sarasota, and Celebration, and stocked the other locations with merchandise. She carried better cigars and expanded the stores' offerings. She could also rely on the Columbia's line of food products: 1905 salad dressing, black beans, yellow rice, sangria mix, seasoning, hot sauce, and coffee.

Back in the corporate office, Lauren didn't feel like she was taken seriously by Richard's financial team. It was a one-woman operation: ordering, unpacking, packaging, and sending product out to the stores. She recruited her mother and sister to help assemble gift baskets and wrap packages.

After some initial research into the gift industry, Lauren attended sales conventions and visited wholesale centers. In order to transition the retail presence away from a reliance on cigars, Lauren went to a giant retail mart in Atlanta. With no permission and no guidance, Lauren and her mother checked into a humble motel down the street from the store.

"I'm trying to be really economical, because I know that they're going to cut off my head for this. Checking in at the Ritz Carlton would not have gone over well." Lauren's mother, Melanie, was not pleased with the accommodations. "That's camping for my mom!" Andrea interjects.

"We felt like we were country bumpkins," Lauren continues, "because we get there and there are three buildings that are twenty stories high of showrooms. We look at each other. I really have no clue what I am doing. I don't know how to buy on this level. I don't know about quantities. I don't know about credit sheets and applications. They are speaking this whole other language that I have had no exposure to. We walk all these floors and kind of figure it out."

The Red Room occupies the site of the Don Quixote Room's bar.

"I finally had transitioned the business beyond cigars. I was bringing in Spanish food products that I could find, which was very hard to do at that point. Back then, nobody cared about Spanish olives and olive oil, all this stuff I was looking for. So when I could find it, I would bring more gourmet-type olive oils and vinegars."

The cheapest and most simple jewelry sells best. While viewing sales reports, Richard would eye best-selling items incredulously. "What the hell is a 'color bar bracelet?'" Richard would ask. Lauren replied, "It's this little bracelet with beads and people really love them. For $3.99, they love it and they'll buy them all day long."

Instead of presiding over a company setback, Lauren initiated growth with her retail efforts. Customers in Sarasota ate lunch at the Columbia and went shopping for souvenirs. After walking St. Armands Circle, they always seemed to end up back at the Columbia's gift shop for their keepsakes.

"I can't describe what we sell because it's a real hodge-podge. I sell home décor, I sell tabletop, I sell jewelry, I sell gourmet food products. You can come in and buy a $350 bronze mermaid or you can buy a $1.99 plastic ring."

Andrea: "When I showed up on the scene, one of the first financial meetings I showed up to, they were like, 'Once again, the retail is an increase.'" Lauren had done well. "I could have just completely screwed it up," Lauren reflects. "But I'm still here and I'm still buying."

The Columbia Hall of Fame

In the 1990s, the Columbia managemernt created its own Hall of Fame, and twenty-three employees have been inducted for excellent service, length of employment, and contributions to the Columbia's legacy. Every other summer, the Columbia holds an annual employee-appreciation dinner, when new inductees are announced. Almost one in five of the Columbia's 775 employees have worked in the company for a decade or more.

Jose Alberto Menendez, who manned the sauté station for thirty-four years, was the first cook to instruct Richard. He came to Tampa from Camagüey, Cuba, in 1954, and came to the Columbia five years later. In 1998, the company inducted Menendez into the Hall of Fame. On Christmas Eve 2006, he died at the age of 84. Pantry man Luis Garcia, who joined the Columbia's ranks in 1965, became an expert in the preparation of the 1905 salad. When Garcia died in November 2006, he was still a full-time employee.

Memories and Ivory

Pianist Henry Tudela walked into the restaurant and fixed himself a cup of coffee. He might smoke a cigarette and have a bite to eat before his first set. He slid onto the bench with the grace of a classical concert pianist, his wrists suspended over the keys just so. The routine began in 1936 and didn't change much over the years.

Henry first pressed the keys of a piano at age six and was immediately smitten with the sound. "I really liked it," Henry said. "My dad decided I should take lessons after that." He studied the playing of greats like Duke Ellington. He played his very first show at the Columbia at age twenty in the newly debuted Don Quixote Room. Henry stayed on for more than sixty years, long enough for the *Guinness Book of World Records* to recognize his gig as the world's longest, from 1936 to 2002, with a three-year interruption when he served in the army during World War II.

Henry's fine musicianship and agreeable manner earned him a position in Cesar's Continental Society Orchestra in 1948. They played upscale clubs all over the Western hemisphere, toured with Liberace, and eventually landed at the Columbia with Cesar. "Henry was Cesar's right arm," Adela remembered. "He always accompanied him while he played the violin, and no one accompanied him like Henry."

Joe Roman served as a Columbia waiter for about fifty years—and then became the restaurant's ambassador.

Whenever Adela entered the Siboney, Henry made her entrance all the more dramatic when he struck up the song that was the room's namesake, her favorite. He played with Cuban composer Ernesto Lecuona when the room first opened.

Accompanied by bassist Nilo Cabrera in recent years, "He helped maintain the aura of days gone by," Casey said. He could pick up a song by ear in just two listenings, and eventually stopped buying sheet music. He lived in West Tampa and enjoyed playing dominoes with the old-timers at the Centro Asturiano.

Henry rarely missed a day of work. Even while being treated for cancer, he'd come straight to the restaurant after medical appointments. He was inducted into the Columbia Hall of Fame in 2000. He died in August 2002 after a twenty-year struggle with cancer, but he went out with his music at the Columbia still ringing in his ears.

The Ambassador

In need of knee-replacement surgery, veteran waiter Joe Roman could no longer wait tables. He retired in 2002. "I did a little part-time, and then I had trouble with the knees and I stopped. I was retired. It was over a year that I didn't do anything."

His wife brought in a modest monthly paycheck, but without his job, they could not make ends meet. Florida's property taxes and insurance priced Joe out of his own home. He only had the funds to hold out for five more years.

"If it wasn't because of Richard and Casey, I would have to sell my house. I never thought I would get to over sixty-five. The [property] insurance for my house went up, and the taxes. Now Richard and Casey give me eight hundred dollars a month."

One day in 2004, Richard met the old waiter in his office, where he insisted on sending Joe and his wife on a vacation. "He gave us a week, for the wife and I, a first-class cruise! We went all the way out to Mexico, Belize. He even gave us money to spend.

"It was a very romantic cruise. I had never been on a cruise before. We've been married for fifty-seven years. A beautiful trip."

Upon his return, Richard asked to see Joe again. Richard asked Joe to become the Columbia's honorary ambassador. Few knew the customers, building, and traditions so well. As ambassador, Joe would mingle with customers and guide tours of the huge facility.

Joe Roman: "Their idea. I never thought of this. I got in all [the] papers and everybody wanted to have an interview with me. I introduce myself a lot of times for all the tables at lunch, and everything. I give them my card, 'We have two shows nightly. Any time, you call in, we'll have your table ready.'"

Because Joe was caring for his ailing wife and has had medical problems of his own, Richard told him only to come in when he could. The ambassador is paid all the same.

The same year Joe was named ambassador, 2004, the Florida Governor's Conference on Tourism gave Joe Roman the Iris D. Larson Hospitality Award for his outstanding career. "I was treated like a king," Roman said. "The

The pianist Henry Tudela played at the Columbia for more than sixty years. He was Cesar's right-hand man on the concert stage.

Gonzmarts even hired a limousine to pick me up and my beautiful wife, Matilda." In 2006, Tampa mayor Pam Iorio declared August 16 as "Joe Roman Day" to observe his half century of service at the Columbia Restaurant.

Lula Mae

For nearly fifty years, Lula Mae Tollaman came to work exceptionally groomed and immaculately dressed in white.

A young Lula served as housemaid in Casimiro Jr.'s home during the 1950s until a new opportunity came up. Having just opened the Siboney Room in 1956–57, Casimiro wanted to make women at the Columbia ever more comfortable. He hired Lula to be the attendant of the ladies' room. At first, she was unclear about her job duties, and arrived to work with a mop she had scrimped and saved the two dollars to buy. She soon began arriving to work with her Bible instead, to read during slow times.

That first year, Lula told herself, "I'm just going to work until Christmas." Then came Easter, when Lula resolved to stay until her daughter graduated high school. The years flew by: her daughter graduated college, became a teacher, and retired. Lula stayed at her post. "I'm working because I love it," Lula beamed in 2005. "I love the Columbia too much to leave."

"Richard is a wonderful boss," she said. "His mother used to bring him in here [to the ladies' room] when he was too young to go in the men's room."

Richard said of Lula, "Here was a person who was so proud, and yet she had a job that most people would say had little importance." Born in Georgia and raised in West Tampa, she was a rare, disarming soul who could talk to and comfort anyone. She addressed friends, strangers, and celebrities with equal warmth and poise.

Tearful, nervous women on dates often sought refuge in Lula's powder room. They could always rely on her sage advice and sympathetic ear. Her basket of hairspray, makeup, and toiletries may have been convenient, but Lula's conversation proved her greatest service. "Women come in, I see them so heartbroken and I tell them, 'Honey, fix your face up and your hair and walk out there. Don't you ever let them see you cry.'"

Over the years, she talked up and listened to a plethora of celebrities. She spoke with Marilyn Monroe for so long that Joe DiMaggio had to retrieve his date from the ladies' room. "She was just like on the screen, so darling and sweet," Lula said. "Eva Gabor was the most darling person. It was just like she lit a candle in here. Have you ever met someone that left such an impression on you?"

Lula Mae Tollaman began working as the women's restroom attendant in the 1950s and wouldn't accept another job at the restaurant. When asked about retirement in her later years, she responded, "I'm just waitin' on Oprah!"

Lula watched many girls grow into women. A young lady came to the restaurant with a Dade City man for an extended period. One night, the woman came in aglow with romance.

"You're so beautiful tonight," Lula said.

The young lover responded, "I'm so in love. Do you think he'll ask me?"

"I don't think he can refuse," insisted Lula. "Keep looking like you're looking."

The couple soon married, had children, and never stopped coming to the Columbia. And Lula Mae was an important part of the experience. She received more mail from friends and fans than anyone at the Columbia. At home, Lula grew roses, cooked for friends and family, and was active in church. She read constantly, and never put down her Bible for long. Three generations of management treasured Lula's charming presence. When management repeatedly offered her promotion, she always refused to leave her post.

When her son became ill in Texas, Cesar paid for her plane tickets. "I went into the bathroom and started crying. That's the way he made me cry, with happiness." She got

the same feeling at her son's funeral when she saw Cesar and Adela standing at one of the church pews. "I tell you I almost crumbled."

Lula attended every Gonzmart family event in her time. She spent time in Casimiro and Carmen's kitchen. She scolded young Richard when he crawled between the stalls of the restaurant's ladies' room. When a teenage Richard met Melanie at the restaurant for their first date, he introduced her to Adela and Lula, and the two greatest women in his life met the third. Richard still calls Lula his second mother. She watched Richard and Casey marry and other relatives pass away. Whenever Richard was troubled, he would seek Lula's counsel. "She'd turn me around like nobody could. Not even my parents could do that."

"When [Cesar] took sick [in 1992]," Lula said, "we went to see him in the hospital. When I got there, he was sitting up in bed and said, 'Oh, Lula.' I started pulling up a chair. He said, 'Oh no, you sit right here by me on this bed.' And we started talking about the old times, oh yes, the old times, and laughing.

Then, Cesar turned back to his longtime employee beside him. "Lula, I hurt so bad and I'm so sick, will you pray for me?"

Left to right: Andrea and Lauren Gonzmart, Lula Mae Tollaman, Joe Roman, and Richard, Melanie, and Casey Gonzmart.

"I was afraid to pray with all the nurses walking around," she remembered years later. She ducked into the ladies' room. "I prayed so hard that day." Before she left, Cesar hugged her one last time and said, "Lula, I love you." Cesar's declaration touched Lula deeply, who insisted that anyone who had not met Cesar had missed part of their lives.

Lula considered leaving when Cesar passed and took his magic violin with him, but Adela convinced her to stay. "Don't go until I'm gone," the matriarch implored.

When Lauren married, Lula sat in the family's pew. "We had family not allowed in the family pews," Richard said.

"They made me part of the family," Lula said. "Nobody could steal me away. Nobody but Oprah. I'm waiting for Oprah to call me now, I really am." In April 2005, she won the Bern Laxer Spirit of Excellence Award for her customer service.

Lula took a vacation in August that year and never returned to work. Richard and Melanie visited Lula at her home, where she was stricken with cancer. Richard saw pictures of his family all over her walls and counters. When he sat at her bedside, Lula kept asking him to come closer. She confessed how much she missed Cesar. Richard gave her a recording of Cesar's music, which she had admired live six days a week for forty years through the bathroom door. She listened to the CD ceaselessly in her final days.

She told tales of the old Columbia and even told a secret or two. When Richard put his hand on Melanie's lap, Lula hoped it wasn't a cue for them to leave. He can't remember how long he stayed that day. Time always flew in Lula's gracious company.

Lula Mae died in November 2005, about three weeks before the Columbia officially turned 100. Management removed Lula's red-cushioned chair from the ladies' room and laid a wreath of white roses tipped with black at the

Adela always said that love kept the Columbia alive during hard times.

door. Melanie wept as she told a reporter, "I realize now how little I knew about Lula, but she knew so much about me. A lot of secrets went down with Lula."

The company will never hire another restroom attendant, because there will never be another Lula Mae Tollaman. (Sadly, she left us just as the interviews for this book were beginning.)

A Woman of Her Time

As a bride in 1946, Adela took to cooking with gusto. She approached her new chore as she would the piano, taking notes, learning techniques, experimenting with flavor. After Adela was married, she bought a small blue recipe book and filled the pages with recipes from her mother, Carmen, and a few clippings from magazines. Her recipe book continues to inspire the Columbia years after her death, a sacred culinary text.

With Ybor Renaissance man Ferdie Pacheco, Adela co-authored The Columbia Spanish Restaurant Cookbook *in 1994.*

"An Affair To Remember"

Adela Hernandez Gonzmart

March of Dimes
Tampa Gourmet Chef's Auction VIII
October 8, 1998

Forever young, Adela's portrait graces her wine label.

As a young boy, Richard did not like to eat rice, which presented a problem in a household where the grain was found with many a dinner. Ybor City's Latin cooking depended on rice for most of its dishes, so Adela wanted her son to enjoy it. Her solution was her trademark "good rice," which is cooked with browned butter, onions, chicken broth, and fresh basil. The result is rich rice packed with flavor and freshness. "The butter is the secret ingredient as far as I am concerned," Richard says, "and the fresh basil." Today, Adela's good rice is served beside a variety of the Columbia's entrees.

Although Adela went for decades with no official title at the restaurant, she carved out a niche no one could fill. She suggested new menu items and recipes, she led Ybor City's social scene, and she participated on a variety of boards and civic groups, such as the Ybor City Chamber of Commerce. Through it all, she never lost the grace and charm that made her popular in the first place. To list her contributions here would require too much ink and paper.

Richard planned a house white wine to be named after his mother. Richard let his mother taste the top contenders without revealing the purpose of the tasting. Adela and Melanie loved one variety, and Richard had already favored another. Without knowing that the wine would bear her name, Adela defended her choice. Richard compromised in a fashion by offering both varieties under the *Adelita* label.

By 1994, a Columbia cookbook was long overdue. Casimiro and journalist Paul Wilder had planned a cookbook in the 1940s and 1950s, but settled on a small pamphlet instead. Teamed up with Ybor City renaissance man Ferdie Pacheco, Adela wrote the Columbia's first cookbook. The book's relaxed style featured the two master storytellers sharing vignettes from their own experiences. Critics and readers loved the cookbook.

In 1998, when the March of Dimes planned its annual Gourmet Chef's Auction, they overlooked more famous chefs and recruited Adela Gonzmart. The 1994 cookbook

After Adela's death, the family paid her tribute with a sculpture.

#10

COLUMBIA CREATIONS

Venture into the heart of Tampa, Ybor City, for this eating adventure for four at the Columbia Restaurant.

~appetizer~
Fondos de Alcachofas a la Carihuela
(Artichoke stuffed with Lobster)

~soup~
Sopa de Novios
(Hen Vegetable Soup)

~salad~
Ensalda Carioca
(Hearts of Palm, Watercress, Pimentos with Vinegarette)

~entree~
Medallions de Solomillo "Don Paco"
(Tenderloin stuffed with a mushroom Truffle Pate)
Filete de Lenguado Glaceado "Escorial"
(Flounder poached in Sherry Wine with a Champagne Sauce)**Sorbete de Parchita**
(Passion Fruit Sorbet)

~dessert~
Gloria de CoCo
(Coconut Pudding)

~beverages~
Cristalino Brut Champagne
Albarino, Martin Codax
Don Cesar Tinto, Rioja 1986
1 after dinner drink per person

Feast Your Eyes On This!!!

Adela was a dedicated philanthropist and was always ready to support a cause in or out of the kitchen.

reminded the community of her contributions to Florida's culinary glory. Adela named the event "An Evening to Remember," and featured black bean "Cuban caviar" with crackers and chopped eggs, a Spanish egg tortilla with potatoes, stuffed mushrooms, shrimp and crab croquettes, the 1905 salad, and paella Valenciana. For dessert, Adela served her special version of *brazo gitano* or "gypsy's arm," rolled sponge cake with cream filling covered in meringue and strawberry sauce, then flambéed with Kirchwasser. Casimiro Sr. had passed on the recipe before he died.

The Lion's Club gave Adela the lifetime achievement award in 2001. She worked with the Ybor Chamber of Commerce, Tampa's symphony, and with artistic organizations to better the community. An optimist with a can-do attitude, Adela did not dwell on the past, but she revered it. "If you want to have Ybor City the way it used to be, you can not. Those people are not there anymore. The only thing that is the way it used to be is the Columbia Restaurant and Max Argintar's," the men's clothing shop, which has since closed. When asked how and why the family maintained the Columbia through good and bad, she answered:

"Love. With us, the Columbia Restaurant is not a business. It's something you carry in your heart. You're looking at tradition; you're looking at family."

By 2001, arthritis had claimed two of Adela's greatest pleasures: playing the piano and cooking. She still managed to make chicken soup when Casey felt ill in early December, 2001. She suffered a stroke two days later on December 8, and could barely speak or swallow. The family took her home under hospice care to die peacefully.

"I told her she would die at home," Richard said, "and she did." The family played Adela's favorite music of Cuban composer Ernesto Lecuona. They whispered that family awaited her on the other side. Adela died on December 22, 2001.

Newspapers eulogized her as one of Ybor City's saviors and greatest boosters. "If there ever was a queen in Ybor City," Richard told the press, "she was the queen." As many as a thousand well-wishers attended her funeral at St. Lawrence Catholic Church. Longtime Jesuit High teacher and family friend Monsignor Lawrence Higgins presided over the service. "There will be a lot of music in heaven," Higgins announced.

Years after her death, Adela still inspires her granddaughter Lauren, who was especially attached to her beloved "Lele." She visited at every opportunity, going so far as to feign illness at school as a child and asking to be picked up by her grandmother. Adela indulged her, taking her home and telling an irritated Melanie later.

Lauren: "She took me back to Davis Island. I can remember her tucking me in the bed, and I was so happy. I remember all the light coming off the bay, and I was just laying there in her bed like a princess. I remember I was really not sick. I just wanted to see my grandmother. My mom was pissed."

When asked what made Adela so special, Lauren said:

"She was kind-hearted, understanding, warm, and caring. You just knew that even if you did something wrong and you screwed up, she couldn't be mad at you. She just didn't have that in her. She'd always help you turn it around, make it better and help to carry you through. She just had a way of making people feel so calm and at ease with themselves."

Former Tampa Mayor Dick Greco remembers Adela's brilliant balance between criticism and nurturing. "She understood Latin men. She'd never admonish you to the point you didn't know she loved you. She did tell you what she thought."

As a woman, Lauren learned a great deal from Adela. "I remember looking at her, and she was always the epitome of a lady. She just was very glamorous, very well spoken, well educated, and was able to communicate and socialize with all walks of life. Everything you want to be as you grow up. If you could have an idol in this world, she was mine. Because she was just everything, she was sophisticated, she was glamorous, she could speak foreign languages, she could cook."

Andrea: "She was also ahead of her time. She was a business woman and had her own visions. She was so involved in the community and the Chamber of Commerce. She was a true leader."

Lauren: "She was philanthropic, but yet she had this business sense, plus she had her family roots grounded. I still wonder and sit back in amazement at how she did it all. How she kept all these bases covered. How she was making sure her children were cared for, her business, her husband, and her social obligations."

Andrea: "And not be exhausted, frustrated and nasty at the end of the day. She was still happy at the end of the day."

Lauren: "I pray to her all the time to help me! 'Lele, give me patience! Lele, tell me how you did it! You forgot to tell me that before you died!'"

Andrea: "You gave me your recipes, but not that!"

Before she died, Adela strongly advised Richard to name Lauren as vice president of the company. The world had changed, and women in the family could take their rightful places working in the family business.

From Tahiti to Sonoma

Richard was enlightened while attending a seminar for business leaders in 1999. Since taking over the company, the business consumed virtually every day of his life. Richard remembers the speaker asking, "When was the last time any of you took a two-week vacation without calling the office?"

"We all looked at each other and said, 'Are you crazy?'" Richard recalls. "He says, 'Apparently, you don't have the right people in place.'

"I start thinking about it, I didn't have the confidence. That's when I realize I had to build the team, so I *could* leave. Not only did I realize I'm a control freak, I realized I *had* to do this. So it took me three years to hire the right people for the right positions.

"You have to plan. You're not indispensable, and if you are, then your family business is destined to fail. Anybody could be replaced. You can be replaced, but can the business survive during that period? You have to prepare someone. You can't sit there and just want to have control.

"For our wedding anniversary [vacation in 2002], I was concerned that if I was too close by, I might not make it. To be successful, I figured we had to go to Tahiti, halfway around the world. It was the best thing I've ever done.

"I could make it two days without calling. I planned this; I'd get on a ship. I knew I would be too cheap to call the United States from a ship because it would be very expensive.

"It was a ten-day cruise. I said, 'Well, this is pretty good, relax and take it easy.' It took me three years to plan this two-week vacation without calling. It made me understand I had to have the right people in place.

"Then, we flew to California the last few days, where we were being entertained by some of our suppliers. We went to the Sebastiani winery, one of the oldest family-owned wineries in California, Sonoma. They're one year older than our family business.

"We're taking a tour of the facility, and we see this woman holding court in the middle of the wine store's gift shop, autographing books.

"She reminded me so much of my mother. She was five feet tall, autographing books, and we start talking to her. I thought I was talking to my mother. We go on and on, and she tells us who she is, and says, 'You want to come to my home?' You can oversee all these vineyards in Sonoma."

Melanie: "It was just gorgeous."

Richard: "I felt like all of a sudden, I was with a family member. I had met this woman just fifteen minutes before. She takes us into her cellar, where she has her wines."

Melanie: "When we left there, the representative of Sebastiani looked at me and Richard and said, 'I cannot believe it. I've never seen her take anyone back to her home.' She obviously felt comfortable. What a very big honor it was."

Richard: "They developed a relationship and friendship with us. Now, her daughter runs the company with her husband, who's the CEO. When they celebrated their one hundredth anniversary in 2004, they came and had dinner with us. As we prepared for our one hundredth anniversary, they gave us a 3-liter bottle with their logo and our one hundredth anniversary logo etched on the bottle.

"We called it the Passing of the Cork. Now we sell about one thousand cases a year, we feature chardonnay, merlot, cabernet, along with everything else. To me, it's just great to be able to maintain that relationship."

Richard returned from his two-week vacation refreshed, energized, and newly inspired.

The flan-eater had come a long way. After a distinguished career in wine sales, he rejoined the Columbia as a wine teacher for new employees.

Wine and Family

The Columbia carried increasing varieties of wine over the years. The first container of Spanish wine arrived from Barcelona in 1974.

Richard Gonzmart: "The Columbia wine list comprised French wines, Italian, German, and maybe three Spanish wines. The Spanish wines weren't very recognized. For a period, I had no wines other than Spanish on the list. People said I couldn't do it. I said, 'Why not?' [Today the list is] 85 percent Spanish."

Curt Gaither always knew Richard as a wine expert. He remembers a conversation shortly after they met. "I was talking with Richard, we were sitting in Cha Cha Coconuts in Daytona. I was a bit mesmerized with Richard, because certainly meeting him on the first occasion is an experience. He said, 'What are your feelings on Spanish wines?'

"I had never seen the wine list. And I remember my response being, 'Spanish wines are kind of scary. I don't think that people are prepared for Spanish wines.' I don't even know if I had drunk a Spanish wine at that point in my life. He kind of laughed. Richard has a passion for the wines. He's much more a wine guru than I am. I don't think I will ever have the knowledge of wine that he has. I think it's an important part of the experience."

Luis Returns

Luis Diaz retired from wine sales, but he still longed to be involved in the Gonzmart family and business. "I always remained close to the Columbia. I went to Spain to look for wine. That's when my relationship with Richard and Casey became very strong. Then Richard became such a tremendous guy in wine, that my services were no longer needed. And slowly, I could see that I [was] fading away forever. I hate to lose the connection with the Columbia.

"So, at that time I told them in a letter which I keep, 'Even if we part from each other, I still have a great deal of affection for the Columbia and for the family, and any time I can be of service, feel free to contact me.'"

In response, Richard asked Luis to be the Columbia's roving professor of wine. Luis educates new employees on wine: vineyards, tasting, and service. The seminars allow employees to ask questions about wine. "I go to seminars monthly. I go to all the operations. I sit down with the guys for an hour, two hours, answering all of their questions that they have. It's a continuous process because the waiters are always changing. It's not like in the past, where a waiter would spend a lifetime. Every three weeks, you got new personnel in the restaurant. It allows me to feel useful in my old age, and allows me to feel happy for the young kids who would never know the wine."

The Unfinished Wine List

As Richard compiled a world-class wine list, the quality and acceptance of Spanish wine increased. The inventory passed one thousand labels by 2007.

Curt Gaither: "In the last ten to twelve years, the whole education and acceptance of the Spanish wines has totally changed. It's not scary anymore. Not because they're out there everywhere, but people have become accustomed to drinking them and appreciating them."

Luis Diaz: "It is by far the finest wine list. I took a copy to Spain. I have a lot of friends in Spain, and I showed it to the guys. They couldn't believe it. They were so amazed by the wines of the Columbia Restaurant. There is no one in Spain that can match the criteria of this wine list."

Richard: "To be named one of the top twelve wine lists in the Unites States by *Wine Enthusiast* makes a statement. If you show concern for having great wines in this service, then it shows you are serious about food."

Richard had been torn between the desire to expand the wine list and the need to stay organized. To help manage his sprawling wine collection, Richard relies upon his daughter Andrea, who has a keen interest in food and wine. "We lost track of the wine list until I came on the scene in 2004," Andrea says. Trying to clean it up has been a slow three-year process. He'll buy stuff that he doesn't tell me he buys, and I don't add it to the inventory."

Richard: "It's a mess and it's my fault. There are certain wines that nobody else can get. I'll buy all there is, but then we have to sell it."

Richard and company arranged the wine list around a map of Spain, and the list is broken down by region, offering the reds and whites of each. The casual wine drinker often finds the list overwhelming. "Now the wine list is impossible to read. It's impossible to select. The white wines aren't all together and the red wines aren't all together." The restaurant began featuring wines daily, along with the lunch and dinner specials. As of the publication of this book, the list is up to over one thousand labels, 280 pages, and still rising. Over thirty thousand bottles, worth over $1 million, reside at the Ybor City location alone.

Marques

In 1970, when a Spanish wine representative found himself in Tampa without a friend, Jose Luis Mugero was welcomed by Cesar Gonzmart at the airport. The Columbia's prince charming had champagne chilling in the limousine. Mugero never forgot the gesture, and declared eternal gratitude. He also sent two bottles of a fine 1925 vintage.

In his quest for the best wines, Richard sought out vintages from Marques de Riscal, Rioja's oldest winery. Every time Richard asked them for old vintages, they said nothing was available, or that they were not selling their older bottles. The winery dismissed the Columbia, and Richard tried to convince someone there that his family had done business with them for the last sixty years. He even visited the winery in person, but got the same response.

The next morning, Richard saw a group of VIPs walking by. The export manager recognized Richard as he walked with the king of Spain's son-in-law, who was touring the Marques de Riscal Hotel, which had just opened. He immediately hugged him like an old friend and said: "I knew your father twenty-two years ago, and I was twenty-one years old. I came to see your father and he picked me up and gave me champagne. Then I called my father and told him how wonderful he was, what a wonderful restaurant and wine list." Richard: "I show him my list. I showed him a collection of a wine called Vega Sicilia and certain things. He can't believe it."

When Richard told Mugero that he had found two bottles of Marques de Riscal vintage from 1925, he responded, "That's because I sent it to Cesar!"

"That night," Richard said, "he calls me and he wants me and Melanie to join them for champagne in their bar. The Marques of Lanzarote from the Canary Islands joins us, and this guy tells the Marques about my wine list and the wines we have, the *Vega Sicilia*."

The Marques said, "There's nobody in Tampa who drinks those wines" with an arrogant air.

When the chairman of the winery finally saw Richard's list, he was "blown away," according to Richard. He asked rhetorically, "Why aren't more of my wines on this list?" Then, he resolved, "We don't sell any of our old vintages to anybody in the U.S., but we're going to send you some of ours."

That kind of recognition is only won through dedication and hard work, two things Richard never seems to run out of. "It's a good feeling to get that respect. I want to be recognized, as I have been told by some of the best wineries and owners, to have the best Spanish list in the world."

Wine Dinners

Richard began to host owners and wine makers from around the world to speak about their products at what the company calls "wine dinners." The guests provide the wine or spirits, and the Columbia prepares a feast featuring the guest's beverage.

Representatives of the featured beverage companies begin the meal with a brief lecture and an aperitif. Wine or spirit selections accompany each course. Columbia chefs feature the beverages in the meal: a splash of wine in a sauce or stock, the punch of bourbon in gravies and frostings. As a great wine salesman, Luis Diaz especially admires the concept of wine dinners. "Right now we are at a stage," he enthuses, "*magnificent*. Incredible ideas and very well done invitations. You feel like, 'Wow, this is an event.' Those [wine] dinners are $50 at the Columbia. They're worth $150.

"Richard wanted the publicity that would come from that. A lot of those Spanish owners and growers go back to Spain and the first thing, 'Oye, I was in Florida. The Columbia Restaurant.' He will start getting letters from all the Spaniards. They want to have dinners at the Columbia." Soon, Italian wineries showed an interest in their own dinners. The idea has caught on.

The conversations leading to each wine dinner are quite interesting. Richard might come up with his own menu during a busy lunchtime meeting. While sipping on the wines, he might create a menu spontaneously. On other occasions, he asks Chef Jerry for his creative input.

Chef Jerry: "What usually happens is Richard comes up with an idea, and I have to translate his idea. Or he'll give me a recipe, and I'll try to make it our own. After these years, I know a lot of his tastes. There are definitely some things Richard doesn't like. 'I tasted cumin in there, definitely not. Oh, you definitely have to cut down.' I know he doesn't like cilantro. I use those products when I have to, but I use them sparingly."

Richard's grasp of wine and food has always impressed Jerry. He knows enough to say what he likes. "I love working with him. I've learned from his knowledge, his experience over the years working here. He was a chef before, so I enjoy talking to him. He actually *makes* me want to work here. He knows a lot about everything, man."

More recently, Richard began asking Jerry to create the wine dinner menus. "He's actually trusting other people more. I take it as a compliment. I appreciate that. The best part is after the wine dinner, he congratulates me, and tells me everything was really good. It really makes me feel good about myself. It makes me feel happy that he's happy, too. Especially on the wine dinners because that's the one point that as chefs, we get to be creative. Especially if he lets us!

"It also lets us know it is up to his standards. That's the other thing; we still have to keep it in a Columbia manner. Not too ornate. If Richard isn't involved, Curt Gaither is involved, and we will make up menus. I will come up with some ideas, whatever I have in my head. It's all just a process."

Sometimes, Richard's instincts surprise Jerry. When Richard described an oxtail dish for a wine dinner, Jerry was skeptical. "I was like ,'Ugh, *oxtail*,' but actually after I made up a recipe, it was one of the best dishes. They actually raved about it."

Richard also enjoys forming the menus by happy hour committee. He invites family members and associates to join him for informal wine tastings at his home. These tastings become spirited debates about the merits of each wine and menu item. Employees and family members sample the wines and nominate dishes to accompany them. Participants often verbally joust over whose dishes should make the cut. "The seared tuna is too strong for this wine," one may contend, while another asserts, "With the sauce, the tuna would be perfect!" It might take a new nomination to shift the argument away from the tuna. Finally,

As a grandfather, Richard cannot help but reflect on the 5th generation of the Columbia. The adults, left to right: Casey Jr., Casey, Jessica, Cassandra, Richard, Andrea, and Lauren. The children: Christian, Marlena, Charlie, Isabella, and Michael.

By the time of the Columbia's centennial celebrations, Richard had raised the company's quality to new heights.

through a wine-induced consensus, the participants agree on the menu, or at least to stop debating it.

New Vintage

In 1998, when Chris Schellman landed a job in Tampa, he visited to find an apartment. When he asked a cab driver where to find a good lunch, the cabbie recommended the Columbia, and Schellman found the food so good that he returned for dinner that night. Years later, Schellman found himself chatting with a brunette in a Clearwater night club.

When he told her about his first Columbia experiences, she said that she worked in the restaurant's gift shop. He searched for her name—Lauren Gonzmart—on the Internet that night and was shocked to learn she was vice

president of the company. She didn't work at a gift shop, but ran the group's entire retail division.

Recently separated, Lauren and her twins were living with her parents. Chris got to know her dynamic parents as the courtship developed. He even shared Richard's fascination with running with the bulls in Pamplona, Spain. In November 2004, Chris joined the Gonzmart family and Columbia associates for a cruise from Barcelona. The night before the party of forty embarked, Chris asked Richard for Lauren's hand in marriage.

Chris proposed on the deck of the liner while they watched the sun set. The Columbia clan knows how to celebrate with style and spirit, and the cruise ship saw many parties on that voyage. In May 2005, while the Columbia celebrated its one hundred years in business, Chris and

Lauren were married. That July, Chris and Richard ran with the bulls in Pamplona. In 2006, Lauren gave birth to a son, Maximilian Cesar. In 2008, Alexander Cole was born.

Now a grandfather several times over, Richard is especially fond of his five new wine cellars, where memories of his own grandfather and hopes for his grandchildren ferment: "Today, we have replaced the kitchen where I began my love affair with the Columbia." Richard moved the seafood cooler in 2004. In its place, he installed one of his greatest loves: a 20,000-bottle wine cellar. "How else could I have replaced that opening that opened my mind about my future? I still have that original cooler door and every time I see it or the opening I recall and give thanks to my grandfather for his love and kindness.

"Today, as a grandfather, I hope that I can help my grandchildren develop the passion to continue in our family business, that they feel the ease to walk freely through the restaurant. If you see a twin brother and sister holding hands and acting like they own the place, it is probably because they will one day. I hope that when they celebrate the 150th anniversary that they will recall a sweet story like this, when their grandfather loved them and taught them all he had to offer."

Running and Sipping for Life

Helping others has always come naturally to Richard. His struggles as a student helped him appreciate persistent underdogs. "I remember first grade, my mom had given me twenty dollars to pay for the tuition. Sister Mary John, first grade teacher, was talking about how we wanted to collect money for the poor in Central America and I gave her the twenty dollars."

Two weeks later, Sacred Heart Academy called, telling Adela she was late with her tuition payment. Cesar and Adela had little money at the time. When she asked Richard what he'd done with the money, he explained. "She couldn't

get mad at that. No matter how much we're suffering, somebody's got it a lot, lot worse."

The Columbia is always involved in philanthropic efforts. The restaurant's chefs have cooked paellas weighing a ton to benefit the Red Cross. But Richard has always found it most meaningful to personally become involved with his favorite charities. He has run for life, sipped for life, coached athletic teams, and mentored sick children.

Philanthropy must be generous—in money or effort—to be meaningful. "I always say if it doesn't hurt, then you haven't done enough. That's my philosophy. That's why I run marathons, because it hurts. You pray and you think about people."

In 2004, Richard first fulfilled his dreams of running with the bulls of Pamplona, Spain. And he wore a University of South Florida Bulls T-shirt. Richard has adopted USF as a place where he can make a difference.

Opened in 1960 as the state's first urban university, the University of South Florida offers high-quality, affordable education to a community hungry for knowledge. Many Floridians never would have attended college without USF. Adela recognized that fact, and she understood the value of education more than most.

In the late 1980s, former USF president Francis Borkowski reached out to the Latin community. Adela responded by supporting Latino scholarships there. She founded her family's own scholarship after Cesar's death; Richard continued the tradition with the Cesar and Adela Gonzmart endowment and Columbia Centenario endowment. Richard was inspired by the story of the 2005 scholarship recipients, Julio and Elsie Rodriguez. Their father had died working in the produce fields.

"They went on to college. He got a 4.0 in engineering. She was summa cum laude, outstanding senior out of four thousand students." With his own memories of classroom difficulties, Richard admired their performances as students. "Both are engineers. She went on to work for a New Mexico nuclear plant. He went to General Electric Aeronautical.

"Julio came to thank me one Christmas. He said, 'When I was a senior at Brandon High School, I was wondering where I would be picking strawberries and tomatoes.' That impacted me. Now Andrea goes to the functions with me, and we have six or seven students. We'll have more as the funding goes in there. That's how you make a difference in this community, the community that supported you."

When Cesar became ill, doctors at USF affiliate H. Lee Moffitt Cancer Center and Research Institute cared for him. "The best surgeons in the world," Richard says. Cesar's experience drove home to Richard how vital USF was in his own life. His daughters earned their degrees there: Lauren in interdisciplinary social science, and Andrea in business. Richard dedicated a fortune of time and money to support scholarships, athletics, and cancer research. Moffitt now has named a unit after Richard and Melanie Gonzmart to recognize their support.

"I've adopted USF. They care, and you make a difference in all the different areas, from the library to athletics to the arts. It is also a huge economic engine. I looked at our receivables today, and I think we have like six different schools that have had functions at the Columbia in the last six weeks. It's good business."

In 2005, USF's Sarasota campus asked Richard to speak in a commencement ceremony to honor the new School of Hotel and Restaurant Management there. Richard earned his degrees in the field: his bachelor's degree in Madrid, his master's in St. Augustine, and his Ph.D. after Cesar passed. "It's not always about the grades. You have to have a passion," he reminded the graduates.

That same year, Richard and Melanie donated the Columbia Restaurant and Gonzmart-Hernandez family collection to USF's Tampa Library. It has since been turned into an archive, a treasure trove of memorabilia. Members of the family and company generously gave interviews for the library's Oral History Program. Through documents, photographs, memorabilia, clippings, ephemera, and interviews, the Columbia collection made this rich book possible. Almost every image in this book comes from the collection or other sources in the USF Tampa Library Special Collections Department.

 ## Excellence

In 1989, while Cesar was still alive, *Bay City Western News* inducted the Columbia into their hall of fame. The recognition stirred mixed emotions in Richard.

"It was a big deal to be recognized by a leading industry magazine. We had not come back from the fall yet, so some maybe thought we shouldn't have won, or we didn't deserve it. It made me work harder to get recognized." After Cesar's death, Richard vowed to win back *Florida Trend* magazine's Golden Spoon Award and the *Holiday* magazine award.

The Columbia's centennial as a family business in 2005 brought an abundance of recognition. Few restaurants last a century, and the Columbia garnered awards that most people and places don't earn until they're long dead. Most impressively of all, state legislators crossed the aisle in a rare display of bipartisan spirit and sponsored bills in the house and senate to formally recognize the Columbia's centennial.

The Columbia won *Florida Trend* magazine's Golden Spoon Award from 1967, the year it was created, until 1973. After a hiatus of more than thirty years, the Columbia reclaimed its prize in 2006. *Florida Trend*'s editors observed in the press, "Florida's oldest restaurant has obviously been doing more than a few things right the past 100 years to soar to the summit of the Golden Spoon achievement."

Richard said, "We are honored and extremely proud of what I consider the premier award given to restaurants in Florida."

The *Holiday* magazine award would be impossible to reclaim, as the publication had ceased to exist. Richard set his sights high for a replacement. The DiRoNA, or Distinguished Restaurants of North America, became Richard's new target. *Holiday* was easy by comparison. DiRoNA's Award of Excellence is among the most prestigious awards in the fine dining industry. Anonymous inspectors scrutinized the Columbia in every conceivable way: for cleanliness, reservation procedures, prices, wine, and food. Inspectors had visited the Columbia years before, but no award came.

Confident he had restored the Columbia to a new glory, Richard had called Hal Staymen, DiRoNA's national director of inspections that same year, 2006. The director was blunt. "The last time I was there, the food wasn't very good, the service was sub-par, and the wine list was not much to be desired."

Richard deeply wanted to restore the Columbia's fine dining credentials once and for all. He replied, "Please have one of your inspectors come."

When Richard traveled to Ft. Lauderdale to be inducted into *Florida Trend*'s hall of fame, he got a call from his assistant: The DiRoNA inspector was trying to reach him. Richard immediately called him. The esteemed judge gushed over the phone, after he personally inspected the Columbia himself. "I was there with my daughter, and what you've done with the Columbia is just amazing. You were so busy, and the food was spectacular, the waiters were so knowledgeable about your outstanding wine list, and you're going to receive the award."

Afraid she would worry, Richard hadn't even told Melanie about the DiRoNA inspection. After thanking the director, Richard admits he was overcome with emotion.

"That man cried," Melanie says. It seemed too good to be true: "for him to re-achieve the Golden Spoon, and then to attain the DiRoNA." He had fulfilled his father's greatest ambitions and served notice to people nationwide that the Columbia was not a relic.

Florida Trend inducted the Columbia into its restaurant hall of fame. At the awards dinner, Richard sat beside the Columbia's old nemesis, editor Robert Tolf. "The legacy I wanted to leave was that I brought the Columbia back to the glory that it deserved," Richard says. "We gained respect."

In another sign of respect, *Wine Enthusiast* magazine named the Columbia's wine list among the top twelve nationally.

Under the Microscope

Richard, who was not an especially good student, became improbably engrossed in a college course. In 2001, the Columbia won the Florida Family Business of the Year Award, which is sponsored by MassMutual. That same year, MassMutual bestowed on the Columbia its National Family Business of the Year Award for large companies. The Massachusetts Mutual Life Insurance Company, which partners with other companies to give the prize, chose the Columbia among eighty applicants. One of the competition's judges, entrepreneur Len Green, taught business as a faculty member at prestigious Babson College in Wellesley, Massachusetts. He asked Richard to answer questions for a case study to be used in a course on family businesses.

The course takes place once a year, and the Columbia has become one of the class's most interesting and enduring subjects. Students pore over the details of the Columbia's improbable journey. They learn that in a family business, every personal and professional decision can affect its legacy. Marriages and children can be especially hazardous, introducing new shareholders and possible business partners.

Too many partners can dilute a company's leadership and unity. "They choose our family business as a case study every year because they say it's classic. My daughters said that to have their name on somebody's exam kind of feels eerie to them. The class was fascinated. They get graded for doing a presentation to the class of about fifty people." A student called Richard for an interview in 2006. He'd been scheduled to run in a relay marathon for charity, but a training injury kept him out of the race. When Richard offered to give the interview in person, the student assumed it was a joke.

Richard Gonzmart: "I decided I should really see this Babson College. I was going to send Andrea there by herself, and she might have been a little intimidated. You can just tell it's a wealthy school. Arthur Blank, the founder of Home Depot and the owner of the Atlanta Falcons, has the Arthur Blank Entrepreneurial School building there.

"The class did not know we were coming. The professor was delighted and excited to see us. He said, 'We are going to start with the Columbia today.'" Students took the stage and shared the Columbia's story with clinical clarity. The lesson plans taught to Babson's business students ask some tough professional and personal questions. Every generation must adapt its own way, they learn. The Columbia's history is still being written, and every year, Babson students study changes at the restaurants. Sensitive family issues were discussed with the same nonchalance as stock options or a corporate merger.

The case study was prepared by Beth G. Silver, Esq., and Sheryl Overlan under the direction of Professor Leonard C. Green in 2003 at Babson College.

The students work off of Green's lesson plan, which is worthy of consideration here. The latest lesson plan—or lesson E—is also the most interesting because all of the issues are unresolved as yet. An abridged lesson plan appears below.

Richard admits that it is difficult having Lauren report to him. Sometimes Richard's wife defends Lauren in disagreements about work and that puts some stress on them as a family. Richard finds it hard to supervise his daughters because he holds them to higher standards than the other employees. He also feels that he is sometimes too lenient when his daughters' personal matters conflict with their jobs.

Richard regrets that he could not convince Lauren and Andrea to work outside the family business before joining Columbia Restaurant. He feels that such experience would be useful in their generating the respect of the other employees.

One challenge that Richard sees in the near future is finding a place in the business for Casey's six children. Casey and Richard have not yet determined whether being a family member entitles one to a job. Casey's older children (ages 21, 19, and 17) work in the restaurants during summers.

Casey and Richard are concerned that it is difficult to instill family values in the next generation.

The company currently has a plan for stock ownership but Richard admits that the plan is subject to change as family circumstances change. For example, one of his daughters is going through a divorce and the current plan provides for Richard's shares to be held in a revocable trust for Richard's grandchildren so that the shares are not involved in the divorce process. Under this plan, profits are currently reinvested in the company.

Casey and Richard have a work ethic that reflects the values instilled in them by their grandfather and father who would quote to them a Spanish saying that translated means: "The eye of the owner fattens the horse," or if you don't watch the business, it will starve. While they are passionate about the need for family leadership in the company in order to continue the family's values, it is unclear who would take over leadership responsibilities should something suddenly happen to take Casey or Richard from the business.

ASSIGNMENT QUESTIONS:

1. What recommendations do you have for successfully incorporating the 5th generation members? Are there policies that should be developed and, if so, when and how should they be implemented?

2. By what means can the Hernandez-Gonzmart values continue to be maintained in 6 locations and with 750 employees?

3. What are the advantages and disadvantages of family members reporting to other family members?

4. If you were judging Columbia Restaurant Group in the Family Business of the Year competition, how would you rate them as a successful family business? Provide reasons for your answer.

5. Bonus Question: Significant research into the patterns of family business indicates that it is unlikely that Columbia Restaurant Group will be able to be successfully passed to the fifth generation. Do you think it will succeed or will it be sold? Provide reasons for your answer.

When the students finished their presentation, Green gestured toward Richard and Andrea in the front row. "You are probably wondering who these people are," he said to the class. He introduced them and offered the podium. Richard spoke first: "Andrea and I talked about the history and the problems. I had concerns about the fourth and fifth generations. Most family businesses don't make it to the second. We're facing that crucial generation transition. My two daughters have been working. The class talked about how so many children [of family businesses] think they get out of college and they're going to earn six figures and they're going to be a vice president, and it doesn't exist."

Richard talked about the challenges of the fifth generation: Casey's children and his own daughters. Casey's eldest daughter Cassandra joined the company in 2006.

It is uncertain whether her siblings will follow: two are currently in college, and three are still too young. Richard warned that there will not be easy breaks for anyone. "I'm very harsh, I realize that, and I'm very honest. I know that is not necessarily good, but people know where they stand. I worked for my dad for twelve years and you have to put in your time."

Every year, Professor Green asks some pressing and difficult questions, and history awaits the answers.

The Glass Ceiling

Having a new generation of two women presents unprecedented difficulties in business and family. Lauren and Andrea have both found it challenging to work as businesspeople unhindered by gender roles. Managers and some people at the corporate office still scoff at the daughters' involvement.

Industrious Andrea always felt guilty that she could not be with her fiancé when she was working. "He used to complain when I was at work. That guilt makes it so much harder. My general manager used to say, 'I love when Sherrod is out of town because you don't worry about going home.'"

A colleague from the Ybor City Chamber of Commerce once asked Andrea to have a drink after work to discuss business. Happy hour, Friday night. As a woman, she felt awkward accepting the invitation of a man. Lauren warned her sister against staying for a drink if her colleague didn't "cut to the chase." When Andrea said the colleague was married, her fiancé said that "was only a yield sign" to most men. When Andrea mentioned it to Richard, he didn't like the smell of it.

Andrea: "Then, he just wanted to talk about the future of the chamber and I'm like, 'God, I'm a moron!' We think he's got all of these ulterior motives. If I was a man, it wouldn't be an issue. Yes, being a woman is a huge problem."

The Columbia presents its own difficulties for a generation yet to participate in upper-level management. Melanie: "Who's going to step up to the plate? Richard did. But do they have enough knowledge? He went through the school of hard knocks. These girls have been living on the sweet street."

Richard tested his daughters. He asked Lauren to open the Celebration location and work there for six months while commuting from Tampa. "She never complained," Melanie says, "and that was a test." When Andrea worked in the kitchen, she earned less than many of her coworkers. More recently, Richard put Andrea in charge of his chaotic wine inventory. Melanie notes her daughter's efforts with understandable pride. "She checked every wine in every unit three times, because she didn't want her father questioning her on anything. That to me was very impressive, and very smart."

As Richard edges toward the idea of retirement, the urgency on behalf of his daughters becomes more acute.

Lauren: "Well, that definitely scares me to death because I've gotten myself out of the loop. I've been having these babies and getting married and all this stuff."

Lauren is concerned that Andrea should be able to have children of her own, while Andrea is afraid to step away from the business for too long during these critical years. Family and business have entwined on a whole new level. When the dominant family line comprises two women of similar age, it presents obvious problems, and something must give: either business or children. The following exchange between the sisters in 2006 brings the conflict to life perfectly.

Andrea: "Right when I'm supposed to have babies is when I'm supposed to be having to do this. I am so young, but I'm not. And that's the problem."

Lauren: "I don't want her to miss out on any of the experience of motherhood and be at home for at least a little while with her babies."

Andrea: "But work comes first."

Lauren: "Well, I hope it doesn't. I really just point-blank said, work is going to be put on hold. I'll do what I have to do during the interim, but I want to be there with my children. I really don't want to miss that much. I want Andrea to have that balance."

Andrea: "I've got no time to kill. I can't afford to have kids at this point." In 2009, Andrea gave birth to a daughter, Amelia.

Melanie has an abiding confidence in her daughters: "They're very smart, I think I've given them the confidence and the knowledge as far as 'woman-ness' goes. They are what they are. It's cooked. I can't change it. They give me hell, so I think I did something right."

Sunshine and Shadows

As young girls, the Gonzmart sisters had no idea that they dwelled in the shadow of the Columbia. "Now your shadow is behind you and you're the full figure," Andrea says, as if she's inching closer toward the spotlight every year. "Now it's scary," Lauren says. "You better dance or get off the stage."

In 2006, at age fifty-three, Richard announced to his family he would retire five years later. Richard wanted "to make them realize that their father will not be here forever. I'm not going to retire. Am I going to sit back and do other things? Yes!"

Andrea admits, "None of us are prepared for that. In the fifth generation, you either survive or you don't. There's going to be a change."

Melanie voiced her concerns to Richard. Melanie: "I don't think you have told the girls enough, you may think you have, but just like what happened with your dad, you need to get more specific. You assume that they know what you're thinking. Put it in e-mail, give it to them in writing. It's very important that the children be prepared."

Lauren: "I'm like, 'Mom what are we going to do?' And she's like, 'Don't worry, your dad was not this brilliant when he was your age.' It seems we've been sheltered and spared some things." Although the Gonzmart sisters work in the business and understand how it functions, upper-level management and high finance can seem overwhelming, just as it was to Richard.

Andrea: "We have Babson College studying us, because they don't know if we're going to survive this generation. I get goose bumps thinking about that. It makes me nervous that I think they're planning on us not succeeding.

"My father is taking care of the fourth generation. He has carried it through. He has made it *more* than successful, better than it probably ever was. I don't know who's *not* amazed by him. So now how do we then make it better? I know I can sustain it. But sustaining is not progress."

Lauren: "Like dad says, 'If you're coasting your going downhill.' It doesn't work."

Andrea: "It makes me nervous because he's not going to always be there. I know Lauren and I will always stand together and that's what we have going for us."

The remainder of the Columbia's story has yet to be told. But as long as it continues, family will hold it together. Great service, food, and drink make it a good profession. Family and history make it a great, contagious passion.

Family may lie at the Columbia's heart, but loyal employees provide the muscle behind every service. Director of Operation Jim Garris, like many of his colleagues, is practically part of the family after working for the company for twenty years.

At the center of the food and service lies family. Led by Richard, the Gonzmart family and Columbia employees restored the restaurant to a new glory.

Jim Garris: "The Columbia is a living, breathing animal. Part of what I love about working here is every day it's different. It changes every day. And the other part I like about it is we really have to think on our feet, you know. Every day it's something different and every weekend it's something different. I don't plan on going anywhere else. I have to work hard. I work six days a week. They take care of me well.

"One of the things that always endeared me to them— even though I was a director of operations—when we were busy as hell, Richard still thought it was important that I went out and coached my son's little league team. The relationship I have with him, Melanie, Casey, and all, that is something special, I think. You have to like where you work. The money's not everything. It can be a crazy freaking place sometimes. Sometimes I go home and tell my wife, maybe once a month, 'That's it! I'm done!' But you sleep on it and you get up the next day and everything's good again. You have a great night and everything goes well, and you're proud of yourself again.

"When I give orientation to the service staff here, I tell them, 'Whether you last a week here or you last ten years here, you're never going to work in another place like this again in your life. The experience you take from here is going to be something you'll remember for the rest of your life.'"

From a small scrappy saloon to a Spanish restaurant empire in Florida, the Columbia has always specialized in making memories: for patrons, staff, and the family. Here's to another Columbia century!

Epilogue

 When I saw the newspaper article on the counter, my heart sank a little.

When I first tried a Cuban sandwich as a teen, I wondered what all the fuss was about. Every day, visitors to Florida wonder the same thing when they find a glorified ham sub. Years ago, I heard someone say that a Cuban sandwich should never cost more than five dollars. The sad fact is that no one can make an excellent sandwich for that kind of money.

Epilogue

 ## The Cuban Sandwich

After hearing and reading about the sandwich's proud history, I wondered how a painstakingly prepared Cuban would taste. Old-timers remember an era when it took all night and day to properly marinate and roast mojo pork. Baking and glazing a ham took hours. Then there's finding decent Cuban bread, which can be a struggle in itself. I once proclaimed that I'd happily spend ten dollars for a sandwich made the old way. These days, I'd spend twenty. When Jeff Klinkenberg of the *St. Petersburg Times* wrote an article about my obsession with finding a Cuban sandwich artisan, I groused about the inferior specimens I had found around Tampa Bay.

Having been chosen to author the Columbia's centennial cookbook, I had wanted to recommend the sandwich there. When I visited the restaurant, I found the sandwich too salty to endorse. I took Klinkenberg to the Museum Café in Homosassa instead, which served the best sandwich I had yet tasted. The article put me in an awkward position. Sandwich slingers around Tampa Bay rebelled online that I would drive so far to eat a sandwich made three counties away. But no one had more reason to be upset than Richard Gonzmart. His archivist and author had snubbed his sandwich.

The day after the article ran, I visited the Gonzmart home to record Richard's interview for the University of South Florida Libraries Oral History Program. Richard's wife, Melanie, welcomed me warmly and congratulated me on the article about my sandwich obsession. When I saw the newspaper article on the counter, my heart sank a little. Richard was in a foul mood and didn't feel good. The interview went well enough, the first of many, and Melanie walked me out. In the kindest possible way, she mentioned that Richard had been surprised that I did not mention the Columbia in the article. When I explained my reason, Melanie thanked me.

For the next two years, among his other duties and responsibilities, Richard felt the weight of three generations of Columbia Cuban sandwiches before him. In later interviews, Richard reviewed the shortcomings of his sandwich in exacting, unflinching detail. He took responsibility for short cuts that everyone else in town had been taking for decades. For example, he bought processed deli pork instead of roasting his own. Through baking, the ham had become overly salty. It was not sugar-glazed the old way. Pre-slicing the ham allowed what juices that remained to evaporate, further concentrating the salt. Only La Segunda Central Bakery's Cuban bread was beyond reproach.

With one eye on tradition and the other on modernity, Richard devised a solution. He began marinating his own pork roasts just for the sandwich. He bought a $35,000

steam convection oven that allowed him to bake the pork in a fraction of the time while retaining the meat's juices and preventing the salt from concentrating. He glazed the ham as well, adding a distinctive flavor reminiscent of the days when the cooks melted the sugar on the ham with a tailor's iron. The smell of glazing ham drew crowds in old Ybor City. Richard even improved his salami, an ingredient that sets Tampa's original creation apart from the Miami interlopers.

When the time came to unveil the Columbia's improved Cuban sandwich, Richard and I naturally invited Jeff Klinkenberg to try one for himself. There is a sense of cosmic justice that my story of looking for the best Cuban sandwich would conclude with Richard's effort to make the best. His efforts to do justice to past generations may yet end with his surpassing them in his own way.

At long last, the lowly sandwich has been elevated to the legendary stature of yore. Pressed in toasted Cuban bread, the Columbia's Cuban sandwich of the twenty-first century is moist, savory, a little sweet, and a little salty. Tampa's mythical sandwich, sullied by complacency and cheap knock-offs, has been restored. Revamping a sandwich might not seem as important as rebuilding a famous restaurant, but they are both part of the same delicious history.

Subject Index

Recipe Index

ANDREW T. HUSE has written for popular and academic periodicals. Huse works as a librarian at the University of South Florida's Special Collections Department and Florida Studies Center in Tampa. He is presently collecting research for a forthcoming book about modern Florida's restaurant culture.

RICHARD GONZMART, fourth generation family member and president of Columbia Restaurant is a devotee of Spanish food and wines. He was awarded the National Restaurant Association's "Humanitarian of the Year Award" for the State of Florida, and the restaurant was voted into Florida's Golden Spoon Hall of Fame.

The Florida History and Culture Series

Edited by Raymond Arsenault and Gary R. Mormino

Al Burt's Florida: Snowbirds, Sand Castles, and Self-Rising Crackers, by Al Burt (1997)

Black Miami in the Twentieth Century, by Marvin Dunn (1997)

Gladesmen: Gator Hunters, Moonshiners, and Skiffers, by Glen Simmons and Laura Ogden (1998)

"Come to My Sunland": Letters of Julia Daniels Moseley from the Florida Frontier, 1882–1886, by Julia Winifred Moseley and Betty Powers Crislip (1998)

The Enduring Seminoles: From Alligator Wrestling to Ecotourism, by Patsy West (1998, first paperback edition, 2008)

Government in the Sunshine State: Florida since Statehood, by David R. Colburn and Lance deHaven-Smith (1999)

The Everglades: An Environmental History, by David McCally (1999, first paperback edition, 2001)

Beechers, Stowes, and Yankee Strangers: The Transformation of Florida, by John T. Foster Jr. and Sarah Whitmer Foster (1999)

The Tropic of Cracker, by Al Burt (1999, paperback, 2009)

Balancing Evils Judiciously: The Proslavery Writings of Zephaniah Kingsley, edited and annotated by Daniel W. Stowell (1999)

Hitler's Soldiers in the Sunshine State: German POWs in Florida, by Robert D. Billinger Jr. (2000)

Cassadaga: The South's Oldest Spiritualist Community, edited by John J. Guthrie, Phillip Charles Lucas, and Gary Monroe (2000)

Claude Pepper and Ed Ball: Politics, Purpose, and Power, by Tracy E. Danese (2000)

Pensacola during the Civil War: A Thorn in the Side of the Confederacy, by George F. Pearce (2000)

Castles in the Sand: The Life and Times of Carl Graham Fisher, by Mark S. Foster (2000)

Miami, U.S.A., by Helen Muir (2000)

Politics and Growth in Twentieth-Century Tampa, by Robert Kerstein (2001)

The Invisible Empire: The Ku Klux Klan in Florida, by Michael Newton (2001)

The Wide Brim: Early Poems and Ponderings of Marjory Stoneman Douglas, edited by Jack E. Davis (2002)

The Architecture of Leisure: The Florida Resort Hotels of Henry Flagler and Henry Plant, by Susan R. Braden (2002)

Florida's Space Coast: The Impact of NASA on the Sunshine State, by William Barnaby Faherty, S.J. (2002)

In the Eye of Hurricane Andrew, by Eugene F. Provenzo Jr. and Asterie Baker Provenzo (2002)

Florida's Farmworkers in the Twenty-first Century, text by Nano Riley and photographs by Davida Johns (2003)

Making Waves: Female Activists in Twentieth-Century Florida, edited by Jack E. Davis and Kari Frederickson (2003)

Orange Journalism: Voices from Florida Newspapers, by Julian M. Pleasants (2003)

The Stranahans of Ft. Lauderdale: A Pioneer Family of New River, by Harry A. Kersey Jr. (2003)

Death in the Everglades: The Murder of Guy Bradley, America's First Martyr to Environmentalism, by Stuart B. McIver (2003)

Jacksonville: The Consolidation Story, from Civil Rights to the Jaguars, by James B. Crooks (2004)

The Seminole Wars: The Nation's Longest Indian Conflict, by John and Mary Lou Missall (2004)

The Mosquito Wars: A History of Mosquito Control in Florida, by Gordon Patterson (2004)

Seasons of Real Florida, by Jeff Klinkenberg (2004)

Land of Sunshine, State of Dreams: A Social History of Modern Florida, by Gary Mormino (2005, first paperback edition 2008)

Paradise Lost? The Environmental History of Florida, edited by Jack E. Davis and Raymond Arsenault (2005, first paperback edition, 2005)

Frolicking Bears, Wet Vultures, and Other Oddities: A New York City Journalist in Nineteenth-Century Florida, edited by Jerald T. Milanich (2005)

Waters Less Traveled: Exploring Florida's Big Bend Coast, by Doug Alderson (2005)

Saving South Beach, by M. Barron Stofik (2005)

Losing It All to Sprawl: How Progress Ate My Cracker Landscape, by Bill Belleville (2006)

Voices of the Apalachicola, compiled and edited by Faith Eidse (2006, first paperback edition, 2007)

Floridian of His Century: The Courage of Governor LeRoy Collins, by Martin A. Dyckman (2006)

America's Fortress: A History of Fort Jefferson, Dry Tortugas, Florida, by Thomas Reid (2006)

Weeki Wachee, City of Mermaids: A History of One of Florida's Oldest Roadside Attractions, by Lu Vickers and Sara Dionne (2007)

City of Intrigue, Nest of Revolution: A Documentary History of Key West in the Nineteenth Century, by Consuelo E. Stebbins (2007)

The New Deal in South Florida: Design, Policy, and Community Building, 1933–1940, edited by John A. Stuart and John F. Stack Jr. (2008)

Pilgrim in the Land of Alligators: More Stories about Real Florida, by Jeff Klinkenberg (2008)

A Most Disorderly Court: Scandal and Reform in the Florida Judiciary, by Martin A. Dyckman (2008)

A Journey into Florida Railroad History, by Gregg M. Turner (2008)

Sandspurs: Notes from a Coastal Columnist, by Mark Lane (2008)

Paving Paradise: Florida's Vanishing Wetlands and the Failure of No Net Loss, by Craig Pittman and Matthew Waite (2008)

Embry-Riddle at War: Civilian and Military Aviation Training During World War II, by Stephen G. Craft (2009)

The Columbia Restaurant: Celebrating A Century of History, Culture, and Cuisine, by Andrew T. Huse (2009)

Ditch of Dreams: The Cross Florida Barge Canal and the Struggle for Florida's Future, by Steven Noll and David Tegeder (2009)